Melusine of Lusignan

Melusine of Lusignan

Founding Fiction in Late Medieval France

EDITED BY DONALD MADDOX AND

SARA STURM-MADDOX

THE UNIVERSITY OF GEORGIA PRESS

ATHENS AND LONDON

Athens, Georgia 30602
www.ugapress.org

Designed by Kathi Dailey Morgan

Most University of Georgia Press titles are
available from popular e-book vendors.

Printed digitally

Library of Congress Cataloging in Publication Data

Melusine of Lusignan : founding fiction in late medieval France /
edited by Donald Maddox and Sara Sturm-Maddox.
vii, 301 p. ; 24 cm.
Includes bibliographical references (p. 289) and index.

1. Jean, d'Arras, active 14th century. Mélusine.
2. Melusine (Legendary character)—Romances—
History and criticism. 3. Civilization, Medieval, in literature.
I. Maddox, Donald. II. Sturm-Maddox, Sara.
PQ1486.J25 M4 1996
841'.1—dc20 95-52471

ISBN-13: 978-0-8203-5710-2

British Library Cataloging in Publication Data available

Contents

Preface

This is the first collection of essays to be devoted in its entirety to the study of one of the most important, though heretofore relatively neglected, literary works of the later Middle Ages. The collection originated from an international colloquium, "Melusine at 600," held at the University of Massachusetts, Amherst, in November 1993 to commemorate the sixth centenary of the *Roman de Mélusine* by Jean d'Arras. The majority of the papers in this volume are revised contributions presented on that occasion.

We owe a special debt of gratitude to our collaborators on this project, for their support in the several phases of its elaboration. We also wish to thank Molly Thompson, editor for the University of Georgia Press, for her valuable assistance in bringing the project to completion. To the two anonymous readers who read the manuscript for the Press, we are most grateful for many thorough and perceptive comments and suggestions.

The reader will note that a list of the most frequently cited primary and secondary works has been included. These works are referred to by the name of the author or editor in parentheses in the individual papers.

Unless otherwise indicated, English translations of citations from the Middle French are those of the authors of individual essays. The editors of this volume are currently preparing the first modern English translation of the *Roman de Mélusine* by Jean d'Arras.

Melusine of Lusignan

Introduction: Melusine at 600

Donald Maddox and Sara Sturm-Maddox

Melusine came to Lusignan and circled it three times, shrieking woefully in a plaintive female voice. Up in the fortress and in the town below, people were utterly amazed; they knew not what to think, for they could see the form of a serpent, yet they heard the lady's voice issuing forth from it. (M 260–61)

Thus does Jean d'Arras, the author of the first *Roman de Mélusine* (1393), describe the leave-taking of Melusine from the city she had founded, the city whose name, like her own, is connected with marvels. Six centuries later, however, readers encountering this text for the first time may well find themselves as perplexed by its hermeneutic strangeness as were the startled citizens of Lusignan who, after Melusine's serpentine metamorphosis, beheld her in her monstrous state and heard her wild lament. For while the work immediately gives more than an inkling of its qualities as a masterpiece of late medieval fiction, it also looms large as a medieval literary monster, a text unsettling on many counts.

Indeed, many of this complex story's most disturbing features become readily apparent from a brief summary of its main lines. The king of Scotland weds a fairy in exchange for his pledge not to see her in childbirth. Unwittingly violating her interdiction, he loses both his wife and his three newborn daughters. Learning later of their father's misdeed, the daughters use their fairy powers to imprison him within a mountain, and are assigned individual punishments by their mother. Melusine, the eldest, will be transformed into a serpent each Saturday; her single hope of escaping this condition, as well as her fairy state, is to marry a man who will observe the interdiction not to see her on Saturday; in any case, she will found a noble and illustrious lineage. She indeed marries a young noble named Raymondin, and is instrumental in the founding of castles and cities in Poitou, notably that of Lusignan, in the meantime giving birth to ten sons. Most of these sons bear physical marks of monstrosity but will extend the dominion of Lusignan through military prowess and through alliance. Some distinguish themselves in the crusading enterprise, and most assume positions of power as lords in Europe and kings in Cyprus and Armenie. One of them, however, the redoubtable Geoffroy, sets fire to an abbey and destroys the monks, among them one of his own brothers. The horror of his deed prompts Raymondin, who has witnessed Melusine's serpentine metamorphosis, to accuse her publicly as a "most false serpent," resulting in her definitive transformation and departure from Lusignan.

The fascination that the *Roman de Mélusine* holds for us as modern readers lies in part in its complex play with the conventions of medieval fictional and historical writing. The romance took shape during a critical phase of the Hundred Years' War and, in keeping with the proprietary claim to Lusignan of its patron, Jean, the duke of Berry, it repeatedly advances truth-claims for its story. On a variety of levels, however, the text proposes an amalgam of disparate elements: of fiction, history, and genealogy, in its account of the founding of the illustrious dynasty of Lusignan and its innovative appropriation of Crusade narratives; of human and fairy, in the marriage of its two central protagonists; of human and monstrous, in the corporeal metamorphoses of its heroine and the grotesque marks borne by her progeny; of folk belief and Christianity; and of romance and epic conventions. The different components of the textual amalgam do not always seem to sit easily together, exacting the reader's vigilance and reflection in the formulation of a response.

Curiously, the Melusinian tradition has been relatively neglected by modern critics. Its popularity during the later Middle Ages is attested by the fact that it served twice to further political designs, once in Jean's prose text, then in an octosyllabic verse version composed under English patronage some ten years later by a certain Coudrette.[1] Its wide readership and international dissemination is evident in the manuscript tradition and the numerous printed editions and translations from the mid-fifteenth to the nineteenth century.[2] Yet it is the "myth of Melusine" that has been the primary object of critical attention: long ago it attracted the attention of European scholars in search of the roots of French folk traditions;[3] a quarter of a century ago, two historians of the *Annales* school took Jean's "Mélusine maternelle et défricheuse," founder of cities and dynasties and provider of wealth and prestige, as a point of departure for the study of late medieval and early modern mentalities (see Le Goff and Le Roy Ladurie). Subsequently, a handful of literary and iconographic studies have appeared in France;[4] recently, and somewhat ironically, a best-selling novel in which it figures as subtext—A. S. Byatt's *Possession*—brought it the widespread if incidental attention of an international audience. Yet we must acknowledge that a great deal remains to be discovered about the *Roman de Mélusine* itself.

Jean d'Arras, recording in his text that on Thursday the seventh day of August in the year 1393 "ceste histoire . . . fu parfaicte" (*M* 307), would seem to be announcing not only its completion but its wholeness, in keeping with the usage of medieval romance whereby the term "perfection" refers to "the attainment of an amalgam that is complete and whole."[5] Yet understood in this sense, the declaration only increases the reader's consternation: open to question is not only its "completion"—which is deferred repeatedly by a lengthy tripartite epilogue—but also its "wholeness." In this and numerous other respects, Jean's *Mélusine* is also a sphinx: elusive and enigmatic, it is a perfect example of what Roland Barthes would call, in contrast with the unproblematic "readerly" fiction destined for mass consumption, a "writerly" text, one whose obstinate resistance to interpretation compels us to engage the full range of our scholarly resources and interpretive faculties in the attempt to capture its essence, master its mysteries.

The readers whose responses to the text are recorded in this volume have identified and confronted a wide variety of hermeneutic challenges. Terms such as "tension," "interference," "ambivalence," "ambiguity," and "paradox" recur throughout these readings; as Gabrielle Spiegel observes at the end of her essay, "at every turn in this complex narrative, Jean proliferates the paradoxes that make it so difficult to interpret the text in any unilinear way." The *Roman de Mélusine* is a text whose fundamental aporias cannot easily be set aside, and these studies are of particular interest because of the variety of scholarly and interpretive resources deployed to engage them. The essays here collected bring to light a wealth of new material and fresh insight, considerably broadening the range of inquiry so as to take account of aspects of this complex work heretofore virtually ignored. A concern for diversification is evident throughout: new perspectives emerge on the text's sophisticated and innovative engagement of learned literary traditions, classical dialectic and rhetoric, philosophical and theological currents, and medieval views of demonology and reproductive biology. Our attention is also drawn to the enigmatic aspects of Melusine's progeny and to the ample segments devoted to her sons' conquests of territory in far-flung lands. Illuminated in these readings are the precise significance of terms, images, and poetic figures; the ambivalent image of the female embodied in Melusine's story; the significance of key episodes; the work's intricate narrative organization; and its eclectic blending of stylistic and generic features.

Contextualizing this multiplicity of inquiries, the essays collectively bring us to an unprecedented understanding of Jean's complex text as a meaningful totality; each in its own way transforms the work's powerfully generative inconsistencies into an illuminating new reading of this remarkable romance. These readings, however, are by no means univocal. Among the various voices heard in this collection, significantly different notes are sounded—differences concerning the success of the "union" of the text's disparate elements as well as the interpretation of the work as a whole. The separate profiles of the individual contributions suggest the rich plurality of the critical issues raised and the multiplicity of methods by which they are productively engaged.

The opening essay by Sara Sturm-Maddox focuses on narrative schemata. It takes as point of departure two early episodes in which an extraordinary destiny is foretold both for Raymondin and for Melusine. The two destinies intersect in a relation of reciprocity, whereby each protagonist is potentially the sole accessory to realization of what is foretold for the other. The ultimate divergence of the two narrative programs raises questions concerning fairy "otherness," a concern heightened here as questions of judgment, punishment, and penance are added to the motifs of interdiction and transgression familiar in the encounters of mortals and supernatural creatures in folklore, lay, and romance. Jean d'Arras's meditation, in his exordium and epilogue, on God's wondrous—and unfathomable—ways both elicits and forecloses on such questions, which concern the relation between the misdeeds of mortals and the fate of fairies and, on a larger scale, the participation of fairies in the workings of the divine plan in the mortal world.

In Douglas Kelly's essay the element of the *merveilleux*, upon which much of the attention previously accorded the *Roman de Mélusine* has focused, becomes a vital accessory to interpretation. Kelly argues that the physical anomalies of Melusine's progeny are conditioned by medieval notions of inheritance according to which the family line is derived from the paternal semen and transmitted through sons, while the maternal blood carries the order to which the offspring belong. That the "mother-marks" of Melusine's sons, as signs reminiscent of her "marvelous, inhuman virtue," do not manifest themselves in the last two sons affords evidence, he suggests, of the progressive humanization of the fairy, a process initiated by her marriage but subverted by her spouse's public betrayal, which permanently consigns her to a supernatural state. The progression illustrates a widespread tendency in medieval romance whereby the marvelous elements of received traditions are "domesticated," leaving only a residue that, like the fairy's tail or her sons' mother-marks, remains as an untamed *surplus de sen*.

The centrality of the marvelous in the *Roman de Mélusine* is confirmed in the remarkable lexical range and frequency of terms indicative of wonderment. But in this text, Rupert T. Pickens argues, wonderment also points to paradox. Noting resonances with biblical intertexts as well as affinities with currents in late medieval linguistic philosophy and its classical antecedents, he cites numerous instances of specific forms of paradox, both in the body of the romance and in the exordium and epilogue. From this sampling a normative pattern emerges, in which Jean's usage of paradox becomes "a means to knowledge and the perception of transcendent truth." If the operations of para-*doxa*, by inducing "wonderment," lead to epistemological certainty, the latter is constantly challenged by *doxa*—received opinion in its many unreliable guises. Pickens argues that this confrontation underlies the events that eventually lead to Raymondin's betrayal of Melusine, her departure, and the decline of the lineage, such that Jean's romance takes shape according to a "poetics of paradox."

In the center of this web of paradoxical strands we find the enigmatic figure of Melusine herself. Affirming that "Melusine's polycorporality is carefully structured in terms of the romance's plot" and that in the plot her metamorphosis results from transgression, Kevin Brownlee offers a close analysis of the two scenes in which her corporeal hybridity is revealed, first to her voyeuristic husband and the reader, then to the public inscribed within the text. These scenes, in his reading, identify her as not only a bodily hybrid—metamorphosing from woman to half-serpent and finally to airborne snake—but also as a composite index of the plurality of traditional cultural resources that fed this voracious literary enterprise. In this light, Melusine is a "discursive composite—a figure constructed out of a set of discourses in unstable contrast with one another: fairy-monstrous, courtly-erotic, maternal, political-foundational, Christian." Although Melusine's hybridity remains a productively destabilizing factor throughout most of the work, Brownlee suggests that, like the hybrid nature of Jean d'Arras's text itself, its modes of signification are emblematic and illustrative of the heterogeneous tendencies of vernacular poetics in late medieval France.

According to Gabrielle M. Spiegel, on the other hand, Melusine's hybrid nature is what marks her progeny as monstrous, as products of a "categorical confusion between the world of humans and the world of animals." Jean's romance, according to her anthropologically informed view, is fundamentally concerned with a "process of desymbolization," with "the plasticity . . . of prevailing cultural categories." Melusine's hybridism threatens the integrity of discrete categories in several respects. Ancient and medieval theories of reproductive biology would make of her twinship a monstrous contravention of the human norm; she moves metamorphically between human and animal states; she is an androgynous creature and lends her name to an agnatic lineage, the "task of males" since the twelfth century. In Spiegel's reading, the romance is framed by Melusine's "parricide" and the "incest" of the Sparrowhawk episode and moves generally from "optimistic dreams of plenitude and legitimation" to "a story of reproductive failure, social loss and monstrous savagery."

Also pessimistic, though for different reasons, is Laurence de Looze's reading of the Lusignan "fall into history" following the betrayal and definitive departure of Melusine. For de Looze she is a fully positive emblem, exemplary, in her *caritas*, of the Christian New Covenant or New Law and Charity incarnate, forgiving of Raymondin's violation of the taboo, until Geoffroy's fratricide remanifests the act of Cain and thus the Old Law. This deed recalls, as *mise en abyme*, Raymondin's unwitting killing of his uncle, likewise evoked by Geoffroy's boarlike "tusk." Unable to recognize Melusine's goodness, Raymondin "misreads" her as a figure of the Old Testament, a serpent, and his misreading dooms Lusignan. The footprint left by Melusine on her departure is "a text that alludes to Raymondin's return to a law written in stone," which at the same time inscribes her place in history. From antithetical points of departure, Spiegel and de Looze thus converge toward a dystopic reading of the text.

Illustrating the romance's rich potential for divergent interpretations, Stephen G. Nichols finds in Raymondin's indictment of Melusine as "phantasme" the accurate perception, however momentary, of a demonic manifestation. In his reading Melusine is not a univocally evil female but an avatar of the ambivalent, late classical "lamia," a female monster; in the miniatures from Arsenal MS 3353 that he examines, she in fact appears both as beautiful female and as miniature dragon. Melusine creates a phantasmagoric world around her husband, while her "lamial status as sabbatical *serpente*" makes even her seemingly benevolent acts irreducibly dual, beyond adjudication. In Jean's text Nichols discerns not merely a pseudohistorical fiction contrived to further the ends of patronage but a wholly new late medieval narrative genre featuring a specific type of political allegory. The peculiar blend of chronicle and romance that would seem to be at odds with Jean's repeated truth-claims is, according to Nichols, founded on a conceptualization of fictional truth in terms not of contemporaneous political events but of their allegorical reconfiguration.

On the other hand, Jane H. M. Taylor proposes that the text fits within the category of genealogy but that as such it is profoundly ambiguous, particularly as regards Melusine's progeny. For example, the lack of physical deformity in the two youngest offspring, also noted by Kelly, is in her reading only one of a number of instances where narrative schemata are activated only to remain unfulfilled. These "blocked schemata" are seen as indicative of a tendency, found elsewhere in late medieval genealogical narratives, to protect the lineage from the potentially negative implications of its founder's eccentric image, here the genealogical ambiguities inherent in the invoking of an ancestor such as Melusine. Thus she suggests that Jean d'Arras, in the interest of "the neutralization, indeed the denial, of genealogy as determinism," may have attempted to foreclose on peripeteia that could be damaging to his patron's cause; hence the text's declared "pragmatic function," which is to support Jean de Berry's claim to Lusignan, is not fully resolved.

Like Nichols, Emmanuèle Baumgartner perceives a profoundly innovative dimension in Jean's narrative. Redressing a notable imbalance in earlier scholarship devoted to the work, she examines the account of how two of Melusine's sons come into possession of Cyprus and lesser Armenia (Cilicia). In the Cypriot episode, she finds that Jean took bold liberties with matters of fact and with the accessible written sources concerning the Lusignan presence in the Near East. This she sees as the design of a tendentious author: "fiction seems to toy with history so as to remodel it to the advantage of the illustrious lineage," relocating it within the context of the Crusades. More is at issue, however: while projecting onto the past an idealized view of the family's achievements, Jean innovatively implements earlier French narrative traditions, "experimenting with a new form of writing" that deftly alloys a story of territorial expansion and conquest with stylistic features of the chansons de geste and motifs of romance. The net result is nothing less than a late fourteenth-century renewal of romanesque prose, prefigurative of the historical novel of a later age.

Michèle Perret demonstrates that despite his protestations of the historicity of his enterprise, Jean relies far more heavily on the discursive properties of fiction. Her detailed stylistic comparison of *Mélusine* with two earlier exemplars of historical narrative, Joinville's *Vie de Saint Louis* and the *Chroniques* of Froissart, highlights the distinctive features of his pseudohistorical style. For the construction of a coherent universe of reference, Joinville and Froissart more frequently make use of "situational reference" to a factual universe, while Jean d'Arras consistently employs "contextual reference" within a closed fictional universe. His text, moreover, abounds with notations in direct discourse, a hallmark of fiction, whereas Joinville and Froissart tend to report discourse in the indirect style typical of historiographic accounts. In the depiction of subjectivity, Jean's recourse to monologues in direct style is not inconsistent with the norms of fiction before the advent of narratives in which focalization on internal process and free indirect discourse predominate.

Scrutinizing the axiological properties of literary discourse as they pertain to this text, Marina S. Brownlee argues that in Jean's "rewriting of popular myth as historical document" certain inconsistencies stem from authorial intention. Citing apparent discrepancies between Melusine's virtuous Christian profile and evidence of her supernatural dark side, she maintains that Jean d'Arras deliberately mediates between myth and allegory, subjecting an allegorical presentation of an exemplary heroine to interference from the mythic background. This, she suggests, is part of a stratagem whereby Jean generates skepticism with regard to Jean de Berry's genealogical link with Melusine while seeking instead to heighten the human stature of his patron, identifying him not with the supernatural but with the earthly lineage of Raymondin, the *roi mondain*.

Less than half a century after Jean d'Arras limned the figure of Melusine, Joan of Arc had come to full prominence. From the respective domains of myth and folklore, on the one hand, and history on the other, both women enter powerful legendary realms, which Nadia Margolis juxtaposes in a literary-typological comparison of perhaps the two most complex and fascinating feminine figures lingering in the collective imagination of the later Middle Ages. Margolis documents a remarkable array of major and minor similarities, finding in both a convergence of popular and learned traditions in the fashioning—

or "self-fashioning" in Joan's case—of a vessel through which the transcendent finds expression in the quotidian in order to modify the course of political events. The Melusinian aspects of Joan's career discerned by Margolis raise interesting questions for further study of late medieval modes of conceptualizing feminine agency in European culture.

Rounding out the collection, Donald Maddox explores the pertinence to Jean's full enterprise of the epilogue in which he commemorates the "perfection" of his *Mélusine*. Maddox finds that all three segments of the epilogue are based on the conventions of the medieval literary *custom* and that each seeks to liquidate ambiguities lingering from the main body of the narrative and ultimately to legitimize Jean de Berry's current claim to Lusignan. Here, moreover, temporal configurations unify the work, culminating in the figure of metalepsis, which assimilates narrated events to the temporality of poet and patron. Thus there emerges a special sense of "perfection": the narrative proper had performed the delicate task of exalting the Lusignan dynasty as it grew, while simultaneously preparing the way for its subsequent decline. The epilogue in turn "perfects" this development, by signifying the decadence of the Lusignan line and, in the ultimate segment, by magnifying the image of the patron and heir capable of restoring Lusignan to the grandeur of its apogee.

Marking the six hundredth anniversary of the first *Roman de Mélusine*, the essays in this volume thus attest to the work's seemingly inexhaustible richness, as well as to the legitimacy of its status as a literary masterpiece of late medieval France. As an ensemble they demonstrate that, unlike the decline of the lineage it depicts, the *Roman de Mélusine* of Jean d'Arras has with increased longevity also waxed in vitality. The many different types of literary and cultural issues brought to prominence in these pages, while constituting the most wide-ranging reception of this work to date, effectively reopen the text to previously untraveled avenues of research. These studies establish the *Roman de Mélusine* as one of a number of major medieval literary works that compel and sustain the kind of methodological diversity that has in recent years revitalized literary study of the Middle Ages. Together, they recommend Jean d'Arras's *histoire* to readers eager to explore the complex dynamics of late medieval culture.

Notes

1. Concerning how the two versions are related, see the introductions to the English translation by Roach and to the modern French translation by Harf-Lancner.

2. On the manuscript tradition see Laurence Harf-Lancner, "La serpente et le sanglier: Les Manuscrits enluminés des deux romans français de *Mélusine*," *Le Moyen Age* 101 (1995): 65–87. The later dissemination is examined by Jennifer R. Goodman, "Mélusine among the Printers," in a paper presented at the 1994 Annual Convention of the Modern Language Association of America, Toronto; see also Harf-Lancner, "Le *Roman de Mélusine* et le *Roman de Geoffroy à la grand dent:* Les éditions imprimées de l'oeuvre de Jean d'Arras," *Bibliothèque d'Humanisme et Renaissance* 50 (1988): 349–66.

3. See, for example, Desaivre, and the bibliographical indications in Stouff, *Essai.*

4. Stouff's *Essai* preceded his edition of the romance. Among more recent contributions, see especially Lecouteux, *Mélusine et le Chevalier au Cygne;* Harf-Lancner, *Fées;* and Clier-Colombani.

5. On "perfection" in this sense, see Douglas Kelly, *The Art of Medieval French Romance* (Madison and London: University of Wisconsin Press, 1992), 134, and the essay by Donald Maddox in this volume.

Crossed Destinies: Narrative Programs in the *Roman de Mélusine*

Sara Sturm-Maddox

In his *Roman de Mélusine* Jean d'Arras sets out, as is well-known, to recount at the behest of his noble patrons "comment la noble et puissant forteresse de Lisignen en Poictou fu fondee par une faee" [how the noble and powerful fortress of Lusignan in Poitou was founded by a fairy] (*M* 5). His is not a gesture without precedent, as supernatural ancestors had been claimed for other noble houses; and certainly the fascination with the intervention of fairy creatures in the world of mortals had been amply manifested, not only in lay and romance but in clerical literature, all of which afford analogues for elements of the story of Lusignan as Jean d'Arras tells it.[1] But Jean's account is distinguished from such analogues in its singular narrative design, one in which the intersection of mortal and supernatural spheres is rendered by the convergence and conjoining of two narrative programs, one with the mortal, one with the fairy as protagonist. Framed by the authorial meditation on God's inscrutable "merveilles" in the exordium and epilogue of his text, this design prompts fundamental questions concerning the fate of fairies and mortals together, questions that, remaining unanswered in the romance, contribute to the often-remarked residue of perplexity with which the reader is left at the story's end.

Curiously, Jean d'Arras draws our attention to these questions in his exordium at the same time that he appears to caution against attempts to resolve them. Concerning the marvels of God scattered throughout the universe, he adds his personal reflection on such matters: "Et croy que les merveilles qui sont par universel terre et monde sont les plus vrayes, comme les choses dictes faees, comme de pluseurs autres" [And I believe that the marvels found throughout the earth and all Creation are the most true, such as the things said to be "fairy," and a variety of others] (*M* 2). The relation between God's works and "les choses dites faees," then, is that these latter are prime examples of the former. But citing the prophet David on the unfathomable nature of God's judgments and punishments, he admonishes us not to strive presumptuously to understand God's works through the exercise of human intellect: "la creature ne se doit pas pener par oultrageuse presumpcion que les jugemens et fais de Dieu vueille comprendre en son entendement, mais y penser et soy esmerveillier" [the creature is not to seek through outrageous presumption to comprehend the judgments and works of God with human understanding, but rather to think upon them and marvel] (*M* 2).[2] We may in fact marvel at the way in which this recourse to Scripture is subtly bent to the purposes of Jean's own project, for the prophet David, of course, refers to the order of human events, not to "choses dites faees." Nonetheless Jean is quite explicit about the relevance of such examples for his own text to follow: "Et ces termes je vous met avant pour les merveilles qui sont en l'ystoire de quoy je vous pense a traictier" [I set these terms before you for the marvels found in the story I intend to treat for you] (*M* 3).

Two principal narrative programs will give shape to that "ystoire," and each has its roots in the exordium. The first is in fact sketched out in Jean's preparation of his reader: he cites reports, from oral tradition sanctioned by the authority of Gervaise of Tilbury, of fairies who take on the form of beautiful women and wed mortal men according to conditions they themselves impose, granting great prosperity to their human consorts until the latter fail to observe the conditions, losing thereby both the fairy and their good fortune.[3] This outline anticipates the dramatic discourse that, early in the text, renders the reaction of Melusine's mother, Presine, to the news that her daughters, using their fairy powers, have shut their father up forever within a mountain:

> La vertu du germe de ton pere toy et les autres eust attrait a sa nature humaine, et eussiés esté briefment hors des meurs, nimphes et faees, sans y retourner. Mais desormais je te donne le don que tu seras tous les samedis serpente du nombril en aval. Mais, se tu treuves homme qui te veuille prendre a espouse, que il te convenance que jamais le samedy ne te verra, non qu'il te descuevre, ne ne le die a personne, tu vivras cours naturel comme femme naturelle, et mourras naturelment. Et, non contretant, de toy ystra noble lignie moult grant, et qui feront de grans et haultes prouesces. Et se tu es dessevree de ton mary, saiches que tu retourneras ou tourment de devant, sans fin, tant que le Hault Juge tendra son siege. Et t'apparras trois jours devant que la forteresse que tu feras et nommeras de ton nom, devra muer seigneur, et aussi quant ly uns des hoirs qui de ta lignie ystront devra mourir.
>
> [The power of your father's seed would have drawn you and your sisters toward his human nature, and you would soon have left behind the ways of nymphs and fairies forever. But henceforth I give you that every Saturday you will be a serpent from the navel down. But if you find a man who wishes to take you as his wife, who will pledge to you that he will never see you on Saturday, or seek you out then or speak of it to anyone, you will live out a natural life span as a natural woman, and die naturally. In any case, a very great noble lineage will issue from you, which will do many great deeds. And if you are separated from your husband, know that you will return to the former torment, without end until the High Judge sits in judgment. And you will appear three days before the fortress which you shall build and endow with your name is to change lords, as well as when one of your descendants is about to die.] (*M* 12–13)

The program set out here will facilitate the reader's journey through the complexities of a story that is extraordinarily rich in peripetiae, from Melusine's initial encounter with Raymondin to her final appearance in the text. But it also refers to a recent past and an indeterminate, remote future, for the misdeed for which Presine castigates her daughters was motivated by her earlier revelation of another misdeed, that of their mortal father Elinas who had himself violated her fairy interdict: "la fausseté de vostre pere, qui vous et moy a mis en grant misere sans fin jusques au jour du Hault Juge, qui punira les maulx et essaucera les biens" [the treachery of your father, who placed you and me in great misery that will not end until Judgment Day, when the High Judge will punish the wicked and reward the good] (*M* 11).

Interestingly, Melusine in exhorting her sisters to punish their father responds to only part of Presine's summary of the critical consequences of his action, emphasizing the immediate consequence alone: "or regardez la grant griefté et misere ou nostre pere a mis nous et nostre mere, qui eussiemes esté en si grant aise et en si grant honnour" [consider the great grief and misery in which our father has placed us and our mother, when we might have enjoyed such great comfort and great honor] (*M* 11); the words, one might imagine, of a princess deprived of the royal lifestyle—the "aise" and "honnour"—to which she is entitled. With Presine's reaction to their own misdeed, however, which reiterates both the "sans fin" of her initial disclosure and the mention of the High Judge, Melusine's reading of the situation is revealed to be inadequate. The gap that opens between her hasty interpretation and her mother's pronouncement concerns both the desirability of escape from the fairy condition and the "grant misere" that is now theirs, resulting from Elinas's violation of a condition set by the fairy herself.

Another story is also foretold early in the romance. Now it is that of Melusine's mortal husband-to-be, Raymondin. The young man has accompanied his uncle, a certain Count Aimery identified as among the wisest and most learned men of his age, in a boar hunt; having far outdistanced the others, they wait together for the moon to rise and shed its light. The count, exceptionally well versed in astronomy, studies the heavens and begins to sigh profoundly. And he says:

> Vrays Dieux, comment sont les merveilles que tu as laissiees ca jus en la vertu de ta chamberiere nature, merveilleuses et diverses en leur expedicion, se tu n'y espandoies ta grace divine, et especialment de ceste merveilleuse aventure que je voy ou cours des estoilles que tu as lassus assises dès le commencement du ciel . . . Mais comment pourroit ce estre raisonnablement, s'il n'estoit en ton invisible jugement, quant par cognoissance humaine que nulz

> homs pourroit avoir bien et haulte honnour par mal faire? Et non contretant, je voy... qu'il est ainsi. Si en suy moult esmerveilliez.
>
> [True God, how strange and diverse are the marvels that you have left here below through your servant Nature, if you do not spread upon them your divine grace! Especially this marvelous adventure that I read in the stars that you have fixed there above since the creation of the heavens... But how could it reasonably be, if not decreed by your invisible judgment, that anyone could receive good and great honor, through evildoing? And nonetheless I see ... that it is thus. I am most amazed.] (*M* 19–20)

The closeness of this phrasing to the terms of Jean's authorial exordium is evident. The stars are God's "merveilles," and witness to Him who made them; he who knows how to read them may find in them the signs of other "merveilles," which may be contradictory to human understanding; yet what cannot be, "raisonnablement," can yet be in God's "invisible judgment"; the result is a confirmation of paradox that, as Rupert T. Pickens points out in his essay in this volume, results in wonderment, "émerveillement." So now is Count Aimery, an exemplary reader of God's wonders in terms of the exordium, "moult esmerveilliez" at the adventure he reads in the stars, which is the following: "Et l'aventure si est telle que, se, a ceste presente heure, uns subjiez occioit son seigneur, qu'il devendroit ly plus riches, ly plus puissans, ly plus honnourez qui feust oncques en son lignaige, et de lui ystroit si tres noble lignie qu'il en seroit mencion et remembrance jusques en la fin du monde" [The adventure is this: that if, at this present hour, a subject were to kill his lord, he would become the richest, most powerful, and most honored of all his line, and from him would issue such a noble lineage that it would be spoken of and remembered until the end of the world] (*M* 21). When the count reveals to Raymondin what the heavens have revealed to him, the younger man refuses to believe it, for, he maintains, "ce seroit contre raison que nulz homs peust avoir bien ne honneur pour faire mortelle trahison" [it would be counter to reason that a man could receive good and honor for mortal treason]; and again, when the count insists: "ce ne croiray je ja, car ce n'est mie chose qui face a croire" [I shall not believe it, for it is not believable]. The adventure will nonetheless come to pass, and Raymondin figures as its principal: he will inadvertently kill his uncle the count, and even before his grief and bewilderment have abated, the narrator confirms "le grant eur qui depuis lui vint de ceste doulereuse tristece" [the great good fortune that came to him afterwards because of this painful sorrow] (*M* 21).

This episode, which in its proleptic function parallels that of Presine's indictment of her daughter, serves very early in the text as a dramatic illustration that human destinies, like those "choses dites faees" of Jean's exordium, may be examples of God's unfathomable wonders and His inscrutable ways. In a very important sense, it distinguishes Raymondin's story in this text from that of the mortal in the typical mortal-meets-fairy story, for the "marvelous" destiny of Raymondin is here inscribed in the stars *prior to* his encounter with Melusine. And in the foretelling of her story by her fairy mother, Melusine too is distinguished from the fairy of conventional lay and romance; for if the events foreseen form a narrative outline familiar in medieval accounts of the interference of fairies in mortal affairs—fairy meets mortal, imposes interdiction, marries mortal, and vanishes when the interdiction is violated, the sequence of Melusine's parents (see Lecouteux, "La structure"; Harf-Lancner, *Fées*)—those elements are framed, as we have seen, with more troubling revelations that endow Melusine with a past, a motivated present, and a future fraught with consequences for herself and for others that will not, like that of the fairy of lay and romance, be determined by her sovereign will. As a result, Melusine acquires a status as protagonist equal to that of her eventual mortal partner. And together the two episodes that preconfigure the stories of Melusine and of Raymondin—one featuring a fairy and one a mortal but both "marvelously" identified as the protagonists of singular destinies—program a double illustration of the lesson of the exordium concerning the working out of God's wonders in the mortal world.

It is only *after* establishing these independent programs that Jean d'Arras engages his two protagonists in the well-known design of the mortal-meets-fairy story.[4] The destinies of these two exceptional individuals soon cross, like their paths, when Raymondin encounters Melusine in the forest. Our suspicion that the encounter is not fortuitous is intensified when Melusine recounts to Raymondin his plight, resulting from his uncle's death, which he has not revealed to her, and continues: "Et saiches de certain que sans moy ne mon conseil tu ne pues venir a chief de t'emprise. Et se tu me veulz croire, toutes les paroles que tes sires te dist te seront, a l'aide de Dieu, achevees, et plus qu'il ne t'en dist, car je te feray le plus seignoury et le plus grant qui oncques feust en ton lignaige, et le plus puissant terrien" [Know for sure that without me and my counsel you will not be able to succeed in what you undertake. And if you believe me, all that your lord said to you will come true, with God's help, and even more, for I shall make you the greatest and most noble man of your line, and the most powerful] (*M* 25–26). But if the latter part of this pronouncement, Melusine's promise of all that Raymondin will gain from alliance with her, resonates clearly with the conventional schema, the manner of its introduction legitimates the question of the way in which the destinies of mortals are intertwined with the fate of fairies. Not only is Melusine aware of the "merveille" concerning Raymondin; she promises to bring about its realization "a l'aide de Dieu." One might well be tempted to exclaim, like the servant to his master in *Le Vair Palefroi*,

> Mien escient, c'est une fee
> Que Dieus vous a ci amenee
> Por restorer vostre domage
> Dont si avez pesant corage.
>
> [In my opinion, it is a fairy that God has brought here to you to repair the harm that weighs so heavily on your heart.] (vv. 1181–84)[5]

Is fairy providence here identical with divine providence? The question is irrelevant in *Le Vair Palefroi*, where in fact there *are* no fairies, but it is central to the *Roman de Mélusine*, for in what follows Melusine is indeed the instrument of the realization of Raymondin's "great good fortune" written in the stars: it is she who tells him how to escape death as a result of the killing of his uncle, how to acquire the vast space necessary for the founding of Lusignan, how to regain his inheritance in Brittany; she who is responsible for the clearing of land and the founding of castles and cities; she who bears the sons who will inaugurate the lineage of Lusignan.[6]

Hence the singular design of Jean's romance, in which the fairy and mortal protagonists are reciprocally related, each to function as auxiliary to the other. At the same time that Melusine offers herself as adjuvant in the narrative program set out for Raymondin, she imposes upon him the precise terms prescribed by Presine. As he eagerly acquiesces, the reader may fairly assume that Raymondin will, by satisfying them, become the instrument of Melusine's escape from the state to which she has been condemned. Thus each entrusts his destiny to the other, and as the two exchange pledges—Melusine will confer prosperity and lineage on her husband, Raymondin will conform unquestioningly to her interdict—the hopes of the mortal and those of the fairy are united. One is tempted to read this congruence of their two stories in Melusine's conferral of the name Lusignan on the fortress where their lineage is founded: her explanation, that the name commemorates its founding "merveilleusement et aventurieusement" (*M* 47), echoes precisely the "merveilleuse aventure" that Count Aimery had read in the stars.

But first a third proleptic passage traces the line of intersection in the stories of fairy and mortal, an intersection that forms the overarching design of a "history" that attributes both a mythic and a heroic mortal ancestor to the house of Lusignan. This one, occurring appropriately between the wedding of Melusine and Raymondin and the consummation of their marriage, takes shape in her own words. She thanks her husband for having thus far conformed perfectly to the conditions she had set him, and goes on:

> Et sachiez de certain que, se vous le tenez desormais ainsi, que vous serez ly plus puissans et ly plus honnourez qui oncques feust en vostre lignaige. Et se vous faictes le contraire, vous et voz hoirs decherront petit a petit, et la terre que vous tendrez alors que vous ferez la faulte, se il est ainsi que vous le faciez, ce que Dieu ne veulle ja consentir, ne sera jamais tenue par nul de voz hoirs ensemble.
>
> [Know for certain that if you always keep your word in this way, you will be the most powerful and honored man of all your lineage. If you do the opposite, you and your heirs will decline slowly, and the land you hold when you commit that fault—if ever you should, and may God not allow it—will never again belong in its entirety to any of your heirs.] (*M* 42)

Melusine's emphasis on the dire consequences of breaking their covenant is essential to Jean d'Arras's project to relate the history of the House of Lusignan because it opens to modification the glorificatory predictions concerning lineage made earlier to both Melusine and Raymondin, thus raising the possibility of the decline of the lineage of Lusignan, which was indeed to take place by the late fourteenth century and to which later episodes of the romance allude.

Yet at the same time this scene admirably serves Jean's narrative design, in its testimony to the conjoining of the two narrative programs, the now-intertwined destinies of the two protagonists. Now Melusine affirms to Raymondin that the dreadful consequences of a failure of their covenant will be shared: "Or gardez que vous ne me failliez de convenant," she tells him, "car vous seriez cellui qui plus y perdroit après moy" [Take care that you do not break your covenant with me, for you would be the one, after myself, to lose the most from it] (*M* 42). Her final comment on the subject, moreover, informs us that despite her fairy powers, she is no more able than Raymondin to see the outcome of their contract. Following his renewed promise, she entrusts herself to her husband, as he has entrusted himself to her: "Mon amy, puis que je me sui mise si avant, il m'en fault attendre la voulenté de Dieu et moy confier en vostre promesse" [My friend, since I have come so far in this, I must await God's will and trust in your promise] (*M* 42). Even while she invokes God's will as decisive, the scene shifts the focus from the divine plan writ large in the heavens to the drama of two individuals in the world below. It will remain there, throughout a long series of trials and triumphs, until the final scene they share in the romance.

In that series of trials and triumphs, there is of course much that is "marvelous," much that reminds the reader that Melusine is indeed different from mortals. Springs appear where there were none before; towers, fortresses, whole cities are built and populated overnight; fabulous wealth is displayed; children bearing strange marks are born to the couple. Yet if we discount those marvels, which are so frequent as to become almost "ordinary," the story of Raymondin and Melusine reads through much of the romance as a family fiction that remarkably anticipates the episodically rich family sagas of a much later age: distant relatives are found and claims of inheritance settled; family lands are developed and administered with attention to practical detail; children grow up, leave home, marry, send word to their parents of their adventures. During this very substantial segment of the romance, the image of Melusine as fairy yields progressively to that of Melusine as mortal woman: devoted wife and mother, capable administrator of estates, bounteous *dame*.[7]

Through the many years of Melusine's and Raymondin's fruitful and prosperous union, no mention is made of the intermittent monstrous state to which Melusine is condemned. That state, however, is not abolished by her marriage to Raymondin; on the contrary, it is the hidden term of her interdict to her husband, and it is highly significant that its fateful discovery will be instigated, in the words of Raymondin's cousin the count of Forez, by a double report of the public speculation concerning her unexplained absences on Saturday. In that report, voiced at this critical moment of the romance, one term presupposes a mortal wife and the other a supernatural creature: "Vous estes mon frere, je ne vous doy pas celer vostre deshonneur. Beau frere, la commune renommee du peuple court partout que vostre femme vous fait deshonneur et que tous les samedis elle est en fait de fornicacion avec un autre. . . . Et les autres dient et maintiennent que c'est un esperit fae, qui le samedy fait sa penance" [You are my brother, I cannot conceal from you your dishonor. Good brother, the common opinion spreading everywhere among the people is that your wife does you dishonor, that every Saturday she engages in fornication with another man. . . . And others say and maintain that she is a fairy spirit, who does penance on Saturday] (*M* 241). While it is the first possibility, that of Melusine's infidelity, that provokes Raymondin's unconsidered reaction "epris de yre et de jalousie" [seized with wrath and jealousy] and leads to the voyeuristic scene in which he discovers not her infidelity but her semiserpentine state, the second hypothesis reminds the reader after a long interval of the "other" dimension of Melusine's story.

What then is the import of that dimension? Is Melusine's transformation on Saturday a confirmation of the speculation concerning "a fairy spirit, who does penance on Saturday"? We recall Jean's citation in the prologue of Gervaise's report concerning fairies who marry mortals that "aucuns convertissoient en serpens un ou pluseurs jours la sepmaine" [some are transformed into serpents one or more days each week], and the hypothesis of his clerical authority: "Et dit le dit Gervaise qu'il creoit que ce soit par aucuns meffaiz secrez au monde et desplaisans a Dieu pourquoy il les punist si secretement en ces miseres que nulz n'en a congnoissance fors lui" [This Gervaise says he believes it is because of some misdeeds, hidden from the world and displeasing to God, that he punishes them with these miseries so secretly that no one knows of it except Himself] (*M* 4).

Is Melusine's serpentine metamorphosis then to be read as a divine punishment? Jean d'Arras himself, with obstinate (and perhaps prudent) discretion, hazards no speculation on this remarkable report. But the term attributed to Gervaise, "ces miseres," recurs in Presine's pronouncement to describe not her daughter's intermittent monstrosity, but the condition to which mother and daughters alike are condemned by the misdeed of her husband, Elinas. And in fact Melusine's serpentine transformation, while it has invited a number of negative readings of her status,[8] is not identical with her fairy nature. Presine has no animal traits;[9] Melusine's animality, moreover, acquired as a punishment specified by her fairy mother, is not shared by her fairy sisters, to whom other punishments are assigned.

Is "being a fairy" itself then some kind of a curse, and their misery the result of a fairy nature whose status is unambiguously malefic within the sphere of divine justice, that of the High Judge? Such is the case for the "Melusines" described by Paracelsus,[10] and there is abundant evidence of misgivings concerning the union of a supernatural creature with a mortal in folklore and in literature as well as in clerical opinion.[11] Particularly pertinent are a group of legends reported in twelfth-century Latin works, in which "the fundamental incompatibility between the figure of the fairy and Christianity" is emphasized in the fairy's strenuous avoidance of "participation in the Mass and all contact with holy water" (cited by Gabrielle Spiegel in this volume). A number of vernacular literary texts, however, confront such suspicions directly and strive to counter their negative potential. Mortal heroes and heroines of lai and romance sometimes request and receive assurances from potential fairy lovers that they are not "de male part"; the fairy lovers of Marie de France's *Yonec* and of the anonymous lai *Désiré* partake of communion to confirm their nonmalefic nature.[12] The example of *Désiré* is particularly pertinent to the treatment of the tension between fairy and Christian spheres in *Mélusine* because in it the tension is confronted by the fairy herself and ultimately resolved publicly, at her behest, through the Christian marriage of fairy and mortal.[13]

Suggestions of such a positive status of Melusine abound in the text. They are pronounced in the assurance she offers Raymondin at the outset of their liaison: "je scay bien que tu cuides que ce soit fantosme ou euvre dyabolique de mon fait et de mes paroles, mais je te certiffie que je suiz de par Dieu et croy en tout quanque vraye catholique doit croire" [I know well that you believe my deeds and words are a phantasm or the work of the devil, but I assure you that I am on God's side and that I believe everything a true Christian must believe] (*M* 25).[14] Apparently any doubts on the part of Raymondin are set to rest by this assurance, and even the most skeptical reader will soon be reassured as well, for along with Melusine's "marvelous" accomplishments in a number of domains there is repeated evidence of the lady's piety, or at least of her full conformity with religious rites. As Donald Maddox notes, her sister Melior attests that she is subject to the Church's jurisdiction concerning marriage.[15] Melusine is married in a church service performed by a bishop, and the same bishop blesses the marriage bed (*M* 39, 41); later, her *chastoiements* to her sons are laced with traditional religious and moral precepts (*M* 84–87; 152–54) and contain the specific instruction: "Tenez les commandemens de nostre mere Saincte Eglise et tous les degrez et commandemens de nostre foy catholique" [Obey the commandments of our mother Holy Church and all the requirements and commandments of our Catholic faith] (*M* 152–53);[16] prior to her ultimate serpentine transformation she laments poignantly that because she will not die "normally" she will not receive Christian sacraments and be buried in the church in Lusignan (*M* 256); following her disappearance, public grief is expressed in the most pious terms, recalling her good deeds and her founding of abbeys, priories, and churches (*M* 261).

It is surely noteworthy that when Raymondin eventually sees Melusine's half-serpentine form he does not consider the possibility of a malefic presence but only laments his culpable betrayal of his wife (248).[17] Nor does the disclosure of her transformation appear to condition the response of Melusine's entourage. Like the emphasis on her status as courtly lady and erotic subject traced by Kevin Brownlee in this volume, the judgment of these lords and ladies receives fullest expression immediately following Raymondin's public revelation of her monstrous state and her acknowledgment of her imminent departure. Now, after reviving "la dame" who has fainted, they lament the separation of these two faithful lovers, "ces deux loyaulx amants," and "s'escrient d'une voix: 'Nous perdons aujour d'uy la plus vaillant dame qui oncques gouvernast terre, et la plus saige, la plus humble, la plus charitable, la mieulx amee et la plus privee a la necessité de ses gens, qui oncques feust veue" [cried out with one voice: "Today we are losing the most valiant lady who ever governed a land, and the wisest, the humblest, the most charitable, the best loved and most attentive to the needs of her people, who has ever been seen] (*M* 257). The single interpretation of Melusine as malefic occurs in Raymondin's private and then public outburst of grief occasioned by the tremendous misdeed of their son Geoffroy, the burning of the abbey of Maillezais and all the monks, including his own brother Fromont, within. The second of these outbursts, Raymondin's accusation of Melusine in which he fatally calls her "tres faulse serpente" [very false serpent] in response to her attempt to attenuate his grief, is carefully explained by the narrator as a result of his uncontrollable anger: "si scet bien qu'elle lui dit voir de quanqu'elle lui avoit dit, et que c'est le meilleur selon raison. Mais il fu se tresperciez et oultrez de yre que raison naturelle s'en estoit fuye de lui" [he knew well that she spoke the truth, and set out the best course according to reason. But he was so filled and overcome with wrath that natural reason wholly abandoned him] (*M* 255).

With this second, definitive moment of Raymondin's betrayal of Melusine, the narrative patterns of the two protagonists definitively diverge. The divergence of their heretofore conjoined stories is announced by the narrator in an uncommon anaphora that underlines its solemnity: "Or commence leur dure departie. Or commence la doulour qui durra a Remond tout son vivant. Or commence la penitence qui durra a Melusigne jusques a la fin du monde" [Now begins their hard separation. Now begins the sorrow that will remain with Raymondin all his life; now begins the penance that Melusine will endure until the world's end] (*M* 254). With this "dure departie" ends the convergence of the two stories that had begun with the encounter of Raymondin and Melusine in the forest, and here the fundamental difference in the two narrative programs is reasserted in the consequences of Raymondin's betrayal. Raymondin has indeed become "the richest, the most powerful, the most honored man in all his lineage," and already the heroic deeds of his many sons have confirmed him as head of a "very noble line" worthy of remembrance, all as Count Aimery had read in the stars, although the decline of that lineage consequent on his betrayal, against which Melusine had warned him, remains to be realized in future generations. Melusine had indeed found in Raymondin "a man who wished to take [her] as his wife, who would pledge to [her] that he would never see [her] on Saturday, or seek [her] out then or speak of it to anyone," the conditions set by her fairy mother, and she had seemed likely to "live out a natural life span as a natural woman, and die naturally"; the "very noble line . . . which will do many great deeds," again, has been amply confirmed. But of course there was more to Presine's prediction—its sequel now to be realized—and in it the equal status implicitly accorded to fairy and mortal throughout their marriage is abruptly and brutally canceled: "And if you are separated from your husband," Presine had told her daughter, "know that you will return to the former torment, without end until the High Judge sits in judgment."

As Melusine cries out to Raymondin, "Las! Mon amy, se tu ne m'eusses faussee, je estoye gettee et exemptee de paine et de tourment," and again, "Or me r'as tu embatue en la penance obscure ou j'avoye long temps esté par ma mesaventure. Et ainsi la me fauldra porter et souffrir jusques au jour du jugement et par ta faulseté" [Alas! my friend, if you had not betrayed me, I would have been saved from pain and torment . . . Now you have thrust me back into the dark penance where I had been so long on account of my misfortune] (*M* 256), one may well wonder why she cannot be excused from a fate foretold for an offense that was Raymondin's and not her own, the violation of an interdict of whose consequences for her he was, moreover, completely unaware. "Fausseté" here echoes Presine's definition of Elinas's similar betrayal and brings again to the fore the unanswered questions of the "misere" to be suffered until the end of time by her and her daughters. Pardon is possible for Raymondin: "Je pry a Dieu qu'il le te veulle pardonner" [I pray to God that He be willing to pardon you], Melusine tells him (*M* 256), and affirms that had he not revealed her serpentine state publicly—thus completing the transgression according to the terms of her interdict and the literal terms set by Presine—God would have forgiven him, as she had already done: "Dieu le t'eust pardonné, car tu en eusses fait la penitence en ce monde" [God would have pardoned you for it, for you would have done penance for it in this world]; and again, "le meffet vous veulle pardonner Cellui qui est vray et tout puissant pardonneur et le droit fons de pitié et de misericorde, car, quant a moy, je le vous pardonne de bon cuer" [may He who is the true and all-powerful pardoner and the fount of pity and mercy pardon you, for as for myself I pardon you with all my heart] (*M* 257). This striking emphasis makes of Melusine an exemplar of Christian charity, as Laurence de Looze observes in this volume. It also emphasizes that God forgives, as she has already declared to Raymondin concerning the heinous sin of their son Geoffroy: "Sachiez qu'il n'a si grant pecheur ou monde que Dieu ne soit plus grant pardonneur et plus debonnaire, quant le pecheur se repent et lui crie mercy de bon cuer et de bonne voulenté" [Know that nowhere in the world is there so great a sinner that God does not extend even greater pardon and goodness, if the sinner repents and cries out to Him for mercy, sincerely and from his heart] (*M* 255). But fairies are apparently subject to the same divine jurisdiction; is there then no pardon for fairies?

The differing nature of the terms that apparently obtain for mortal and fairy within that jurisdiction is further brought out in the penance to which both Melusine and Raymondin are now subjected. Raymondin's penance for his misdeed, in fact if not in detail, is explicitly recorded in the text, and his expiation begins almost at once. Overcome with grief following Melusine's departure, he makes a pilgrimage to Rome and confesses his sins to the Pope himself; the Pontiff, "quant de ce qu'il s'estoit parjurez envers sa femme" [with regard to his having broken his oath to his wife] duly assigns him a penance, whose nature is not disclosed: "lui charga tel penitence qu'il lui plot" [set him the penance that he found appropriate] (*M* 270).[18] Geoffroy too will confess to the Pope and be assigned acts of penance (*M* 275). But Christian concepts of penance are evidently relevant to Melusine's state as well: her farewell to the assembled company, "A Dieu vous commant, tous et toutes, et vous plaise a prier Nostre Seigneur qu'il Lui plaise a moy alegier ma penitence" [I commend you to God, one and all; may you pray Our Lord that it please Him to ease my penance] (*M* 259), obviously resonates with the Christian notion of Purgatory evolving in the period, as do the terms with which Raymondin announces to the Pope his desire to become a hermit: "Et la prieray Dieu qu'il lui plaise faire allegement a ma moillier" [I shall pray to God to alleviate my wife's pain].[19]

What, then, is the status of fairies in a mortal world ruled by divine providence? In her response to Raymondin concerning Geoffroy's burning of the abbey, Melusine evokes God's design fulfilled in the event with an almost exact reprise of Jean's own words in the exordium concerning the secret nature of God's judgments, "que nul cuer mondain ne les puet comprendre en son entendement" [that no mortal heart can comprehend them in its understanding] (*M* 255). It would appear that God's secret judgments, hidden from mortals, are at least partially accessible to fairies, for Melusine is fully aware of her own fate. In this she is like her mother Presine, who told her husband following his act of betrayal "Et me fault partir soubdainement" [I must leave at once], words suggestive of constraint rather than of the exercise of her free will in her departure. Unlike Presine on that occasion, Melusine now offers her husband an explanation: "Mais quant de ma demouree," she tells the sorrowing Raymondin who entreats her to remain, "c'est pour neant, car il ne plaist pas au Hault Juge" [But as for my remaining, there can be no question of it, for it does not please the High Judge]; and again: "je ne puis plus demourer avec vous, car il ne plait pas a Dieu, pour le meffait que vous avez fait" [I can no longer remain with you, for it does not please God, on account of your misdeed] (*M* 257); and again: "ainsi fault qu'il soit, puis qu'il plaist a Cellui qui tout puet faire et deffaire" [it must be so, because He who can make and unmake everything so desires it] (*M* 258). But this explanation, like Presine's references early in the text to the High Judge, is no more that an affirmation that Melusine is subject to divine jurisdiction; her revelation of her lineage immediately prior to her departure as a flying serpent—"je suiz fille au roy Elinas d'Albanie et a la royne Presine, sa femme, et sommes iij. seurs qui avons esté durement predestinees et en griefz penitances" [I am the daughter of king Elinas of Albanie and queen Presine his wife; I am one of three sisters who have been condemned to a cruel destiny and grievous penance](*M* 260)—does little to dispel the mystery of her fate.

Melusine's fate, like Raymondin's, is not happy. Unlike the alliances of mortal and fairy in the lais of *Yonec* and *Désiré*, for example, their alliance does not result in a positive resolution. Melusine does not achieve the human condition to which she aspires, the human condition that would release her from perpetual torment; Raymondin lives out the last years of his life as a grieving hermit after divesting himself of his lands in favor of his sons. What remains? Lineage of course remains, the single point of intersection of the two major narrative programs and Jean d'Arras's avowed project, the glorification of the noble house of Lusignan, although its foretold decline has now begun. But there remains also, for the reader, a residue of questions at the story's end.

At the story's end, in his epilogue, Jean d'Arras reiterates his defense of the truth of his "history of Lusignan" in terms almost identical to those of the exordium:

> Je repute ceste histoire et la cronique a estre vraye, et les choses faees. Et qui dit le contraire, je dy que les secrez jugemens de Dieu et les punicions sont invisibles a congnoistre a entendement humain, car il est trop gros pour entendre l'espite espirituelle, ne comprendre que c'est. Et la puissance de Dieu y puet adjouster ce qu'il lui plaist, comme on raconte, en pluseurs histoires, de pluseurs faees, avoir esté mariees et avoir eu enfans. Comment ce se puet faire ne puet savoir humaine creature, car ces poins et autres a Dieu retenu en son secret, et en monstre les exemples es lieux et aux personnes ou il lui plaist.
>
> [I maintain that this story and the chronicle are true, and the fairy things. If anyone says the contrary, I say to him that the secret judgments of God and His punishments are invisible to human sense and understanding, which is too coarse to understand what is spiritual, nor comprehend it. God's power can transform whatever pleases Him; a number of stories tell of fairies having married and had children. How that can be is something that human creatures cannot know, for these things and others God keeps secret, and shows us examples where and to whom He pleases.] (*M* 310–11)

We may ponder these examples, but further, Jean tells us at the very end of his very long text, we may not—cannot—go.

Thus in the *Roman de Mélusine*, where the mysteries are writ large, the reader's questions remain not only unanswered but unframed, forestalled by Jean's disclaimers and his invitation to "marvel" instead at his story's illustration of God's unfathomable ways in the world. Yet in its very design, in the conjoining and then divergence of the fates of his mortal and fairy protagonists, Jean's text invites us to frame the questions upon which he would summarily foreclose. What is the place of fairies in the divine order? What is the relation between the misdeeds of mortals and the fate of fairies? What is to happen to Melusine on that fateful day, so often evoked, when the High Judge will sit in judgment?[20]

The answer to the latter question, critical to the resolution of the others as well, is denied us by the very terms of Melusine's story, whose closure is deferred until Judgment Day—at the end of time.[21] In the meantime, at least for modern readers, the enduring interest of Jean's romance may result less from the "marvelous" founding of the house of Lusignan that it is designed to illustrate than from his creation of a most uncommon fictional universe, one in which mortal creatures and fairy creatures attempt to work out their singular destinies together, and from our inability to find completely satisfying answers to the questions that he declines to frame.

NOTES

1. For a summary of both, see Laurence Harf-Lancner's introduction to her modern French translation of Coudrette, 1–19.

2. Jean cites Psalms 35 and 91: "David le prophete dit que les jugemens et punicions de Dieu sont comme abysme sans rive et sans fons, et n'est pas saige qui les cuide comprendre en son engin" [The prophet David says that God's judgments and punishments are like a boundless, bottomless abyss, and he is not wise who thinks to comprehend them with his understanding].

3. Jean refers to the *Otia imperialia* (1209–14); he will go on to tell one specific story found in Gervaise, that of "Rogier du Chastel de Rousset, en la province d'Auxci, qui trouva une faee et la voult avoir a femme" [who found a fairy and wanted to have her as his wife] (*M* 4).

4. The fact marks a major difference between his text and that of Coudrette, where Melusine's "past" is not revealed until the end of the narrative, which begins with the adventure of Count Aimery.

5. Huon le Roi, *Le Vair Palefroi*, ed. Arthur Langfors (Paris: Champion, 1957); the hero is informed of the return of his horse, bearing a young woman.

6. See Rupert T. Pickens in this volume on Melusine's power to accomplish the paradoxical by showing Raymondin the way out of his dilemma.

7. See Douglas Kelly's observations in this volume on the lack of "mother-marks" in her last two sons as indication of her progressive approach to a human state.

8. Examples are cited by Robert J. Nolan, who includes, among others, John of Salisbury's *Policraticus* that "the children of the union of a man and a lamia are cursed." Nolan himself concludes that Melusine is a demon, the revelation of whose nature "serves the same function as an act of exorcism," in keeping with iconography and clerical commentary; her deferred departure "further places Melusine's 'benevolent' qualities at the romance's periphery and, supplementing iconography and Church commentary, gives added weight to the idea that the demonic theme functions as a central element in the romance." See "The Origin of the Romance of Melusine: A New Interpretation," *Fabula* 15 (1974): 192–201 (here 197).

9. Harf-Lancner observes that "La fée entièrement humanisée ne manifeste pas la moindre tendance à reprendre une forme animale," which renders her taboo meaningless (*Fées* 159). Spiegel argues in this volume, on the other hand, that giving birth to triplets is in itself a marker of Presine's monstrosity.

10. Paracelsus is cited by Stouff (*Essai* 15), here translated by Nolan: "Melusines are the daughters of kings who are tormented because of their sins. Satan seized them and transformed them into phantoms, evil spirits, horrible ghosts, and frightful monsters. They live without a rational mind in a fantastic body, which is formed from the elements, to which they will return at the Last Judgment unless they marry a mortal being. Through this union they can die a natural death, since they live a normal life in their marriage. It is believed that these phantoms inhabit deserts, forests, ruins and tombs, empty vaults, and the edge of the sea" ("The Origin," 192–93).

11. Fairy interdicts such as those formulated by Presine and Melusine are frequently a precaution against the disclosure of fairy otherness, designed to protect the supernatural creature against these misgivings; see Lecoutoux, "La structure," 297.

12. On *Yonec* see Francis Dubost, "Yonec, le vengeur, et Tydorel, le veilleur," in *Et c'est la fin pour quoy sommes ensemble. Hommage à Jean Dufournet, Professeur à la Sorbonne Nouvelle. Littérature, Histoire et Langue au Moyen Age* (Paris: Champion, 1993), 1:449–67. Here, he suggests, the tension occasioned by the liaison between mortal woman and fairy lover is resolved in a "légalité merveilleuse" in which God is repeatedly implicated, with the result that "le système du merveilleux" offers in this text "une cohérence sans défaut. Il unifie dans une visée totalisante les aspirations humaines, la magie verbale, la féerie bretonne et la Providence divine" (453).

13. See *Les lais anonymes des XIIe et XIIIe siècles*, ed. Prudence Mary O'Hara Tobin (Genève: Droz, 1976), 157–206, and the observations of Jean Subrenat,

"L'aveu du secret d'amour dans *Le lai de Désiré*," in *Mélanges de langue et littérature françaises du Moyen Age et de la Renaissance offerts à Charles Foulon* (Rennes: Université de Haute Bretagne, 1980), 1:371–79.

14. The declaration in Coudrette mentions specifically the articles of the faith: "J'ai une foi inébranlable en tous ces articles, dont rien ne me ferait douter" (50).

15. Melior, lady of the Sparrowhawk Castle in the epilogue, will not acquiese to marry the young king who demands her because she is his aunt and therefore, even if she were to wish it, "the Church would not allow it," confirming the efficacy of its jurisdiction; see Donald Maddox's analysis of the episode in this volume.

16. Marina Brownlee notes in this volume the importance of the latter speech, which occurs at the midpoint of Jean's text, underlining Melusine's Christian rather than her supernatural identity.

17. The allegorical connotations of the terms of his lament, casting her as "la licorne precieuse" [the precious unicorn] and himself, her betrayer, as "le faulx crueux aspis" [the false cruel serpent] further suggest her positive status in the axiology of "good" vs. "evil."

18. That penance, remaining incomplete, will serve in the epilogue to explain another "merveille" at Lusignan; to end it, Geoffroy will agree to found a hospital and a chaplaincy for the peace of his father's soul. See the analysis of the episode by Donald Maddox, who points out that the intervention of a mysterious figure who affirms that he is "de par Dieu" (*M* 298, 300) offers the reader further evidence that Melusine was not a malefic creature.

19. On "the logic of Purgatory" see Jacques Le Goff, *The Birth of Purgatory*, trans. Arthur Goldhammer (Chicago: University of Chicago Press, 1981), 209–34.

20. It is tempting to see reflected here the question of the state of "monstrous" creatures in the Resurrection, one engaged by Augustine, for example, in the *City of God;* see the discussion of John Block Friedman, *The Monstrous Races in Medieval Art and Thought* (Cambridge, Mass.: Harvard University Press, 1981), 121.

21. For the increased emphasis on the Last Judgment as reflected in religious drama and especially iconography from the twelfth century, see Pamela Sheingorn, "'For God is such a Doomsman': Origins and Development of the Theme of Last Judgment," in *Homo, Memento Finis: The Iconography of Just Judgment in Medieval Art and Drama* (Kalamazoo: Medieval Institute Publications, 1985), 15–58.

The Domestication of the Marvelous in the Melusine Romances

DOUGLAS KELLY

Les merveilleuses aventures

Qui aviennent aux creatures.

Savoir est excellente chose.

[Marvelous adventures that happen to creatures: to know them is a very fine thing.] (Coudrette, vv. 29–31)

In each of the Melusine romances in French, that by Jean d'Arras and that by Coudrette, Melusine assumes two principal roles: she is a mother of sons and a builder of buildings. She is the "Mélusine maternelle et défricheuse" described by Le Goff and Le Roy Ladurie. The marriage, births, and constructions found the Lusignan family. At the same time, the two romances relate in part the progress of Melusine's metamorphosis from an inborn fairy nature to humanity, a progress initiated and abetted by her marriage to Raymondin.

Melusine's mysterious nature and power are no doubt the source of the fascination that her story and that of the Lusignan family she founds continually exert. That fascination cannot be accounted for by the writings of Jean d'Arras and Coudrette alone. Laurence Harf-Lancner and

Gaël Milin have shown that folktales like the Aarne-Thompson folktale motif type 782[1] have a long tradition in Breton folklore and that one or the other such tale may have become attached to the Lusignan family line from its beginnings in Brittany.[2] Nor is the Lusignan legend unique: Le Goff has noted other medieval families that trace their line back to animal or supernatural origins and found on them their claim to be an extraordinary and thus, in romance terms, marvelous lineage.[3] The name Melusine itself, we are told, means "merveilles ou merveilleuse" [marvel or marvelous woman] (*M* 47).[4]

Marvels are indeed the primordial stuff—the *hyle*, as it were—of romance. However, romances tend to domesticate their marvels. Domestication occurs when the marvel enters the realm of custom;[5] the accommodation of marvel to custom is characteristic of most medieval history and romance. Yet this kind of "euhemerization" of marvels in romance is rarely total: there not infrequently remains at least a residue of the extraordinary, noncustomal that is no doubt an essential element in the romance aesthetic.[6] We are left, as in the lays of Marie de France and in all works of the "Ancients," with a hidden *surplus de sen*.[7] That extraordinary quality in marvels that they bring along in their passage into historical or pseudohistorical narrative may make even the customary extraordinary.

That is the effect of Melusine on the Lusignan family she founds, on its genealogy and its history. Melusine contributes the major elements that found the family: wife, children, architecture, and a name. The fate of the family is in turn intimately tied to her own failure to persist in the metamorphosis by which she might achieve humanity and mortality. For Melusine's transformation aborts. As Léo Desaivre long ago pointed out, and as Louis Stouff recalled, relying on the Poitevin traditions that Desaivre recorded and that Le Roy Ladurie again studied, "Il en est des ouvrages de Mélusine comme de ses fils; il y a dans les uns et dans les autres quelque chose de manqué et d'incomplet."[8] Melusine never attains humanity, all but two of her sons are physically disfigured or morally and physically deformed, and the whole family and its foundations are destined to slow decline and ultimate extinction. Melusine prophesies as much just before leaving Raymondin: "Sachiez que après vous jamais homs ne tendra ensemble le pays que vous tenez, et auront moult voz hoirs aprez vous a faire. Et sachiez que aucuns par leur folie decherront moult d'onneur et de heritaige" [Rest assured that, after you, no one will keep together the country you hold, and that it will be very difficult for your heirs after your death. Know too that the honor and inheritance of some will decline greatly because of your folly] (*M* 257–58; cf. Coudrette, vv. 3965–80).

To be sure, Melusine does make considerable progress in the gradual transformation of herself and her family, a transformation that makes her both founding mother and almost human. Her last two sons, Thierry and Remonnet, have no marks like their older siblings, nor are they morally or emotionally unstable.[9] But the other brothers are not necessarily repulsive or even unattractive. Even the wives of the older brothers see the nobility of their spouses despite their disfigurement; at least, none seems to object to it and some find excuses in the wonderful prowess the oddities seem to them to betoken. As Hermine, daughter of the king of Cyprus and wife-to-be of Urian, puts it: "se il avoit le visaige plus contrefait .c. foiz que il n'a, si est il tailliez, pour sa bonté et pour sa prouesse, d'avoir la fille du plus hault roy du monde a amie" [Even if his features were deformed far more than they are, still, his noble qualities and prowess would make him worthy of the daughter of the grandest king in the world] (*M* 104). The first five sons easily find heiresses broad-minded and aristocratically perceptive enough to live out their respective versions of Beauty and the Beast with neither regret nor disgust. "Bontez vault mieulx que beautez" [Excellence is of greater worth than beauty] (*M* 104), it seems, in Melusine's world.

The "bontez" of the next three sons and brothers is more problematic. Geoffroy Big-Tooth, Fromont, and Horrible never marry. They are the three sons born directly before Remonnet and Thierry, the last two brothers, who are "normal." The three celibates are especially unusual morally and socially. Geoffroy is courageous and fears no one, but he is also cruel. He not only confronts and defeats giants and puts to flight hoards of Saracens, he also burns a monastery to the ground with its monks, one of whom is his brother Fromont, inside, and causes the death of his uncle, the count of Forez. Fromont himself is as devout and God-fearing as Geoffroy is wild and determined to keep his brother from God; Geoffroy fears neither heaven above nor any of its agents here below, as his last adventure, the duel of the Tour Poitevine tribute, illustrates. Horrible too is cruel, but his violence is more intimate. Jean d'Arras reports that before Horrible is four years old he has, as it were, suckled to death two of his nurses; later, while still young, he kills two of his servants (*M* 80; not in Coudrette's version). Each of the three celibate brothers is marked by a physical abnormality, like their older siblings: Geoffroy has the great tooth that becomes part of his name; Fromont has a hairy mother-mark on his nose; Horrible has three eyes, one in the middle of his forehead.

Since Remonnet and Thierry have no physical abnormality, does not the absence of a mark betoken Melusine's progress in metamorphosis into a mortal? Not only do Remonnet and Thierry lack the marvelous features of their older brothers and mother, they also seem to escape their father's tragic fate and that of some of their older siblings: Antoine's cruelty, Geoffroy's irascible temper, Horrible's violence and mysterious moral flaw that requires that he be asphyxiated while still young in order to protect the Lusignan family and its possessions from destruction.

Let us return to the marvel and Melusine's place among the romance marvels that are related to her. As a common, defining feature of both medieval history and romance, the marvel initiates an adventure that leads to the achievement of that marvel. The achievement permits the integration of the marvel into a conventional world, while it defines and distinguishes, in both senses of the word, that world and its achievers. Although the marvel can be a supernatural or magic phenomenon, as is the case with Melusine, it is not necessarily so. Moreover, a marvel, even when it is supernatural or magic in origin or at the outset, may change its nature. This is what Melusine herself hoped would happen to her over time because of her marriage to Raymondin. Finally, the marvel may simply be an extraordinary natural phenomenon. This is the case in some of Marie de France's *Lais*, for example *Equitan, Milun,* or the *Laüstic.* It is also the case with Melusine's sons, and with the Lusignan family she founds and sends out into the world.

In the Melusine romances the fay in the woods attempts to move into the human world rather than draw someone into her otherworld, as in most lays and in Antoine de la Sale's *Paradis de la reine Sibylle*, a late medieval text. Melusine hopes to become human and mortal in this way. Whether success would also entail loss of her supernatural knowledge, attributes, and powers is not made clear. Her failure is the fault of her human husband Raymondin, and, because of it, Melusine is banished from future intercourse with him, in both senses of the word. Yet, while still his wife Melusine has interesting, important, even enduring effects in the human world: she establishes the Lusignan and Parthenay families, contributes her sons to many other families while linking those families by the male seed to her own, and civilizes large stretches of wild, uninhabited forests with the constructions that are the source of the family's name and geographical mark of its establishment, importance, and durability. Melusine's constructions are virtual mother-marks on the landscape and in the Lusignan patrimony.[10]

The ritual "domestication" of the marvelous, the assimilation of the marvelous that Melusine initiates, and the catastrophic effects of her failure all focus on the interrelated matters of birth and construction. How does domestication of the marvelous occur through the intervention of fairy powers? Melusine's birth and childhood, told at the beginning of Jean d'Arras's romance (*M* 9–10) and interpolated into Coudrette's narrative (vv. 4919–32), will serve as point of departure, model, and partial illustration of domestication and its failure.

The marvelous, yet problematic offspring of the union of fay and human marks the beginning of the Lusignan family. There are three examples of such unions in Jean d'Arras: Melusine and Raymondin themselves, Melusine's parents Presine and Helinas, and Hervy de Leon and a fountain lady in Forez. All illustrate the union of a female fay and a male human. (There is no example of the opposite, that is, the union of a human woman and a fairy or otherwise supernatural husband, as in Marie de France's *Yonec.*) The last example, Hervy de Leon and the fountain lady, found only in Jean d'Arras, can be dealt with quickly. Hervy de Leon, Raymondin's father, went to Forez after being driven from his lands in Brittany, lands Raymondin will recover later at Melusine's instigation. Upon arriving in Forez he met a lady by a fountain—"une dame de laquelle je ne vous vueil pas parler" [A lady I don't wish to speak about], affirms the narrator (*M* 50). Hervy and she separate after she helps him settle Forez and establish himself there with castles and cities. There is no mention of children. After the separation, Hervy marries the sister of the count of Poitou. Their third son is Raymondin. Raymondin is therefore the human son of human parents. He has no marvelous features, or mother-marks.

The second example is chronologically the first in the Melusine romances: the marriage of Helinas and Presine. Helinas, king of Albanie, or Scotland, marries twice. But he reverses Hervy's sequence of wives-from fairy woman to human woman. Helinas first marries a human female and has a human son, Mataquas. This son, like Raymondin, has therefore a human mother and father. And like Raymondin, Mataquas has no inborn physical or moral defect. In fact, he becomes the grandfather of Philip of Macedonia and great-grandfather of Alexander the Great through his own son Florimont, the titular hero of Aimon de Varennes's romance.[11] When Helinas's first wife dies (a not uncommon occurrence in the Melusine romances), he marries the fay Presine. Helinas meets Presine by a fountain, much as Raymondin will meet Melusine. Together they have three daughters, in order: Melusine, Melior, and Palestine (Coudrette reverses the order: Palestine, Melior, Melusine).

Unlike Mataquas, who is exclusively human, the three daughters inherit their mother's fairy nature, or "faee condicion" (*M* 12; cf. Coudrette, vv. 4979–98). However, as Presine explains to them later, the daughters could have gradually slid from their fairy nature into humanity through the action of their paternal seed: "La vertu du germe de ton pere toy [= Melusine] et les autres [= Melior and Palestine] eust attrait a sa nature humaine, et eussiés esté briefment hors des meurs, nimphes et faees, sans y retourner" [The virtue of your father's seed would have drawn you and the two others to his human nature, and you would have divested yourselves, in short time and once and for all, of your nymphlike, fairy ways] (*M* 12). In a short time, therefore, all three would have metamorphosed into humans. That is, they would have achieved their father's humanity and with it, presumably, access to salvation upon death.

Events, however, take a different turn. Helinas promised upon marrying Presine never to attend her in childbirth or see her during her confinement, or *gesine*. Mataquas's enmity toward his newborn half-sisters provokes him to trick Helinas into breaking his vow, causing the father to lose his fairy wife. When they learn of their father's betrayal, Melusine, Melior, and Palestine seek to avenge their mother and punish their father's indiscretion by having him magically enclosed for life in an underground prison.[12] Yet the vengeance angers Presine in turn. As punishment, she halts the metamorphosis of the daughters into humans and imposes a curse on them that makes the eventual attainment of humanity impossible or, in Melusine's case, difficult. Presine's magic stabilizes Melusine's serpentine nature. Only love and a Christian marriage with a human offer Melusine the prospect of escaping from her otherwise permanent "faee condicion."

The possibility of domesticating the marvelous by human love interests both Jean d'Arras and Coudrette. To be sure, in the Melusine romances love in human marriages is more familial than courtly (Melusine is somewhat of an exception to this; see Hoffrichter, 70). Nonetheless, both romances embody typical plots in that the marvelous, not the human, side of the family provides interest and leads to narrative elaboration. Thus, Mataquas's sisters' stories are related, not his own. In Jean d'Arras, the Florimont story, not that of Melusine's sons, is set aside; "nostre histoire n'est pas emprise pour lui, et pour tant nous en tairons nous et procederons en nostre hystoire et vraye matiere" [Our story is not written for his sake. We shall therefore cut short his account in order to get on with our story and true subject] (*M* 10). Jean d'Arras's *histoire* is "la vraye histoire des merveilles du noble chastel de Lisignan en Poictou" [the true account of the marvels of the noble Lusignan castle in Poitou] (*M* 14–15; cf. Coudrette, vv. 47–120). These two features distinguish the plots of the romances by Jean d'Arras and Coudrette: they are marvelous, and they are about the Lusignans. Mataquas is neither marvelous like fairies' sons, nor does he belong by seed to the Lusignan family.

We may appreciate Jean d'Arras's and Coudrette's predilection for the marvelous and its domestication by further comparing Raymondin's fate with that of his distant relative Mataquas, as well as the conditions and lives of Raymondin's sons by Melusine with that of Mataquas's son Florimont. In Aimon de Varennes's romance, Florimont also meets a fay, the Pucelle de l'Ille Perdue, or Avalon. But, according to Jean d'Arras, the Pucelle is Presine's sister. The sister will avenge Presine on Mataquas (*M* 9–10). But in fact, like his distant ancestor Hervy de Leon, who becomes count of Forez, Florimont leaves the fay and later marries the daughter of the Macedonian king, Romadanaple in Aimon de Varennes's romance. Alexander the Great loses thereby a supernatural ancestor; still, Florimont's human wife preserves the Macedonian line from disfigured children.

Siblings that are the offspring of fays are all of one sex in the Melusine romances. Presine's children are all daughters. Melusine has only sons. But there is a major difference between the daughter and the son of a fairy mother. Melusine's offspring, all sons, inherit more of their father's humanity than do Helinas's daughters. Melusine's sons are human and therefore mortal, as Fromont and Horrible show when each is murdered, within the family, as it were. Helinas's and Presine's children, all female, inherit their mother's fairy nature.

Daughters inherit their mother's nature despite the paternal seed, whereas sons do not inherit that nature, but only a mark of her nature that shows as a physical or moral blemish. Here we must take into account medieval notions of inheritance relating the father's seed or semen with the mother's blood, as well as the phenomenon known as mother-mark, birth-mark, or *envie de mère* in French.[13] These phenomena mark features of Melusine's children as well as the Lusignan landscape. Both reveal the desire of a fairy mother for a human family and children. Both mother-marks—those on the landscape and those on the children—come about mysteriously. The births seem normal, just as do the constructions. Yet the generation of the disfigurement is a *surplus de sen* that is never elucidated, any more than we learn the origin of the armies of workers that Melusine musters so quickly and the buildings that rise up so rapidly at her instigation. Like, for example, the Lusignan fortress, which "a esté fondee merveilleusement et aventureusement," for the workers "fesoient . . . tant d'ouvrage et si soubdainement que tous ceulx qui la passoient en estoient esbahiz. . . . Ne nulz homs ne savoit dont cilz ouvriers venoient, ne dont ilz estoient"; all onlookers are equally "esbahiz comment si grant ouvraige povoit estre en si pou de temps faiz ne achevez" [was founded in a marvelous, adventuresome way. . . . They accomplished so much so quickly that all who passed that way were astonished. Yet no one knew where those workers came from or who they were. . . . They are equally astonished that so great a construction could rise up and be completed in such short time] (*M* 46; cf. Coudrette vv. 1309–30).

According to folklore and legend, ancient medicine and medieval genealogy, the mother-mark comes about during pregnancy. It occurs as an effect of an unusual or extraordinary desire—the *envie de mère*—or fear that accompanies the pregnancy. The strong emotions leave a mark on the child, a mark that usually resembles the object of desire or fear. In its usual manifestation, the desire is gastronomic, and the mark is an image of the object of desire: a strawberry, an olive, a pickle. It may also express anxiety by the image of a wolf, rat, or other frightening encounter or threat. When, however, the mother is not human, or when she unites with a nonhuman male, a mother-mark may also appear on the child as a sign of his or her marvelous parent. Melusine and her children fall into this category. Of course, the mother-marks of these children are more extraordinary or marvelous than most. They evoke astonishment, horror, and curiosity from almost everyone except their eventual wives. This places them in a special category of mother-marks, like the marks that Stith Thompson identifies as "marks of royalty" (type H71), such as the royal ray of light issuing from Havelok's mouth. Melusine's mother-marks are also marks of the fairy. In the case of Melusine and her children, no special gastronomic desires or frightening experiences are recounted to explain the marks.

What is remarkable in the case of Melusine and her children is that Melusine's fairy nature manifests itself once a week over the lower half of her body, even during pregnancy, whereas the analogous physical marks in the sons appear in and on their heads. Whatever the nature of the relationship between the marks and the mother, it is clear that that relationship exists at least until the births of Remonnet and Thierry. Raymondin himself makes Melusine responsible for the disfigurement of the eight other brothers in the outburst that aborts her progress toward mortality: "Par la foy que je doy a Dieu, je croy que ce ne soit que fantosme de ceste femme, ne ne croy pas que ja fruit qu'elle ait porté viengne a perfection de bien; elle n'a porté enfant qui n'ait apporté quelque estrange signe sur terre" [By my faith, I think that that woman is nothing if not supernatural, nor do I believe that her offspring would ever fully develop; none of her children has been born without some strange mother-mark] (*M* 253).[14] *Signe*, like *tache* elsewhere in the Melusine romances, can mean mother-mark in Old and Middle French (see Jaberg, 292–99). Raymondin claims in his outburst that all his children are marked. But, as I have noted, no marks are found on the last two sons in either Jean d'Arras or Coudrette.

In unions of female fay and male human in the Melusine romances, each partner contributes something of his or her own "virtue" to the offspring of the union. Thus, before they took vengeance on their father, Melusine, Melior, and Palestine could hope someday to metamorphose into a mortal but human being. No longer fay or nymph, they would assume human nature, or "virtue," without fear of returning to their former fairy condition. The misdeed of the three sisters—that is, the vengeful imprisonment of Helinas—angers Presine, whose decree leaves open for Melusine alone a single hope of redemption, through a husband who abides by a marriage contract analogous to that made between Presine and Helinas. Her husband may neither witness, nor a fortiori reveal, her Saturday-night assumption of a mermaid's appearance—scaly body and tail from the waist down—which is the sign or mark of the fairy virtue she inherited from Presine. Palestine is imprisoned in Mount Canigou with her father's treasure until Geoffroy comes there (Coudrette, vv. 5023–37), but she is not present in that episode when Geoffroy arrives (cf. *M* 13); according to Coudrette, Geoffroy dies before he can achieve the adventure (vv. 6602–38). Melior, made guardian of the Sparrowhawk Castle, may never marry or know human love, yet must maintain the custom of the castle, which stipulates that any knight who achieves the adventure by passing three nights in the castle without sleeping may claim as reward anything he desires—anything except Melior's hand or her body. All of these effects on the daughters are mother-marks that illustrate inheritance along the matrilinear line. Like their mother, the daughters have a fairy "virtue" from which they may escape—and escape is desirable—only under select, exceptional circumstances and in conformity with prescribed rituals and taboos. The patrilinear effect, through which they might acquire humanity, is interrupted in every case, including Melusine's. The fault is with the husband—with Helinas and with Raymondin, because each breaks his vow.

The effect of the maternal and paternal "virtue" on Melusine's sons is not the same as on Presine's daughters. From Urian, the firstborn, to Thierry, the last, all the sons are human, not fairy, in virtue and thus in species. None must undergo metamorphosis in order to achieve the apparently desirable, if accident- and error-prone humanity and mortality of their father. Still, their mother is a fay. Just as Helinas's *germe* works on his daughters' fairy nature, so Melusine's inhumanity finds expression in eight of her ten sons. None may lose or outgrow his physical or moral mother-marks, which are ingrained in their humanity.

How are we to account for the similarities in inheritance in the offspring of human and fay, and for the differences between the fairy virtue of the daughters and the real, albeit marked, humanity of the brothers? Two medieval factors seem to me important: seed and blood. Traditionally, the family passes to the offspring through the father's semen.[15] The sons preserve that seed and transmit it in turn to their own children. This occurs as the name of Lusignan, derived from Melusine, passes through the five sons who marry to their own sons and daughters. Their children become ipso facto part of the horizontal Lusignan family in the different lands of the marriages. This holds for the children, male and female, of Urian, Eudes, Guyon, Antoine, Renaud, as well as those of Remonnet and Thierry. Fromont, Horrible, and Geoffroy, as noted, have no children. When a son dies without male offspring, that branch of the family dies out with him. If all die in this way, as occurs at the end of the romances with the death of the deposed Armenian king in Paris, the family disappears (Coudrette, vv. 6198–6216).[16]

Daughters are also the product of the father's seed, but they do not transmit that seed. They transmit blood. Blood carries the order to which one belongs. It is more or less blue—or fairy—blood. It determines therefore whether the child will be ducal or royal, burgher or peasant, fay or human. In the cases of Melusine and Presine, the daughters transmit their mother's nature, the sons transmit the father's family. Yet each acquires, but does not transmit, the effect of the opposite-sex parent. In daughters, the paternal seed effects a slow humanization if no supernatural force intervenes. In sons, there are signs of the marvelous, inhuman virtue of the mother. These *signes*, or mother-marks, appear on all but the last two sons of Melusine: misshapen features, huge ears, three- or one-eyed monstrosities, a patch of hair on the nose or a lion's paw on the cheek, a single large, protruding tooth.

The first five sons are nevertheless remarkable by chivalric standards. Their nobility, acquired by their mother's blood, is extraordinary. But they belong to humanity. Urian, Guyon, Eudes, Renaud, and Antoine all marry well despite their extraordinary mother-marks, and four of them distinguish themselves and their family in feudal wars and in wars against the Saracens. Despite a certain cruel streak or fierceness (*fierté*) attributed to some of them (*M* 91, 93, 159, 165), partly because of their features, they nonetheless conduct themselves properly by the feudal and chivalric standards Melusine herself articulates in an extensive *chastoiement* pronounced when Guyon and Eudes set out for Cyprus (*M* 84–88). Her admonitions are reminiscent in some ways of those given by the Lady of the Lake, another faylike creature, to Lancelot before he leaves for Arthur's court in the Lancelot-Grail cycle. All five sons are good warriors, good fathers, good—if not especially loving—husbands.

It is surprising that the sons' virtues and vices become more unusual among the next three, Geoffroy, Fromont, and Horrible, than among the first five. As we have seen, Geoffroy's ferocity and irascibility incline him as often to doing wrong as to doing good. The giant-killer also burns monasteries; the knight who restores his father's feudal rights in Ireland also causes the death of his uncle. Yet there are ambiguities too. Did Geoffroy actually do wrong in burning the monastery at Maillezais? To be sure, Geoffroy recognizes and regrets his act almost immediately afterwards. Although he seems to exact violent vengeance on his uncle, the count of Forez, he also governs the Lusignan lands well and gently despite his "fierté," a word associated in part, as I have suggested, with his appearance. Melusine declares him innocent for burning the monastery, as she reproaches Raymondin for his inordinate anger and despair upon learning of the arson: "Sachiez que de certain c'est pour le pechié des moines, qui estoient de mauvaise vie et desordonnee; et en a Nostre Seigneur voulu avoir la punicion" [Rest assured that it came about because of the monks' sin, that is, because of their evil, disordered life. Our Lord wanted them to be punished for that reason] (*M* 255; cf. Coudrette, vv. 4003–24). For her Geoffroy is an agent of divine justice on errant monks, a bit like Galahad at Carcelois in the *Queste*. Fromont, however, the brother who perishes in the fire, seems innocent of ecclesiastical corruption, as was Perceval's sister in the leprous lady episode of the *Queste*. Is there a mysterious link between Fromont's death and Horrible's? Horrible seems born with the very devil's rot in him and must, therefore, be put to death before he comes of age, stifled by the orders of his own mother in order to preserve the family. He seems a more sinister Balain. Geoffroy, Fromont, and Horrible all have striking physical and moral mother-marks.

It is just as remarkable, then, that neither Remonnet nor Thierry have such marks. It would appear that, despite apparent throwbacks in the cases of Geoffroy and Horrible and an irregularity in Fromont's case, Melusine's virtue is actually progressing toward a real humanity at the time her last two sons are born, before Raymondin breaks his marriage contract and openly reveals her Saturday-night metamorphoses. The last two sons, Remonnet and Thierry, besides having no marks identified in the texts, also evince a decidedly humane, almost placid moral self. Remonnet inherits the county of Forez on the death of his uncle, Thierry that of Parthenay when the count dies without heir. Geoffroy never marries but inherits Lusignan, which passes to Thierry on the older brother's death.

Human mothers do not have children with mother-marks like those of a fairy mother. This is evident not only in the children born to Melusine's sons and daughters-in-law but also in their descendants' own offspring. Yet Melusine's curse lingers in the various branches of the family, reinforced in the Armenian branch by the disastrous visit of an ancestor to the Sparrowhawk Castle guarded by Melior. The curse prevails until the family's final extinction in the time of Jean d'Arras and Coudrette. All the sons' marriages produce predominantly male offspring. Here the human father, with or without mother-marks, is united to a human mother, and together they produce human, albeit excellent and noble, children like Mataquas. The union of Presine's child Melusine, who was still a fay, did not have this effect, except for Melusine's last two children. This permits the hypothesis proposed above: the children born without mother-marks suggest the growing humanization of their mother. Humanity has so imbued her nature or virtue that she is almost entirely human and can begin to bring forth unmarked sons just as her daughters-in-law will do in Cyprus, Armenia, Luxembourg, and elsewhere.[17]

Raymondin's betrayal of her secret halts the metamorphosis, and Melusine reverts to her serpentine nature wholly and for all time. A serpent from the waist up and down, she no longer has any human appearance. Yet fairies may feel love. This is evident in her sorrow and care for the two last sons while they are still infants. Melusine also continues to care for her larger family. She returns on occasion, to announce death and disaster in the Lusignan family three days before the event is to occur. Thus both Jean d'Arras and Coudrette satisfy the romance tendency to domesticate or customize the marvelous, but not entirely. A *surplus de sen* remains, a residue hidden like Melusine's serpentine appearance and fairy appearances as well as the Lusignan family curses. For such creatures the "merveilles qui sont par universel terre et monde . . . les choses dictes faees" are real and true. Nor are we expected to understand them. In Jean d'Arras's words, "la creature ne se doit pas pener par oultrageuse presumpcion que les jugemens et fais de Dieu vueille comprendre en son entendement, mais y penser et soy esmerveillier" [marvels spread out over the earth and through the universe, the so-called fairy occurrences. . . . The creature must not strive outrageously and presumptuously to understand God's judgments and deeds with a human mind, but rather to consider them and marvel] (*M* 2).[18]

Notes

1. Annti Aarne, *The Types of the Folktale: A Classification and Bibliography*, 2nd rev. ed., trans. and enlarged by Stith Thompson, FF Communications 184 (Helsinki: Suomalainen Tiedeakatemia-Academia Scientiarum Fennica, 1964), 782: "Midas with ass's ears," or, more generally, the prince with an animal trait. The supernatural wife motif is treated, pp. 128–40 (types 400–424).

2. Harf-Lancner, especially ch. 4; Gaël Milin, *Le roi Marc aux oreilles de cheval* (Geneva: Droz, 1991), 209–21.

3. Le Goff, 595–98; see also Milin, 212–13, and Anna Mühlherr, "Geschichte und Liebe im Melusinenroman," in *Positionen des Romans im späten Mittelalter*, ed. Walter Haug and Burghart Wachinger (Tübingen: Niemeyer, 1991), 329–32.

4. Cf. Coudrette, vv. 1343–44 and 364 note.

5. On what follows, see Donald Maddox, *The Arthurian Romances of Chrétien de Troyes: Once and Future Fictions* (Cambridge: Cambridge University Press, 1991); and Douglas Kelly, *The Art of Medieval French Romance* (Madison and London: University of Wisconsin Press, 1992), 240–46.

6. See Daniel Poirion, "Théorie et pratique du style au moyen âge: le sublime et la merveille," *Revue d'histoire littéraire de la France* 86 (1986): 15–32.

7. Marie de France, *Les lais*, ed. Jean Rychner (Paris: Champion, 1966), Prologue v. 16. On this important expression, see Alfred Foulet and Karl D.

Uitti, "The Prologue to the *Lais* of Marie de France: A Reconsideration," *Romance Philology* 35 (1981): 242–49; and Kelly, *Art*, 110–14.

8. Stouff, 77 (Desaivre was not available to me); Le Roy Ladurie; Perret.

9. Neither Jean d'Arras nor Coudrette identifies any blemish in the last two sons. This important difference between Melusine's last two sons and their older siblings has often been overlooked. See, for example, Le Goff, 591; Claude Lecouteux, "Zur Entstehung der Melusinensage," *Zeitschrift für deutsche Philologie* 98 (1979): 74; Milin, 216. Leo Hoffrichter appears to have noticed the difference, but his words are tentative: "Alle ihre [Mélusine's] söhne sind wie Urien irgendwie gezeichnet; doch wird ihr aussehen im laufe der zeit immer menschlicher, und die letzten kinder Melusines haben eine schöne menschliche gestalt. Dies scheint darauf zu deuten, daß der fluch, der auf ihr und ihren nachkommen lastet, langsam zu schwinden beginnt"; see *Die älteren französischen Bearbeitungen der Melusinensage,* Romanistische Arbeiten, 12 (Halle/S.: Niemeyer, 1928), 17.

10. On constructions and the establishment of the family after the twelfth century, see Karl Schmid, "Zur Problematik von Familie, Sippe und Geschlecht, Haus und Dynastie beim mittelalterlichen Adel: Vorfragen zum Thema 'Adel und Herrschaft im Mittelalter'," *Zeitschrift für die Geschichte des Oberrheins,* 105 (1957): 30–36. Useful background studies on the relation between the dwelling and literary production: Karl Hauck, "Haus- und sippengebundene Literatur mittelalterlicher Adelsgeschlechter von Adelssatiren des 11. und 12. Jahrhunderts her erläutert," in *Geschichtsdenken und Geschichtsbild im Mittelalter: ausgewählte Aufsätze und Arbeiten aus den Jahren 1933 bis 1959,* ed. Walther Lammers (Darmstadt: Wissenschaftliche Buchgesellschaft, 1965), 165–99 (for the later medieval period, see the bibliography, 167–68 n. 8); and Joachim Bumke, *Mäzene im Mittelalter: die Gönner und Auftraggeber der höfischen Literatur in Deutschland 1150–1300* (Munich: Beck, 1979), especially ch. 2, which includes examples from French literature.

11. How did Jean d'Arras know about Mataquas and Florimont? All surviving prose versions of Aimon's *Florimont* seem to date from the fifteenth century except Tours 954, a fourteenth-century fragment unfortunately destroyed in 1940. See Brian Woledge, *Bibliographie des romans et nouvelles en prose française antérieurs à 1500* (Geneva: Droz, 1954), 43, and the *Supplément (1954–1973)* (Geneva: Droz, 1973), 38–39; Charity C. Willard, "A Fifteenth-Century Burgundian Version of the *Roman de Florimont,*" *Medievalia et Humanistica,* new ser. 2 (1971): 21–46. Georges Doutrepont, *Les mises en prose des épopées et des romans chevaleresques du XIV*[e] *au XVI*[e] *siècle* (1939; rpt., Geneva: Slatkine, 1969), 264–75, confuses the manuscripts of two versions in his classification (see 265–70). His first prose version (= Woledge §59) is represented by Paris BN

fr. 1490 and Paris Arsenal 3476; they should be grouped together. The version in Paris BN fr. 12566 (=Woledge §58) is different from them, as Willard shows in her article.

12. His fate is therefore analogous to that of the knight in the *Paradis de la reine Sibylle;* see Perret, 26.

13. See especially Karl Jaberg, "Das Muttermal in Sprache, Volksglauben, Sitte und Literatur," in his *Sprachwissenschaftliche Forschungen und Erlebnisse: neue Folge* (Bern: Francke, 1965), 282–322.

14. Cf. Coudrette, vv. 3806–10, 3879–80, and Mühlherr, 332, 336. Melusine's actual progress toward humanity, which Raymondin does not recognize here, stands out more strikingly when compared with the tendency of the fay to arrest normal development, an effect just as deleterious when the father resists giving away his daughter; see Elisabeth Schmid, "Mutterrecht und Vaterliebe: Spekulationen über Eltern und Kinder im *Lanzelet* des Ulrich von Zatzikhoven," *Archiv für das Studium der neueren Sprachen und Literaturen* 229 (1992): 241–54. The exogamic marriage of Melusine and Raymondin and the marriages of their sons are healthy.

15. This is the Aristotelian theory of conception. See David C. Lindberg, *The Beginnings of Western Science: The European Scientific Tradition in Philosophical, Religious, and Institutional Context, 600 B.C. to A.D. 1450* (Chicago and London: University of Chicago Press, 1992), 65. For much of what follows I am indebted to Elisabeth Schmid, *Familiengeschichten und Heilsmythologie: die Verwandtschaftsstrukturen in den französischen und deutschen Gralromanen des 12. und 13. Jahrhunderts* (Tübingen: Niemeyer, 1986). See also Dorothea Kullmann, *Verwandtschaft in epischer Dichtung: Untersuchungen zu den französischen "chansons de geste" und Romanen des 12. Jahrhunderts* (Tübingen: Niemeyer, 1992); R. Howard Bloch, *Etymologies and Genealogies: A Literary Anthropology of the French Middle Ages* (Chicago and London: University of Chicago Press, 1983), esp. ch. 2.

16. Jean d'Arras does not report this incident, which occurred after the date on which he completed his version of the romance; cf. *M* 306–7, and Eleanor Roach in Coudrette, 60–61.

17. For example, Hervy and Griffon, sons of Urian and Hermine (*M* 140, 238; Coudrette, vv. 1769–70, names only Griffon); Bertran and Lohier, sons of Antoine and Crestiane (*M* 170, 195; Coudrette, vv. 2723–26); Olliphar, son of Renaud and Aiglentine (*M* 192); Remond, son of Guyon and Florie (*M* 238); Bernardin, son of Eudes and the daughter of the count of La Marche (*M* 289).

18. Perret also points this out.

The Poetics of Paradox in the *Roman de Mélusine*

Rupert T. Pickens

A prominent lexical feature of Jean d'Arras's *Roman de Mélusine* is a prevalence of words denoting marvel, the marvelous, and the effects of experiencing the marvelous: wonder, wonderment, to wonder at, to wonder. In fact, the vocabulary of wonderment seems to dominate the romance and to subsume the exquisite courtliness of Jean's voluminous dialogue, a major focus of his artistry, and the romance's conventional lexicon of *aventure*, as well as the romancer's self-conscious references to his composition and especially to its truthfulness. In the first hundred pages after the exordium in the edition of Louis Stouff, the frequency of words relating to wonderment averages better than two per page; in some key passages the concentration rises to four and five per page. The implications of these facts are far-reaching when we read Jean's romance in view of his commentary in his exordium and epilogue.

The bibliography of scholarly studies devoted to the *Mélusine* is relatively short, but it embodies a wide variety of critical methods that have shed light on the romance's historical and cultural contexts, its genealogical values, its psychological implications, its wealth of folkloric, legendary, and mythic content, its structure as a folktale and *conte merveilleux*, its rich contributions to the history of art and manuscript illustration, and so forth.[1] However, with a few notable exceptions,[2] scant attention has been paid to the romance's language and rhetoric, that is to say, its very bases as a work of literary art. In the present study I propose to analyze a prominent feature of the romance's "literariness" that is implicit in the dominance of the vocabulary of wonderment. As we shall see, Jean explores wonderment as a function of paradox. In so doing, he lays bare the foundations upon which his romance is constructed; at the same time, he marshals the forces of ancient and medieval intellectual and poetic tradition to fashion his work as a romance of paradox.

The dominant lexicon centers on the noun *merveille* as an object or event that inspires wonderment (*M* 14, 19, 23, 30, 34, etc.), which recurs in the adverbial phrase *a merveille(s)* ["marvelously"] (*M* 9, 28, 46, 55, etc.) and interesting verbal expressions like *(se) donner merveille* ["to strike/(be struck) with wonder"] (*M* 30, 36, 52, 55, 78, etc.) and *avoir merveille* ["to feel wonderment"] (*M* 93). The adjective *merveilleux* ["wonderful," "wondrous"] (*M* 11, 18, 19, 20, 21, 23, etc.) also occurs frequently, the derived adverb *merveilleusement* (*M* 46) less so. Most common, however, are pronominal verbs denoting the mental and emotional processes of wonderment: *s'esmerveillier* ["to marvel," "to wonder"] (*M* 7, 25, 29, 37, 38, 39, 40, etc.), *se merveillier* (*M* 81), and the inchoate *se prendre a merveillier* ["to be taken with wonderment"] (*M* 33); significantly, the passive *estre esmerveilliez* ["to be wonderstruck"] is also very common (*M* 20, 28, 30, 55, etc.). Shadings in the meaning of these verbs range from "the subject is thunderstruck" to "the subject wonders about" something in perplexity.

Other degrees of wonderment, ranging from astonishment to dread, are denoted in Jean's somewhat less frequent use of the verb *esbahir* ["to astound"] in constructions that exactly parallel his use of *esmerveillier*: *s'esbahir* (*M* 39, 48, 54, 55, 60, etc.) and *estre esbahiz* (*M* 6, 8, 9, 10, 20, 25, 33, 34, 36, etc.); the verb *esbahir* is more flexible than *(es)merveillier* in that it can be used transitively (*M* 18). Finally, the field is broadened still further by related concepts such as surprise (*souspriz* ["taken by surprise"] [*M* 8]), the uncanny (*estrange* ["strange"], *estrangement* ["strangely"] [*M* 28, 39, 49, 80, etc.]), and bewilderment, uncertainty about where one is or what one should do (*ne sçavoir* ["not to know"] [*M* 6, 114]).

Such emphasis on the lexicon of wonderment befits a romance whose heroine's name, Melusine or Melusigne, means "merveilles ou merveilleuse," according to one character (*M* 47); this heroine in turn gives her name, in the anagram form Lusignan, both to the castle she has built, to commemorate that "elle [la forteresse] a esté fondee merveilleusement et aventurieusement" [it was marvelously and providentially founded], and consequently to the noble family whose founding ancestor she is and whose origins Jean's romance records and celebrates (47).[3] Thus, a very large segment of the vocabulary of wonderment connotes Melusine herself. The very fact that the heroine's name is so pervasively suffused in the text is, of course, highly significant. As the exordium suggests, however, Jean's preoccupation with the marvelous also points to a fundamental problem in romance writing generally that looms all the larger when the text functions as a genealogy: the question of truth—Michèle Perret's *invraisemblable vérité*. Obviously, truth and truthfulness constitute an even more important issue when the founding ancestor is *merveilleuse*: she is part human, part fairy, she has the form of a woman who changes into a serpent from the waist down once a week, she eventually becomes wholly reptilian as she metamorphoses into a flying dragon, and in Jean's own day she continues to haunt the castle she has established.

Jean confronts the issue of truth by introducing paradox as a means to knowledge and the perception of transcendent truth. It is paradox that provokes wonder and wonderment when it opposes to commonly held opinion (Greek *doxa*) a statement or a condition that runs counter to that opinion. Or else, in another mode, paradox can seem to ascribe equal validity to opposed statements or conditions so that common opinion finds it irrational and meaningless. It would not be overly facetious to recall that the *doxa* that is challenged in paradox is what Roland Barthes held in such contempt that he felt compelled to revolt against it.[4] Similarly, Jean d'Arras, in asserting the truthfulness of his history, favors the paradoxical and valorizes the wonderment it produces. Paradox, wonder, and truth are the primary topics in Jean's exordium and the complementary epilogue. In his commentary Jean in fact develops a poetics of paradox that pervades and gives shape to his entire romance, just as the name Melusine, the marvel she is, the wonders she works, and the wonderment she inspires permeate every page of his text.[5]

Jean's opening paragraph is a richly complex tapestry of interwoven themes and topoi that are significant in their own right, of course, as befits the formal exordium. These commonplaces include an invocation of the Deity, expressions of authorial humility, acknowledgment of noble patronage, references to the history of the work at hand with mention of sources, the command to write, even the date when the project began.[6]

Other exordial themes also emerge as prominent in the Melusine romance itself. Appropriate in the topicality of the prologue is Jean's implication that his literary project is a humble imitation of the divine creative act. In the opening sentence—at the beginning of Jean's work as in the beginning of the created world ("En toutes choses commencier" [In beginning all things] (*M* 1)—God is evoked as "le Createur des creatures, qui est maistre de toutes les choses faictes et a faire" [the Maker of all creatures, who is master of everything created and yet to be made] (*M* 1). Similarly—but in dim reflection of the divine enterprise, for he is a creature ("Si prie a mon Createur" [So I pray my Creator] (*M* 1) who depends upon a source and works at a patron's behest—Jean says of his achievement: "[j']en ay fait le mieulx que j'ay sceu" [I have done the best with it that I knew how] (*M* 1), "je l'ay fait au plus justement que j'ay peu" [I have made it as right as I could] (*M* 2). This conventional comparison is further projected beyond the exordium and into the romance itself, where the theme of superhuman creativity dominates particularly in the character of the heroine as builder of marvelous cities and castles and as mother of extraordinary sons. Thus Melusine's work reflects that of Jean d'Arras, his imitates hers, and both are well-intentioned but refracted distortions of the divine model.

Jean also implicates God's creative powers with certain moral issues: God is "maistre de toutes les choses faites et a faire, qui doivent tendre a perfection" [master of all things created and yet to be made which must bear toward perfection] (*M* 1),[7] while He punishes those things that do not "bear toward perfection" "selon les vices des creatures" [according to the creatures' vices] (*M* 1). The issue of tending toward perfection and goodness, and consequently salvation, or toward corruption, and therefore perdition, is central in acts of assessment throughout the romance—in making judgments about the products of creative acts, including Jean's as well as Melusine's, and most especially about the nature, character, and ambiguous destiny of Melusine herself. Jean also relates the matter of judgment and punishment to the thematics of paradox.

Jean implicitly broaches the subject of paradox by evoking a set of ideas associated with the state of mind that is provoked when human reason confronts paradoxical statements: *émerveillement*. He introduces his theme in references to Psalms 35 and 91:[8] "David le prophete dit que les jugemens et punicions de Dieu sont comme abysme sans rive et sans fons, et n'est pas saige qui les cuide comprendre en son engin" [David the prophet says that God's judgments and punishments are like a boundless, bottomless abyss, and he is unwise who pretends to understand them through his intellect] (*M* 2). In Jean's statement, the Psalm text "Justitia tua sicut montes Dei, judicia tua abyssmus multa" (Ps. 35:7) is linked to "Quam magnificata sunt opera tua, nimis profundae factae sunt cogitationes tuae; insipiens non cognoscit, et stultus non intelliget haec" (Ps. 91:6–7).[9] Moreover, through the medium of expressions like "magnificata opera tua," "profundae cogitationes tuae," "montes Dei," and the verb *cognoscere*, Jean's text further implies association of these with other Psalm texts, such as 138, where the Psalmist exclaims: "Mirabilis facta est scientia tua ex me; confortata est, non potero ad eam" (Ps. 138:6) and "mirabilia opera tua, et anima mea cognoscit" (Ps. 138:14).[10] Contemplation and acknowledgment of *mirabilia* causes the sensation of wonderment; and, while God's knowledge is wonderful—*mirabilis*—in and of itself, the Psalmist's own feelings of wonderment when facing God's *mirabilia* can lead him to greater knowledge ("insipiens non cognoscit," but "anima mea cognoscit").

Jean recognizes a relationship between *mirabilia* in the created world and truth: "Et croy que les merveilles qui sont par universel terre et monde sont les plus vrayes" [And I believe that the wonders that exist throughout Earth and all Creation are the things that are truest] (*M* 2). In the first direct reference to the exact nature of the matter of the romance to come, Jean gives as the prominent example of such *merveilles vraies* "les choses dites faees" [the things that are called fairy] (*M* 2).[11]

Jean goes on to warn his reader that creatures should not strive in outrageous presumption to understand God's judgments and works through their intellect (*entendement*), but they should contemplate them and "marvel at them" as though wonderstruck. As in the Psalms, when the mind explores the limits of human reason and then crosses beyond, it is struck with wonderment, and this experience can lead to perception of eternal truth: "et, en soy esmerveillant, [l'être humain doit] considerer comme il saiche douter et glorifier Celui qui si celeement juge" [and, as they feel wonderment, (people) must consider how they might fear and glorify the One who judges so secretly/invisibly] (*M* 2).

Jean further develops this theme by conjoining with it two distinct currents in medieval intellectual history. On the one hand, he cites Aristotle and Saint Paul as authorities who explicitly posit a relation of signification linking the visible world, where wonders are produced, and the invisible world, where God acts "si celeement" (*M* 2). Jean remarks: According to what Aristotle says concerning invisible things, the rational creature of God should understand that, with respect to the distinctions among the [visible] things He has created here below, these things by their presence here make Him known through their essence and nature.[12] Jean reinforces this Aristotelian commonplace with a reference to an equally well-known passage from Saint Paul's Epistle to the Romans: "Invisibilia enim ipsius a creatura mundi per ea quae facta sunt, intellecta, conspiciuntur: sempiterna quoque eius virtus et divinitas" (Rom. 1:20).[13] As demonstrated by Peter Lombard's *Sententiae*,[14] as well as commentaries by William of Ockham and others, the Pauline text is one of the bases of traditional theological speculation, as it posits the means by which it is possible to gain knowledge of God.

On the other hand, Jean returns to the question of paradox by relating his reflections on the links between the visible and invisible worlds to the tradition of sophistic disputation, which also has Aristotelian origins. He accomplishes this by evoking ways in which authoritative works can stimulate the reader's imagination. Aristotle's "rational creature of God," who understands that visible creation bears the signifying imprint of the invisible Creator,[15] is, for Jean d'Arras, an ideal reader of books: he reads books—more explicitly, "*voit* les livres lire" [*sees* books being read] (*M* 2, my emphasis)—and brings to this reading a certain "foy es atteurs, entendre les anciens" [faith in the Authorities (*auctores*), which is to say, the Ancients] (*M* 2–3). Such a reading experience is tantamount to visiting faraway "provinces, lands, and kingdoms" (*M* 3).[16] Circling back to his initial elucidation of relevant texts from the Psalms, Jean suggests that it is precisely in these realms that the reader encounters novelties and wonders ("merveilles . . . si nouvelles" [marvels so new] [*M* 3]) which, exactly like the *mirabilia* that moved David to wonder at the powers of God, compel the reader to acknowledge that "les jugemens de Dieu sont abisme sans fons et sans rive" [God's judgments are a bottomless, boundless abyss] (*M* 3). In this new, more learned context, however, Jean explicitly qualifies wonderful events as occurring contrary to ordinary human experience and beliefs, that is, contrary to *doxa*: such events are "merveilles, selon comm[un]e estimacion" [wonders, according to common opinion] (*M* 3). Jean's use of this term literally recalls the definition of Greek *paradoxon*; thus, he places his argument squarely in the classical dialectical tradition.[17]

Before continuing with an account of that tradition, it will be helpful to look at two relatively simple forms of paradox that inform the *Roman de Mélusine*.

Mirabilia and Wonderment

Very frequent in Jean's romance are references to objects and events, described as *merveilles* or construed to be *mirabilia*, which, because they are unusual and extraordinary, provoke bewilderment or wonderment in a way that is direct and uncomplicated.

I have already anticipated Melusine's construction of the castle of Lusignan and its name. As Melusine builds her castle, its foundations are "si fors que c'estoit merveilles a veoir" [so strong that it was a wonder to behold]; her workers are so quick and accomplish so much that "tous ceux qui par la passoient en estoient esbahiz" [all who passed by there were astounded by (what they saw)]; the castle's posterns are "fors a merveilles" [wondrously strong]; the whole castle is "grant et fort a merveille" [wonderfully great and strong] and all who see it "furent tous esbahiz comment si grant ouvraige povoit estre en si pou de temps faiz ne achevez" [were all amazed at how such a great work could be built and finished in so little time] (*M* 46).

Later Melusine asks for help in naming the castle so that "il soit memoire a jamais comment elle a esté fondee merveilleusement et aventurieusement" [it may be remembered forever how it was wondrously and providentially established] (*M* 46). When she invents the name Lusignan, the young count of Poitiers exclaims: "ce nom lui affiert tres bien pour deux cas, car vous estes nommee Melusigne d'Albanie, et Albanie en gregois vault autant a dire comme chose qui ne fault, *et Melusigne vault autant a dire comme merveilles ou merveilleuse*. Et aussi ceste place est fondee *merveilleusement*, ne je ne croy mie que jamais, tant comme elle durra, qu'on n'y treuve *de merveilleuses choses*" (*M* 47, my emphasis; see note 3).

The seduction of King Elinas by Presine provides an example of protracted wonderment. When Elinas encounters the fairy Presine at a remote fountain, he is "tous esbahiz de la beauté qu'il perceut en [elle]" [utterly amazed at the beauty he saw in her]; he is bewildered and perplexed: "si abusez tant du doulz chant que de la beauté de la dame qu'il ne scet s'il dort ou veille" [so greatly confounded by the singing as much as by the beauty of the lady that he does not know whether he sleeps or wakes] (*M* 6). As there is no castle nearby except his own, Elinas wonders where Presine has come from: "Et pour tant, *m'emerveil je* de quel part si belle ne si gracieuse creature . . . puet estre cy venue, si seule de compaignie" [And thus *I wonder* where such a beautiful and graceful creature . . . can have come here from all by herself] (*M* 6, my emphasis). Further, when he sees her palfrey, its rich trappings leave him "tous esbahiz" [utterly amazed] (*M* 7).

When he finds her again, he is "si souspriz de s'amour" [so overwhelmed by love for her] that he does not recognize her; she calls him by name, but he is "moult esbahiz, car il ne congnoissoit celle qui parloit à lui" [quite thunderstruck, for he did not recognize the woman who spoke to him] (*M* 8). Their eventual marriage also provokes wonderment: "ly pays du royaume d'Albanie estoient moult esbahiz qui celle dame estoit" [the land of the kingdom of Albanie was dumbfounded as to who that lady might be], and their three baby daughters, the eldest of whom is Melusine, are "tant belles qu'a merveilles" [so beautiful it was a wonder] (*M* 9).[18]

Doxa and Para-*doxa*

Jean also frequently portrays a juxtaposition of *doxa* and a contradiction of *doxa*. The discovery of Melusine's secret exemplifies paradox as an opposition of a common and a more elite opinion.[19] When Raymondin's brother, the count of Forez, tells him what people are saying about Melusine, his statement opposes two explanations for her weekly disappearances: "la commune renommee du peuple court partout que vostre femme vous fait deshonneur et que tous les samedis elle est en fait de fornicacion avec un autre. Ne vous n'estes si hardiz, tant estes vous aveugliez d'elle, d'enquerre ne de savoir ou elle va" [the common story among the people runs everywhere that your wife dishonors you and that every Saturday she commits fornication with another man. Nor are you man enough, you have been so blinded by her, to ask or to find out where she goes] (*M* 241). This is *doxa*, "la commune renommee du peuple." He continues: "Et les autres dient que c'est un esperit fae, qui le samedy fait sa penance" [And the others say that she is a fairy spirit that does its penance on Saturdays]. What "the others say" is manifestly not the common opinion. Thus, as a proposition, it is literally para-*doxa*; yet, because we have been privy to the words of Presine's curse,[20] we know that para-*doxa* expresses the truth. Appropriately, as he contemplates the contradiction, Raymondin's brother is perplexed: "Or ne scay lequel croire" [Now I don't know which one to believe] (*M* 241).[21]

As Jean always affirms the truth in paradox, so the *doxa* is false and Raymondin eventually witnesses the truth, perhaps without understanding it, when he spies on Melusine in her bath.[22] Raymondin is not amazed by the sight of his half-reptilian wife, but he is grief-stricken that he has betrayed her (*M* 242). The reason why his sense of betrayal overwhelms any wonderment must be that the rage and jealousy that have beset him and provoked him to violate his oath stem from the *doxa* he has embraced, the common view of infidelity and cuckoldry. This is why Raymondin calls his brother's statement a false accusation ("faulx enortement" [*M* 242]). It is not false in and of itself, however, although the *doxa* it transmits is false; the statement is "merely" paradoxical.

Other modes of paradox in Jean's text require more elaboration. Some useful guidelines are provided by a recent definition of paradox by the philosopher Howard P. Kainz, who recognizes three distinct kinds of paradox: the religious, the literary, and the philosophical.[23] Philosophical paradox is a species of dialectical argumentation; it "challenges received opinion . . . [and] value systems." Literary paradox, which Kainz restricts to oxymoron, is also dialectical in that it can yield opposing propositions, but it "depend[s] on insight and intuition rather than argument." He continues: "Oxymorons such as 'loving hate,' 'darkness visible,' [etc.] . . . in the very brevity which is essential to their formulation, seem to preclude any argument whatsoever. Presumably literary paradoxes *could* be argued for; but they would lose their aesthetic appeal and literary value if this happened." Religious paradox is also dialectical, but in it contradictions follow from a particular "belief-system or mystical experience or state of enlightenment."[24] Of the three, literary and philosophical paradox are the most germane to the present discussion.

Oxymoron as Antithesis or *Contentio*

Juxtaposition of opposites without syntactical linking at the level of phrase and sentence is discussed in medieval arts of poetry as antithesis or *contentio*, as in Mathieu de Vendôme.[25] But Geoffroi de Vinsauf provides some particularly compelling examples of oxymoron when he takes the trope beyond simple juxtaposed opposites to compose richly meaningful sentences: "Numquam fessa manus, nisi quando quiescit"; "Ante Dei faciem devota silentia clamant."[26] It is especially noteworthy that, when he proposes far more extended discourses, his statements resemble plot summaries. For example:

> Litibus alternis quando bellantur amantes,
> Crescit in hoc bello linguarum pax animorum;
> Hoc odio conditur amor.[27]

Significantly, Geoffroi considers both kinds of structures, his sentences and his extended plots, to be paradoxical by the effect they produce in his reader. Marking his transition from the simple to the more complex, he bids his reader: "Consule res alias, et idem mireris in illis."[28]

In Jean d'Arras's romance, emotional and other kinds of conflicts are frequently expressed in oxymoronic juxtaposition or *contentio*. In the struggle for control of Cyprus, for example, the Sultan's spies in the besieged city of Famagouste inform him "que secours venoit au roy et que le peuple de la ville en fut *fort resbaudiz*, et aussi comment le roy estoit navrez, dont la cité fu *moult troublee*" [that help was coming to the king and that the townspeople were *much gladdened* because of it, and also how the king had been wounded, at which the city was *greatly troubled*] (*M* 110, my emphasis). After the Sultan is eventually defeated, the Captain of Limassol enters the city "et lors trouva les gens par la rue dont *aucuns faisoient grant joye* pour ce que ilz se veoient delivrez des Sarrasins, et beneissoient l'eure que les enfans de Lusignen [Urian et Guyon] furent onques nez, et l'eure que ilz estoient arrivez ou pays; et *l'autre partie faisoient grant douleur* pour la blessure du roy, dont on disoit que il n'y avoit remede nul qu'il ne perdist la vie" [and then he found the people all about the street *some of whom were heartily celebrating* because they saw themselves delivered from the Saracens, and they blessed the hour when the boys from Lusignan [Urian and Guyon] had been born, and the hour when they came to that country; and *others were deeply grieving* because of the king's wound, about which people said that there was no remedy to keep him from losing his life] (*M* 114, my emphasis).[29]

Later when the dying king of Cyprus tells his daughter Hermine that Urian wishes to marry her—"elle ot si *grant joye ou cuer* qu'elle ne scot que faire"—her joy perplexes her. "Mais elle n'en monstra nul semblant. Ains monstre qu'elle sente *grant douleur ou cuer*, et si faisoit elle" [she felt such *great joy in her heart* that she did not know what to do. But she showed no sign of it. Rather, she appeared to feel *great grief in her heart*, as indeed she did] (*M* 116, my emphasis).

An exemplary occurrence of *contentio* raised to the level of plot occurs in the narrator's remark after Raymondin accidentally kills his benefactor, Aimery, count of Poitiers; the *contentio* extends to the plot of his entire romance: "Or commence *la doulour et la grant tristece Remondin* et *le grant eur qui depuis lui vint de ceste doulereuse tristece*, si comme la vraye histoire le nous raconte" [Now begin *Raymondin's grief and his great sadness* and *the great happiness that afterwards came to him from this baleful sadness*, just as the true history tells us] (*M* 21, my emphasis). Another comes in Melusine's *plainte* after Raymondin betrays her: "Las! Mon amy, or sont noz amours tournees en hayne, noz doulceurs en durté, noz soulaz et noz joyes en larmes et en plours, nostre bon eur en tres dure et infortuneuse pestillence" [Alas! My friend, now our love has turned to hatred, our tenderness to hardness, our solace and our joy to tears and weeping, our happiness to harsh, luckless sickness] (*M* 256). The terms in which Melusine expresses her grief transcend the present moment in the history and project her conflict past the end of Jean's romance and the time of its writing until Judgment Day when her penance will be over.

Hypomone

Another form of literary paradox, the figure of speech called *hypomone*, functions differently from oxymoron. As the minor rhetorician Julius Rufianus defines it, hypomone occurs when "meaning [is] suspend[ed] and something the audience does not expect happens instead."[30] The Latin terms for this figure emphasize the bases of its effects: *sustentatio* (forbearance) suggests the possibility of unaccustomed novelty, while *inopinatum* (something unexpected) stresses the element of surprise. The importance of the unexpected is discussed in Aristotle's *Poetics*. Jean d'Arras cannot have known the *Poetics*, which was not published in the West until just over a hundred years after the *Roman de Mélusine*, but Aristotle's development is instructive in a general way. The unexpected occurs in the most noteworthy tragic plots (*Poetics*, ch. 9, §§11–23): the inspiration of pity and fear "is best produced when the events come on us by surprise."[31] Aristotle's phrase translated as "by surprise" points precisely to paradox: παρα τὴν δόξαν (contrary to common opinion). And the state of mind provoked in the spectator is wonderment—τὸ θαυμαστὸν, *mirabile*, which S. H. Butcher translates as "*tragic* wonder" (my emphasis). Later (ch. 24, §§8–9) Aristotle remarks that the illogicality—τὸ ἄλογον—on which wonderment depends is even better suited for the epic, that is, for narrative, than it is for tragedy. There is nothing unexpected in the *doxa*; surprise results from the para-*doxa*, and it produces wonderment.

To return to *hypomone*, Julius Rufianus's remarks suggest an interruption in the orderly laying out of an argument; this clearly raises the issue of natural vs. artificial order. Geoffroi de Vinsauf counsels artificial order as nobler, better befitting the public realm ("civilior" [l. 99]; "large prior" [l. 100]). Most significantly for our purposes, in his exuberant verse Geoffroi also associates artificial order with paradox. The notion of order is bifurcated; natural order, he asserts, is sterile, but the "second branch," that is, artificial order, is fertile:

> et mira succrescit origine ramus
> in ramos, solus in plures, unus in octo.[32]

Thus, the eight forms of artificial organization Geoffroi recognizes all stem from a wondrous original. More generally, then, anything unusual or unexpected in a literary structure can be paradoxical.

Two examples of hypomone in the *Roman de Mélusine* are particularly outstanding. Jacques Le Goff has already pointed out one when he notes a most significant exception in the way Jean d'Arras constructs his romance. Jean's work clearly partakes of the *conte merveilleux*: "Une des caractéristiques du conte merveilleux, c'est la *happy end[ing]*" (Le Goff and Le Roy Ladurie, 598). Yet, as Le Goff observes, "*Mélusine* finit mal." In fact, he sees in Jean's romance a turn toward "le poème héroïque, dont l'accent est souvent tragique" (598).

Geoffroy's murder of the monks at Maillezais along with his brother Fromont constitutes another surprising and important turn of events. Although Geoffroy is foolhardy and often callous, nothing in his character and nothing in Jean's plot—not any form of antimonasticism, not a hint of hatred for his brother—anticipates such an effusion of cruelty. Jean introduces the episode with a double paradox. In an exemplary *contentio*, he reports that the monks at Maillezais rejoice at Fromont's arrival: "Mais se lors orent joye de la venue Fromont, depuis en orent grief doulour" [But if they now felt joy at Fromont's arrival, afterwards they came to great grief because of it]. He comments that the "grief doulour" happened not because of anything Fromont did but "par une moult merveilleuse adventure que je vous diray ci avant en une histoire" [through a wondrous happenstance which I will tell you in a story farther along] (*M* 248). What is *merveilleux* about the *adventure* is the element of surprise in Geoffroy's unexplained attack on the monastery as well as the enormity of his unexpected crime; in other words, the *aventure* is hypomonic.

In opposition to the will of Raymondin and Melusine, who have consented to Fromont's vocation,[33] stands Geoffroy's conviction that the monks at Maillezais are vile men ("ces lecheours moynes") who have enchanted Fromont and taken him there to raise their status ("pour mieux valoir") (*M* 250); but this view is not justified by the context and appears paradoxical. Later Geoffroy turns aside, with another unexpected expression of antimonasticism, Fromont's explanation of his motivation, which is consistent with the attitude Jean attributes to his parents;[34] Geoffroy answers that Fromont will be burned with the others: "ne il me sera ja reprouvé que j'aye moine a frere" [and it will never be held against me that I have a monk for a brother] (*M* 251). The paradoxicality of Geoffroy's accusations is further underscored by the abbot's assertion that, in effect, Fromont's vocation is not irrational: "Haa sire, dist l'abbé, pour Dieu, mercy, veuillez vous informer de raison" [Ah, my lord, said the abbot, for God's sake, take pity, please find out the truth for yourself] (*M* 251). Geoffroy steadfastly refuses to listen to reason, and he is condemned by his companions.[35]

The fact is that Geoffroy's unmotivated attack on the abbey introduces a whole complex of paradoxes leading to the romance's climax and conclusion; we shall return to this episode.

Sophismata: Paradox and Knowledge

In *Sic et Non* Abelard cites Cicero, as well as Saint Augustine, as his authority on paradox and the paradoxicality of language, although Abelard does not use these terms.[36] This treatise, we recall, lists contrary opinions on doctrinal points, each of which claims authoritative validity. Clearly, perplexity produced by such confrontation in antinomy invites a skepticism that is endemic to dialectical paradox. Most interesting, however, are the antithetical paradoxes that invite the mind to move beyond skepticism to perceive an apparently transcendent truth that embraces both opposites—as, for example, in confronting antinomies in the doctrine of the Trinity (a Father and His Son are coeternal) (Questions 5–7).[37]

Along different lines, Aristotelian paradox emerged in the thirteenth and fourteenth centuries as a pedagogical device in the study of dialectics; perhaps the most relevant example is Jean Buridan's *Sophismata*.[38] The sophistic exercise involves approaching a single problem from opposite directions. According to Aristotle, the experience of working through the exercise to face an apparently insoluble paradox produces in the student a state of *aporia*, or perplexity, at which point the process of learning can begin to take place.[39] I would suggest that the kind of wonderment that the sophistic method produces in order to create conditions conducive to learning is closely akin to the wonderment provoked by Abelard's antinomies and antitheses: in the one case, *aporia* results in the desire to know, in the other, the sense of wonderment results in belief. Both outcomes are suggested in context with the Greek Bible's only use of the term *paradoxon* (translated as *mirabilia* in the Vulgate). When Jesus heals the paralyzed man whose bed had been lowered through the roof, the witnesses gain knowledge about the nature of Jesus and are led to belief in his divinity: they are astonished and filled with terror, yet they praise God "quia vidimus mirabilia hodie" [We have seen strange things today] (Douay Version: Luke 5:26). This is precisely the quality that Jean d'Arras ascribes to *mirabilia* when he appeals to the authority of David, Saint Paul, and Aristotle.

Sophistic paradox is prominent especially at the beginning of Jean's romance, as might befit a young hero's education. Melusine's trick with the stag's hide playfully takes the form of the sophism based on connotation (*appelatio*), that is, on how the same terms connote differently in different contexts. Melusine instructs Raymondin that, when he sees the young count of Poitiers, he must ask him a boon: "si lui demandez autant de place en ceste roiche et en ce desrubant comment un cuir de cerf pourra enclourre" [ask him for as much space on this crag and on this cliff as can be enclosed by a stag's hide] (*M* 21). According to *doxa*, the hide of a single stag does not define a large area, so Raymondin's request seems insignificant and easy to grant. But Melusine creates paradox by posing a second context where the initial statement is shown to be false: a stag's hide cut into a single lanyard can define an area two leagues around (*M* 34): "Et quant vous aurez tout fait, l'endemain, vous trouverez un homme qui portera en un sac un cuir de sers courree a alun, et achetez le tout ce qu'il le vous fera, puis en faictes taillier un corion tout d'une piece soubtilment, le plus delié que on pourra bonnement" [And when you have done everything [I have said], the next morning you will come upon a man carrying in a sack a stag's hide tanned with alum, and buy it for the full price he names, then have a strip, all of one piece, carefully cut from it, the thinnest possible] (*M* 21). Relevant examples from Jean Buridan's *Sophismata* include "An old man will be a boy" and "You know the one approaching," which are both true and false. The former is true of the Antichrist, as the equivalent of "he who is old or will be old will be a boy," but it is not true of old men generally (Buridan is not concerned with metaphor or with oxymora like the *puer senex*) [111, 120]; the latter is false if you do not recognize the one approaching but true if it is your father and his face is hidden [124, 127].

As Jean d'Arras transforms Melusine's sophism into narrative, it continues to produce wonderment: when the workmen see that the hide has been cut into a single long strip, "ilz en furent tous esbahiz" [they were all astonished by it] (*M* 33). Her stratagem also produces other wonders, as in the process of measuring Raymondin's land, which is fraught with paradoxical encounters: the workmen see the beginnings of Melusine's construction project (trees cut down, deep trenches dug), "dont ilz se prindrent fort a merveiller, car onques mais n'y avoient veu trenchiez" [at which they began to wonder greatly, for they had never seen ditches there before] (*M* 33); and when the first stake is driven into the ground to mark the perimeter, a great stream gushes out: "dont cilz qui livroient la place furent moult esbahiz, tant du ruissel qu'ils virent courre soubdainement comme de l'enceinte que ly cuirs de cerf tenoit, car il comprenoit deux lieues de tour" [at which those who were clearing the land were greatly amazed, as much for the stream they saw suddenly flowing out as for the amount of space which the stag's hide contained, for it reached two leagues around], repeated in a reprise (*M* 34).

Finally, Jean portrays the generation of narrative accounts of the wonders. Workmen returning to Poitiers tell the young count and his mother about "ceste merveilleuse adventure" [this marvelous happening] (*M* 34). Later the young count asks Raymondin to explain the "grant merveille [qui] est advenue" [great wonder (that) has happened] (*M* 34). He responds by affirming the truth in the workmen's story: "se cilz qui ont esté avec moy ne vous en ont compté fors ce qu'ilz en ont veu, il est tout vray de la place que ly cuirs de cerf enceint au roont. Et quant des deux hommes qui l'ont mesuré et du ruisseau qui y est sours soubdainement, c'est toute verité" [if the men who were with me have told you about it only what they saw, the story about the space enclosed by the stag's hide is completely true. And as for the two men who measured it off and the stream that suddenly sprang up there, it is all the truth] (*M* 35). Appropriately, the young count is wonderstruck: "Par foy, dist ly contes, veez cy grans merveilles" ["In faith," said the count, "this is a great wonder!"] (*M* 35).

Another key episode is especially interesting because it is a *mise en scène*, or rather *mise en récit*, of the master-pupil situation in which sophistic paradox was used in the Middle Ages. It is Aimery, count of Poitiers, the young Raymondin's noble protector, who plays the *magister abstractionum*.[40] Count Aimery reads the stars, which foretell his death. The stars themselves are *mirabilia*, "merveilleuses et diverses" [wondrous and strange] in their courses ("expedicion") (*M* 19). In them he sees foretold a "merveilleuse aventure" [marvelous happening] that could not happen according to any reason except God's own "invisible jugement," since "par congnoissance humaine" [according to human understanding], that is, according to *doxa*, no one should achieve wealth and high honor through an evil act (*M* 19); yet he knows what will happen thanks to his knowledge of astronomy, which God has bestowed on him as a gift, and he is wonderstruck ("moult esmerveilliez") (*M* 19–20).

Raymondin reacts with the skepticism that constantly emerges within, and threatens to close off, the sophistic exercise: "laissiez telx choses ester. Il n'appartient point a si hault prince comme vous estes, mettre cure d'enquerre de telz arts, ne de telz choses" [leave such things alone. It does not behoove a prince of such high station as you to bother finding out about such arts or such things]; moreover, it is not worth upsetting oneself over things that cannot help or hurt (*M* 20). Aimery nevertheless urges acceptance: "Haa, folz, . . . se tu savoies la grant et riche et merveilleuse adventure que je voy, tu en seroies tous esbahiz" [Ah, fool, . . . if you only knew about the great, powerful, wondrous happening that I see, you would be utterly amazed] (*M* 20).

Eventually Aimery states the paradox his pupil has resisted comprehending: "Et l'aventure si est telle que, se, a ceste presente heure, uns subgiez occioit son seigneur, qu'il devendroit ly plus riches, ly plus puissans, ly plus honnourez qui feust oncques en son lignaige, et de luy istroit si tres noble lignie qu'il en seroit mencion et remembrance jusques en la fin du monde; et saiches que c'est vray" [And the "adventure" is such that if, right now, a vassal killed his overlord, he would become the most powerful, the strongest, the most honored man ever in his family line, for he would be talked about and remembered until the end of the world; you can be sure that this is true] (*M* 21). This paradox is nothing less than a proleptic summary of the *Roman de Mélusine* that extends past the time of Jean's writing to Doomsday.

Once more Raymondin responds with skepticism born of *doxa*: "Lors respondy Remondin que jamais ne le pourroit croire que tel chose feust veritable, car ce seroit contre raison que nulz homs peust avoir bien ne honneur pour faire mortelle trahison" [Then Raymondin answered that he could never believe that such a thing was true, for it would be against reason for any man to have riches or honor for committing mortal treason] (*M* 21). Aimery feels compelled to believe, but for Raymondin: "ce n'est mie chose qui face a croire" [it is not a thing that is to be believed] (*M* 21). When the paradoxical prediction does come true in the fight with the wild boar, however, Raymondin, in his grief, rejects that truth as he again yields to *doxa*: "Messire, qui la gist mort, me dist, se telle adventure m'evenoit, que je seroie ly plus honnourez de mon lignaige. Mais je voy bien tout le contraire, car je seray ly plus maleureux et ly plus deshonnourez, et certes c'est bien droit" [My overlord, who lies dead there, told me that if such an "adventure" happened to me, I would be the most honored man of my family line. But I see just the opposite, for I shall be the most unfortunate and the most dishonored, and that is indeed right!] (*M* 22). It is precisely Melusine, in showing Raymondin the way out of his dilemma, who has the power to set everything aright in terms of the forecast and to accomplish the paradoxical.

A Panoply of Paradox

The biography of Melusine in human and half-serpentine form ends in a starburst of paradoxical display; her fate is played out in an elaboration, intertwining, and enfolding of a multiplicity of paradoxes. The immediate impulse propelling the *dénouement* is Geoffroy's destruction of the abbey at Maillezais, which has already been offered as an example of hypomonic paradox because Geoffroy's rage comes unexpectedly, his antimonasticism apparently conflicts with the piety implied in his parents' consent to Fromont's vocation, and he lacks reasonable conscious motivation.

The messenger who informs Raymondin about the disaster offers a rational, naturalistic explanation for Geoffroy's bewildering behavior, blaming it on melancholy and grief (*M* 254).[41] In light of the messenger's interpretation, it is significant that Nicole Oresme, anti*mirabilia* naturalist *par excellence*, also observes that melancholia stemming from grief can lead to errors in judgment that can indeed seem to be wondrous.[42]

Melusine eventually provides a retrospective interpretation that puts Geoffroy utterly in the right—hypomonically, unexpectedly. What the messenger takes to be the effects of a judgment-impairing disease has an even more astonishing cause: Geoffroy committed his outrage "par son courage merveilleux et fort" [through his wondrous and great courage] as a punishment for the monks' sins (*M* 255). Moreover, it was a punishment ordained by God "combien que ceste chose soit incongnoissable quant a humaine creature" [however much this thing is unknowable to a human creature]—that is, according to *doxa*. And here Melusine echoes the words of Jean d'Arras's exordium and epilogue: "car les jugemens de Dieu sont si secrez que nul cuer mondain ne les puet comprendre en son entendement" [for God's judgments are so secret that no mortal heart can understand them through its intellect] (*M* 255; cf. 2–3, 311). Thus the tables are turned again, and condemnations of and explanations for Geoffroy's behavior expressed in the text up to this point are revealed to be *doxa*. The paradoxicality of Melusine's statement is compounded by her startling claim that she knows the mind of God. As her words recall those of Jean's commentaries, she widens the gap that her dual nature creates between her and ordinary human beings.

Raymondin's response to Melusine's words is also irrational, as it is paradoxical, but it is not wholly unexpected.[43] As Jean reports, Raymondin recognizes the truth in Melusine's speech; thus, he acknowledges the transcendence of the paradoxical. However, he is so overcome with grief and frustration that his inborn reason ("raison naturelle"), which would bid him to embrace the wondrous, "s'en estoit fuye de lui" [had flown from him] (*M* 255).

Raymondin challenges Melusine's miraculous nature and her achievements by advancing the very *doxai* against which they have appeared as wonderful. Every phrase in his retort (*M* 255) illustrates the process: 1) "tres faulse serpente" [most false serpent] (snakes are traitorous [*doxa*], but Melusine is faithful [para-*doxa*]); 2) "ne toy ne tes fais ne sont que fantosme" [you and your deeds are but enchantments] (ordinary spirits and their works lack substance, but Jean's romance attests to the concreteness of Melusine's achievements and to her material existence both as a beautiful creature and then as a fearful dragon); 3) "ne ja hoir que tu ayes porté ne vendra a bon chief en la fin" [no offspring you have borne will ever finally come to a good end] (a logical conclusion according to Raymondin's premises, which regard Melusine as evil, but history confirms the contrary); 4) "Comment raront les vies ceulx qui sont ars en grief misere, ne ton filz qui s'estoit renduz au crucefix?" [How will those who are burned up in grievous suffering have their lives back, or your son who had yielded to the cross?] (Melusine admits that nothing human can undo the harm wrought by Geoffroy, but God creates and destroys at will: "Voulez vous arguer contre la voulenté du Createur des creatures?" [Do you wish to argue against the will of the Maker of creatures?] (*M* 255); 5) "Il n'avoit yssu de toy plus de bien que Fromont" [No worthier child has come from you than Fromont] (*M* 255) (Jean's romance proves the contrary by recounting, in much greater detail than the single Fromont episode, the wondrous heroic exploits of her five eldest sons; Eudes is the exception, and Raymondin eventually has him slain at Melusine's behest [*M* 258, 261]; Geoffroy is a benevolent prince, the last to hold the Lusignan domains intact); 6) "Or est [Fromont] destruit par l'art demoniacle, car tous ceulx qui sont forcennez de yre sont ou commandement des princes d'enfer; et par ce fist Gieffroy le grant et horrible et hideux forfait d'ardoir son frere et les moines qui mort ne avoient point desservie" [Now (Fromont) has been destroyed by the Devil's art, for those who are driven out of their minds by wrath are under the sway of the princes of Hell; and this is how Geoffroy committed the great and horrible crime of burning his brother and the monks who had not deserved death] (not true according to Melusine's account; on the contrary, she has attributed the disaster to the will of God).

The flood of *doxa* in Raymondin's denunciation overwhelms Melusine, and she falls in a faint as she comprehends that the betrayal it embodies has sealed her fate. Raymondin's immediate repentance and the couple's reaffirmation of love cannot prevent the inevitable outcome. Melusine's history ends in the still more spectacular *mirabilia* of her hideous transformation into a dragon, her fiery flight into the night, and her eventual returns to haunt the castle she built.

We have seen in example after example that Raymondin, despite some successes and often despite his best efforts, is a champion of *doxa* in the face of *mirabilia* that point the way to knowledge and truth. He proves to be the failed pupil of a *magister abstractionum* when he refuses to believe his benefactor's forecasts, he accepts the popular story accusing Melusine of adultery, he assails her with commonplace insults and thereby condemns her to a horrific purgatory. The history of Raymondin and Melusine is that of a failed marriage of the ordinary and the *merveilleux*—or rather *le commun* and *la merveilleuse*. It is the double sin of embracing *doxa* and rejecting para-*doxa*, which leads to error, instead of rejecting *doxa* and embracing para-*doxa*, which leads to truth, that Raymondin spends the rest of his life expiating, hidden away in his monk's cell in Catalunia. Meanwhile, Melusine remains an unhappy and monstrous but living reminder of the transcendence of the marvelous, the emblem of the truth in Jean's history, and the affirmation of the special greatness of her progeny.

Notes

1. Beginning with Stouff's pioneering *Essai sur Mélusine* and continuing with the study, responsible for renewed interest in the romance, by Le Goff and Le Roy Ladurie; see also Lecouteux, Markale, and especially Clier-Colombani.

2. Especially Perret, "L'Invraisemblable vérité," who broaches the subject of paradox in her analysis of the use Jean d'Arras and Antoine de La Sale (in *Le Paradis de la Reine Sibylle*) make of exordial and linguistic strategies for conveying truthfulness, which she calls *garants de crédibilité, preuves métonymiques,* and *témoignage médiatisé.*

3. When Melusine names her castle Lusignan, the young count of Poitiers exclaims: "ce nom lui affiert tres bien pour deux cas, car vous estes nommee Melusigne d'Albanie, et Albanie en gregois vault autant a dire comme chose qui ne fault, *et Melusigne vault autant a dire comme merveilles ou merveilleuse.* Et aussi ceste place *est fondee merveilleusement*, ne je ne croy mie que jamais, tant comme elle durra, qu'on n'y treuve de *merveilleuses choses*" [this name suits it very well for two reasons, for you are named Melusine of Albanie, and Albanie in Greek means the same as something that does not fail, *and Melusine means the same as wonders or wondrous.* And so this place has been *wondrously established,* and I do not believe that, as long as it lasts, people will ever (fail to) find *marvelous things* here"] (*M* 47, my emphasis).

4. Roland Barthes, *Roland Barthes,* Ecrivains de Toujours 96 (Paris: Seuil, 1975): "La *Doxa* . . . c'est l'Opinion publique, l'Esprit majoritaire, le Consensus petit-bourgeois, la Voix du Naturel, la Violence du Préjugé" (51); "Formations: une *doxa* (une opinion courante) est posée, insupportable; pour m'en dégager, je postule un paradoxe; puis ce paradoxe s'empoisse, devient lui-même concrétion nouvelle, nouvelle *doxa*, et il me faut aller plus loin vers un nouveau paradoxe" (75); etc. This attitude reflects that of the ancient Stoics, according to

Cicero's *Paradoxa stoicorum* (*Les Paradoxes des stoïciens*, ed. and trans. Jean Molager [Paris: Les Belles Lettres, 1971]). But see also Barthes, *L'Aventure sémiotique* (Paris: Seuil, 1985): in his lectures on "L'Ancienne Rhétorique" from ten years earlier, he discusses in terms of *doxa* questions of verisimilitude (96) and exordial forms and topoi (150–51).

5. As I have attempted to demonstrate elsewhere, paradox functions in Chrétien de Troyes's last romance, but in very different ways than in the *Roman de Mélusine.* See Rupert T. Pickens, *The Welsh Knight: Paradoxicality in Chrétien's Conte del Graal* (Lexington, Ky.: French Forum, 1977). As will be seen, Jean d'Arras conflates Christian *miracula* and natural *mirabilia* despite the distinctions maintained by one of his principal sources, Gervaise of Tilbury's *Otia imperialia;* see John Bloch Friedman, *The Monstrous Races in Medieval Art and Thought* (Cambridge, Mass., and London: Harvard University Press, 1981) 118–22; and Stouff, *Essai*, 51–58, 155–59.

6. The Wednesday before Saint Clement's Day in the winter of 1392, that is, the Wednesday before either November 23, for Saint Clement of Rome, Pope Clement I, or December 5, for Clement of Alexander. The ambiguous dating may well be related to the workings of paradox. In any case, it appears significant that, in his epilogue, Jean regards as a function of his romance's *perfection* a movement from ambiguous dating in terms of the liturgical calendar to precision in reference to the civil calendar: "ceste histoire . . . fu parfaicte le jeudi vij^{e} jour d'aoust l'an de grace Nostre Seigneur mil ccc. iiij^{xx} xiij" [this history . . . was brought to an end / perfected on Thursday, the seventh day of August in the year of Our Lord's grace 1393] (*M* 307).

7. Perfection is possible for Melusine's marked sons; for example, it is said of Antoine and Renaud "que les enfans ne povoient faillir, se Dieu leur donnoit vie, de venir a grant perfection de bien et de tres haute honneur" [that the children could not fail, if God granted them life, to come to great perfection in worthiness and in very high honor] (*M* 156); this contrasts with Raymondin's false observation concerning Melusine: "ne croy pas que ja fruit qu'elle ait porté viengne a perfection de bien; elle n'a porté enfant qui n'ait apporté quelque estrange signe sur terre" [I do not believe that any fruit that she has borne will ever come to perfection in worthiness: she has never given birth to a child who did not bear some unearthly strange mark] (*M* 253). Finally, Jean's romance can achieve perfection: "Et encores jusques au jour de la perfection de ceste histoire, qui fu parfaicte le jeudi" [Moreover, until the day of the perfection of this story, which was brought to perfection on Thursday"] (*M* 307; see above, n. 6).

8. Psalms 36 and 92 in the Authorized Version and other Bibles.

9. "Thy justice is as the mountains of God; thy judgments are a great deep" (Douay Version; Ps. 36:6, A.V.); "O Lord, how great are thy works! and thy

thoughts are exceedingly deep. A senseless man shall not know, nor will the fool understand these things" (D.V.; Ps. 92:5–6, A.V.).

10. "Thy knowledge is become wonderful to me; it is high, and I cannot reach to it" (D.V.; Ps. 139:6, A.V.); "wonderful are thy works, and my soul knoweth right well" (D.V.; Ps. 139:14, A.V.).

11. The gradual introduction of matter into an exordium reflects a process of insinuation, as ancient rhetoricians advised for difficult or controversial themes. According to Barthes: "si la cause est extraordinaire, suscite l'étonnement en se situant très loin de la *doxa* (par exemple: plaider contre un père, un vieillard, un enfant, un aveugle, aller contre la *human touch*), il ne suffit plus d'une action diffuse sur le juge (d'une connotation), il faut un vrai remède, mais que ce remède soit cependant indirect, car il ne faut pas affronter, choquer ouvertement le juge: c'est l'*insinuatio*, fragment autonome (et non plus simple ton) qui se place après le début: par exemple, feindre d'être impressionné par l'adversaire" (*L'Aventure sémiotique*, 151).

12. The text is difficult and perhaps garbled: "La creature de Dieu raisonnable doit entendre, selon que dit Aristote, que des choses invisibles, selon la distinction des choses qu'il a faictes ça jus, et que par leur presence de leur estre et nature le certifie" [God's rational creature must understand, according to what Aristotle says, that, concerning invisible things, according to the distinctness of things He has created here below, [they] attest to Him, through their presence, with their existence and nature] (*M* 2). Perret translates: "La créature de Dieu, si elle est raisonnable, doit prendre garde que, comme le témoigne Aristote, il y a des choses invisibles, selon la distinction qu'il a faite des choses de ce monde, et que par leur existence et leur présence, ces choses témoignent pour Lui" (14–15).

13. "For the invisible things of him [God], from the creation of the world, are clearly seen, being understood by the things that are made; his eternal power also, and divinity" (D.V.).

14. Magistri Petri Lombardi, *Sententiae in IV libris distinctae*, 2 vols. (Grottaferrata: Editiones Collegii S. Bonaventurae ad Clares Aquas, 1971–1981), vol. 1, pt. 2 (1971), 68–69 (= Liber I, distinctio 3, ch. 1). I owe much insight into the implications of paradox in ancient and medieval philosophy to discussions with my colleague, Alan R. Perreiah, whose generosity I gratefully acknowledge.

15. See Peter Lombard, 1.3.2 ("Concerning the image and likeness of the Trinity in the human soul: [193–97]). Also Nicole Oresme, *Le Livre du ciel et du monde*, ed. Albert D. Menut and Alexander J. Denomy, trans. Albert D. Menut (Madison and London: University of Wisconsin Press, 1968), 48–50.

16. The text is elliptical in its summary use of infinitive constructions (in the last two cases): "C'est l'omme qui voit les livres lire et adjouste foy es atteurs, en-

tendre les anciens; les provinces, terres et royaumes visiter" [It is the man who sees books being read and acquires faith in the Authorities [*auctores*], which is to say, visits [distant] provinces, lands, and kingdoms] (*M* 2–3). However, Perret translates: "Ainsi fait l'homme qui prend connaissance des livres, prête foi aux auteurs, écoute les Anciens, visite les provinces et les royaumes" (15).

17. Jean's prologue continues by suggesting that wonders, as visible signifiers of the invisible, are a condition of the Fall: wonders have been so widespread in time and space that only Adam can have had "parfaicte congnoissance des euvres invisibles de Dieu" [perfect knowledge of the invisible works of God] (*M* 3). He then cites wonders (fairies, *lutins*, and other spirits) recounted by "*noz* anciens" [*our* Ancients] (*M* 3, my emphasis), that is, recent witnesses, primarily Gervaise of Tilbury, on whom Jean confers an *auctoritas* equivalent to that of David, Saint Paul, and Aristotle (on Gervaise see Stouff, *Essai*, 155–59). Jean's epilogue (*M* 307–12), which mirrors the exordium, accordingly contains an "appendix" that details such wonders (*M* 294–311).

18. Finally, in a more complex manifestation of wonderment, when Elinas breaks his promise not to visit Presine in her confinement and he loses her and his three daughters, "il fu si esbahiz qu'il ne scot que faire" [he was so astounded that he did not know what to do] (*M* 10); this state of mind leads to melancholia and a perceived state of madness. This relates to the paradoxical state of mind later ascribed to Geoffroy when he massacres the monks of Maillezais, including his brother Fromont.

19. The episode of the giant Gardon of Guérande, interlaced with this episode, introduces the theme of *doxa*. Geoffroy tells the inhabitants of Guérande that he and his men are bringing the giant the only tribute he will ever have from his father Raymondin; it will come "en la pointe du fer de ma lance" [on the tip of my lance]. The people express their fears: "vous vous entremettez de grant folie, car telz cent que vous estes n'y pourroient durer" [you are undertaking great foolishness, for a hundred men like you could not last against him] (*M* 240). They are too much afraid of him to repeat their warning. The para*doxa* occurs, of course, in the fact that Geoffroy defeats the giant.

20. "Tu, Melusigne . . . c'est par toy . . . que ceste dure chartre et prison a esté donnee a ton pere, et pour ce en seras tu la premiere punie [des trois soeurs]. La vertu du germe de ton pere toy et les autres eust attrait a sa nature humaine, et eussiés esté briefment hors des meurs, nimphes et faees, sans y retourner. Mais desormais je te donne le don que tu seras tous les samedis serpente du nombril en aval. Mais, se tu treuves homme qui te veuille prendre a espouse, que il te convenance que jamais le samedy ne te verra, non qu'il te descuevre, ne ne le die a personne, tu vivras cours naturel comme femme naturelle, et mourras naturelment. Et, non contretant, de toy istra noble lignie

moult grant, et qui feront de grans et haultes prouesces. Et se tu es dessevree de ton mary, saiches que tu retourneras ou tourment de devant, sans fin, tant que le Hault Juge tendra son siege. Et t'apparras trois jours devant que la forteresse que tu feras et nommeras de ton nom, devra muer seigneur, et aussi quant ly uns des hoirs qui de ta lignie ystront devra mourir" [You, Melusine, . . . it is because of you . . . that this harsh prison was given to your father, and for this you will be the first [of the three sisters] to be punished. The power in your father's seed would have drawn you and the others to his human nature, and in a short time you would all have been beyond the custom [of] nymphs and fairies, never to return. But henceforth I grant you this gift: that every Saturday you will be a snake from the navel down. But, if you find a man who will take you as his wife, and if he swears to you that he will never see you on Saturdays or look where you are hiding or tell anyone, then you will live out the natural life of a born human woman, and you will die naturally. But whatever happens, from you will issue a very great noble line, and they will accomplish great and high deeds of prowess. But if you are separated from your husband, know that you will return to your former torment, endless until the High Judge takes His seat. And you will appear three days before the fortress, which you will build and name with your name, is to change lords, and also when one of the descendants issued from your line is about to die] (*M* 12–13; cf. 256). Melusine's redoubled dual nature (fairy, mortal; human, snake) is paradoxical in its conjoining of opposites.

21. The count's statement is actually much more complex because it manifests antinomy in opposing the two explanations for Melusine's weekly disappearances. Moreover, his perplexity in not knowing which of the explanations to believe suggests the effects of the *sophisma* (below). Finally, what the second proposition refers to, Melusine's wondrous nature, is also paradoxical, as Jean d'Arras has repeatedly said elsewhere.

22. Jean's reader knows that Melusine's transformation is, in accord with the paradoxical statement, a form of penance in that it is a punishment that can eventually result in her living and dying as a natural mortal; Raymondin does not find this out until Melusine's later confession (*M* 256).

23. Howard P. Kainz, *Paradox, Dialectic, and System* (University Park and London: Pennsylvania State University Press, 1988), 40. All subsequent quotes are from this page.

24. Statements like "the first shall be last and the last shall be first" (Matt. 19:30) and "He who saves his life shall lose it and he who loses his life shall save it" (Matt. 10:39) "can make sense only if one accepts the belief-system of the Gospel, including the doctrine of an afterlife and the redemptive effects of humiliation, suffering, and death" (40).

25. *Antithetum* is a conceptual juxtaposition of opposites that distinguishes them without an attempt to conjoin them, as in Ovid's "Frigida pugnabant calidis" (*per nomina adjectiva*) or as in "Audeo, formidas; fugo, cedis; milito, cessas" (*per verba*). Mathieu de Vendôme, *Ars versificatoria*, in Edmond Faral, ed., *Les Arts poétiques du XIIe et du XIIIe siècle: recherches sur la technique littéraire du moyen âge* (1924; rpt., Paris: Champion, 1962), 173–74; cf. also 178.

26. "Never is the hand as busy as when it lies quiet" (*Poetria nova*, l. 877), "Before the face of God the devout silences cry out" (l. 878), in Faral, 224.

27. "In case after case, when lovers quarrel, their spiritual peace grows in the war of tongues; in this hatred love is founded" (ll. 880–82).

28. "Consider these other things, and you will likewise wonder at them" (l. 879).

29. The captain is perplexed when confronted by this paradox: "Si ne scet le cappitaine que penser, car il ne savoit pas que le roy feust blessez" [And the captain did not know what to think, for he did not know that the king had been wounded] (*M* 114).

30. "Hoc schema [paradoxon vel hypomone] suspendit sensum, deinde subicit aliquid eo, contra expectationem auditoris," *De figuris sententiarum et elocutionis liber,* in *Rhetores latini minores,* ed. Carolus Halm (Leipsig: B. G. Teubnerus, 1863; rpt., Frankfurt am Main: Minerva, 1963), 46. Quoted in Pickens, 156–57, n. 7.

31. Text and translation are taken from *Aristotle's Theory of Poetry and Fine Art,* 4th ed., ed. and trans. S. H. Butcher (1894; rpt., New York: Dover, 1951).

32. "and this branch, from its wondrous origin, grows out into other branches, the single into many, the one into eight" (ll. 102–3).

33. "Fromont . . . tant pria a son pere et a sa mere, qu'ilz lui accorderent qu'il seroit rendu moyne en l'abbaye de Maleres, et y fu vestu par l'accord de son pere et de sa mere" [Fromont . . . begged and begged his father and mother until they agreed that he would become a monk at the Abbey of Maillezais, and he was committed there with his father and mother's consent] (*M* 248).

34. "Lors sault Fromont avant, qui moult bien cuida appaisier l'ire de Gieffroy, et lui dist: Mon chier frere, par l'ame que j'ay a Dieu a rendre, il n'a personne ceans qui oncques le me conseillast, car je l'ay fait de moy propre, sans conseil d'autrui et par droicte devocion" [Then sprang forth Fromont, who was sure he could calm Geoffroy's anger, and said to him, "My dear brother, by the soul that I must give up to God, no one here advised me to do this, for I have done so by my own free will, without anyone else's counsel, and in proper piety"] (*M* 251).

35. The ten knights in Geoffroy's company "moult le blasmerent et dirent que Fromont estoit en bon propos, et que encores par son bien fait et par sa

priere il povoit faire grant allegement aux ames de ses amis" [harshly blamed him and said that Fromont was in his right mind and, moreover, that through his good works and prayer he could bring great comfort to his friends' souls]. After Geoffroy curses the monks another time, "Lors se partent les chevaliers de lui, et lui dirent que ilz ne vouloient pas estre coulpables de ceste mesprison" [Then the knights left him and told him that they did not wish to be guilty of this crime] (*M* 251).

36. Peter Abailard, *Sic et Non: A Critical Edition*, ed. Blanche B. Boyer and Richard McKeon (Chicago: University of Chicago Press, 1977). As Eleonore Stump demonstrates, it was primarily Boethius who transmitted Ciceronian as well as Aristotelian dialectics to the medieval tradition; see her essays in her translation of Boethius's *De topicis differentiis* (Ithaca and London: Cornell University Press, 1978).

37. Or, one might add, in commonplace references to the Incarnation, such as a woman becomes the mother of her Father, yet she remains eternally virgin. See, for example, Mary the Egyptian's confession to the Virgin (Version *T*, ll. 451–64), where she says that the relationship just described is "merveilleuse cose." *La Vie de Sainte Marie l'Égyptienne*, ed. Peter F. Dembowski (Geneva: Droz, 1977), 42–43.

38. Theodore Kermit Scott, trans., *Jean Buridan: Sophisms on Meaning and Truth* (New York: Appleton-Century-Crofts, 1966).

39. See Alan R. Perreiah, "Aristotle's Axiomatic Science: Peripatetic Notation or Pedagogical Plan?" *History and Philosophy of Logic* 14 (1993): 87–99, esp. 91–92 and nn. 19–20.

40. The title belonged to a certain Ricardus Sophista. See Paul A. Streveler, "A Comparative Analysis of the Treatment of Sophisms in Mss Digby 2 and Royal 12 of the Magister Abstractionum," in *Sophisms in Medieval Logic and Grammar*, ed. Stephen Reed, Nijhoff International Philosophy Series 48 (Dordrecht, Boston and London: Kluwer, 1993), 144–84.

41. Jean had remarked that "il *sembloit* mieux forsenné que autre" [he *seemed* to be more out of his mind than anything else] (*M* 250, my emphasis).

42. Bert Hansen, *Nicole Oresme and the Marvels of Nature: A Study of His "De causis mirabilium" with Critical Edition, Translation, and Commentary* (Toronto: Pontifical Institute of Medieval Studies, 1985), 156 and n. 30. For the rarity of Oresme's admission of *mirabilia* that cannot be explained naturalistically, see Hansen's ch. 4, 49–73.

43. Raymondin says of Geoffroy's cruel act: "Et ores en es tu du tout desmis par ta cruauté. Par la foy que je doy a Dieu, je croy que ce ne soit que fantosme de ceste femme [Melusine], ne ne croy pas que ja fruit qu'elle ait porté viengne a perfection de bien; elle n'a porté enfant qui n'ait apporté quelque estrange

signe sur terre. . . . C'est aucune esperite ou c'est toute fantosme ou illusion qui m'a ainsi abusé; premiere foiz que je la vy, ne me scot elle bien a dire toute ma mesaventure?" [And now you are brought low by your cruelty. And by the faith I owe God, I believe that it is just a spell [cast] by this woman [Melusine], nor do I believe that any fruit she has borne will come to perfection in worthiness; she has not given birth to one child who has not borne some unearthly strange mark. . . . She is some sprite, or else everything is an enchantment or an illusion that has so beguiled me; the first time I ever saw her, was she not able to tell me all my ill fortune?] (*M* 253). Perhaps inappropriately—hypomonically (?)—Raymondin's example of Melusine's monstrous offspring is striking in its Rabelaisian grotesqueness: "Ne veez la Oruble qui n'a pas vij. ans acompliz, qui a ja occiz deux de mes escuiers, et avant qu'il eust trois ans, avoit il fait mourir deux de ses nourrices par force de mordre leurs mamelles?" [And what about Horrible who is not yet seven years old and has already killed two of my squires, and who, before he was three, had killed two of his nurses by biting their teats?] (*M* 253). However, the exaggeration seems to suggest the diabolical rather than the comic: Oruble, or Horrible, is the only one of her sons whom Melusine considers evil, and she orders him killed (*M* 258).

Melusine's Hybrid Body and the Poetics of Metamorphosis

KEVIN BROWNLEE

Jean d'Arras's *Roman de Mélusine* (1393) is centered on the identity of its eponymous heroine, presented as the founding mother of the House of Lusignan.[1] It is her hybrid status—both inside and outside history[2]—that allows the figure of Melusine to lend prestige and authority to the Lusignan lineage, while at the same time legitimizing the appropriation (by military conquest in 1374) of the fortress of Lusignan by Jean de Berry, Jean d'Arras's patron and, along with his sister Marie de Bar, the romance's explictly named dedicatee.[3] This privileged political status is represented in the text by Melusine's hybrid body.

In this essay I explore the implications of Melusine's corporeal hybridity by focusing on the two key narrative moments that stage her metamorphoses. On the one hand, I analyze how these densely patterned and carefully structured sequences function as such; on the other hand, how (in effect) they read each other, how they are linked. These close readings strive to reveal the various discursive components of the composite figure of Melusine in their dynamic (and unstable) juxtapositions and interrelations. I am par-

ticularly concerned with the potent female-gendered categories of the erotic and the "natural"; the courtly and the Christian; the human and the monstrous—and how the text purposefully stages their ultimately unresolvable contradictions.

At the same time, it is important to stress at the outset certain broader literary and cultural implications of the notions of hybrid and metamorphosis utilized by Jean d'Arras. For Melusine functions as a kind of master figure for his discursively and generically hybrid text as a whole. And in this capacity, she also can be seen as a figure for the overtly and problematically hybrid poetics of the late Middle Ages. Both Melusine the female subject in Jean d'Arras's romance and that romance as a whole are constructed from—built up out of—radically divergent generic, rhetorical, and narrative components. The final textual result is paradigmatic with regard to fourteenth- and fifteenth-century vernacular poetics in France.[4]

Melusine is a genealogical hybrid, born of a fairy mother and a human father. And Jean d'Arras's text represents this hybridity as a tension. In corporeal terms, this tension is figured by means of Melusine's three bodies: 1) a woman's body; 2) a mixed body, half-woman and half-snake; and 3) the body of a flying snake. Melusine's polycorporality is carefully structured in terms of the romance's plot. Indeed, it may be said to constitute the very basis of the plot. At issue are two different kinds of metamorphosis, each resulting from a different sort of transgression. At the level of plot, we thus have a kind of transgressive causality, with female corporeal consequences.[5]

First there is the transgression that the human-bodied Melusine commits against her human father, Elinas: imprisoning him for life in Mount Brumbloremllion in Northumberland (*M* 11–12).[6] The punishment visited upon her by her fairy mother involves Melusine's first metamorphosis, into a periodic double corporality.[7] This is initially presented indirectly as Presine explains the transformation that her daughter will undergo beginning in the diegetic present and extending for an (as yet) indeterminate time into the diegetic future. The defining terms of this transformation are those of Melusine's hybridity, whose two constitutive parts are henceforth to be set in a fundamentally unstable, tension-laden relation, which replaces the (now

irrevocably lost) progressive resolution of hybridity into unity that would have been Melusine's fate:

> La vertu du germe de ton pere toy et les autres eust attrait a sa nature humaine, et eussiés esté briefment hors des meurs, nimphes et faees, sans y retourner. Mais desormais je te donne le don que tu seras tous les samedis serpente du nombril en aval. Mais, se tu treuves homme qui te veuille prendre a espouse, que il te convenance que jamais le samedy ne te verra, non qu'il te descuevre, ne ne le die a personne, tu vivras cours naturel comme femme naturelle, et mourras naturelment . . . Et se tu es dessevree de ton mary, saiches que tu retourneras ou tourment de devant, sans fin, tant que le Hault Juge tendra son siege.
>
> [The power of your father's seed would have attracted you and your sisters to its human nature, and you would have been, before too long, definitively detached from the world of nymphs and fairies. Now, however, I give you the gift that you will become a serpent from your navel down every Saturday. But if you find a man who will marry you with the proviso that he will never look upon you on Saturday, nor reveal your secret, nor tell it to anyone, then you will live out your natural life as a natural woman, and you will die naturally . . . And if you are betrayed by your husband, know that you will return to your previous torment until the Last Judgment.] (*M* 12–13)

The second sequence of transgression and metamorphosis grows directly out of the conditions of the first, which, however, it both reverses and elaborates. Here, it is Melusine's husband Raymondin who transgresses against her by violating his oath (*M* 26, 42) not to see her on Saturday, the oath that had enabled their marriage to occur in accord with the requirements of Melusine's first metamorphosis.

This transgression takes place in two stages: first visual and then verbal. In each case the initial impetus comes from outside, rather than originating within Raymondin's own psyche. In each case also, it is a question of a fraternal crime. The two scenes are thus linked by various parallels, at the same time as a dramatic telescoping obtains: the second elaborates and intensifies the first.

The first stage of Raymondin's transgression against Melusine is introduced by the narrator's intervention: "Las! Or commence une partie de la doulereuse tristece Raimond" [Alas! Now begins a part of Raymondin's painful sadness] (*M* 241). It takes place during a Saturday night visit by his brother, the count of Forez, who recounts two rumors concerning his sister-in-law's (necessary) absence (one, in fact, false, the other, true): people are saying that Melusine's hidden Saturday activities involve either illicit sex ("tous les samedis elle est en fait de fornicacion avec un autre" [*M* 241] or an illicit nonhuman identity ("c'est un esperit fae, qui le samedy fait sa penance" [*M* 241]).

Raymondin reacts to the first (false) rumor: instantly "espris de yre et de jalousie" [overcome by rage and jealousy] (*M* 241), he uses his phallic sword to penetrate the door behind which Melusine is concealed. This metaphoric scene of aggressive sexual penetration has a purely visual climax. Furthermore, suspense is built up by a careful deferment of this climax, titillating the reader by witholding the image of Melusine: "quant il appercoit l'uis, si tire l'espee et mist la pointe a l'encontre, qui moult estoit dure, et tourne et vire tant qu'il y fist un pertuis; et regarde dedens, et voit Melusigne qui estoit en une grant cuve de marbre, ou il avoit degrez jusques au fons . . . Et la se baignoit Melusigne en l'estat que vous orrez cy aprez en la vray histoire" [as soon as he saw the door he drew his sword and placed its point against the door's surface, which was very hard, and turned and twisted it until he made a hole; then he looked inside and saw Melusine who was in a large marble tub with steps down to the bottom . . . And Melusine was bathing there in the condition which you will hear recounted hereafter in this true story] (*M* 241).

Into this sequence of scopic eroticism at the level of plot is interposed a series of recalls of the basic textual situation that work to break the mimetic illusion: the distancing writerly perspective of the locutionary relationship between narrator and reader; the evocation of "time of reading" ("cy aprez") in contradistinction to "time of narrative event"; the explicit recall of the reader's status as reader, whose "metaphoric" gaze is both mediated by and detached from the "literal" gaze of the character Raymondin. This textual self-consciousness is heightened by representing the reader's experience of the text (the naked body of Melusine) in an auditory mode ("en l'estat que vous orrez") which involves a further "disruptive" contrast with the visual erotic mode of the story line at this climactic moment.

This "disruption" is compounded by an additional—and carefully strategic—double intrusion of textual materiality between the transgressive gaze of the male subject and the visual image of the female object. First there is interposed an authorial rubric, graphically marked and functioning to establish material and interpretive divisions within the body of the text qua book. On fol. 130, r., col. 2 (of Paris, Arsenal BL 234 [3353]) we find "Comment Remond vit Melusigne baignier, par l'enhortement de son frere le conte de Forests, et lui failly du covenant qu'il lui avoit prommis" [How Raymondin saw Melusine bathing, through the prodding of his brother the count of Forez, and how he broke the oath he had sworn to her] (*M* 242). In addition, the return to the plot line is introduced by yet another evocation of the extradiegetic literary speech situation, followed by a deliberately repetitive second description of the special physical activities that enable Raymondin to arrive at the (still for the moment deferred) spectacle of Melusine's naked body: "En ceste partie nous dist l'ystoire que tant vira et revira Remond l'espee qu'il fist un pertuis en l'uis ou il pot adviser tout ce qui estoit dedens la chambre" [Here the story says that Raymondin turned and twisted his sword until he had made a hole in the door through which he could see everything inside the room] (*M* 242).

It is only at this point that the reader's gaze (following that of Raymondin, but carefully distanced from it) is allowed to see Melusine's transformed body "directly," that is, to observe both the body and Raymondin's transgression in gazing upon it: "et voit Melusigne en la cuve, qui estoit jusques au nombril en figure de femme et pignoit ses cheveulx, et du nombril en aval estoit en forme de la queue d'un serpent, aussi grosse comme une tonne ou on met harenc, et longue durement, et debatoit de sa coue l'eaue tellement qu'elle la faisoit saillir jusques a la voulte de la chambre" [and he saw Melusine in the tub: from her head to her navel she had the form of a woman and was combing her hair; and from her navel down she had the form of a serpent's tail, as thick as a herring barrel, and very long, and she was splashing her tail in the water so much that she made it shoot up to the ceiling] (*M* 242).

The careful preparation for this vision of Melusine's metamorphosed, hybrid body has created in the reader the anticipation of an erotic spectacle. The scene of the voyeur gazing through a secret perforation in the door leading to a lady's bath is a stylized generic convention within the context of late fourteenth-century French romance narrative.[8]

Perhaps the most significant anterior example from the point of view of Jean d'Arras's *Mélusine* occurs in the key scene of Gerbert de Montreuil's *Roman de la Violette* (ca. 1227–29),[9] in which Gondree, the old serving woman of the heroine Euriaut, plots to provide Lisïart with evidence that the latter can use to demonstrate—falsely—Euriaut's sexual infidelity to Gerart, the romance's hero. Gerart has foolishly agreed to wager his lands against those of Lisïart depending on the latter's success in seducing Euriaut within a week. In the scene in question, Gondree, after discovering (vv. 574–605) that Euriaut bears a sign ("*saing*" [598]) on her body whose concealment is the guarantee of her sexual fidelity to Gerart (in a *"couvens"* [601] between the lovers), proceeds to spy upon her mistress in her bath. The old servant first pierces a hole in the door: "L'aisié . . . / a lués perchié d'un percheoir; / par la fera son mireoir / a sa damoisiele esgarder" [she then pierced the door with an awl to make the peephole through which to see her lady] (637–40). Next, she gazes through it:

> mis son oel au pertruis;
> Sa demoisiele esgarde el baing,
> Et tantost a coisi le saing,
> Et voit sor sa destre mamiele
> Une vïolete nouviele
> Inde paroir sor la car blanke.
> La vielle vit cele samblanche,
> Molt par li vint a grant merveille.
>
> [she put her eye to the peephole; she looked at her lady bathing and immediately recognized the sign as she saw on her right breast a fresh violet whose purple was set off against the white flesh. The old woman marvelled greatly at this image.] (vv. 645–52)

Finally, Gondree has Lisïart repeat her voyeuristic procedure:

> La vielle le prent, si l'adreche
> Au pertruis qu'elle fait avoit.
> Li quens i met son oel et voit
> Desor sa destre mamelete
> Indoier cele vïolete.
>
> [The old woman took him and placed him before the peephole that she had made. The count looked through and saw upon her little right breast the purple hue of the violet.] (vv. 663–67)

It is also suggestive, in terms of *Mélusine*, that the treacherous Lisïart in the *Violette*—who causes the betrayal of the heroine's corporeal secret, which leads to her separation from her beloved—is the count of Forez, just like Raymondin's brother in *Mélusine*.

The visual climax of this classic version of the voyeuristic scene in the *Violette* is doubly erotic: Euriaut's semantically overdetermined naked breast, marked by the metonymic sign of her sexual identity.[10] In addition, this intensive, fetishistic, reductive focus on a single anatomical detail signifying female sexuality incorporates the conventional erotic detail of Euriaut's "car blanke" (650), whose force is heightened by the sensual contrast with the violet birthmark.[11]

By contrast, the transgressive spectacle of Melusine's body voyeuristically viewed is de-eroticized in a way that receives special emphasis because of the generic *horizon d'attente* with which it is introduced. First, her hybrid quality is carefully stressed: she appears as a rhetorical figure, analogous to Dante's Gerione in *Inferno* 17.[12] Thus the "secondary" nature of the physical manifestation of her composite identity is emphasized: she is not simply half woman and half serpent but rather half "*en figure* de femme" and half "*en forme* de la queue d'un serpent." Of particular importance in this context is the comparison of her tail to "une tonne ou on met harenc." Not only does this metaphor de-eroticize Melusine's composite body, it also transposes that body abruptly and comically out of the courtly register.[13] She is portrayed not only as a monster but as a somewhat comical monster. The playful splashing of the tail heightens this effect.

Within the context of Jean d'Arras's story line, however, the de-eroticized revelation of Melusine's hybrid body to her husband is immediately recuperated in a courtly erotic context. Not only does the physical spectacle of his wife's half-human, half-fairy identity instantaneously convince Raymondin of her innocence of the charges of sexual transgression hypothetically adduced against her by his treacherous brother, the count of Forez, but this same spectacle gives rise to a courtly erotic lament by Raymondin for what he believes to be the irrevocable loss of his lady. His reaction to the sight of Melusine qua female monster is to bemoan his loss of Melusine as courtly lady.

At this point in the plot, there is no overt reaction by Raymondin to Melusine's corporeal status as hybrid monster, nor to her "existential" status as fairy. It is as if the text temporarily suppressed any reaction to this identity as such, deferring its full implications until later.[14] Rather, Raymondin's extended lament here presents his transgressive violation of his fairy pact with Melusine as a courtly *mesfait* against a courtly *dame*. Particularly important in this construction of Melusine are the standard courtly epithets Raymondin uses to refer to her. He begins by exclaiming: "Hay, . . . *m'amour*, or vous ay je trahie" [Alas . . . my love, now I have betrayed you] (*M* 242). He goes on to characterize her to his brother as "la meilleur et la plus loyal dame qui oncques nasquist" [the best and most loyal lady ever born] (*M* 242).[15] The "piteux regrez" (*M* 243) with which the now bedridden Raymondin concludes are dense with courtly constructs and are rhetorically structured around three standard courtly vocatives: 1) "Haa, Melusigne, . . . *dame* de qui tout le monde disoit bien" [Ah, Melusine . . . lady about whom everyone spoke well]; 2) "Aveugle *Fortune*, dure, sure et amere" [blind Fortune, harsh, certain, bitter]; 3) "Las, ma tres doulce *amie*" [Alas, my very sweet friend]. Both the language and the structure of Raymondin's *complainte* belong to the system of fourteenth-century courtly discourse embodied most authoritatively in Guillaume de Machaut, especially in his *Remede de Fortune*.[16]

The most strikingly characteristic feature of this highly distinctive and highly conventional discourse (clearly perceptible as such to Jean's audience of the 1390s) is the catalog of courtly and ethical virtues attributed by Raymondin qua courtly *amant* to Melusine qua courtly *dame*, lost through his *mesfait*: "Or ay je perdu beauté, bonté, doulcour, amistié, sens, courtoisie, charité, humilité, toute ma joye, tout mon confort, toute m'esperance, tout mon eur, mon bien, mon pris, ma vaillance, car tant pou d'onneur que Dieu m'avoit prestee me venoit de vous, *ma doulce amour*" [Now I have lost beauty, goodness, sweetness, friendship, judgment, courtliness, charity, humility, all my joy, all my comfort, all my hope, all my happiness, my fortune, my worth, my courage, for the little honor that God had lent to me came from you, my sweet love] (*M* 243).[17]

The net effect of Raymondin's reaction is to intensify Melusine's human side at the very moment that her hybrid corporeal identity has been most graphically presented in the text up till now. The spectacle of Melusine's monstrous body is juxtaposed to Raymondin's construction of her in poignantly human terms, by means of courtly discursive conventions. At the same time, Melusine as female fairy monster is de-eroticized, while Melusine as courtly human lady is re-eroticized. The culmination of this program occurs after Raymondin's despairing lament, at dawn on Sunday. The retransformed Melusine enters the couple's bedroom "et celle se despoille et se couche toute nue delez lui" [and she undressed and lay down completely naked next to him] (*M* 243).

Within the context of the plot, the naked human female body of Melusine signals that her second and definitive metamorphosis has not yet taken place, that Raymondin's transgression does not constitute an effective violation of the pact. This is explained by the narrator by way of contrasting Raymondin's incorrect assumption of Melusine's ignorance of his deed with the reality of her full and complete knowledge: "elle scet bien tout. Mais pour ce qu'il ne l'ot descouvert a nullui, elle s'en souffry et n'en monstra semblant" [She knew everything. But because he had not revealed it to anyone, she tolerated his transgression, and gave no sign that she knew] (*M* 244). Raymondin's final expression of happy relief is couched in the same conventional courtly terms as his earlier lament: "Par ma foy, *m'amie et ma dame*, je me sens tous assouagiez de vostre venue" [By my faith, my friend and my lady, I feel entirely healed by your arrival] (M 244).

The passage as a whole works to heighten the contrast (and the tension) between Melusine's two bodies. The first direct presentation of her hybrid body calls forth contrastively (by way of "response") a more elaborate and intensive presentation of her human (courtly erotic) body (and identity) than virtually anywhere else in the text before this point. What is given particular emphasis is the bivalent (bidirectional) character of her first metamorphosis.

To sum up: the first—visual—betrayal of Melusine by Raymondin involves doubting, questioning, her status as wife. Raymondin's second—verbal—betrayal of Melusine will involve questioning, doubting, her status as mother. The first stage of Raymondin's transgression is against the uxorial Melusine in terms of her sexual conduct. The second will be against the maternal Melusine in terms of her offspring. Together, they constitute a "full" *mise en question* of her status as *woman*.

Furthermore, the first time, Melusine's monstrous hybrid body constitutes absolute proof of her sexual, uxorial fidelity, which is, as it were, guaranteed by her (part-)fairy identity and its corporeal manifestation—neither of which are mentioned at all in Raymondin's reaction. The second time, this same hybrid body (remembered by Raymondin in a kind of delayed reaction) will provoke his reproach against Melusine's maternity, as a function, precisely, of his now explicit articulation of her status as fairy, as monster, as serpent.

The fraternal crime that motivates the second stage of Raymondin's betrayal of Melusine—the second stage of his violation of his oath to her, which causes her second metamorphosis—is Geoffroy's murder of his brother Fromont. This narrative sequence is initiated by Raymondin's letter to Geoffroy recounting Fromont's decision to enter a monastery, introduced—as was Raymondin's first transgression—by the narrator's intervention, this time more explicit, more elaborate, and more intensely affective: "Helas! Tant a male heure le fist. Car ce fu la cause de sa tres cruel doulour et de la perte de sa moillier, dont puis n'ot joye au cuer, ainsi comme vous orrez" [Alas! He did it in an evil hour. For this was the cause of his very cruel suffering and of the loss of his wife, because of which he never felt joy again, as you will hear] (*M* 248).

It is his definitive discovery of Geoffroy's crime that causes Raymondin to condemn and reject Melusine's identity as a mother, as a fairy, and as a woman. His first articulation of this is private:

> Par la foy que je doy a Dieu, je croy que ce ne soit que fantosme de ceste femme, ne ne croy pas que ja fruit qu'elle ait porté viengne a perfection de bien; elle n'a porté enfant qui n'ait apporté quelque estrange signe sur terre . . . Et ne vy je leur mere, le samedy que mon frere de Forests m'acointa les males nouvelles, en forme de serpente du nombril en aval? Si fiz, par Dieu. C'est aucune esperite ou c'est toute fantosme ou illusion qui m'a ainsi abusé.
>
> [By the faith I owe God, I think that this woman is nothing but a phantom, and I do not believe that any fruit she has borne can grow to perfection . . . And did I not see their mother, on the Saturday when my brother of Forez brought me the evil tidings, in the form of a serpent from the navel down? Indeed I did, by God. She is some kind of spirit, or else a total phantom or illusion who has thus deceived me.] (*M*, 253)

The immediate narrative cause of the ensuing public articulation of Raymondin's condemnation of Melusine is the message his barons send to her to come from Nyort to Meurvent in order to comfort her husband. This provokes the third and most elaborate commentary by the narrator: "Las! Tant mal le firent, car ilz les mirent tous deux en grief tourment et en grief misere. Or commence leur dure departie. Or commence la doulour qui durra a Remond tout son vivant. Or commence la penitence qui durra a Melusigne jusques a la fin du monde" [Alas! They acted badly, for they plunged both of them into painful suffering and bitter affliction. Now begins their harsh separation. Now begins Raymondin's pain which will last all his life. Now begins Melusine's penitance which will last until the end of the world] (*M* 254).

Melusine's opening words to her husband involve a Christian explanation of Geoffroy's crime (and its possible expiation), which echoes Jean d'Arras's prologue in terms of the topos of the inscrutability of God's judgments (*M* 2). Raymondin's fatal response is thus implicitly set up as constituting a sin. This becomes explicit in the careful presentation of Raymondin's reaction, both internally (in psychological-moral terms) and externally (in affective-descriptive terms). He knows that his wife speaks the truth (*voir*) and according to reason ("le meilleur selon raison"), but he is completely possessed by the sinful emotion of anger ("si tresperciez et oultrez de *yre*") and rejects his own "raison naturelle": his actual words are presented by the narrator as spoken in "une tres crueuse voix" [a very cruel voice].

The final and definitive stage of Raymondin's transgression against Melusine is his explicit, public, condemnatory articulation of her fairy identity, which proceeds as follows in a pseudological chain: 1) her serpentine corporeal status; 2) her illusory, mendacious metaphysical status; 3) her necessarily flawed offspring; 4) the generally diabolical context in which both she and her children operate: "Hee, tres faulse serpente, par Dieu, ne toy ne tes fais ne sont que fantosme, ne ja hoir que tu ayes porté ne vendra a bon chief en la fin. Comment raront les vies ceulx qui sont ars en grief misere, ne ton filz qui s'estoit renduz au crucefix? Il n'avoit yssu de toy plus de bien que Fromont. Or est destruit par l'art demoniacle, car tous ceulx qui sont forcennez de yre sont ou commandement des princes d'enfer; et par ce fist Gieffroy le grant et horrible et hideux forfait d'ardoir son frere et les moines qui mort ne avoient point desservie" [Ah, most false serpent, by God, you and your

deeds are nothing but phantoms, and no heir whom you have borne will come to a good end. How can those who were cruelly burned come back to life, including your son who took holy orders? You bore no child more worthy than Fromont. Now he is dead through demonic art, for all those who are mad with rage are under the power of the prince of hell; and it was in this way that Geoffroy committed the enormous, horrible and hideous crime of burning his brother and the monks who did not deserve to die] (*M* 255).

Even as he speaks these words, however, Raymondin undercuts the judgmental (as opposed to the merely descriptive) aspects of his (thus overtly limited and inadequate) characterization of Melusine. Two ironic contradictions are built into his condemnation: the assertion of Fromont's goodness undermines the global condemnation of Melusine's offspring; the condemnation of Geoffroy's "yre" undermines the validity of Raymondin's own words, since this is the essence of his affective state as he speaks.

This verbal transgression of Raymondin, a literally correct but spiritually inadequate description of Melusine, will, within the context of the romance's plot, cause her second, and putatively definitive, metamorphosis.

The scene (*M* 256–60) that immediately precedes Melusine's actual physical transformation (*M* 260) is perhaps the most dense in the entire book. Narratologically, it both parallels and elaborates Raymondin's monologic reaction to the first (visual) stage of his betrayal of Melusine, with a significantly more complex dialogic reaction to the second (verbal) stage of this same transgression. At the same time, the discursive situation at this second stage is compounded by the intradiegetic presence of a courtly public audience, as well as by Melusine's own explicit articulation of the public (and political) consequence of Raymondin's second-stage transgression against her. Mimetically, this scene constitutes the high point of Melusine's self-representation as a desiring female subject in courtly erotic terms, in other words, as a human female body. Of particular importance to my present reading is the fact that this extreme intensification of Melusine's human female corporeal identity immediately precedes and thus is strategically juxtaposed with the diegetic moment that most dramatically emphasizes the opposite extreme with regard to her corporeal identity: her

metamorphosis into a nonhuman, nonfemale, nonerotic monster—a flying snake.

The scene is structured by a repeated pattern of courtly behavioral and linguistic constructs, in particular, the faint, the embrace, and the stylized amorous vocative. In each case, repetition works to heighten the rhetorical (and the erotic) effect. The initial reactions are paradigmatic: Melusine faints; Raymondin repents, but this time it is too late, as the narrator explicitly tells us, and as Melusine's corporeal reaction qua courtly lady guarantees intradiegetically. Her ensuing *complainte*—the first direct discourse of the scene—makes explicit her *retrospective* status as desiring subject: "Haa, Remond . . . Mal vy oncques ton gent corps, ta facon, ne ta belle figure, mal convoitay ta beauté . . . Las! Mon amy, or sont noz amours tournees en hayne, noz doulceurs en durté, noz soulaz et noz joyes en larmes et en plours, nostre bon eur en tres dure et infortuneuse pestillence" [Ah, Raymondin . . . Alas that I ever saw your noble body, your manner, your beautiful face, alas that I desired your beauty . . . Alas! My friend, now our love has turned to hate, our sweetness to bitterness, our pleasures and our joys to tears and sobs, our happiness to most harsh and luckless pestilence] (*M* 256). Her speech of regret now proceeds to rearticulate the two conflicting components of her hybrid identity from what appears to be the temporal perspective of a definitive—though negative—resolution: first, the human, that is, her now-lost hypothetical status as "femme naturelle" in an explicitly Christian context; and second, the fairy, presented as a "penance obscure" that is about to be fully and definitively revealed in terms of her body. The scene's first segment closes as Raymondin faints, his corporeal reaction to Melusine's words concerning the full implications of her hybrid body thus paralleling her initial reaction to his transgressive condemnation of the temporary metamorphosis of her body, whose full significance he had misunderstood.

What ensues is a symmetrical exchange in courtly terms. First, Raymondin asks his wife's pardon, addressing her as "Ma chiere amie, mon bien, mon esperance, mon honneur" [my dear friend, my treasure, my hope, my honor]. Next, Melusine responds by explaining that her freely granted pardon is subordinate to the divine necessity that ordains her departure, addressing him as "Mon doulz amy" (*M* 257). There follows one of the most explicit corporeal erotic moments between the

two protagonists in the romance up till now, initiated, significantly, by Melusine: "le lieve, et l'embrace et l'acole de ses bras, et s'entrebaisent" [she raised him up, and embraced him and hugged him in her arms and they kissed each other] (*M* 257).[18] This erotic reciprocity is now refigured in the courtly gestural register as the third instance of the "faint motif": the two lovers—having each fainted alone in sequence—now faint together, their bodies commingled: "ilz cheirent eulx deux pasmez" [they both fell together into a faint] (*M* 257).

The inscribed courtly audience reacts to this spectacle with an affirmative articulation of the couple's courtly erotic identity, designating them as "ces deux loyaulx amans." A discursive shift begins, however, in their ensuing proleptic lament for the loss of Melusine qua political ruler: "la plus vaillant dame qui oncques gouvernast terre" [the bravest lady who ever ruled a state] (*M* 257).[19]

Her next speech involves the locutionary stance of ruler—of founding mother—as she provides a set of prophecies and instructions, initiated by the courtly vocative "Mon doulz amy" (*M* 257). Significantly, this speech is preceded by a careful "undoing" of the "lovers' faint motif," which emphasizes Melusine's dominance as acting subject: it is she who first awakens from the swoon and then revives and physically raises up her lover: "le lieve et drece en son estant." Her prophetic instructions involve a chiastic structure in which two positive (maternal) components are framed by two negative ones: first, the House of Lusignan after Raymondin will not hold together; second, the postmetamorphosis Melusine will continue—indirectly—to take care of Raymondin himself during his lifetime; third, this same postmetamorphosis Melusine will intervene directly—"en forme femmenine"—to take care of her two youngest children; fourth, her eighth child, Horrible, must be put to death in order to preserve her geopolitical legacy.

There follows the final direct exchange of words between the couple, and the culmination of the courtly erotic status of Melusine's human body. Raymondin, addressing her as "ma doulce amour," one last time begs her to remain; Melusine, addressing him as "mon doulz amy," again explains the necessary subordination of her own desire to stay with him to the will of God, "Cellui qui tout puet faire et deffaire" [He who can do and undo all things]. Her rearticulation of this divine necessity leads (as it had the first time [*M* 257]) to the second and final erotic embrace

between the lovers, again initiated by Melusine: "et lors, a ce mot, Melusigne le va acoler et baisier moult doulcement" [and then, having said these words, Melusine went to embrace and kiss him most tenderly] (*M* 258).

The ensuing definitive farewell by Melusine rewrites in a positive future mode the negative past evocation of her erotic appreciation of Raymondin's body that had opened the scene (*M* 256): "Adieu, mon tres doulz amy, mon bien, mon cuer et toute ma joye. Et saches encore que, tant comme tu vivras, j'auray toujours recreacion en toy veoir" [Farewell, my most sweet friend, my treasure, my heart and my entire joy. And know that for as long as you live I will always take pleasure in seeing you] (*M* 258–59). Melusine as female (courtly) desiring subject is thus definitively established in the text at the very moment of her disappearance in this capacity. All of this functions, of course, as part of the romance's larger program of valorizing Melusine by "neutralizing" the threat of her female erotic desire—and, most particularly, within the context of her fairy identity. She is thus consistently presented as not a succubus, not an undine.[20] Melusine's final words to Raymondin in this context reaffirm her "safely" double erotic status. While she will continue to gaze upon him with the eyes of female desire, he will be protected by virtue of not being able to reciprocate, owing to her impending metamorphosis: "mais, moy de cy partie, tu ne me verras jamais de nul jour en forme femmenine" [but once I have departed from here you will never see me in the form of a woman] (*M* 259).

The end of the reciprocal farewell scene between Melusine and Raymondin is signaled as she changes her physical location, moving to a windowsill—an intermediate space that isolates her both from Raymondin and from the assembled courtly multitude. It is from this liminal space that Melusine will deliver the last (and qualitatively different) part of her final speech, already, as it were, halfway between her human and her serpentine form, as she is (within the stylized spatial configuration of the scene) halfway between the floor and the sky. Significantly, Melusine's jump onto the windowsill already involves a proleptic metaphoric corporeal transformation that anticipates (and prepares) the literal metamorphosis that she is about to undergo: she "sault sur l'une des fenestres de la chambre . . . aussi legierement comme se elle volast et eust esles" [jumped up onto one of the windows of the room . . . as lightly as if she were flying and had wings] (*M* 259).

Melusine's final speech in her human body—from the liminal space of the windowsill—involves a series of increasingly intense and explicit affirmations of the different aspects of her human identity. First, she speaks as courtly erotic desiring subject, addressing Raymondin (for the penultimate time) as "mon doulz amy," as she gives him a pair of magic, protective rings, in a gesture that is at once amorous and maternal (at once human, as love token, and *merveilleux*, as magic fairy power). This is, of course, a stylized recall of her first lover's gift to him at the time of their first meeting (*M* 27), which simultaneously recalls the various protecting gifts to her children made in the interim.

Next, she speaks as founding mother in geopolitical terms, regretting Lusignan, the domain she has created, in the same erotic terms she had used to characterize her (soon to be lost) pleasure in Raymondin's body: "Hee, doulce contree, j'ay eu en toy tant de soulas et de recreacion, et y estoit ma beneurté . . . Helas! Je en souloye estre dame clamee" [Ah, sweet land, I have had such pleasure and delight in you, and my happiness has been here . . . Alas! I used to be called its lady] (*M* 259). This lament for her positive past political status quickly turns into an anticipatory lament for her contrastively negative future political status, imagined from the perspective of her former subjects reacting to her postmetamorphosis monstrous body: "ceulx qui me souloient faire grant joye quand ils me veoient, se deffuiront de moy, et auront paour et grant hidour de moy quant ilz me verront" [those who used to make merry when they saw me will flee from me and will be afraid and terrified when they see me] (*M* 259).

At this point, Melusine addresses these very subjects ("vous . . . tous et toutes") in terms of the two complementary aspects of her human identity: her Christian soul and her human lineage. First, she asks them to pray for her. Then she proceeds to explain her identity in terms of her human genealogy: "je vueil bien que vous sachiez qui je sui ne qui fu mon pere, afin que vous ne reprouvez pas a mes enfans qu'ilz soient filz de mauvaise mere, ne de serpente, ne de faee, car je suiz fille au roy Elinas d'Albanie et a la royne Presine, sa femme" [I want you to know who I am and who my father was, so that you will not reproach my children with being the sons of a bad mother or of a serpent or of a fairy, for I am the daughter of King Elinas of Albanie and of Queen Presine, his wife] (*M* 259–60). Even as her metamorphosis is about to take place, therefore, Melusine reinscribes herself into her human lineage, between

her parents and her children. At the same time she speaks as a political mother, attempting to protect her heirs. And her verbal strategy here constitutes a specific response to Raymondin's reproaches against her maternal identity, the reproaches that had motivated the verbal transgression of his pact with her (*M* 253, 255) which is about to lead to the very metamorphosis she is here preparing for. But this affirmation of Melusine's human status is simultaneously (for the reader) a reminder of her fundamentally hybrid nature: the daughter of a human father and a fairy mother, both explicitly named in her genealogical self-description. In addition, her explicit rejection of a maternal identity contaminated by *faee* and *serpente* components is of course about to be dramatically contradicted by the physical transformation she is on the verge of undergoing.

The final words of farewell from her human body, the discursive signs of closure for this stage of her polycorporeal life, are addressed to Raymondin. Her final vocative, "Adieu, mon amy" (*M* 260), constitutes a discursive frame with the opening vocative of the concluding section of her speech ("mon doulz amy" [*M* 259]), at the same time establishing a parallel with the opening and closing vocatives of the first part of that speech ("Haa, Remond . . . Adieu, mon tres doulz amy" [*M* 256, 258]). In addition, this final vocative definitively reemphasizes her status as courtly lady, as wife, while the final instructions that follow reemphasize her status as political mother.

The elaborate and "extreme" establishment of Melusine's identity as courtly-erotic and human-maternal in the farewell scene sets up a striking contrast vis-à-vis the ensuing description of her metamorphosis into a monster. This contrast functions to present Melusine even at the moment of her transformation as still fundamentally hybrid. A series of other rhetorical, mimetic, and structural devices work to elaborate this presentation. The point of departure is the brilliantly Ovidian touch in which the physical sign marking the place of Melusine's metamorphosis into a flying snake is the last mark of her corporeal identity as a walking woman: "Et lors fist un moult doulereux plaint et un moult grief souspir, puis sault en l'air, et laisse la fenestre, et trespasse le vergier. Et lors se mue en une serpente grant et grosse et longue de la longueur de XV. piez. Et sachiez que la pierre sur quoy elle passa a la fenestre y est encores, et y est la fourme du pié toute escripte" [And then she groaned most mournfully and sighed most painfully, then she

jumped into the air, and left the window and crossed the orchard. And then she was transformed into a great serpent, fifteen feet long. And know that the stone windowsill from which she left is still there, with her footprint inscribed upon it] (*M* 260).[21]

The process of metamorphosis is thus contrastively linked with (and guaranteed by, in pseudohistorical terms) the stasis of the footprint. The empty trace of the now absent human body points toward the monstrous presence of the serpentine body, and vice versa.

But in the text of Jean d'Arras, this metamorphosis is not definitive. First of all, the narrator immediately characterizes the snake as itself a hybrid by the use of phrases such as "la dame, en guise de serpente" and "Melusigne en guise de serpente" (*M* 260).[22] Second, there is the overtly hybrid combination of Melusine's serpentine body with her still-human voice.[23] As she flies around the towers of Lusignan she "se lamentoit de voix femmenine" [lamented with a woman's voice] (*M* 260), to the consternation of the local inhabitants, who "voient la figure d'une serpente et oyent la voix d'une dame qui yssoit de lui" [saw the form of a serpent and heard the voice of a lady issuing from it] (*M* 260–61).

Both of these markers of Melusine's postmetamorphosis hybridity recur when she reappears at Lusignan to announce Raymondin's death. Again, her serpentine body is presented in contrastive combination with her human voice: "la serpente se monstra sur les murs, si que tous la povoient veoir, et ala tout autour par trois foiz. Et puis se mist sur la Tour Poictevine, et la faisoit si griefz plains et si griefs souspirs qu'il sembloit proprement a ceulx qui la estoient que ce feust la voix de une dame, et si estoit ce, si comme dist l'ystoire" [the serpent appeared on the walls, so that everyone could see her, and she flew around them three times. Then she alighted on the Poitevin Tower where she lamented and sighed so piteously that it seemed to those present that it was a lady's voice, and indeed it was, as the story recounts] (*M* 288). The human (maternal) component of Melusine's identity is further emphasized by her sons' reaction to this human voice: "Gieffroy et Thierry en orent grant pitié, car ilz savoient bien que c'estoit leur mere, et commencent a plourer moult tendrement" [Geoffroy and Thierry were struck with pity, for they knew that it was their mother, and they began to weep most tenderly] (*M* 288). In addition, the narrator again utilizes "figurative" language that stresses Melusine's continuing hybrid status: "fut Melusigne grant espace sur la Tour Poittevine, en guise de serpente" [Melusine stayed quite some time on the Poitevin Tower, in the form of a serpent]. The final depiction of Melusine in this passage highlights her hybridity by emphasizing in sequence her human affective identity, as she cries in maternal tenderness for her children (thus mirroring their affective reaction to her, as she appears to weep "moult tendrement"), and her serpentine corporeal identity, as she flies off to Montferrat: "et lors prist son chemin par my l'air, et s'en va le droit train d'Arragon, et avoit la queue longue a merveilles, et toute burlée d'azur et d'argent" [and then she made her way through the air, proceeding directly to Aragon, and her tail was wondrously long, striped in azure and silver] (*M* 288–89).[24]

The third and most dramatic marker of Melusine's postmetamorphosis hybridity is the bivalence of the metamorphisis itself, the fact that the serpentine Melusine is able to turn back into a woman, to reattain her human body, under various sets of circumstances.

Initially, these involve her maternal obligations to her two youngest children, Remonnet and Thierry, while explicitly excluding her husband: "Melusigne venoit tous les soirs visiter ses enfans, et les tenoit au feu, et les aisoit de tout son povoir; et la veoient bien les nourices, qui mot n'osoient dire . . . Mais quant Remond scot par les norrices que Melusigne venoit visiter ses enfans tous les soirs, si lui alega moult sa doulour pour l'esperance qu'il ot d'encore recouvrer et ravoir Melusigne. Mais pour neant y pense, car jamais il ne la rara, ne ne la verra en figure femmenine, combien que pluseurs lui ayent depuis veue" [Melusine came every evening to visit her children, holding them by the fire and taking care of them as well as she could . . . But when Raymondin learned from the wet nurses that Melusine came to visit her children every evening, his pain was much assuaged by the hope that he could recover her. But his thoughts were in vain, nor would he ever recover her, nor see her in the form of a woman, although others have since seen her like this] (*M* 261–62).

The final key instance of the bivalence of Melusine's metamorphosis is even more explicit—and serves to link Jean d'Arras's patron to Lusignan, that is, to Melusine as history, as subject matter, and as text. Melusine's hybrid body—with a direct description of her bivalent metamorphosis—reveals itself to announce Jean de Berry's imminent capture of the fortress of Lusignan, in the first, most elaborate, and most spectacular of the sightings of Melusine adduced by Jean d'Arras as "proof" of her historicity: at the moment of Jean de Berry's siege of Lusignan (1373–74, approximately twenty years before the writing of the text). Cersuelle (Creswell), who holds the fortress for the English, is in bed with his mistress Alixandre de Sancerre. There is thus an eyewitness guarantee for the following: "Il vit, ce disoit il, apparoir, presentement et visiblement, devant son lit une serpente, grande et grosse merveilleusement, et estoit la queue longue de vij. a viij. piez, burlee d'azur et d'argent[25] . . . Et aloit la serpente, debatant de sa queue sur le lit, sans eulx mal faire" [He said that he saw appear clearly and visibly before his bed a marvelously large serpent with a tail seven or eight feet long, striped in azure and silver . . . And the serpent went beating its tail on the bed without causing them any harm] (*M* 308).[26]

Alixandre identifies the snake as "la dame de ceste forteresse, et qui la fist fonder" [the lady of this fortress, she who founded it] (*M* 309). What follows is a set of bivalent metamorphoses, marked for historical specificity. After some time passes, "elle se mua en figure de femme aulte et droicte, et estoit vestue d'un gros burel, et ceinte dessoubz les mamelles, et estoit affublee de blans cuevrechiez a la guise du viel temps" [she transformed herself into the shape of a woman, tall and well-carried, dressed in coarse freize, belted under the breasts, and she wore white head gear in the style of days gone by] (*M* 309). Cersuelle further says "qu'elle s'en ala asseoir sur le banc au feu, l'une heure le viaire devers le lit et le doz au feu, si que ilz povoient tout a plain veoir sa face, et bien leur sembloit qu'elle avoit esté moult belle, et l'autre heure retournoit le visaige devers le feu, et gueres de temps ne se tenoit en un moment . . . Lors se transfigura en guise de serpente comme devant, et s'en ala debatant de sa queue autour du lit et sur leurs piez, sans nul mal faire, et puis dist qu'elle se party, et la perdy si soubdainement qu'il ne scot oncques par ou" [that she took a seat in front of the fire. Sometimes she turned her head toward the bed with her back to the fire, so that they could plainly see her face, and it seemed to them that she had been very beautiful; sometimes she turned her face back toward the fire; and she did not long remain in the same position . . . Then she transformed herself into the shape of a serpent as before, and started beating her tail about the bed and upon their feet, without doing them any harm. Then Creswell said that she left, disappearing from his sight so suddenly that he had no idea where she had gone] (*M* 309).

Our final image of Melusine's body thus spectacularly recapitulates the double nature that has been her defining feature from the beginning of Jean d'Arras's narrative. She is first two natures in one body, then a hybrid body, and finally, two alternating bodies. What remains problematically constant is her hybridity as a female figure of power. It is, I think, no exaggeration to speak of her body as a kind of secularized female version of metamorphosis that evokes—contrastively but powerfully—the Incarnation. Both the spiritual glosses of the *Ovide moralisé* and the Dantean use of the Griffin as hybrid animal body to represent Christ's double nature in *Purgatorio* 31 are highly relevant here in terms of how Melusine must be read in a fourteenth-century literary and political context.[27]

Jean d'Arras's Melusine is a discursive composite—a figure constructed out of a set of discourses in unstable contrast with each other: fairy-monstrous, courtly-erotic, maternal, political-foundational, Christian. This discursive hybridity, of course, makes Melusine a figure for Jean d'Arras's text as a whole: a hybrid mixture of the discourses of *conte de fée*, courtly romance, crusade-epic, political historiography, travelogue/pilgrimage, popular theology, Hundred Years' War propaganda. And in Jean's text, as in the figure of Melusine, this hybridity remains unresolved, unstable. Thus Melusine's corporeal identity remains polymorphic to the end. Her final metamorphosis is not definitive but open-ended. And as such, it serves to illustrate (to "embody") a particularly fourteenth-century poetics—and politics—of hybridization.

Notes

An earlier version of this essay appeared in *Yale French Studies* 86 (1994).

1. For Melusine's identity as founding mother in anthropological (and comparative folkloric) terms, see the seminal article by Jacques Le Goff and Emmanuel Le Roy Ladurie.

2. For Jean d'Arras's manipulation of "historiographic" discourse, see Perret, "L'Invraisemblable vérité."

3. For the historico–political dimension of Jean's *Mélusine* and its links to Jean de Berry, see Harf-Lancner's magisterial study, 170, 176–78 (as well as the "Introduction" to her translation of Coudrette, esp. 30); and Louis Stouff, *Essai*, esp. 89–118. See also Emmanuèle Baumgartner, "Fiction et histoire: l'épisode chypriote dans la *Mélusine* de Jean d'Arras," in this volume.

4. See Kevin Brownlee, "Generic Hybrids. 1225: Guillaume de Lorris Writes the First *Roman de la Rose*" in Denis Hollier et al., eds., *A New History of French Literature* (Cambridge, Mass.: Harvard University Press, 1989), 88–93; and "The Ideology of Periodization: Auerbach's *Mimesis* (ch. 10) and the Late Medieval Aesthetic," in Seth Lerer, ed., *Literary History and the Challenge of Philology* (Stanford: Stanford University Press, 1995), 156–75.

5. For the basic structure of Jean's *Mélusine* in terms of the tripartite pattern "rencontre-pacte-transgression," see Harf-Lancner, *Fées,* 156–78. Cf. also Lecouteux, "La structure," and G. Pillard, "Les thèmes initiatiques dans les romans de Mélusine" in *Mélanges Dontenville* (Paris: Maisonneuve et Larose, 1980), 218–45.

6. All references and citations are from the edition of Louis Stouff. I have consulted with profit the modern French translation by Michèle Perret.

7. For metamorphosis as a figure in Jean d'Arras, cf. Sylvie Roblin, "Le sanglier et la serpente: Geoffroy La Grant' Dent dans l'histoire des Lusignan" in Laurence Harf-Lancner, ed., *Métamorphose et bestiaire fantastique au moyen âge* (Paris, 1985), 247–85. Cf. also, in the same collection, Francine Mora-Lebrun, "Métamorphoses dans *Le Paradis de la Reine Sibille:* Des archétypes mythiques aux jeux d'une écriture," 287–315.

8. Cf. also the famous case of Ginevre in Boccaccio's *Decameron* 2.9.

9. See esp. the luxury ms. C (St. Petersburg, Bibl. publ., fr. F.r. XIV, no. 3, in which the *Violette* is followed by the *Dit de la Panthere*), written 1400–1420. Citations from the *Violette* are from the edition of D. L. Buffum, *Le roman de la violette ou de Gerart de Nevers par Gerbert de Montreuil* (Paris: Champion, 1928); translations are mine.

10. Cf. the rose-shaped birthmark on Lïenor's thigh in Jean Renart's *Roman de la Rose.* See Michel Zink, *Roman rose et rose rouge: le Roman de la Rose ou de Guillaume de Dole de Jean Renart* (Paris: Nizet, 1979).

11. Also significant in this regard is the erotic diminutive "mamelete," v. 666. Cf. *Aucassin et Nicolette* 12, where the "mameletes dures" of Nicolette function as part of the eroticized description of her body.

12. See Teodolinda Barolini, *The Undivine "Comedy": Detheologizing Dante* (Princeton, N.J.: Princeton University Press, 1992), 58–79.

13. Cf. the function of herring in the noncourtly food code in Adam de la Halle's *Jeu de Robin et Marion.* See Kevin Brownlee, "Transformations of the

Couple: Genre and Language in Adam de la Halle's *Jeu de Robin et Marion*," *French Forum* 14 (1989): 419–33; and Jean Dufournet, "Complexité et ambiguïté du *Jeu de Robin et Marion:* L'ouverture de la pièce et le portrait des paysans" in *Études de philologie romane et d'histoire littéraire offertes à Jules Horrent* (Liège, 1980), 141–59.

14. Cf. Harf-Lancner, *Fées,* 172–74.

15. This epithet ends with a suggestive comparative evocation of the Virgin Mother, thus activating both Melusine's maternal and her Christian sides: "après celle qui porta Nostre Createur" (242).

16. See Kevin Brownlee, *Poetic Identity in Guillaume de Machaut* (Madison: University of Wisconsin Press, 1984), 37–62.

17. It is interesting that this catalog ends with the statement "J'ay fait le borgne" (*M* 243), which both evokes the figure of Machaut in the *Voir-Dit* and suggestively elaborates the thematic network of spying and visual perception/misperception/transgression that looms large in this entire sequence. See Jacqueline Cerquiglini, "Le clerc et le louche: Sociology of an Esthetic," *Poetics Today* 5 (1984): 479–91. See also the subsequent characterization of Fortune in *Mélusine* as "faulse borgne," as well as Raymondin's earlier attempt to undo his visual violation by closing up the peephole (metamorphically equivalent to attempting to restore virginity): "Il court en sa chambre, et prent la cire d'une vieille lettre qu'il trouva, et en estouppa le pertuis" (*M* 242).

18. The first of these (quite rare) erotic moments had been (at least superficially) initiated by Raymondin as he took his leave of Melusine after their first meeting: "en la acoulant moult doulcement, et la baisa tres amoureusement . . . car il estoit ja si sousprins de s'amour que quant qu'elle lui disoit, il lui affermoit toute verité; et il avoit raison, si comme vous orrez ca avant en la vraye histoire" (*M* 27). Cf. also the nonerotic presentation of their wedding night (*M* 42); with the single—but significant—final indirect designation of the couple in courtly erotic terms: "Tant furent et demourerent *les deux amans* ou lit que ly soulaux fu levez" (*M* 42).

19. Cf. Harf-Lancner's discussion of this scene in *Fées*, 175, and in particular, of how Jean d'Arras here inflects "une fois de plus, le schème folklorique dans un sens favorable à Mélusine. Le même souci de laisser de l'ancêtre des Lusignan une image pure et rassurante, malgré la métamorphose en serpente, se retrouve dans le dernier plaidoyer de Mélusine."

20. See the typology of female fairies in Jean d'Arras's prologue (*M* 3–4).

21. Cf. Harf-Lancner, *Fées,* 166–67, on the suggestively unstable iconography of Melusine's metamorphosis found in different mss: "car d'un manuscrit à l'autre, la fée s'envole sous la forme d'un serpent, d'un dragon ou d'une sirène."

22. This recalls the overtly "figurative" language used to describe Melusine's explicitly hybrid body in the bath as viewed transgressively by Raymondin (*M* 242).

23. Cf. the initial female voice/body dichotomy, positively—and erotically—deployed in Elinas's first encounter with Presine (*M* 5–7).

24. Melusine's postmetamorphosis appearances to indicate that the lordship of the chateau is about to change also suggest a sequence that sets up and valorizes Jean de Berry as the final legitimate Lusignan "heir equivalent." See *M* 13, 289, 307–10.

25. Worth noting is the variable length of Melusine's tail (cf. the "XV piez" of *M* 260), as well as the tail's status as coat of arms, cf. *M* 289.

26. Cf. the serpentine metamorphosis of Cadmus and Harmonia in the *Ovide moralisé,* ed. Cornelius de Boer, Verhandelingen der Koninklijke Akademie van Wetenschappen te Amsterdam. Afdeeling Letterkunde, n.s. 15, 21, 30, 37, 43 (Amsterdam: Müller, 1915–38), 4.5116–5381 (*Met.*4.563–606), esp. v. 5192, "ne n'orent talent de mal faire."

27. Cf. for the *Ovide moralisé,* Rita Copeland, *Hermeneutics and Translation in the Middle Ages: Academic Traditions and Vernacular Texts* (Cambridge: Cambridge University Press, 1991); and Renate Blumenfeld-Kosinski, "The Scandal of Pasiphaë: Narrative and Interpretation in the *Ovide Moralisé,*" *Modern Philology* (forthcoming). For *Purg.* 31, see Peter Armour, *Dante's Griffin and the History of the World* (Oxford: Clarendon, 1989).

Maternity and Monstrosity: Reproductive Biology in the *Roman de Mélusine*

GABRIELLE M. SPIEGEL

To the casual, first-time reader, the *Roman de Mélusine* presents itself most obviously as a myth of transgression. Not merely does the plot turn on the breaking of a vow, the transgression of a quasi-sacred promise that attains the status of a taboo, but the tale's principal constituent elements entail the transgressive uniting of a supernatural and a natural being, of the universe beyond and the here and now, the human and the animal, virtuous and evil, savage and civilized. Even the geography of the *roman* is classically liminal—those woods and fountains that anthropologists have taught us to recognize as sites of exchange between the world of humans and creatures of the uncertain realms that lie beyond mortal ken.[1] If ever there was an exemplary case of the meaning of liminality—that zone of marginality and permeability—the *Roman de Mélusine* would appear to be it.

And yet, let me as a relative outsider, a liminal figure myself—historian among *littérateurs*—begin by articulating my perplexities in the face of this most obvious reading of the *roman* or *soi-disant histoire*. To begin with, and most conspicuously, the actual transgression of the taboo placed upon the relationship between Melusine and Raymondin has no immediate consequences. It is only the public declaration of the transgression—the speech, not the deed—that produces the expected punitive response. At that, no one seems the least dismayed to discover that Melusine is a serpent; not Raymondin upon first viewing her, nor her children, nor the assembled company upon learning of her identity.

Odder still, no one seems to think that she represents a threat of magical pollution, despite her clear provenance from another world and although she clearly is not a fully human figure. Earlier Melusine narratives in Latin had, in fact, emphasized the fundamental incompatibility between the figure of the fairy and Christianity, since in these texts the fairy strenuously avoids participation in the Mass and all contact with holy water. For example, in the tale of Henno cum dentibus recounted by Walter Map in the *De Nugis Curialium*, written between 1181 and 1193,[2] Henno's wife, despite her pretensions to piety, studiously avoids the beginning and end of Mass, thereby evading the aspersion of holy water and communion. When Henno's mother espies her daughter-in-law bathing in the form of a dragon and reports it to her son, he has the priest sprinkle her with holy water, whereupon she jumps through the roof and disappears into the air with a great howling. A comparable story is told by Gerald of Wales (ca. 1217) in his *De Principium Instructione*, 3.27, to explain the diabolical origin of the Plantagenets. In Gerald's version, it was noticed that a certain countess of Anjou (ancestor of Geoffrey Plantagenet, father to Henry II) rarely attended church and that, when she did so, never remained throughout Mass to celebrate the consecration of the host. One day he had her restrained by four sergeants. She escaped and flew away through a window, in the sight of all, and never reappeared.

Similarly, Gervaise of Tilbury, writing between 1200 and 1214, records in his *Otia Imperialia* (Tertio Decisio, 62) the story of the Dame du Château de l'Épervier (*De domina castri de Esperver*), whose custom was to arrive sufficiently late for Mass so as to miss the celebration of the Eucharist. One day, restrained by her husband and his servants in the church at the moment of the consecration of the host, she shed the cloak by which they were holding her and flew away through the roof, destroying in the process a part of the chapel, whose ruined tower was still visible, according to Gervaise, in his own day. Virtually the same story is found in Philippe Mouskés's *Chronique Rimée,*[3] in this version recounted of the count of Toulouse.

All these writers take pains to accent the diabolical nature of the fairy-wife. Gerald of Wales uses his tale to explain the diabolical origin and character of the Plantagenets, while Gervaise of Tilbury opens his account with a quotation from 2 Corinthians, "frequens est ut angeli satanae in angelos lucis se transforment et in humanis mentibus aliquid diabolicae immisionis nutriant," and says that the Dame was lifted *spiritu diabolico* to take flight from the church. Walter Map employs the term *pestilentia* to designate fairies, while Philippe Mouskés, narrating her moment of flight, clearly denominates the wife of the count of Toulouse as a devil:

> Mais quant perciut l'aigue benoite
> et le provoire ki s'esploite
> pour le prendre, moult l'en caut,
> fors de lors mains à force saut.
> Diables iert et com diables
> desrompi couvertiure et tables
> fors de la glise s'esforça. . . .[4]

In sharp contrast, in Jean d'Arras's version, Melusine entertains wholly amiable relations with the Church, the clergy, prayer, Mass, and holy water. And this notwithstanding the marks of deformity that appear on her progeny, which might logically have aroused suspicions of diabolical forces at work. Even Horrible is not recognized as too horrible to let live, until Melusine finally insists upon his murder. Did his own prior annihilation of two nurses while still a suckling infant simply go unnoticed, hence unworthy of concern or punishment?

Even if we set aside Melusine's physical duality, is it not strange that no one seems dismayed to learn of her initial act of vengeance against her father, for which act, in fact, she has assumed the curious dual state she inhabits, if secretly? On the contrary, we are repeatedly told that upon hearing the story of Elinas d'Ecosse, Geoffroy, Raymondin, et al. rejoice in the discovery of his royal status, which bequeaths a legacy of social prestige to his descendants. But the fact that this socially prestigious origin is mediated by a mother who was the instigator of a vengeful plot against this very same ancestor goes unremarked,[5] part of a larger pattern in which no one seems to register what they read or are told, a failure of insight that significantly marks the narrative as a tale of illusion and duplicity.

What is one to make of these confounded expectations? This is a text that appears to violate every rule of narrative construction as well as every norm of medieval religious thought. Although proleptically broadcast, the consequences of transgression fail to occur. In place of rational norms and anticipated developments, illusion, duplicity, and ambiguity reign throughout. In *Mélusine*, the intricate patterns of the narrative weave a skein of illogic, unpunished deeds, unmotivated violence, self-delusion, and inexplicable events.

Perhaps, in the end, this is a tale not so much about transgression per se as about boundaries, or more precisely about the transgression not of taboo but of category. For the one transgression that has gone virtually unexplicated, if not entirely unnoticed, in scholarship on the *Roman de Mélusine*, is a phenomenon that involves the reproductive biology so essential to the tale's economy: the fact that Melusine is a twin. I would like to propose a reading of the *Roman de Mélusine* that is critically informed by the fact of her twinship, and the doubling—on all levels of the text—that is the narrative analogue and enactment of this cardinal characteristic. In order to understand the particular valence that twinship carries in the *roman*, it is necessary to see it against the background of more general conceptions of reproductive biology that prevailed in the High Middle Ages, and most especially in the light of Aristotelian notions of biological and zoological categorization that formed the central strand of medieval biological thinking down to the end of the medieval period and beyond.

Aristotle presents his theories on the biology of twins in the context of an exposition of the generation of *monstra* in general; thus, by implication twins are some kind of monsters. For Aristotle, twins are monstrous for two reasons. First because of their rarity, since Aristotle defines a monstrosity as that which belongs to the class of "things contrary to nature," although it is contrary not to Nature in her entirety but only to Nature in the generality of cases.[6] Twins are natural, therefore, in that they occur, if infrequently, in the natural course of human reproduction. But they are "monstrous" (second reason) in that they constitute anomalies not only by virtue of their rarity but because—like, indeed, all animals that occupy more than one zoological category (seals, sea anemones, hermit crabs, ostriches, etc.)—they are said, in Aristotelian terms, to dualize.[7] Twins "dualize" by confounding the categories animal/human. This they do by violating the basic typology (and teleology) of the animal kingdom, which ordains that humans replicate themselves singly, while animals do so in multiples.[8] Hence, for Aristotle, twins are a "natural monstrosity"; no matter how biologically neutral such multiple births might be, they menace the order by which human society organizes and understands itself.

This Aristotelian linking of multiple births and the monstrous was to have a long life in the Middle Ages, little affected by Galenic modifications to Aristotle's reproductive biology that were beginning to make their appearance in the thirteenth century under the impact of Arabic translations of Galen's corpus by Avicenna and others. Thus a clearly derivative and hybrid text such as Pseudo-Albert's *De Secretis Mulierum*, despite its deployment of both Aristotelian and Galenic ideas of human conception, continues to view twins as monstrosities, an unfortunate and threatening occurrence that, given this author's obsession with menstrual blood, should be attributed to maternal causes, a position, of course, totally consistent with Aristotle's own beliefs.[9] If anything, the notion that twins were fundamentally monstrous in nature was strengthened in the High Middle Ages in the work of Albertus Magnus, who added to Aristotle's exposition a much more sophisticated discussion of the biological processes through which the generation of twins and other monstrous beings took place.[10] Since, for Albert, there is no cause of monstrosity other than matter (*causa monstruositatis non est nisi in materia*), and since matter in reproductive generation is that which is supplied by the maternal *menstruum*, it follows again that the responsibility for monstrosity as well as twinning lies with the mother, opinions we would do well to keep in mind in reading the *Roman de Mélusine*.

To the classical medical conceptions concerning the biology of twinning we can add insights garnered from anthropological fieldwork, where once more we learn that what is biologically neutral is more often than not seen to be socially and culturally threatening. Although so-called primitive societies entertain widely divergent beliefs about twins, rarely are they accepted as socially neutral. Most societies profess the classificatory assumption that human beings bear only one child at a time; twins, therefore, pose an immediate challenge, if not outright threat, to kinship and other classifying schemata. In Africa and elsewhere, as Victor Turner has shown, it is widely held that children born during a single parturition are mystically identical. Thus the Ndembu rituals that Turner has investigated seek to confront the paradoxes inherent in twinship that what is physically double is structurally single and what is mystically one is empirically two.[11] Not only are twins, thereby, a "classificatory embarrassment" (the term is Turner's), but they and their parents are considered to be potentially polluting for the whole of society. Among the Nyakyusa, for example, the parents of twins are held to be contaminated by "bad" violence, and they are compelled to submit to rites of separation and purification lest their dangerous contagion spread.[12] The ritual seeks to prevent the spread of social violence that the birth of twins portends by its abolition of cultural distinctions through formless and unassimilatable duplications and sinister replications.[13] It is, in my view, precisely the fear of such processes of duplication and replication—and with them the erasure of cultural/categorical boundaries—that runs throughout the *Roman de Mélusine*, both on the level of plot and on the level of theme, duplications that take the form not only of doublings but more exactly of splittings off.

The most obvious, if not necessarily most significant, level on which duplication takes place in the *Roman de Mélusine* is that of the narrative economy of the tale. Jean d'Arras's prefatory narrative of the marriage of Presine and Elinas d'Ecosse, its inexorable failure with the king's hapless violation of the taboo whose observance was the condition of possibility for the union, and the consequent separation of the couple, leading to the daughters' revenge and punishment, functions as an almost exact double of the narrative of Melusine.[14] The differences are, in fact, reciprocal, in that Presine has only daughters, whereas Melusine has only sons. In both instances, it is the intervention of a male relative that precipitates the breaking of the taboo, leading to the dissolution of the marriage and the ultimate failure of the lineage. The mother lacks only the sign of monstrosity that will be the daughter's curse, unless one is willing to acknowledge—as I would be—that just as Raymondin is forbidden to see his wife's monstrous tail, the sight of which constitutes the violation of the taboo, so Elinas is forbidden to witness his wife's parturition, suggesting that it is the very gestation of triplets that itself constitutes her monstrosity.[15]

Strikingly, Jean d'Arras redoubles the central tale yet again by furnishing an account of Raymondin's father, Hervy de Leon, who, like his son, enters the narrative as an exile adjudged culpable of having committed a murder, from whose consequences he is redeemed by his marriage to a fairy, as is Raymondin's accidental murder of the count of Poitiers by his marriage to Melusine.[16] And it goes without saying that within the main narrative itself, Geoffroy functions as a double of *both* Raymondin and Melusine, while Melusine's sisters, Palestine and Melior, are aspects of their sister split off, points to which I will return. Moreover, the repetitive Oedipal structure characterizing Melusine's enclosure of her father, Hervy's slaying of the King of Briton's nephew, and Raymondin's killing of his overlord connects all three as displaced, sinister duplications of a single form of transgression, namely parricide.[17] That Jean d'Arras offers us three separate instances of this most monstrous form of violence as introduction to the story of Melusine must be accorded its full narrative and symbolic weight.

Parricide, we know from the work of anthropologists, violates not only the moral code against murder that lies at the root of all social organization, but, in attacking the foundation of the family, attacks the source and bulwark of all forms of social distinctions. The parricide usurps the place of the father, and in so doing unravels the hierarchical distinctions that subtend social structures of authority. Like twins, the parricide seeks to occupy two places and two categories at the same time, and so threatens irreparable confusion of both classificatory and social schemata. The parricide who successfully usurps the place of the father effaces key structural differences within the family, and it is this lack of differentiation that serves, as Girard points out, to symbolize the dissolution of family distinctions, in other words, to desymbolize. Indeed, for Girard, twins are even more powerful agents of desymbolization than parricides. Whereas parricide entails the commission of an act, the mere appearance of twins sets off the process of desymbolization, portending what he calls the "sacrificial crisis," that is, the desymbolization of symbolic rivalry and its descent into actual violence that engulfs the whole of society.[18] To the degree that order, peace, fecundity and social progress depend on cultural distinctions, the loss of such distinctions unleashes a process of desymbolization that terminates in the abolition of all meaningful categories.

On some deep level, the *Roman de Mélusine* is about this process of desymbolization, or what I would prefer to call the plasticity—the threatened formlessness—of prevailing cultural categories: of form and nature, body and spirit, human and animal, history and myth, appearance and reality. In a word, of culture. Melusine herself is, in effect, the very emblem of such plasticity. Not only is she clearly an androgynous figure, both *maternelle* (in Le Goff's rather romantic reading of the *Roman*) and phallic, but she functions socially in highly ambiguous—and androgynous—ways. It is she who is responsible for the construction of the Lusignan domains, who builds castles, clears lands, provisions households, endows churches and, most important, gives her name to the agnatic *lignage*, which, since the twelfth century at least,[19] had been the principal and exclusive genealogical task of males. From this perspective, it is hardly accidental that she gives birth to male children alone, a narrative mimesis of the agnatic lineage that since the late eleventh century had operated as the organizing structure of aristocratic families and households. In eleventh- and twelfth-century genealogies and genealogical histories, as in the *Roman de Mélusine*, the social capital of the family resides on the female side, but—unlike *Mélusine*—that social capital is captured by and for males and serves as the foundation of an agnatic lineage that is semiotically marked with the man's name and emblem. Thus, the characteristic genealogical myth of eleventh- and twelfth-century families involves the rape or seduction of a daughter of the count of Flanders, who in marrying the social upstart that abducts her establishes the social prestige of the family, thereafter organized along agnatic lines.[20]

The plasticity of social identity that Melusine represents, first as a twin and then in her social functioning, is most powerfully emblematized in her physical nature, which at its simplest level represents a transgressive union of female/human and serpent (phallic)/animal form. But even this transgressive doubleness is only the beginning, for by the end of the tale she is further transmogrified into a dragon, initially chthonic and finally aerien, an additional mixing of categories that suggests that, ultimately, Melusine is best understood as a figure of the hybrid *tout court*.

It is precisely this hybrid nature that marks her progeny as monstrous. The physical deformity with which each child is marked replicates the categorical confusion between the world of humans and the world of animals that is the distinguishing feature of Melusine's own physicality. From this perspective, what is transgressive about the union between Melusine and Raymondin, as physically embodied in their progeny, is not the uniting of a human and a supernatural being but the more debased union of man and *subhuman* being, who approximates animality both in her status as a twin and in her embodied, punitive form.

That Jean d'Arras intends the *tares* borne by each of Melusine's children to be understood as monstrous and to underscore their hybrid nature is supported by the fact that according to one strand of medieval biological thinking, a fundamental cause of monstrosity is the "mixing of semens"—that is, hybridization.[21] Monsters are, therefore, quintessentially hybrids, and lest we forget the monstrous nature of Melusine herself in the rather romantic readings that the *roman* seems to engender, she too is the hybridized product of the union between a fairy and a human, in which the two elements vie for mastery over the child's nature. As Presine reminds her daughter at the moment of pronouncing her curse: "La vertu du germe de ton pere toy et les autres eust attrait a sa nature humaine, et eussiés esté briefment hors des meurs, nimphes et faees, sans y retourner." [The force of your paternal insemination might have drawn you and your sisters into the sphere of a human nature; you would have been bound to the law of nymphs or fairies only for a short time, without ever returning] (*M* 12). In this contest between humanity and animality, it is animality that triumphs.

The physical deformities that disfigure Melusine's progeny are noteworthy for the ways in which they emphasize the children's visible monstrosity, underlining their ugliness, despite their putatively heroic nature, a fact that serves to de-aestheticize the *roman* in a fundamental fashion. In addition to their gigantism,[22] a trait characteristic of all the sons, they variously display huge ears,[23] differently colored eyes wrongly spaced upon the face (Urian and Eudes); upon the cheek of one a lion's paw that, after eight years, begins to grow hair and nails (Antoine); an enormous, animal-like tooth (Geoffroy); a single eye (Renaud); or three eyes (Horrible). Even the pious Fromont participates in animality in the nature of his skin, hairy like a mole's, linking him to a blind, paradoxically earthbound creature, among nature's most primitive. It is as if the fragmented detritus of the animal kingdom were strewn upon their bodies, physical testimony to the monstrous (if not actually demonic[24]) maternity that gave them life.

Moreover, the lack of bodily perfection and integrity signals the potential possessed by Melusine's children as agents of pollution,[25] betokening their essentially impure state and designating them as dangerous for the whole of society. Although current scholarship on the *Roman de Mélusine* professes uncertainty about whether or not these deformities should be considered totems, it is difficult to avoid the conclusion that they function as residual totemic marks since, like totemism, they serve to connect the world of humans and animals, to bind the society of men to the realm of nature, to locate, as Lévi-Strauss defines it, "hors de notre univers, et comme par un exorcisme, d'attitudes mentales incompatibles avec l'exigence d'une discontinuité entre l'homme et la nature, que la pensée chrétienne tenait pour essentielle."[26] In that sense, the totemism of Melusine's offspring replicates the biological confusion already signified by the mother's twinship. They, too, represent the "dualizing" tendency of hybrids, which transgresses the boundary between the human and the animal. From a symbolic perspective, it would appear that the only pure type in the *roman* is Horrible, not because he is free of the biological (hence categorical) confusion that affects the entire family, but because he alone is what he seems to be, a personality "equal to himself" (to borrow a phrase from Bakhtin), without initiative or internal contradictions, who offers to others a view of himself that coincides completely with their view of him. He is, therefore, a wholly "authentic" person, in the sense that his essential and externalized nature are one, unique only insofar as he typifies in extravagant ways the attributes for which he stands. Within this tale of illusion and duplicity, he functions as the sole transparent sign, an emblem of the (anti-) heroic, in that he shares with the hero the fullness and flatness of a violent being.

If Horrible is the antitype to Melusine, the visible contradiction to the *roman*'s fantasies of the generativity, prosperity, and benevolence that she can bestow, her double, clearly, is Geoffroy. Geoffroy's role in the *Roman de Mélusine* is both central and complex. His attributes and functions appear to link him at times with Raymondin and at others with Melusine. His physical deformity—the "Grand Dent"—figures his status as "le plus fier et le plus courageux et le plus hardy" [the proudest, most courageous and boldest] (*M* 197) of all Melusine's progeny and connects him symbolically to the wild boar,[27] in pursuit of which his father had accidently slaughtered the count of Poitiers, making him a sinister, displaced replication of Raymondin. Moreover, and in sharp contrast to the other brothers whose deforming marks are mitigated by their chivalric posture, in the case of Geoffroy his inherent brutality is commented upon by all. Thus, when Geoffroy comes to the aid of his brothers against the Sultan of Barbary, the interpreter to the Sultan warns the latter against engaging in a fight with "la grant, horrible et resoingneuse fierté de cellui au grant dent, son frere" [the great, horrible and awesome ferocity of he with the large tooth, his brother] (*M* 226). Similarly, on learning that Geoffroy has taken Beyruth, the Sultan of Damascus proclaims: "Par Mahon . . . je croy que cellui au grant dent a le deable ou corps" [By Mohammed . . . I think that he with the large tooth has the devil in him] (*M* 227).

On this level, he is brutality and evil incarnate, the embodiment of the underlying malevolence that runs through all the members of this strange and salient *lignage*, for the most part masked by the charitable and chivalric deeds through which they seek to redeem their blemished nature. Although Geoffroy will also seek to redeem himself ultimately by the reconquest of his father's lands and the rehabilitation of his father's memory, he is singularly unsuited to the task, for he is, as he asserts, a person who "ne scay ne ne vueil enquester des choses passees" [does not know nor does he wish to inquire into events of the past] (*M* 239). Despite being the sole protagonist in the *Roman* who can possibly be connected with a historical figure,[28] and the one child destined to rehabilitate the family's paternal memory and recuperate its maternal past, he is nonetheless on principle antihistorical, yet another of the paradoxes that make this text so difficult to grasp.

Geoffroy's centrality to the *Roman de Mélusine* derives from his narrative linking with his mother, for it is his actions that initiate the unraveling of the plot and force the public disclosure of Raymondin's transgression of the taboo and Melusine's own transgressive nature. Nor is it accidental that the deed that unleashes Raymondin's fury, and with it his denunciation of Melusine, entails an act of fratricide, Geoffroy's narrative analogue to Melusine's earlier parricide. Strikingly, it is only after Geoffroy's brutal and unmotivated burning of the monks of Maillezais in the fire that consumes his brother, Fromont, that Raymondin is moved to such demented fury that he publicly reveals his knowledge of Melusine's secret nature, knowledge acquired by having broken the taboo that forbade him to see her at her ablutions on Saturdays, whose public articulation constitutes a doubling of the transgression.

The terms of Raymondin's denunciation are noteworthy, both for the ways in which they echo Melusine's presentation of herself upon their first encounter in the forest and for the ways in which they centrally interrogate the whole reproductive structure of the myth. Upon hearing what has happened at Maillezais, Raymondin becomes deranged with fury and curses son and mother, placing into question Melusine's benevolence (which, the reader will recall, he had insisted upon in his lament after his initial transgression of the taboo)[29] and the nature of her progeny: "Par la foy que je doy a Dieu, je croy que ce ne soit que fantosme de ceste femme, ne ne croy pas que ja fruit qu'elle ait porté viengne a perfection de bien" [On the faith that I owe God, I believe that this woman is a mere phantom, I do not think that the fruit of her womb can be perfectly good] (*M* 253). And, indeed, it is precisely this monstrous reproductivity—the inherently bad biology—that accounts for the unfolding tragedy, for as Walter Map had already recognized, children born of the union between mortals and fairies rarely or never come to a good end.[30]

In designating Melusine a "fantosme," whose great deeds are illusory, given her nature as "fausse serpente," Raymondin recalls her original introduction of herself, in which she had carefully sought to allay any suspicions concerning her possibly diabolical nature by reassuring him that "Je scay bien que tu cuides que ce soit fantosme ou euvre dyabolique de mon fait et de mes paroles, mais je te certiffie que je suiz de par Dieu et croy en tout quanque vraye catholique doit croire" [I know that you think that my deeds and words are the product of a fantastic or diabolical work, but I certify that I belong to God and believe in everything that a true Catholic ought to believe] (*M* 25). Moreover, Raymondin draws the correct conclusion concerning the ways in which Melusine's

"fantastic" nature casts its shadow upon her children and upon the history of their life together: "Elle n'a porté enfant qui n'ait apporté quelque estrange signe sur terre. Ne veez la Oruble qui n'a pas vij. ans acompliz, qui a ja occiz deux de mes escuiers, et avant qu'il eust trois ans, avoit il fait mourir deux de ses nourrices par force de mordre leurs mamelles? Et ny vy je leur mere, le samedy que mon frere de Forests m'acointa les males nouvelles, en forme de serpente du nombril en aval? C'est aucune esperite ou c'est toute fantosme ou illusion qui m'a ainsi abusé; premiere foiz que je la vy, ne me scot elle bien a dire toute ma mesaventure?" [She has brought into the world infants marked with a strange sign. Is there not Horrible, who before he was even seven had already killed two of my squires; and before the age of three had killed two of his nurses from having chewed their breasts? . . . Did I not see their mother, the Saturday when my brother the count of Forez told me about the rumors which were circulating, in the form of a serpent from the belly button down? This is an evil spirit, or an apparition, or an illusion which has abused me thusly; the first time I saw her, did she not know how to tell me everything that would happen?] (*M* 253). With a logic born of despair, he curses "l'eure que Gieffroy fu nez ne onques engendrez" [the hour that Geoffroy was born and conceived] (*M* 253), thus placing in question Melusine's entire *fonction maternelle*.

Curiously, Melusine continues to insist upon the wholly human, hence "natural" character of her maternity, even after the public disclosure of her serpentine appendage. In a parting lament to Raymondin and the assembled company, she persists in denying her status as a fairy and seeks to assure in her children the purely human condition that eludes her: "Je vueil bien que vous sachiez qui je sui ne qui fu mon pere, afin que vous ne reprouvez pas a mes enfaans qu'ilz soient filz de mauvaise mere, ne de serpente, ne de faee, car je suiz fille au roy Elinas d'Albanie et a la royne Presine, sa femme, et sommes iij. seurs qui avons esté durement predestinees et en griefz penitances. Et de ce ne vous puis je plus dire, ne ne veuil." [I desire that you know who I am, and who my father was, so that you will not reproach my children for being the sons of an evil mother, or a fairy or a serpent. I am the daughter of King Elinas of Scotland, and of Queen Presine his wife. We were three sisters to whom was assigned a cruel destiny, a terrible penitence. And I cannot, nor do I wish to tell you more] (*M* 259–260).

The futility of this gesture is underscored by her own prophecy of the future failure of the Lusignan, whose fantasies of territorial power and social prestige now stand revealed as illusory, a "fantosme" like the maternal image upon which they were engendered. Melusine can no more recuperate her childrens' humanity than she can prevent her final metamorphosis into an entirely animal state; before their eyes she is transformed "en une serpente grant et grosse et longue de la longueur de xv. piez" [into a huge and fat serpent, fifteen feet in length] (*M* 260). With this final transformation Melusine fulfills her destiny, enacting the curse that had been placed upon her by her mother, in the light of which her relationship with Raymondin constitutes merely a detour.

A pressing question remains. Why does the fulfillment of the broken taboo, already broadcast at the opening of the tale, occur only with its public disclosure, rather than as a result of the actual transgression itself? On this point Jean d'Arras is decisive. Although Raymondin supposes that Melusine is unaware of his breaking of the taboo, Jean carefully informs the reader that "Mais pour neant le cuide, car elle scet bien tout. Mais pour ce qu'il ne l'ot descouvert a nullui, elle s'en souffry et n'en monstra semblant" [He was mistaken about that, for she knew everything. But since he had not told it to anyone, she tolerated it and pretended that nothing had happened] (*M* 244). There can be no question here of narrative suspense, since the reader has long been informed of what will come to pass, inexorably, a destiny embedded in the very nature of the *roman*, not to mention the mythic structures on which it is based. If the taboo exists to be broken, why doesn't its transgression inaugurate the unleashing of those consequences that the reader knows and desires should follow, as justice demands?

The answer to this question lies in the recognition that the fundamental transgression occurs not in the betrayal of the vow and the breaking of the taboo but in the hybridization of categories that Melusine stages. Categories are by nature public and social constructions; no form of human life ever conforms perfectly to them, and the resulting confusion can be sustained as long as it does not openly conflict with dominant social norms. Private tolerance for ambiguity, in other words, can be extensive. But the public effacement of socially important categories, those that function as tacit forms of social rules, will ultimately generate levels of anxiety that require the reassertion of

cultural distinctions, at least to the extent that the transgression of those categories took the form of the erasure of crucial systems of differentiation structuring social life and the values that attend it. What is necessary is the reestablishment and revalorization of precisely the categories at issue, a "cleaning up of categories" that reassembles both the latent and overt structures on which all societies are constructed, a patrolling of the borders that prove most permeable to slippage and mixing, to the invasion of "foreign" matter.

This is the meaning of Melusine's final disavowal of her fairy nature. In denying her own hybrid status (a failed attempt at best, since she can hardly expect the reader not to remember that Presine, too, was a fairy) she seeks to create a "pure," unitary category for her children to inhabit, free of the categorical confusion that she herself most profoundly exemplifies. Only after the human categories are restored and in place is Melusine ready to become herself wholly animal, never to be seen again, as she affirms, in human form.[31]

The price of this boundary drawing is Horrible, who becomes in effect a sacrificial victim to the reestablishment of social order and the reassertion of distinctive (if never entirely distinct) cultural categories. Not because his deeds are incommensurably more horrible than Geoffroy's—indeed, what is the murder of two squires and two nurses when set against Geoffroy's act of fratricide and the burning of a whole abbey of monks, even if less than wholly pious ones? Rather, Horrible falls victim to the demands of culture precisely because he alone is a pure type, categorically coherent in the very horribleness of his being and cultural label, a person in whom, as we saw above, appearance and reality are one. By virtue of his very awfulness, he alone can redeem the transgressions of category that his mother and siblings embody. Only with his death is there hope for the future, as Melusine warns Raymondin: "Beaulx siegneurs, gardez, si chier que vous avez vostre honneur et vostre chevance, que, si tost que je seray partie, que vous faciez tant qu'Eudes [sic. Horrible] nostre filz qui a trois yeulx, dont l'un est ou front, soit mort priveement, car sachiez en verité, que il feroit tant de maulx que ce ne seroit pas si grant dommage de la mort de telz xx^m. que de la perte que on auroit par lui, car certainement il destruiroit tout quanque j'ay ediffié, ne jamais guerre ne fauldroit ou pays de Poittou ne de Guyenne" [My lord, if you desire to maintain your honor

and prosperity, make arrangements so that Horrible, the one of our sons who has three eyes, one of which is in the middle of his brow, is killed secretly, for you should know the truth, namely that he will do so much evil that the loss of twenty thousand men would be as nothing compared to the sorrows that you will deplore because of him. You can be sure that he will destroy all that I have built and that [if he lives] war between Poitou and Gascony will never cease] (*M* 258). And, in keeping with the workings of cultural production, the manner of his murder symbolically replicates Melusine's attack on Elinas, for Horrible is enclosed in a cave and then suffocated with smoke from the burning of damp hay (*M* 261).

This mode of reciprocal, symbolic exchange is subsequently restaged between Geoffroy and Melusine, in that Geoffroy is redeemed only when Melusine is damned. His monstrous nature is rectified when she descends entirely into the realm of animals, in both cases a process that recuperates the coherence of category and represents the redrawing of boundaries. Yet, although Geoffroy becomes human, he is nonreproductive so that, to the extent that he is the emblematic figure of the Lusignan lineage, his failure to reproduce signals the beginning of the family's decline.

That decline is sealed by the concluding incident that Jean d'Arras invents to frame his narrative: the episode concerning Melusine's second sister, Melior, and the Château de l'Épervier, whose name, we know, Jean borrowed from Gervaise of Tilbury's account of the *Domina castri de Esperver* in his *Otia Imperialia.*[32] Melior, the reader will recall, as her punishment for participating in the imprisonment of Elinas, had been consigned to pass the rest of her days in a beautiful and powerful castle in Armenie, where her task was to administer the adventure of the sparrowhawk. Any knight who succeeded in watching the sparrowhawk during a period extending from the eve of the day before through the whole day of June 25 (the feast of Saint Jean) without falling asleep would be rewarded with a gift of some worldly prize by Melior, on condition that he did not demand her body, her love, or her consent to marriage. Those who failed the test were condemned to be enclosed within the castle for the remainder of their lives, while those who articulated the forbidden requests were to be cursed until the ninth generation and their lineage doomed to witness the decline of its prosperity (*M* 303).

What we have here is both an adventure—in effect, a test—and a taboo. Remembering that Melior is, by virtue of her twinship with her sister, an aspect of Melusine split off, the taboo—as it works out—is effectively an incest taboo, since the only reported contestant in the ordeal of the sparrowhawk is Guyon, a young king of Armenie and Lusignan cadet, whom Jean describes as "beaulx jeunes homs et en chaleur de force et de vigour, et moult plain de sa voulenté, et de grant cuidier, et hardiz et aspres comme un lyon" [a handsome youth, bubbling with strength, of an energetic and decisive character, extremely thoughtful, and bold and ardent like a lion] (*M* 302). Upon arriving at the Château de l'Épervier, Guyon seeks permission to undergo the adventure of the sparrowhawk, at which point an old man restates for him the conditions of the test and the limits placed on the rewards that can legitimately be requested upon its successful conclusion. After eating and drinking moderately from the meal prepared for him, Guyon passes through the halls of the castle, where frescos of stories, with inscriptions below explaining the matter depicted, adorn the walls. Among the stories recounted in image and word is that of the history of King Elinas, Presine, and their three daughters "from beginning to end" (*M* 303). Jean thus centrally ties the episode of the Château de l'Épervier to the preceding narrative of Melusine, making it function as a gloss to the tale as a whole.

Once Guyon has successfully completed the adventure of the castle, he proceeds to make his request: the prohibited demand to marry Melior. She reiterates the impossibility of granting it and implores him to make another, but the king of Armenie repeats his demand for her hand, assuring Melior that he wishes no other gift. She warns him of the evil that will befall him and his descendants if he persists, but he closes his ears to her admonitions. In the face of his intransigeance, Melior informs him as emphatically as possible that a union between them would constitute incest since, as she lays it out for him: "n'es tu pas descendu de la lignie du roy Guion, qui fu filz Melusigne, ma seur, et je suis ta tante, et tu es si prez de mon lignaige, posé que je me voulzisse assentir a toy avoir, que l'eglise ne s'i vouldroit pas accorder. Et puis lui compte de chief en chief comment vous l'avez ouy dessus ou chappitre du roy Elinas, et aussi des hoirs de Lusegnen" [Are you not descended from King Guyon, who was the son of my sister Melusine? I am your aunt, and you are so closely related to my family that, even supposing that I wished to consent in accepting you, the Church would never permit it. And she recounted to him from beginning to end the whole history, just as it has been related to you in the chapter concerning King Elinas as well as in the history of the Lusignans] (*M* 305). Moreover, she stresses the misfortune that will befall his lineage if he continues in his illicit demands, sketching the inexorable decline that will overtake the family as a result of his rash and intemperate actions: "Toy et les tiens decherront de terre, d'avoir, d'onnour et de heritaige, jusques a la ix^{e} lignie; et perdra par ta fole emprise le ix^{e} de ta lignie le royaume que tu tiens. Et portera cellui roy nom de beste mue" [You and your family will see their lands, fiefs, possessions and patrimony steadily diminish through the ninth generation; and, because of your unreasonable behavior, your ninth descendent will lose the realm that you now govern. And he will bear the name of a savage beast] (*M* 305).

Unmindful of these consequences, Guyon, instead of renouncing his "foolish error," attempts to take Melior by force, to commit, therefore, an act of incestuous rape. This attack is prevented by Melior who, like Melusine, vanishes into the air, while Guyon is beset from all sides with blows struck by invisible assailants and finally ejected from the castle. As prophesied, he never again experienced joy and, despite a long reign (usually a sign of prosperity), was forced to witness the daily degradation of his estate, a process that continued to afflict his heirs until the very extinction of the Lusignan line, whose last representative was the Armenian king, Léon VI of Lusignan, the "bête mue" or savage beast predicted by Melior.[33] In the end, then, the Lusignan—born of a dual heritage both human and animal—revert to the animality that so powerfully marks their line, apparent equally in the totemic signs they bear upon their persons and in the savage character that they exhibit. Léon, the mute (hence savage) beast, names this destiny, which is at the same time a return to origins.

That Jean d'Arras elects to frame his tale with narratives of parricide and incest is not to be taken lightly. I would argue that it is precisely these framing stories that establish the meaning of the tale as such, whatever its mythic or learned sources; indeed, that it is *because* of its mythic and learned sources that Jean d'Arras attempts to reinterpret whatever traditional significance might have adhered to it by means of the frame, which evacuates from the central narrative its optimistic dreams of plenitude and legitimation and recasts it as a story of reproductive failure, social loss, and monstrous savagery. Moreover, if we accept Girard's notion that parricide and incest betoken the abolition of differences, the propagation of "formless duplications, sinister replications, a dark mixture of unnameable things" (75–76), then their connection to the fact of Melusine's twinship becomes clear, since all three threaten the confusion of category and effacement of cultural distinctions.

"Monstra quia monstrant" runs an ancient adage. Monsters are so called because they demonstrate the nature of things. In this light, Jean's utilization of the *conte* of Melusine becomes more understandable. As Mary Douglas has taught us, in times of crisis societies often fall back on bodily metaphors to express their sense of confusion. Such societies tend to have cultures that anthropologists term "autoplastic," in that they seek to achieve or express their desires and fears through self-manipulations upon the body. As Douglas puts it: "far from using bodily magic as an escape, cultures which frankly develop bodily symbolism may be seen to use it to confront experience with its inevitable pains and losses" (120).

Although displaced to the level of metaphor, Jean's adaptation of the *conte* of Melusine uses her bodily plasticity as a means of expressing the mutability of character, fortune, and fate, the fragility of social hierarchy, and the permeability, hence arbitrary nature, of social categorization. Melusine is the figure of this confusion, a representative of the androgynous, hybridized, dangerous, and polluting elements that menace social order and hierarchy by the obliteration of necessary categorical differences, an erasure of distinctions that abolishes social identity itself.

Written toward the end of the Hundred Years' War, the *Roman de Mélusine* confronts the crisis of legitimacy and the bestiality that lie at the heart of that age. In tracing the descent of the Lusignan into animality, Jean articulates the belief that there is nothing more monstrous than *l'homme animalisé*; nothing more threatening than the abandonment of social conventions and prohibitions in the pursuit of gain; nothing more terrifying than the blurring of boundaries. Yet the very ambiguity with which he sets forth this critique makes even this statement problematical. At every turn in this complex narrative, Jean proliferates the paradoxes that make it so difficult to interpret the text in any unilinear way.

But perhaps, in the end, that is appropriate, for as Matthieu-Castellani reminds us, there is "rien de plus ambigu qu'une rêverie sur l'ambiguïté."

Notes

1. The classic ethnographic description of such a medieval site is, of course, Jean-Claude Schmitt's *The Holy Greyhound: Guinefort Healer of Children since the Thirteenth Century* (Cambridge: Cambridge University Press, 1983).

2. Ed. M. R. James (Oxford: Clarendon Press, 1914).

3. Ed. Baron de Reiffenberg (Brussels: M. Hayez, 1836–38), ll. 18798–807.

4. On these texts see Le Goff and Le Roy Ladurie; Stouff, *Essai;* Lecouteux, *Mélusine et le Chevalier au Cygne,* "La structure des légendes mélusiennes," and "Zur Entstehung der Melusinensage," *Zeitschrift für Deutsche Philologie,* 98 (1979): 73–84; Markale; Henri Fromage, "Recherches sur Mélusine," *Bulletin de la Société de Mythologie Française,* 86 (Juillet–Sept., 1972): 42–75; Harf-Lancner, *Fées;* and Josef Köhler, *Der Ursprung der Melusinensage: Eine ethnologische Untersuchung* (Leipzig: E. Pfeiffer, 1895).

5. Thus Geoffroy, when he finally comes to understand that the tablettes he discovers recounting the story of Elinas and Presine relate to him, and that he and his brothers are their descendants through Melusine, reacts with pride: "si s'en tint plus chiers" [they felt even prouder] but without the slightest indication that Melusine's actions were blameworthy; see *M* 268.

6. *Generation of Animals*, ed. A. L. Peck (1942; rpt., Cambridge, Mass.: Loeb Classical Library, 1990), 770b, 9.

7. On animals that dualize see, for example, the sea anemone (see *Parts of Animals*, 681b1); apes (ibid., 689b 32); ostriches (ibid., 669b 15); the pig (*Historia Animalium*, 499b 12); the hermit crab (ibid., 529b 24); and the seal, whom Aristotle calls an "inveterate dualizer" (ibid., 566b 27, and *Parts of Animals*, 697b 1). See also J. M. Thijssen, "Twins as Monsters: Albertus Magnus's Theory of the Generation of Twins and Its Philosophical Context," *Bulletin of the History of Medicine* 61 (1987): 237–46.

8. Thus, in the *Historia Animalium*, Aristotle's basic discussion of the classification of the animal kingdom, he notes that "Some animals produce one and some produce many at a birth, but the human species does sometimes the one and sometimes the other. As a general rule and among most nations, the women bear one child at a birth, but frequently and in many lands they bear twins, as for instance in Egypt"; in *The Complete Works of Aristotle: The Revised Oxford Translation*, ed. Jonathan Barnes, vol. 1, Bollingen Series 71.2 (Princeton, N.J.: Princeton University Press, 1984), 584b, 28. The reference to

Egypt goes back to Aristotle's earlier statement (584b, 7) that in Egypt women are wont to bear multiple offspring.

9. Thus Pseudo-Albert maintains that "all types of monsters can be reduced to two categories: those caused by disobedience of matter [menstrual blood] and those caused by insufficiency of matter. . . . By disobedience I mean indisposition, which takes place when the matter [the *menstruum*, or female seed] is not well prepared [in Aristotelian terms, not well "concocted"] and therefore does not obey the agent [i.e., the male seed, or sperm]." See *Women's Secrets: A Translation of Pseudo-Albertus Magnus' De Secretis Mulierum with Commentaries*, ed. and trans. Helen Rodnite Lemay (Albany: State University of New York Press, 1992), 119. Twins, for Pseudo-Albert, who here follows both Aristotle and Albertus Magnus, fall into the category of the monstrous caused by disobedience of matter. In Aristotle's opinion, twins are produced by virtue of an excess of the material residue, i.e., menstrual blood. See *Generation of Animals*, 772a, 35.

10. This is not the place to review Albertus Magnus's complicated exposition of the generation of twins, but for an excellent overview see J. M. Thijssen, "Twins as Monsters."

11. See Victor Turner, *Ritual Process Structure and Anti-Structure* (Ithaca, N.Y.: Cornell University Press, 1977), 45.

12. Turner here relies upon the work of Monica Wilson, *Rituals of Kinship among the Nyakyusa* (London and New York: Oxford University Press, 1957). See p. 47. For our purposes, a interesting case is that of the Lele studied by Mary Douglas in *Purity and Danger: An Analysis of the Concepts of Pollution and Taboo* (London and Boston: Ark Paperbacks, 1984), 168. Like many peoples, the Lele assume that human births are single, in contrast to the natural fecundity of animals. Human couples who produce twins or triplets, therefore, are thought to have transcended normal human limitations, to have broken through the boundaries of the human in a way that is anomalous, but not necessarily inauspicious. What is exceptional about the Lele is that the parents of twins are paired with their exact counterpart in the animal world—a benign "monster" to whom the Lele devote a formal cult and who is symmetrically anomalous with the parents of twins. This "monster" is the pangolin, or scaly anteater, a creature that contradicts all the most obvious animal categories. It is scaly, hence fishlike, but climbs trees; it behaves reproductively like an egg-laying lizard, yet it suckles its young like mammals. Unlike most other small mammals, however, and most significant, all its young are born singly.

Lele veneration of the pangolin acknowledges the reciprocal contradictions to their categories human/animal posed by the parents of twins and by anteaters and allows the Lele momentarily to confront the inherent ambiguity of experience, to which the pangolin becomes a sacrificial victim. Initiates of the Pangolin cult ceremonially hold, kill, and devour the pangolin, whose power for good is released in its dying. In embracing the pangolin, the Lele embrace the fortuitous and contradictory nature of life and death, human and animal, good and evil, and disclose the intrinsically conventional nature of all categorization.

13. This understanding of the cultural implications of twins I borrow from the formulations of René Girard, *Violence and the Sacred,* trans. Patrick Gregory (Baltimore and London: Johns Hopkins University Press, 1977), 56.

14. This doubling works on both sides of the equation, that is to say, for both Presine/Melusine and Elinas/Raymondin. In the latter case, both husbands experience profound sorrow at their wives' departures, equally withdraw from the governance of their realms—Elinas bequeathing the government of the kingdom of Scotland to Mataquas and Raymondin passing the governance of his lands to Geoffroy—and both end their days enclosed: Elinas in the magic mountain of Brumborenlion and Raymondin in the monastery of Montserrat. For the account of Elinas's sorrow and relinquishment of government, see *M* 10.

15. Harf-Lancner stresses the absence of any mark of monstrosity in Presine: "La fée entièrement humanisée ne manifeste pas la moindre tendance à reprendre une forme animale; elle n'est pas affligée d'un trait animal dans son aspect ou sa conduite." In Harf-Lancner's opinion, this fact renders her taboo meaningless, since there is no apparent reason that she cannot be seen (59). Clier-Colombani, on the other hand, sees the dragon depicted in the Arsenal manuscript of the *Roman de Mélusine* (Arsenal 3353) as Presine's totem and double, a double that she transmits by heredity to her daughter Melusine, who is also accompanied in the Arsenal illuminations by a dragon, into which, of course, she later transforms herself at the time of her metamorphosis. On the basis of this illustrative detail in the Arsenal manuscript, Clier-Colombani infers that the reason Presine refuses to be seen when she gives birth is that at that moment she assumes her natural form of a dragon (111). There is, of course, absolutely no textual evidence for this, and the accompanying dragon represents a later, interpretive illumination to Jean's narrative. Even in the Arsenal manuscript, there is nothing to suggest that Presine herself ever assumed the form of a dragon, which appears more as an independent mascot than as an attribute. The inference that it represents Presine's "animal form" seems to me quite illegitimate and in any case fails to explain Jean d'Arras's reticence about specifying Presine's condition, a reticence that is clearly absent almost everywhere else in the text.

16. So parallel are the stories of Hervy and Raymondin that Harf-Lancner claims that Jean d'Arras presents Raymondin "comme un héros prédestiné par

l'histoire de son père à une aventure similaire" (*Fées,* 161). For those who believe this story is directed at legitimizing Jean de Berry's acquisition of Poitou, one should note how very odd it would be to do so by beginning with a narrative of the count's murder.

17. Jean Markale, with a characteristically indulged tendency to psychologization, interprets Melusine's imprisonment of her father in the mountain as an act of castration (28). But structurally it seems to me to be closer to parricide. Markale acknowledges that it is more usual in popular *contes* for the daughter to induce a young man she loves to kill the father rather than commit the act of murder (or to perform a castration) herself. Melusine's imprisonment of Elinas, therefore, partakes of both parricide and castration, but fits neither case perfectly. If, structurally, Melusine's imprisonment of her father takes the place of the expected parricide, her acquisition of a tail would seem to suggest the transfer of this phallic member from father to daughter. The implied castration and Melusine's acquisition of a phallus are, to be sure, central to Markale's interpretation of Melusine as an androgynous figure, although there are more securely based textual grounds for seeing her in this way that do not require the imprisonment to be treated as a symbolic castration. On this see below.

18. Rêne Girard, *Violence and the Sacred,* 62–65.

19. What is curious about these genealogical tales is that the story of an illicit union between a social unknown and—typically—a Flemish "princess" often displaces the known, and wholly licit, origins of the family as its founding myth.

20. On the genealogies and genealogical histories see Georges Duby, "Remarques sur la littérature généalogique en France aux XIe et XIIe siècles," in *Hommes et Structures du Moyen Age* (The Hague and Paris: Mouton, 1973), 287–98; Léopold Génicot, *Les Généalogies* (Turnhout: Typologie des Sources du Moyen Age Occidental, 15, 1975); Gabrielle M. Spiegel, "Genealogy: Form and Function in Medieval Historical Narrative," *History and Theory* 22 (1983): 43–53; R. Howard Bloch, *Etymologies and Genealogies: A Literary Anthropology of the French Middle Ages* (Chicago: University of Chicago Press, 1983).

21. See Marcel Sendrail, "Sur l'origine des monstres," *Concours Médical* 77 (1955): 306.

22. For Markale, the gigantism of the sons links them to figures like Hercules, also born of the union of a god and a mortal (52) and serves to connect Melusine to the Celtic tradition of the Déesse-Mère, the Primordial being who gave birth to the human race and to the race of gods. The notion of Melusine as an avatar of the Déesse-Mère appears in virtually all the folkloric studies of the *roman;* see for example Henri Dontenville, *La Mythologie française* (Paris: Payot, 1948), and *Les dits et récits de Mythologie française* (Paris: Payot,

1950); Henri Fromage, "Recherches sur Melusine," *Bulletin de la Société de Mythologie Française* 86 (Juillet-Sept. 1972): 442–75; Léo Desaivre, "Notes sur Melusine," *Bulletin de la Société des Antiquaires de l'Ouest,* 2ème sér., 20 (1899): 204–34; Marcelle Richard, *Mythologie du Pays de Langres* (Paris: Picard, 1970); F. Thouvenet, "Melusine en Gâtinais?" *Bulletin de la Société de Mythologie Française* 90 (Juillet–Sept. 1973): 73–76. For an apparently exhaustive account of all the possible mythic prototypes of Melusine, Markale and Clier-Colombani are not to be shunned.

23. Claude Lecouteux traces this motif back to classical antiquity and the myth of the Panotéens. See his "Les Panotéens: sources, diffusion, emploi," *Etudes Germaniques* 35 (1980): 253–66. See also Lecouteux, *Mélusine,* 50.

24. In the opinion of Harf-Lancner, the physical deformities of the children betray their demonic orgin, and thus belie Melusine's image as a benevolent fairy (*Fées,* 177). They are, of course, in the most literal sense, the "mark of the beast."

25. On the idea of bodily wholeness as part of holiness (or the sacred) and therefore of imperfection or lack of bodily integrity (wholeness) as defilement see Douglas (*Purity and Danger,* 49–53). Christianity retained this notion in its requirement that candidates for priesthood be "integral" in order to receive ordination, hence the practical as well as symbolic vengeance that Héloïse's uncle Fulbert enacted upon Abelard in castrating him, effectively barring him from further clerical advancement.

26. Claude Lévi-Strauss, *Le Totémisme Aujourd'hui* (Paris: Presses universitaires de France, 1962), 4.

27. As almost all commentators have remarked. See, for example, Michèle Perret, who notes that "sa grande dent l'apparente en effet à la bête monstrueuse, dont il a aussi le caractère brutal, violent, et direct, la force et la sauvagerie, la cruauté instinctive" (Postface, *Le Roman de Mélusine,* 330). For Markale, Geoffroy is the new incarnation of the wild boar killed by Raymondin, making him "le Dieu Sanglier dans toute sa sauvagerie, comme il apparaît encore dans les traditions bretonnes ou gauloises" (49–51).

28. That is, the thirteenth-century Geoffroy de Lusignan, d. 1250.

29. In his monologue contemplating the losses that his intemperate actions will produce, Raymondin dwells at length on Melusine's goodness and the great well-being that she has conferred on him, a speech that in principle confirms the image of Melusine as treated to this point in the *roman.* Thus, Raymondin excoriates himself for having betrayed his wife, a woman "de qui tout le monde disoit bien, or vous ay je perdue sans fin. Or ay je perdu joye a tousjours mais. Or ay je perdu beauté, bonté, doulcour, amistié, sens, courtoisie, charité, humilité, toute ma joye, tout mon confort, toute m'esperance, tout

mon eur, mon bien, mon pris, ma vaillance, car tant pou d'onneur que Dieu m'avoit prestee me venoit de vous, ma doulce amour." [of whom everyone speaks well, now, I have lost you forever. Now I have lost joy forever. Now I have lost all beauty, goodness, sweetness, friendship, sense, courtesy, charity, humility, all my joy, all my comfort, all my hope, work, goods, prowess, vaillance, since whatever little honor God granted me came from you, my sweet love] (*M* 243). Harf-Lancner insists upon the importance of Raymondin's response to the sight of Melusine in distinguishing Jean d'Arras's text from the earlier Latin "contes mélusiniens." In her view, Jean's account of Raymondin's lack of horror at the spectacle of Melusine *qua* serpent, indeed his renewed love and tenderness toward her, places his narrative closer to the primitive myth, in which ambitious *lignages* who endowed themselves with fairies for ancestors were much more sensitive to the glory to be derived from a supernatural filiation than to the disturbing character of a pagan prodigy. See Markale, 172.

30. *Audivimus demones incubos et succubos et concubitus eorum periculosos; heredes autem eorum aut sobolem felici fine beatam in antiquis historiis aut raro aut nunquam legimus.* This opinion forms the conclusion to Walter Map's account of the story of Edric the Wild, in the *De Nugis Curialium*, trans. M. R. James and E. S. Hartland (London: Cymmrodorion Record Series, no. 9, 1923), 2.12.77.

31. She proclaims to Raymondin: "tu ne me verras jamais de nul jour en forme femmenine" [You will never see me again any day in the form of a woman] (*M* 259).

32. See the text of the *Otia Imperialia* reprinted in Stouff, *Essai,* 155–59. A French translation of bk. 3 of the *Otia Imperialia* under the title *Le Livre des merveilles* has been published by Annie Duschesne (Paris: Les Belles Lettres, 1992).

33. The main branch of the Lusignan was extinguished in 1308, but the Armenian branch continued until the time of Léon VI, who was dethroned in 1375. In 1384 he placed himself under the protection of Charles VI, dying in Paris in 1393, just as Jean d'Arras was completing his narrative of Melusine, finished, as he tells us (*M* 303) on Thursday, 7 August 1393. At the end of the fourteenth century, only the kingdom of Cyprus remained in the hands of the Lusignan, who retained it until 1473. On Léon VI of Armenia see Stouff, 98, and Harf-Lancner, 176.

"La fourme du pié toute escripte": Melusine and the Entrance into History

Laurence de Looze

In her article "L'Invraisemblable vérité" Michèle Perret has called attention to how Jean d'Arras's *Mélusine*, like so many fourteenth-century works, is concerned with the ways in which truth can be occulted by appearances. Perret has quite rightly pointed out that *Mélusine* is aware of its own status as writing, particularly with respect to the author. One might add, as a corollary to this authorial self-consciousness, that at another level of diegesis—at the level of plot—the work is also insistently and incessantly interested in *re*writing: each important element of the work is repeated, multiplied to excess. This aesthetic of repetition is an aesthetic of self-conscious mimesis; the Greek *mimoumai*, whence *mimesis*, refers after all not just to imitation but also to reenactment and repetition.[1] Mimesis is imitation because it reseeks ("re-peto") the world, and vice versa.

Let me give some examples from Jean d'Arras. By the time Raymondin meets his fairy princess Melusine in the woods, there have already been several such encounters in the work: first, the general cases mentioned by Gervaise of Tilbury and re-cited by Jean d'Arras; second,

Elinas's meeting with Presine by a forest fountain; finally, the meeting of the count of Forez, Raymondin's father, with a magic "belle dame" (*M* 15)—perhaps Melusine herself—also by a fountain. Similarly, the sequence of battles that lead to the marriage of Melusine's sons is repeated with little variation in the cases of Urian, Guyon, Antoine, and Renaud. Also, it is the implausible profusion of orphaned princesses, one after another, that has provided the material for Jacques le Goff's well-known article, "Mélusine maternelle et défricheuse," in which he analyzes this plenitude as indicative of a wish-fulfillment economic system. More interesting from my point of view is that these trials follow what Tzvetan Todorov, speaking of Galahad's role in the Grail Prose Cycle, has called a "ritual logic" in which the outcome of putative "trials" is never in doubt because they are in reality just reaffirmations of a character's worth.[2] Even the crimes against genealogical lines become repetitive. Melusine's crime against her father returns in mutated form with Raymondin's murder of his uncle and surrogate father. Geoffroy will continue the "family tradition" by substituting fratricide for patricide. This soap-opera aesthetic of repetition might be reason for us to argue à la Peter J. Rabinowitz against close reading;[3] the literary menu or paradigm matters here more than the individual choices or syntagmas.

Now, in contrast to repetitive features such as the transgressions against the genealogical line are the elements that are—or appear to be—*sui generis*. For example, the fear of a genealogical misalignment is balanced by a fascination with the *mulier* who appears to all and sundry to be *ex nihilo*. The question of where the title character Melusine comes from haunts the work: she is found beside a *source*, but it is precisely her source that is unknown. At the marriage festivities Raymondin is pushed to frustrated anger by the question, put to him by the counts of Forez and Poitiers, "de quel lignie vostre femme est" [what genealogical line is your wife from?] (*M* 43). Equally unanswerable is where the workers and the materials come from for the speedy edification of Melusine's building projects. The initial question regarding where Melusine comes from is restated, after she marries Raymondin, as one of where she goes. The question of origins and genealogy (*unde venis*?) becomes translated into a question of geography in the form of Melusine's sabbatical disappearances (*quo vadis*?). Raymondin cannot, of course, answer either query.

One of the features that ensures, however, that the series of repetitions will not be endless is Raymondin's initial promise not to inquire after Melusine. Melusine's conditions are clear: "Vous me jurerez sur tous les seremens que preudoms doit faire, que le samedi vous ne mettrez jamais peine a moy veoir ne enquerre ou je seray" [You must swear by all the oaths a noble man should use that you will never make an effort on a Saturday to see me nor to try to find out where I am] (*M* 26). Melusine, in turn, promises to do nothing that does Raymondin dishonor. From that moment on, the reader/audience of course expects the necessary telos: the end is given with the beginning, and the pleasure of the text, as Peter Brooks would point out,[4] is in frustrating or deferring our arrival at the scene of betrayal.

In the best Melusine manuscript, that of the Bibliothèque de l'Arsenal, this deferral lasts from folio 12 to about folio 130. It comes to an end during the portion of the narrative devoted to the adventures of Geoffroy. In the middle of Geoffroy's giant-slaying adventures, the narrative switches back to Raymondin and Melusine. While the couple is visiting the Morvan, the count of Forez falsely informs Raymondin that Melusine may be doing him dishonor every Saturday by having "fornicacion avec un autre" [fornication with another] (*M* 241). Goaded by the charge that he is too weak and blind to *enquerre* as to her whereabouts, Raymondin becomes suspicious that she has broken the terms of her promise to him. He therefore goes to the spot where she is, peeks through a hole, and spies her in her half-serpent form. A Freudian analysis could undoubtedly make quite a bit out of the voyeurism in this scene.[5] Somewhat differently, I wish to concentrate on the lack of immediate ramifications.

For if the tension should snap at this point, something goes amiss. According to all expectations, including both the reader's and Raymondin's, Raymondin should now lose his wife straightaway. Yet he doesn't, nor does the narrative offer any explanation for this, even though Raymondin has clearly betrayed the pact he made with Melusine. It is surely curious that after having set up a narrative code so carefully Jean d'Arras seems willing to let it just fall by the wayside. Raymondin even begins lamenting his impending loss when Melusine comes to join him in bed, but he stops when she gives no sign of being aware of his transgression. Raymondin thinks this is because she is unaware of his *parjuration*, though we (and later he) are specifically told this is not the case.

The question I wish to ask is: why? Why, if the pact is perfectly clear, are there no consequences to be suffered when Raymondin so evidently breaks it by both seeking after Melusine and seeing her on a *samedi*? Raymondin suffers no loss whatsoever, life returns to normal, and the suspension of consequences that already lasted 118 folii is renewed for another seven.

During this suspension is narrated the adventure (if it can be called that) in which Geoffroy burns to death his own brother Fromont along with one hundred other monks in the abbey of Maillezais. Only after all this does Raymondin, in a fit of anger, utter that he has seen Melusine in her bath, half-serpent and half-woman, and at that moment Melusine becomes lost to him. The betrayal of Melusine is thus split into two parts—action and then utterance—and the consequences, when they finally arrive, are anticlimactic. Should we view what in musical terms one might call this "suspended cadence" as a flaw in Jean d'Arras's narrative, or might it have meaning for our overall understanding of the work? Put in the simplest terms: why are the betrayal and loss split into two parts, and why is Geoffroy's terrible crime intercalated between these two parts?

Let me return to the excessive nature of the tale as a whole, to which I alluded earlier. Thirteenth- and fourteenth-century narratives push sequences of adventures to an extreme, to be sure, as is evident in the almost interminable episodes of the Grail Prose Cycle, Froissart's *Méliador*, and the work at hand, Jean d'Arras's *Mélusine*. Repetition always implies difference, however, and Geoffroy's actions are qualitatively different from those of his preceding brothers. His extreme nature is both a concentration and a repetition of the Raymondin tale overall: a microcosmic *mise-en-abyme*. If the boar of the work's beginning can be read as a signifier of uncontrolled and uncontrollable violence, violence that becomes displaced to Raymondin in an oedipal murder, Geoffroy Big-Tooth can in turn be read as the return of the boar. His great tooth, which evokes his father's crime by resembling a boar's tusk,[6] is also a metonymic sign of the excessive violence Geoffroy incarnates—a violence directed finally against God and his brother. Geoffroy's crime against Fromont is much more than mere cleric-knight rivalry, though it is also that, more even than Raoul de Cambrai-ish immoderation. In murdering his brother and burning the house of God—which is a crime against the supreme Father—Geoffroy's actions rearticulate the earlier offenses against genealogy: the crime of Cain is mixed here with a blasphemously oedipal rebellion. Moreover (and I shall return to this), it is this very crime that pushes Raymondin himself to rearticulate what he saw the day he spied on Melusine.

I have not yet answered the questions I posed earlier: why should Raymondin's betrayal be intertwined with Geoffroy's adventures, and why should Raymondin's *declaration* that he broke faith with Melusine, rather than the actual betrayal itself, lead directly to castigation?

As a way of approaching an answer, I would like to begin by suggesting that the two questions are really one. Let me observe also that what Melusine asked of Raymondin was faith above all. He needed to have faith in her. He needed to have faith that her service was to God: "car seurement je suiz de par Dieu," she tells him. But Raymondin—as well as some modern critics—cannot believe that she is an agent of good. A long tradition regards serpents necessarily as signifiers of evil, as though the bond between signifier and signified were not arbitrary and conventional but rather material. Raymondin also needs to have faith that when Melusine disappears on Saturdays, it is not to do him any dishonor. As she tells him, "jamais cellui jour je ne feray ja chose qui vous puist estre atournee fors a toute honneur" [on those days I will never do anything that does you other than great honor] (*M* 26). Raymondin swears to all her terms: "Et Remondins lui jure ainsi" (*M* 26). Only after he has sworn this troth does Melusine tell him what story to contrive regarding the accidental murder of his uncle. Following her advice, he manages to blame the death on the boar and is absolved.

Now just as *Mélusine* reveals a keen interest in what we would now categorize as Freudian questions (the boar as a sign of oedipal violence), *Mélusine* also gives evidence, like so much medieval French literature, of a fascination, even an obsession, with matters of law and justice. This is part of the concern for truth and appearances that characterizes a new evidentiary dimension in late medieval judicial processes. The (perhaps faulty) judicial system plays a role in both Raymondin's absolution for the murder of his uncle and in his reclaiming of his father's heritage in

Brute Bretagne. Melusine proves extremely instrumental in both instances. One could rephrase the matter of truth and appearances as intention and action or true signified and ambiguous signifier. A similar example from another work that comes to mind is the two accusations of Guenevere in *La Mort le Roi Artu*. Guenevere commits a crime in action but not in intentions when she unknowingly hands Mador de la Porte's brother a poisoned apple; but if she is innocent in that instance she should surely be found guilty when, caught with Lancelot in her bedchamber, she contends that there is no evidentiary proof of an adulterous act but only suspicious circumstances. Guenevere's action *appears* to make her guilty, though her intentions are blameless, in the first instance; in the second, her intentions are surely criminal even if apparent evidence is lacking. To return to Melusine, she bases her legal advice on a consideration of intentions: she helps Raymondin uncover the culprit who intentionally murdered his father, yet she helps Raymondin escape punishment for the death of his own uncle, since his intention did not participate in the action. In this sense Melusine truly moves, as she claims, in God's service, even if this means skewing the terrestrial judicial process, which, derived from Germanic law, still placed great weight on a consideration of actions.

This focus on intentions as the all-important criterion for framing guilt or innocence, sin or no, goes back of course to Saint Augustine. Given also Melusine's concern for intentions and her insistence that Raymondin have faith in her, we can see that Melusine repeats and even parodies (though with no ridicule implied) the Christian New Covenant or New Law: a law of love, written in the flesh of the heart and not in stone.

Without wishing to labor the obvious, we should recall that the Christian New Testament juxtaposed the stony lettricity of Moses' tablets with Jesus' law of the spirit. Second Corinthians 3:6 is justly famous for succinctly synthesizing this view of "a new covenant, not of the letter but of the Spirit; for the letter kills, whereas the Spirit vivifies." Furthermore, this distinction between Old Testament and New Testament law was developed most powerfully for the Latin Middle Ages by the West's greatest semiotician, Saint Augustine.[7]

The power this distinction between the spirit that brings life and the letter that kills had for medieval writers is well-known. For Saint Augustine, to read "charitably" is to seek always the spirit and to privilege the divine signified over the terrestrial signifier through which it passes, while to read "cupiditously" is to be overly concerned with the letter of the law rather than with the divine truth the letter can signify (see *De Doctrina Christiana*, bk. 2, esp. 1, 2, 6, 8–10, and *Confessions*, bk. 4). Moreover, divine grace is the refusal by God to concentrate solely on the letter of the law when on Judgment Day he weighs our souls and tempers a potentially harsh judgment of our inevitable transgressions by considering also our intentions. Though Dante is perhaps the writer who most consistently harps on this distinction—the gate to Hell, for example, is a supremely "stony" text, Medusa stands as a way of reading that turns men to stone[8]—many others come to mind as well. Part of the humor (and the pleasure) of the staged oath scenes, whether in the twelfth-century *Tristan et Iseut* or the fourteenth-century Icelandic *Grettissaga Asmundarsonar*, is that they dare suggest that God might uphold the letter of the truth even when to do so travesties the spirit of the truth.

I wish to suggest that this same distinction is crucial for the questions I have posed here. There is no doubt but that Raymondin violates the terms of the covenant he has established with Melusine. He knows it and she knows it. In the overall scheme of things, however, this is but one small transgression in a marriage of many *samedis*, and Melusine responds charitably with forgiveness, choosing to ignore Raymondin's breaking of the specific terms of the covenant. As she will explain later: "Combien que tu t'estoies parjurez envers moy quant tu mis paine a moy veoir, mais pour ce que tu ne l'avoies descouvert a personne, je le t'avoye pardonné en cuer, combien que je ne t'en eusse point fait de mencion, et Dieu le t'eust pardonné, car tu en eusses fait la penitence en ce monde" [Despite the fact that you had become a liar toward me when you took steps to observe me, nevertheless, because you had not revealed this to anyone, I pardoned you in my heart, even though I made no mention of it to you; and God would have pardoned you also, for you would have done penitence in this world for your offense] (*M* 256).

The terms of this explanation are significant. Because the infraction went no further and was not articulated, and above all because Raymondin felt genuine contrition, Melusine (like God) pardoned him *in her heart* (*en cuer*). Melusine contrasts here his breach of the outward covenant with her concern for both his and her *intentions*.

After Raymondin learns Melusine's secret and discovers that he has not lost her as a result, the Raymondin-Melusine episode is suspended in favor of Geoffroy's final "adventure" in which he burns his brother Fromont and Fromont's fellow monks to death. This series of actions culminates, in other words, in a return to the oldest biblical crime and a wholesale overthrowing of the New Law. The originary Old Testament crime of fratricide coalesces with an attack on the (New Testament) Church. Following this, we return to Raymondin and Melusine, and Raymondin now compounds his earlier violation by uttering what he has seen. Indeed, it is precisely Geoffroy's outrageous crimes that push Raymondin to accuse Melusine of responsibility for having created a diabolical son. When Raymondin's ire (*yre*) replaces his *raison naturelle* [natural reason] (*M* 255), he accuses Melusine of being a "faulse serpente" [false serpent/snake] (*M* 255), whose only good work was Fromont. This attempt to fix the iconography of the serpent sign in terms of the Garden of Eden casts Melusine as an Old Testament enemy of the Church who has been reincarnated in Geoffroy (rather than reading Geoffroy as a personification of Raymondin's own offenses).

There are obvious problems with Raymondin's formulation. First is that Geoffroy is their jointly created son, and, man inevitably being tainted with transgression, it is hubristic for Raymondin to raise himself above the law and claim no participation in sin's transmission. Second is that Raymondin fails to see his boar-son as a sign of his own violent transgression, also represented by a boar. Finally, Raymondin proves himself a slave to the signifier here, for he focuses entirely on Melusine as serpent-sign and not at all on her intentions. Accusing her of being Old Testament in nature, Raymondin is in fact the one who proves *himself* an Old Testament type of interpreter. Serpents, after all, are no more true or "faulse" than any other signifier. Indeed, in Christian semiotics, a signifier is neither good nor bad, but interpretation makes it so. Even the *serpent* of the Garden of Eden did not deprive Adam and Eve of choice; they could have used the temptation as an opportunity to reaffirm their faith instead of losing it. The inscrutability of the sign is conveyed to us by the fact that the half-serpent Melusine says she is doing God's work, and we see this confirmed by her *caritas* in even the most difficult situations.

If the half-serpent Melusine becomes the sign of the New Law, it is (paradoxically) Raymondin's accusation that returns to Old Law: he announces that he has transgressed the letter of the law. Raymondin compounds his earlier violation by now *revealing* what he saw. He returns linguistically to the Old Testament terms that characterized the intervening crime of Geoffroy. At the level of lettricity, this is an analogous rejection of the new, charitable love and faith Melusine has offered him. For Augustine the temporality of speech is of course one of the primary markers of man's fall from Edenic grace and into the "syllables of time";[9] Raymondin brings about his own "second fall" in a second, voluntary articulation of his betrayal of the covenant.

As a result of this mock "judgment" in which Raymondin recondemns himself as he tries to condemn Melusine, he loses her for all time, just as the man who refuses God's teaching by choosing to fall a second time in this world will lose God eternally. It is in this light that I read Melusine's transformation. What Raymondin refuses (or is unable) to do is to read his wife charitably as a sign of God. Instead, he banishes her to Old Testament serpentine status. Her transformation, in other words, responds to and literalizes his act of reception. It is as though Dante's contrapasso were operating here. Raymondin would deny his wife her wife's status and turn her wholly into a serpent; his punishment is that precisely this comes to pass. It is also in this light that I read Melusine's departure from Lusignan castle.

Let me recall the extraordinary description of her departure: "Et lors fist un moult doulereux plaint et un moult grief souspir, puis sault en l'air, et laisse la fenestre, et trespasse le vergier. Et lors se mue en une serpente grant et grosse et longue de la longueur de xv. piez. Et sachiez que la pierre sur quoy elle passa a la fenestre y est encores, et y est la fourme du pié toute escripte" [And then she gave a very painful cry and a deep sigh; after that, she leaps into the air, leaving the window, and flies over the orchard. Then she changes into a great and enormous reptile, fifteen feet long. Know that the stone on which she stepped at the window is still there, and the shape of her foot is perfectly written there] (*M* 260). I submit that when she departs, Melusine leaves behind a text that alludes to Raymondin's return to a law written in stone; I am of course speaking of "la fourme du pié toute escripte" [the shape of the foot perfectly written] Melusine inscribes in the windowsill as she changes into a serpent. I submit also that in this corporeal inscription history, historicity, and historiography quite literally find a "foothold" (if one will permit the pun). This deliberate fixing of the Melusine tale in scripture is also a writing of and into history—into, as Augustine would say, the syllables of time.

At the same time, however, Melusine becomes the protoauthor of the Melusine text. If man's post-Edenic existence is a writing of history in the clay of the earth—what has been called the book of the world—Melusine inscribes her text in this world as she steps from Raymondin's world and back into timelessness. The entry of her story into history and into historiography takes its *premier pas* in the form of the written foot, which, as Jean d'Arras tells us, may still be seen in the windowsill.

This scripture of Melusine's departing step is also a text of Raymondin's fall. Throughout the tale Melusine has defied the temporality of this world. Her ability to make things from nothing or with impossible speed could only be owing to a divine power or a diabolical one. The temporality of man's creative processes and the resistance of earthly media are reminders of man's fallen state; creation by God, in contrast, is immediate and effortless.[10] Raymondin failed to see the ways in which Melusine hinted at an impalpable world beyond the temporal order. With Melusine's departure, that world is lost, and Lusignan falls into history.

This is important because the inscription at the window also serves to authorize Jean d'Arras's text. Jean d'Arras's book, we should remember, is associated with, among other things, a new *translatio* of the Lusignan property; it serves to legitimize the origins of a property that passes in the late 1300s into the possession of the duke of Berry. At the level of authorship, Jean d'Arras, by this clever authenticating turn, manages to anchor his writing in the most authoritative scripture of all: Melusine's own testimonial scripture in stone. Melusine becomes for Jean d'Arras both *auctoritas* and primal historiographer.

Moreover, because Melusine's writing is in stone—that is, in the very stone of her (former) dwelling—this corporeal inscription bridges the distance between text and referent, between book in the world and book of the world, between literature and reality. The historical referent becomes in the most literal sense the first *writing* about that experience and an autobiographical text to boot. To return to the ideas of Michèle Perret with which I began, let me say that the written form of the foot bridges from vision and speaking to testamentary writing. It is a momentary stasis of both the foot and the hand at the very moment that oral culture passes into writing. Jacqueline Cerquiglini argues in her masterful *Un engin si soutil* that oral culture is of the foot in the clay (coming from dance and song), whereas written culture is a culture of the hand.[11] The Melusinian "body politic" here describes a transitory and precarious balance in which text and referent are momentarily one and the same, as the foot writes the text of Raymondin's fall.

If my reading of these events of *Mélusine* is correct, then our understanding of the work gains, I believe, in several powerful ways. First, we have the means to explain the structuring of the most crucial events of the work, namely the discovery and denunciation of Melusine's secret. The resuspension of Raymondin's betrayal and the intercalation of Geoffroy's fratricide point to both delicate framing and deep meaning, rather than being a tedious flaw in a long text. In fact, to place Geoffroy's crime precisely here could not be more apropos since, as Jacques Le Goff has noted ("Mélusine maternelle," 595), Geoffroy is the one almost certifiably historical character among Melusine's sons, and his crime really took place (ca. 1232). History truly *is* inscribed here. Moreover, by a kind of conservation of critical literary mass, every element becomes meaningful: Melusine's delay, the nature and terms of both Raymondin's accusation and her response, her imprint left in the stone of the castle, and the extraordinary metaphor chosen by Jean d'Arras: "la fourme du pié toute escripte." We are given the means for understanding how actions become inscribed in history in our (necessarily) fallen world. At the same time, Jean d'Arras authenticates and authorizes his own text, placing it under the rubric of Melusine's protowriting. This is a powerful political gambit, which speaks at once to the past, to Jean d'Arras's contemporary world in which legitimacy of possession is intricately related to legitimacy of inscription, and to us as modern scholars concerned with questions of text and referent. Finally, Jean d'Arras resurrects and resolves at the textual level the question of genealogical usurpation that was so problematic in the plot of the work. Todorov once remarked that every literary work recounts its own genealogy.[12] Jean d'Arras daringly makes his text a direct descendant of that supremely fertile matrix, Melusine.

Notes

1. I owe this observation to Professor Greg Nagy's *Poetry as Performance: Ancient Greece and Beyond* (forthcoming), chs. 1, 2 n.5, and 3. I am grateful to Professor Nagy for having made his typescript available to me.

2. Tzvetan Todorov, *Poétique de la prose* (Paris: Seuil, 1971), 140–42.

3. Peter J. Rabinowitz, *Before Reading: Narrative Conventions and the Politics of Interpretation* (Ithaca, N.Y.: Cornell University Press, 1987), 230–31.

4. See Peter Brooks, *Reading for the Plot* (New York: Knopf, 1984).

5. I fully concur with the analysis by Kevin Brownlee in this collection.

6. The Spanish translation of Jean d'Arras makes the association overt. Describing Geoffroy at birth, the fifteenth-century Spanish version says that he "nacio con vn diente muy grande que le salía fuera de la boca, como vn colmillo de puerco montes" [was born with a great tooth that issued from his mouth like a wild boar's tusk] (Corfis, *Historia*, 51).

7. In recent years Augustine's thinking has been elucidated by Eugene Vance in an important series of essays. I am particularly indebted here to his essay "Augustine's *Confessions* and the Grammar of Selfhood," *Genre* 6 (1973): 1–28, and to the first two chapters of his *Mervelous Signals: Poetics and Sign Theory in the Middle Ages* (Lincoln: University of Nebraska Press, 1982).

8. On these instances in Dante, see John Freccero, *Dante: The Poetics of Conversion* (Cambridge, Mass.: Harvard University Press, 1986), chs. 5 and 7.

9. In his *Confessions* Augustine sees the blessed in heaven as "reading God's face without the syllables of time" ("et ibi legunt sine syllabis temporum" [13.15.18]). See Vance, *Mervelous Signals,* ch. 2.

10. Alexander of Hales notes à la Aristotle that "ars respicit operationem" [art is concerned with its operation] in a way that divine creation never needed to be. Subsequently, Thomas Aquinas pointed out that the resistance of the artist's medium, the elaboration of artistic creation over time, and the difference both of these factors introduce into the artist's initial conception are elements wholly alien to divine creation, which knows no resistance of matter and which is instantaneous. For discussion, see de Brugne, *Etudes d'esthétique médiévale*, 3 vols. (Brugge: De Tempel, 1946), 3:114 and 3:318–46.

11. See Jacqueline Cerquiglini, *"Un Engin si soutil": Guillaume de Machaut et l'écriture au xive siècle* (Geneva: Slatkine, 1985), ch. 2, esp. pp. 181–200.

12. Tsvetan Todorov, *Littérature et signification* (Paris: Seuil, 1967): "Toute oeuvre, tout roman raconte, à travers la trame événementielle, l'histoire de sa propre création, sa propre histoire" (49).

Melusine Between Myth and History: Profile of a Female Demon

STEPHEN G. NICHOLS

Allegory thus would reach the highest plane in a symbolism that conveys the action of the mind.—Angus Fletcher

Sometime between 1387 and 1392, a court poet named Jean d'Arras invented a proto-Gothic romance for one of the most powerful and famous literary patrons of the age: Jean, the duke of Berry, count of Poitiers, suzerain of Languedoc and Guyenne, and tutor to the young king, Charles VI of France. Jean d'Arras called his book the *Roman de Mélusine*, after the name of a new kind of heroine, part fairy, part human, whom he made up from a dazzling mélange of Latin, Celtic folklore, and local legend. In one stroke he synthesized a millennium of controversy revealing popular and learned ambivalence, not to say fear, regarding the power of images.

From the extraordinary character of his female monster, Melusine, and her ten grotesquely marked sons, Jean d'Arras constructed a puissant allegory of history showing the illusory nature of English claims to the French throne as they had, for example, recently been set forth by Jean Froissart in his popular and authoritative *Chroniques*. But however compelling contemporary political concerns might have been for Jean d'Arras's powerful patron, Jean himself seems to have been fascinated by the chance to construct a vast encyclopedia of images—an "image theater," consisting of fantastic exotica.

Fascinating and necessary as these iconic elements of *Le Roman de Mélusine* may be, none compares with the conception of the fairy herself. One might claim this simply on the incredible afterlife Melusine has had, not only in the Middle Ages and Renaissance but also for her role in modern times. Many fascinating female figures were invented in the late Middle Ages who have passed from all but scholarly memory. Not so Melusine. But if she has gripped the Western imagination for the last five hundred years, it must have to do with the way Jean d'Arras conceived her: what he invented and how. Above all, her hold stems from the way she synthesizes a millennial tradition of learned and folkloric speculation about female monsters, those demonic agents who appeared human, who had passionate souls like humans, but who shared with the gods eternal life and an aerial abode, though, like gods, they could and often did choose to descend to earth when they bore an illusory human (female) body. Jean did not so much invent Melusine, in other words, as turn to history for his raw material and then, through his work, return her fully formed to the historical record.

In Jean's romance, then, Melusine is about the feminization of the image; or rather the evil that images of history, conceived as feminized, can provoke. He also asks us to speculate on the the deplorable necessity for illusion in life. In what follows, I would like, first, to show just how thoroughly Melusine incarnates a problematic demonology of image; then, to trace the "philology" of this feminized personification beyond the usual and by now familiar analogues in Gervaise of Tilbury; and finally, to examine the pictures in one of the principal manuscripts of Jean's romance to illustrate how it constructs an allegory of history where iconic representation dramatizes the ambivalence of historical memory.

Melusine: A Demonology of Image

Who says Melusine says image; visual image, certainly, but also verbal image in its myriad permutations, such as symbol, connotation, metaphor, and analogy. The visual image of Melusine, the quintessential medieval fatal attraction, is, of course, that of the siren, mermaid in the more anodyne form, except that Melusine, like the dragon with which she is also associated, has wings as well as the piscine tail.

Like the *sirènes bifides* or split-tailed sirens carved on the corners of Romanesque capitals, Melusine's image has two complementary parts, two morphologies, really, since they apparently represent two distinct body images. Her "signature-image" is that of the winged siren, a beautiful, blonde, full-breasted woman down to the waist, with the dragon wings and fishtail filling out the rest of the picture. This is not the image of Melusine that one first encounters in her narratives, however; we first see a beautiful princess, a seemingly normal woman, sumptuously gowned in the fashion of the later Middle Ages, standing beside a well or spring.

In her human form, one may also find Melusine in the midst of a building site, authoritatively directing the construction of one of the handsome castles legend credits her with erecting in record time and with the same regularity that she gave birth to sons. Occasionally, she may be shown with one or two of her ten sons, many of them distinguished by a visually striking deformity, such as Geoffroy Big-Tooth's tusklike incisor, or Horrible, her eighth son, unnamed at birth, distinguished by three eyes and the fact, we are told, that he would, before the age of three, kill two of his wet nurses by biting their breasts off.

Melusine's dual morphologies are not accidental. They constitute a deliberate doubling of her nature, a narrative and not simply a biological twinning. Within the culture of the period, her attributes formed a perfectly natural aspect of the character and narrative of one who was simultaneously monster, hero, and demi-demon. This drama of biological and philosophical boundary violation offers a stunning instance of the Middle Ages' confidence in its power to transcend the limits of representation.

The paradox of the work, for a modern reader though perhaps not for a medieval public, lies not in the apparent exoticism of Melusine and her sons but in their systematic correlation to contemporary structures of thought. Melusine incarnates ambivalence, both physiologically, as part of her genealogy, that is as part of her narrative of creation (for genealogy and narrative are one), and naturally, as a readily explicable example of category mixing.

Now, one of the most significant facts of Jean's work, and one contributing to the force of his allegory, is the historical disparity between Melusine's name—local and recent—and the species the name connotes. Jean brilliantly succeeds in co-opting under the particular name, "Melusine," associated with the Lusignan family by parochial and largely unrecorded legend, an anonymous category, the "lamia," a species of female monster, of which there exists a long and voluminous tradition from the late classical period down to Robert Burton's *Anatomy of Melancholy* (1621) and John Keats's striking poem, "Lamia" (1819).

Keats's poem has a wonderful description of the ambiguous gestalt of the lamia that captures the horrific fascination—and the unmistakable pathos—by which early modern Europe conjured the feminine demonic:

> The God, dove-footed, glided silently . . .
> Until he found a palpitating snake,
> Bright, and cirque-couchant in a dusky brake.
> She was a gordian shape of dazzling hue
> Vermilion-spotted, golden, green, and blue;
> Striped like a zebra, freckled like a pard,
> Eyed like a peacock, and all crimson barr'd;
> And full of silver moons, that, as she breathed,
> Dissolv'd, or brighter shone, or interwreathed
> Their lustres with the gloomier tapestries—
> So rainbow-sided, touch'd with miseries,
> She seem'd, at once, some penanced lady elf,
> Some demon's mistress, or the demon's self.
> Upon her crest she wore a wannish fire
> Sprinkled with stars, like Ariadne's tiar:
> Her head was serpent, but ah, bitter-sweet!
> She had a woman's mouth with all its pearls complete:
> And for her eyes: what could such eyes do there
> But weep and weep, that they were born so fair?
>
> (ll. 42, 45–62)[1]

With Keats's ekphrastic evocation in mind, let us first look at the way Melusine configures narrative, including the way she becomes a narrative agent deflecting the story to her own ends in some key scenes.

Witnessing her "active" role in the narrative production of images will help us to grasp better her ontology, that is the ontology of the sign "Melusine."

Morbid passion played an important role in the polemic surrounding demonology during the late classical and medieval period. In his treatise on demons, *De Deo Socratis*, the second-century philosopher, Lucius Apuleius, better known for his *Metamorphoses* (*The Golden Ass*), advances Plato's doctrine that demons are aerial creatures residing midway between earth and the heavens, who serve as messengers between the gods and humans.[2] Demons have responsibility for all mysterious divinations or presages by which gods convey signs to human beings: Sleep and Love, for example, are noncorporeal demons.

Apuleius ascribes five qualities to demons: 1) movement, 2) the faculty to reason, 3) a passionate soul, 4) a body composed of air, and 5) eternal life. They share the first three with humans, are unique in the fourth, and have the fifth in common with gods. Apuleius notes the passionate nature of their souls—their ability to love, hate, feel jealousy—for he sees this quality as assuring the efficacy of religious observances.[3]

Plato and Apuleius argue the centrality of the passionate soul as a motor not only in human relations but also in human-divine exchanges. For them, at least in this economy, passion does not shut out reason nor circumvent it but is ancillary to it. Consequently, pathos is not necessarily morbid in the Greek tradition. The Judeo-Christian situation presents quite another picture of the same interaction, however. Early Christian apologists, and notably Saint Augustine, viewed the passionate soul, when ascribed to superhuman beings, as decidedly pathological.

The same mental turmoils (*turbationes mentis*) that for Plato and Apuleius made empathy possible between demons and humans struck a raw chord in Saint Augustine, who devoted considerable space in books eight and nine of *De Ciuitate Dei* to attacking the concept that demons, rather than angels, mediated between heaven and earth. The doctrine of a passible soul in demons appeared particularly perverse: "to deal with . . . Apuleius' statement that demons have in common with us a mind subject to emotion, I ask why it should happen that the minds of demons are tossed by the whirlwinds and tempests of emotion. For *perturbatio* (disturbance) is what the Greeks call *pathos*, and that is why he chose to call the demons *passiva* or subject to emotion, because the word *passio* (emotion) for the Greek word *pathos* means a mental agitation which is contrary to reason."[4] We shall return to these issues later, particularly to the contradictory views, sympathetic and negative, accorded demons in the Greco-Christian tradition bequeathed to the Middle Ages. Suffice it to note for the moment the charged nature of the pathological mind within this tradition as we consider Melusine's ontology.

Once we understand what she actually does in the text, we may better conceive how these narrative representations of Melusine translate theoretically into what we may call a demonology of the image. We will find four major characteristics of the demonic image that must be taken together in context:

(1) *Irresolvable Duality,* represented as morbid variation in the appearance and behavior of the same being. Melusine is always herself, but what is the true nature of that self and which of her morphologies represents "the bottom line" of her ontology?

(2) *Compulsive Repetition,* the key to the pathology of the demonic image lies in the manner by which it repeats the same kind of events or actions. If the demonic agent be characterized by irresolvable duality, its actions betray sameness, an identity independent of the agent's intention, indeed, sometimes the opposite of the agent's stated purpose. The basic narrative armature of the romance itself, in which human males marry female demons or demi-demons through several generations and where the shadow of parricide recurs, affords teasing examples of repetition as key to the production of image.

(3) *Distorting Perspective,* central to the demonic image is the skewed or oblique nature of its vision. Louche itself in its off-centered voyeurism, it also *looks askance*, compelling a furtive and surreptitious gaze on the part of the onlooker or participants. The prohibition against seeing so crucial to the basic legend, the injunction "not to look at specified times or occasions," thereby suggesting that there is "something dirty" or discredible *to see*, characterizes the pathological image. It also sets the stage for the denouement of the work. The most famous single example of the principle of off-centered voyeurism, of course, is the scene of Melusine's husband, Raymondin, peering lasciviously at her

nude body bathing through a hole he has pierced in the door of her chamber.

(4a) *Illusion,* the demonic image is never what it seems. Grounded in the ontology of the demon whose incorporeality substitutes the *appearance* of a body for the body itself, the demonic image calls into question the very possiblity of truth in images, that is, reliable cognition based on aesthetic or sensory perception (*pathos*) as opposed to reason. Conscious of the asymptotic relation between authentic model and its pathological deformation, the demonic image displaces the question of authenticity, or otherwise distracts attention from it.

(4b) Since the illusion of corporeality of demons was thought to be the product of light refracted through the varying density of air, and since light and air were also the media through which image properties had to pass before being processed as sense perception, it was inevitable that visual images be suspect. The signature case of the pathology of illusion in the romance is Melusine in her bath. In place of the anticipated erotogenic body, Raymondin sees the monstrous hybrid: a female torso terminating in a lithe and outsize phallus displaced as a fish's tail. Her human form, like the *integumentum* or covering of a medieval metaphor, conceals a concatenation of disparates, making Melusine signify the demonic *one-of-the-many*, rather than the theological *one-in-many*. Neither monad nor unit, Melusine offers an ontology of dispersion, the original chaos.

"Melusine" as/and Narrative

At first blush, Jean appears to have taken pains to present Melusine as benign, even pious within the frame of her life in France with her husband Raymondin of Lusignan. Certainly by comparison with some of the more sanguinary exploits of her husband and sons, Melusine's concern for constructing family castles and founding religious institutions would seem to signal a pious bent: "Et fist Melusigne faire fonder par le païs mainte eglise, et renter et moult d'autres biens qui ne sont mie a mettre en oubly" [And Melusine caused many churches to be founded and endowed in the region, and many other good works that should not be forgotten] (*M* 80). Her husband, for example, founds his fortune when he kills his benefactor, Aimery, count of Poitiers, accidentally it is true, but in accordance with a prophecy. Melusine's son, Geoffroy, in many ways the "hero" of the romance and successor to his father, Raymondin, as lord of Lusignan, exhibits such a capacity for slaughter that he frightens even the Saracens.

But the most sanguinary defining exploit for Geoffroy has a much more familiar religious aura: that of Cain slaying Abel. At a crucial moment in the narrative, a moment that will lead to the public unmasking of Melusine, Geoffroy learns that his brother, Fromont—Melusine's seventh son and thus the next younger brother of Geoffroy (sixth in birth order)—has become a monk at the Abbey of Maillezais near Lusignan. Geoffroy, whose taste runs to massacring Saracens and slaying giants, reacts with unbridled fury to the news that his brother, Fromont, has taken holy orders. In his wrath, he sets fire to the abbey using the flame from votive candles in the church, burning alive his brother and the hundred-odd monks within. That Geoffroy's actions at Maillezais directly implicate Melusine cannot be missed since Jean observes: "Ce fu la cause de sa tres cruel doulour et de la perte de sa moillier" [This was the cause of his cruel misfortune and of the loss of his wife] (*M* 248).

The denouement results less from the undeniably monstrous acts in this section, however, than from the pathology of the thought process that sets the acts in motion and proceeds by cause and effect to scar every major player in the story. Each event begins with a narrative act that initiates a cognitive process producing a picture in the mind of the interpreter quite different from the "reality" that a neutral observer, the reader, for example, might infer from the same narrative. In each instance, a pathological mutation of affection to hatred motivates the construction of a fatally erroneous picture of reality: love transmuted to hate by suspicion, inserting itself obliquely as a sense that all is not as it appears.

Jean seems to be saying that in a lineage based on the violation of category boundaries—where fairies lie with mortals to produce monsters—lucidity will always be clouded by pathos.

After burning the abbey and immolating his brother and the monks, Geoffroy quits the scene. At once the ambiguity of his being and status reassert themselves: reverting to his dominant human nature, Geoffroy realizes his transgression and feels keen remorse.

His extravagant grief, however, asserts the status of the Maillezais massacre as narrative, in fact as interactive narrative. Geoffroy, the first reader of his father's news about Fromont's monking, has now added a macabre twist to it that must, in turn, be told to Raymondin. Each iteration, of course, increases the dimension of the tale, but without necessarily adding to its symbolic or metaphysical meaning as one might expect in a romance. We see instead a static repetition; the same or similar events leading to a denouement that decreases rather than augments the symbolic capital. The further one proceeds in the story-within-the-story, in other words, the less potential for meaning do the characters possess.

What else could one expect? The ontology of the demonic sign is based on negation, diminishment. It is a pyramid scheme in which the demonic agent perpetually borrows from one to repay another and from another to repay the first. There's no narrative capital, no accumulation of meaning, only the illusion of capital. As long as the number of participants expands, the illusion continues, but when the players begin to shrink, the whole pyramid collapses. This is why Melusine must continually bear sons who go to the far corners of the medieval world, fighting Saracens in the Mediterranean, giants in central Europe, settling scores in the Celtic marches, and so on. Through these exploits, she succeeds in promulgating the myth of Lusignan supremacy. At last, however, Fromont asserts a religious vocation that fatally crosses the line separating the undemanding secular world where wealth, or the appearance of it, provides its own justification, into the cold light of true metaphysical accounting. From that moment, negation commences. More exactly, revisionist assessment of the entire legend gets under way.

Melusine's husband, Raymondin, begins the revisionist trend by his violent reaction to Fromont's murder at Maillezais. Like Geoffroy, he becomes enraged, but Raymondin's anger leads to insight: he immediately links Geoffroy's fratricide to Melusine's demonic origin.

Historical event for the Middle Ages is always a sign that joins narrative and interpretation. Jean d'Arras here insists that the narrative mode must receive the same careful scrutiny as the interpretive process. The origin of the sign, he would seem to assert, will certainly affect meaning. Prior to the Maillezais moment, Melusine had sought to diffuse questions regarding her shadowy origins by offering to Raymondin a conventional genealogical narrative: "I am the daughter of the king of Scotland and come from a long and distinguished lineage." This has always sufficed for Raymondin, who has deflected the world's curiosity by repeating her own account. No longer.

Jean now focuses on the mode of Melusine's historical narrative and the way outcomes may be used to demonstrate its essential fallaciousness. The Maillezais moment, then, serves as a proof scene for the whole allegorical enterprise, which is really as much a battle over modes of historical discourse as it is an account of the failure of the Lusignan dynasty. The issue is not historiography, at least not in any modern sense, but rather calls into question interpretive narration when used for political ends.

Raymondin will interpret the Maillezais events as pointing directly to his wife's origins by his insight that Geoffroy, the perpetrator, simply functions as the agent of some more powerful force. Raymondin does not hesitate to locate that agency in his wife, and in the demonic powers she incarnates. At least this is where Raymondin's reasoning grounds itself when he uses technical terms from demonology like "fantosme de ceste femme" [phantasm of this woman].

The Ontology of Melusine

Raymondin's anger leads him to reevaluate what has until now been one of Melusine's chief accomplishments: her success in bearing male heirs and thus founding an apparently secure lineage. Suddenly, this asset is cast in a new and more somber light:

> Par la foy que je doy a Dieu, je croy que ce ne soit que fantosme de ceste femme, ne ne croy pas que ja fruit qu'elle ait porté viengne a perfection de bien; elle n'a porté enfant qui n'ait apporté quelque estrange signe sur terre. Ne veez la Oruble qui n'a pas vij. ans acompliz, qui a ja occiz deux de mes escuiers . . . Et ne vy je leur mere, le samedy que mon frere de Forests m'acointa les males nouvelles, en forme de serpente du nombril en aval? Si fiz, par Dieu. C'est aucun esperite ou c'est toute fantosme ou illusion qui m'a ainsi abusé; premiere foiz que je la vy, ne me scot elle bien a dire toute ma mesaventure?

> [By the faith that I owe to God, I think that this can only be a phantasm of this woman, nor do I believe that fruit borne by her may ever ripen to the perfection of goodness. She's never given birth to a child who did not bring some strange sign into the world with him. Look at Horrible who's not out of his seventh year and has already killed two of my squires and didn't I see their mother, that Saturday when my brother, the count of Forez told me the evil reports [about her], in the form of a serpent from her navel on down? Certainly I did, by God. She's some kind of spirit or a phantasm or an illusion who has taken advantage of me. Why the very first time I ever saw her didn't she know enough about my mishap to tell me all about it?] (*M* 253)

Raymondin scrutinizes Melusine and her progeny here. For the first time, he turns an analytic gaze on the phantasmagoric world she has constructed around him with his all too willing consent. Now, shocked into a skeptical frame of mind, he calls up before his mind's eye the anomalous or aberrant marks of the pathological image, what the text calls "phantasm." He recognizes that for once he can look at his wife and children without her surrounding gloss, using the technique of "coloring with the truth as we understand it" described by Jean in his prologue [pour coulourer nostre histoire a estre vraye, comme nous le tenons] (*M* 3).

All the events earlier in the narrative, indeed, were foreseen by Melusine, who instructed Raymondin how to behave when the predicted event actually arrives. Maillezais, however, deconstructs or forecloses extenuating gloss. It reveals starkly—if belatedly for him—how naked and insubstantial appears the phantasm without its enveloping gossamer of duplicitous language, a discourse of seduction, distracting the victim from seeing what really lies before him. Raymondin recognizes that Melusine's language of love, her authoritative managing of his life, has been a blind, an illusion to distract him from turning his gaze on her and her progeny, who consequently owe their existence to his liaison with illusion. Maillezais reminds him that the phantasm's true pathology lies not in the illusory image itself but in the pernicious delusion that phantasms of any sort can provide a key to resolving personal, social, or political problems.

We cannot understand the denouement these events precipitate

without recognizing in Raymondin's and Melusine's final confrontation elements of an allegory representing two orthogonal attitudes toward history and its interpretation. For Melusine, the present being composed of phantasms, acts based on illusions, once those acts will have occasioned unfortunate consequences, she must endeavor to repudiate any causal link between the original event and subsequent eventuality. Deflecting or distracting glosses advance plausible explanations. Prime among these is the discourse of fatalism that ascribes the link between cause and effect to supernatural intervention rather than an initially erroneous human agency.

So in the case of Maillezais, Melusine suavely adduces God's will, divine justice in the face of impious behavior on the part of the monks, as the cause of the conflagration: "the judgments of God are so hidden that no earthly being may comprehend them using human understanding." Resignation, fatalism in effect, can be the only reasonable course open to Raymondin, in her view [car les jugemens de dieu sont si secrez que nul cuer mondain ne les puet comprendre en son entendement] (*M* 255). She drives home the lesson by arguing that between them they have more than enough wealth to rebuild the abbey, to endow it more richly than before, thereby enabling it to admit even more monks. Instead of this inordinate chagrin, she concludes, her husband should busy himself with the work at hand.

To Melusine's fatalism, Raymondin opposes causal analysis, insisting on clearly naming the event for what it is. This speech does not merely rend the veil once and for all from Melusine's disguise, beginning as it does with the sibilent epithet, "Hee, tres faulse serpente," it also lumps Melusine, Geoffroy, and Horrible together as demonic manifestations, making all too evident the sons' true identity as allegorical personifications of the mother. They bear not the mark of Cain but the mark of Melusine, signaling that they too arise from the phantasmic, the demonic: "Hee, tres faulse serpente, par Dieu, ne toy ne tes fais ne sont que fantosme, ne ja hoir que tu ayes porté ne vendra a bon chief en la fin. Comment raront les vies ceulx qui sont ars en grief misere, ne ton filz qui s'estoit renduz au crucefix? Il n'avoit yssu de toy plus de bien que Fromont. Or est destruit par l'art demoniacle, car tous ceulx qui sont forcennez de yre sont ou commandement des princes d'enfer; et par ce fist Gieffroy le grant et horrible et hideux forfait d'ardoir son

frere et les moines qui mort ne avoient point desservie" [O false serpent, by God, you and your deeds are nothing but phantasms, and no heir that you have ever borne will turn out well in the end. How will those who were burnt with such painful suffering ever regain their lives, including your own son who dedicated his life to Christ? Fromont was the only good thing that ever came from you. Now he's destroyed by demonic arts, for all those maddened with rage do the bidding of the princes of hell; and so it was that Geoffroy committed this great and heinous crime of burning his brother and the monks who never for a moment deserved such a death] (*M* 255).

By joining his public revelation of her monstrous being to a denunciation of her sons, Geoffroy and Horrible, Raymondin unites the three—mother, son, and evil sprite—in a demonic trinity. This triune grouping recalls Melusine's own status as triplet, but it also signifies the unnatural morbidity of this family given to parricide, fratricide, and infanticide.

No matter how much Raymondin, as a man, lover, and husband, may subsequently regret his act of moral forthrightness, he has restored historical perspective to the work. We recognize that, like Raymondin, we have been bewitched by Melusine, who has enormous credibility, especially from her quiet dignity. She exits the work with a series of observations that demonstrate her human qualities, the qualities of empathy and pathos that link her kind to humans. Nevertheless, the story she forces on the work from her appearance at the forest fountain when Raymondin was out hunting with his benefactor, the count of Poitiers, has been a fairy tale in the original sense of the term. Melusine's preferred literary mode is not that of history but that of romance. As a romancer, she seeks to impose otherworld dimensions of seeing, seeing not what is really here but what desire foists on everyday reality, what desire wishes the world were like, for that's what phantasm means.

This duality of vision constitutes a relativity toward the commonplace in keeping with Jean d'Arras's stated intentions in the preface to his work. There he points to this narrative ambivalence when he claims to be writing a true chronicle of local events for Jean, the duke of Berry, but then makes veiled references to the work we actually find, a political allegory. His confection of Melusine from the irresolvable duality of opposing accounts of demonology given by Apuleius and Augustine, whom we looked at earlier, provides the other level of narrative ambiguity. That fertile ambiguity toward the female demon seems idiosyncratic with Jean d'Arras, for we do not find it in Jean's precursors. They all seem content to adopt Augustine's censorious view of *lamiae*, or female demons.

Jean himself, adopting the more tolerant view of Apuleius, refuses so reductive and doctrinal a reading. Instead, he takes a more philological approach, going back to the root of the demonological debate to rediscover the cultural duality toward demons in the Latin West, very much kept alive in medieval folklore on the subject, which he then takes as the basis for his narrative. This is one reason for the work's fascination, its compelling eccentricity, in a sense. It also allows him to develop the two conflicting narrative modes of *historia* and allegory.

These two modes imprint themselves in the narrative image of Melusine. Her mother, Presine, with her courtly manners, elegance, and concern for her husband's (King Elinas) welfare, clearly represents the "good fairy," or benevolent demon-soul, the first category of demon described by Apuleius. Presine is that genre of virtuous soul that attaches itself to a body, the kind of demon Apuleius calls "genius," as when one speaks of someone's having a "good genius." In a striking phrase, Apuleius cites the act of praying on one's knees to the genius, a god in a virtuous soul, as the very image of the beneficent integration of body and soul whose commingling defines humans.[5]

A second form of this benevolent demon includes departed souls freed from their bodies and set to watch over their descendants. Called *lemures* (lemurs) in archaic Latin, such demons were of two types: those virtuous souls whose powerful, tranquil, and continuing presence brought well-being to the families they watched over; and those unvirtuous souls condemned to wander eternally who made nocturnal mischief in less virtuous households. The first sort of lemur was called "Lar familiaris," or domestic deity, the second, "larva."[6] Lexicographers see "lemur" as akin to the Greek λαμια, "lamia," which brings us back to Melusine.

That Melusine should emulate her mother in certain respects fulfills the condition of compulsive repetition in the narrative economy of the pathological image. Intergenerational repetition, patterns of repeated actions or characteristics, constitute an important marker of identity for demons, especially female demons. Yet Melusine differs from her mother in one major respect: she is technically a monster, that is a hybrid, born of mixing the demonic and human categories represented respectively by Presine and Elinas. Accordingly, one may expect to find more actively negative events associated with Melusine, in contrast to her mother. As we have seen, such events tend to occur through the agency of her sons, lamial surrogates, just as the disasters befalling Scotland are not Presine's doing but those of her and Elinas's children.

Monster, from Latin *monstrum* from the root *monere* "to warn," traditionally connoted something terrible or portentous. Presine decrees Melusine's monstrous morphology as retribution for her daughter's unfilial attack on her father. Her monstrous morphology is not a birth defect but a redefinition of Melusine's body and the ontology imprinted on her by her mother in a coming-of-age ceremony, a kind of puberty ritual or social rebirth.

The "lamia factor" does not simply connote an abstract potential or predisposition toward certain pathological kinds of behavior, then. Marked on her body as an historical record of a terrible deed, Melusine's lamial status as sabbatical *serpente* imprints all her acts, even those seemingly most benevolent, with irresolvable duality, an ambivalence impossible to adjudicate, though ever-shaded with a distorting perspective and a strong sense of illusion.

Three Pictures of Melusine's Mythical Ontology

That ambivalence permeates the pseudomyth of Melusine constructed by Jean d'Arras, imparting a power, and interest, to Jean's text resolutely absent from his analogues in Gervaise of Tilbury, Giraldus Cambrensis, and the others. In the guise of a conclusion to our exposition of Jean's construction of Melusine as pseudomyth, we might note briefly how the principal manuscript used by Stouff for his edition, Paris, Arsenal MS 3353, manages to convey in pictures Melusine's dual ontology while also posing successfully the problematic (and pathological) nature of the image.

Interestingly enough, Arsenal 3353 limits pictures of Melusine to the early part of the romance and then to the long denouement: the bathing scene, the scene where she flings herself from the window while metamorphosing into a "serpente," and scenes of her flying, in the guise

Figure 1. Presine chastises her daughters Melusine, Melior, and Palestine for their transgression against their father, King Elinas. Rubric: "Comment le roy Elinas fu esbahy quant il les vit ainsi partir." Jean d'Arras, Le roman de Melusine. *Paris, MS Arsenal 3353, f. 4v. Photo: Service Photographique, Bibliothèque Nationale.*

of a winged serpent, around the Poitevin Tower of the Lusignan castle. Three early miniatures, however, clearly establish her identity in an unusual iconic manner not found in other manuscripts. The three miniatures in question, fol. 4v, 18r, and 22v, show the denouement of the prehistory (4v), Melusine's marriage to Raymondin (18r), and Melusine constructing the Lusignan castle, particularly the Poitevin Tower that figured prominently as the contemporary inspiration and venue for the legend of Melusine (22v).

Each illumination has interesting characteristics in its own right, but all have in common a unique iconic trait: the dual representation of Melusine in her human form as beautiful woman and as a rampant, miniature dragon. Space will not permit discussing all three illuminations in detail. I suggest that we look closely at the first while simply adumbrating the salient points of the second two.

The first picture (fig. 1) depicts a composite scene between Presine and her daughters that illustrates dramatically the ways in which visual art may conflate or condense sequential narrative both for dramatic economy and by way of stressing ambivalence.[7] The actual scene is simple enough. Presine, on the left, tall and dressed as a married woman of fashion, appears to address her three daughters, or so her upraised index finger would suggest. The young girls, Melusine, Melior, and Palestine, their status indicated by bare heads and simple dress, face her on the right. They stand one behind the other, rather than side by side, indicating a hierarchy of responsibility. Melusine, the first, also holds her hand upraised in the gesture that usually indicates speech.

Each figure seems to be recoiling from the one facing it; in any case, the space between daughters and mother is not neutral, for in the lower part we see a dragon standing on its hind legs with its back toward Presine, looking up at Melusine, the first in the daughter-group. The latter has its collective back to a cave whose large entrance clearly shows in the right-hand margin. This represents the cave in "the wondrous mountain in Northumberland called Brumbloremllion," the site chosen by Melusine for their father's life imprisonment: "Et j'ay advisié, se il vous semble bon, que nous l'enclouons en la merveilleuse montaigne de Norhonbelande nommee Brumbloremllion, et de la n'ystra de toute sa vie" [I thought, if it seems fine with you, that we shut him up in the wondrous mountain in Northumberland called Brumbloremllion, whence he will never escape during his lifetime" (*M* 11–12).

These two apparently ancillary details, the dragon and the cave mouth (mountain), frame the sisters, particularly Melusine, the animate figure. These framing details, far from providing simple local color, a kind of neutral background, furnish the visual energy of the scene as well as point to its drama. Melusine never appears alone in pictures but always in a setting that plays off her figured appearance, suggesting that there *is* a story to tell. The iconic role of the "background" or setting in representations of Melusine in this manuscript stands as the visual equivalent of what I earlier called the distorting perspective of the pathological image in the narrative. The need to situate Melusine vis-à-vis backgrounds that interpret or qualify the foreground suggests the aura of loucheness, or off-centered voyeurism, the looking askance that we found as an aspect of the pathological image.

Here, in figure 1, rampant dragon and cave-mouth convey the ambivalence of Melusine's parricide. Ostensibly undertaken to avenge Presine, Melusine presents the plan to entomb Elinas as an act of filial piety, almost a duty: "Et vindrent a leur mere et lui dirent: Mere, il ne te doit chaloir de la desloyauté de nostre pere, s'il l'a t'a faicte, car il en a son paiement, car jamais n'ystra de la montaigne de Brumbloremllio, ou nous l'avons encloz, et la usera son temps en doulour" [Mother, you should not worry about the disloyalty of our father, if he did it to you, for he has now received full payment; for he will never escape from the mountain of Brumbloremllion, where we have shut him up and where he will pass his time in pain] (*M* 12).

Presine sees the event very differently. She perceives the moral outrage of the act committed at the bidding of a "false and arrogant spirit" [faulx et orguilleux couraige]. Naming the transgression an unpardonable aggression committed against their father, she condemns her daughters to live as *lamiae*.

No one has the moral high ground in this demonic kinship, for, in her own anger, Presine commits the same kind of familial aggression she condemns in her daughters. If we cannot quite call her curse infanticide, neither is Melusine's immuring of Elinas quite parricide. Both impose irreversible limits on the victim; both suspend the victim in a perpetual state of contradiction: perpetrator and victim of violence against a close kin (wife or child). Presine and her daughters inhabit a world where passions reign in a setting of logical justice, but without the possibility for redemption.

Figure 1 captures Presine and her daughters suspended in contradiction. The tension between intention and judgment, Melusine as *lar* or as *larva*, defines the role of visual image as it does of narrative. Besides signifying Presine's curse, the presence of the dragon here records this mythic rite of passage where the daughters are admitted to the mother's fellowship, her demonic status.

But it is the cave that proves most fertile in signaling the incredible diversity of Melusine's multiple meanings, her true mythic vigor. The shadowy cave signifies the unfilial transgressive act, the beginning of Melusine's story, but it also represents its ending, a concluding chapter when Melusine's son Geoffroy will kill the giant whom Presine places as an eternal guardian over her husband's tomb. Only a son of one of the three daughters can kill this giant, thereby revealing to the world the chthonic and British provenance of the family.

The cave also symbolizes the feminine body forsaken by Melusine in assuming, in the place of the female sex, the serpent's tail, itself a form of usurpation of male authority. She has, after all, returned her father to the womb and symbolically assumed the male roles of master builder (of towers, as the pictures in this manuscript repeatedly stress), founder

Figure 2. Raymondin of Lusignan weds Melusine of Albanie. Rubric: "Comment Remondin espousa Melusigne a grant noblesse." Jean d'Arras, Le roman de Melusine. *Paris, MS Arsenal 3353, f. 18. Photo: Service Photographique, Bibliothèque Nationale.*

of a lineage, and strategist for the conflicts in which her husband engages.

In sum, this first image of Melusine effectively illustrates how she is always contextually defined in conjunction with an element of the earth or feudal landscape: cave, castle or tower, or the mountain on which the Lusignan castle, her signature, will be constructed (figs. 3–5). Indeed, one may construe the Lusignan castle as a modern surrogate for the chthonic cave with Melusine as Sibyl.

The second picture (fig. 2) shows Melusine's marriage to Raymondin of Lusignan. This picture also suspends her between symbols of real life and the mythic underworld. Again we find reversal of the apparent meaning. To the left, we see the festive tent that houses the bridal couple prior to the construction of their castle by Melusine. The tent ostensibly signals the courtly world to which Raymondin's rank will admit her. On the right we find not the cave this time, but the cavernous church with its portal open like the entrance to the cave in figure 1. Between these architectural symbols stand the participants in the wedding: a bishop holding Raymondin's hand ready to join it to that of

Melusine. Below, at her feet, almost hidden by the drapery folds of her gown, stands her double, the telltale dragon.

This single detail transforms the ostensible meaning of the image as a whole into something quite different. We sense the illusion and distorting perspective brought about by this reminder of Melusine's irresolvable duality. Hovering between ecclesia and domus, church and house, neither of which she can serve in the normal way, Melusine is not the obedient, virtuous bride but in fact the instigator of the whole narrative scenario. It is *her* material wealth that will admit Raymondin to the status and title of the Lusignan dynasty; *her* strategy indeed that has preserved him from the wrath of the family of the count of Poitiers, secured for him the grant of land that will allow him to found his domain and pretend to this auspicious union. It is, in short, the dragon icon that simultaneously literalizes and ironizes the rubric: "Comment Remondin espousa Melusigne a grant noblesse" [How Raymondin married Melusine with great nobility]. What ironic force falls on the single concept *grant noblesse!*

The third picture, the last dragon-icon picture (fig. 3), relies less on the viewer's intuiting illusion or a distorting perspective in favor of a straightforward depiction of a scene that is itself anomalous: the female master builder. In the foreground on the left, we see a more matronly Melusine directing the work of stonecutters beside her and masons on scaffolding on the castle wall in the upper register. Hodcarriers bring the cut stone to the masons on a cleated, wooden access plank. In fine, the construction details, including the largely completed chateau, could hardly be more realistic, down to the garb worn by the workmen. Even Melusine, hand upraised in the "speech-gesticulation" sign of imaged discourse, stands where a real-life foreman of the works might be found.

The absence of any other humans but Melusine and the male workers plunges the image deep into an irreality, an aura emanating from the tiny dragon icon standing behind its feminine double. We are struck by the verticality of the towers, by Melusine herself who stands below them so that some literally make a continuation of her upright figure. Against this scenario, her prominent breasts and protuberant stomach on which she appears to rest her right hand contrast sharply.

This emphasis on her female reproductive and nurturing attributes represents in all probability one of her regular pregnancies, but it also

Figure 3. Melusine directs the construction of the principal Lusignan castle. Rubric: "Comment la noble forteresse de Lusignen en Poitou fu fondee par Melusigne." Jean d'Arras, Le roman de Melusine. *Paris, MS Arsenal 3353, f. 22v. Photo: Service Photographique, Bibliothèque Nationale.*

grounds the rubric, indeed the whole picture, in androgyny, or perhaps it would be more accurate to say it drives home to the viewer her double sex role. She produces children and castles in the absence of Raymondin: as we see her here, pregnant, alone, directing the construction of the family seat, literally founding the lineage: "Comment la noble forterecse de Lusegnen en poittou fu fondee par Melusigne" [How the noble fortress of Lusignan in Poitou was founded by Melusine].

Raymondin will later discover her usurpation by spying on her bath within this very castle. Yet again we face the interior/exterior dichotomy, cave and reality. Outside the castle, Melusine appears isolated but balanced between female form, male role, and dragon double. Later on, in the inner precincts at the heart of the castle/cave she has built, the male voyeur will discover something more sinister: a body unified, no longer divided, bearing the monstrous shape of the phallic-female. It is this anticipation that gives to this third picture its secret fascination. We know that the chateau whose construction she directs is both the stage for her own drama and the setting for her folkloric manifestation as the flying *serpente* who may be seen circling the master tower as an omen of the lord's approaching death (figs. 4–5).

We can now begin to see the logic of the ontology of Melusine in Jean's romance. By making folkloric manifestations like *lamiae* and their passions stand as allegories for psychological reality, he can deploy a broad historical and cultural consciousness in his work. The pathological image instructs by its refusal to accept easy categorization. Despite her disquieting aspects, despite her metaphysical sentence to eternal serpentdom, Melusine remains a fascinating, sympathetic figure in Jean's work. She is not rejected out of hand like the *lamiae*, *nuitons*, or *larves* found in his pretexts. Above all, she captures the reality of conflicting and demonic motivations in a contemporary setting intensely preoccupied with legitimacy, authority, and their usurpation, above all the latter.

After all, Jean d'Arras's patron, the duke of Berry, named count of Poitiers in 1356, was the most recent possessor of the castle of Lusignan, an historical event Jean's work was meant to celebrate. Himself a great builder of palaces in Paris, Bourges, Poitiers, Mehun-sur-Yèvre, and elsewhere, Jean de Berry could perceive himself as inaugurating a new, properly French and royal lineage in place of the Lusignan hybrid British line.

Figure 4. Melusine bathing as Raymondin watches surreptitiously. Rubric: "Comment Remond vit Melusigne baignier par l'enhortement de son frere le comte de Forests et lui failly du convenant qu'il lui avoit promis." Jean d'Arras, Le roman de Melusine. *Paris, MS Arsenal 3353, f. 130. Photo: Service Photographique, Bibliothèque Nationale.*

Brother of Charles V, Lieutenant of Languedoc from 1380 to 1390, and, with his brother the duke of Burgundy, a major power in the early years of Charles VI's reign and then during his madness in 1392, the duke of Berry made himself, in the words of Michelet "his own kingdom in France, ruling Languedoc and Guyenne as an absolutist."[8] Does not Jean say that none other than his patron himself told him that it was Melusine in person who foretold the duke of Berry's royal succession to the castle of Lusignan when she mysteriously appeared one night in the master bedroom, first as serpent then as beautiful woman, to tell the last English tenant of the castle that it must be handed over to its besieger, the duke of Berry?

Le roman de Mélusine plays out a Francocentric fantasy that at last, after centuries of alienation in the hands of a British hybrid lineage, Languedoc, Poitou, Guyenne (Aquitaine), have returned to French royal hands. The setting is not entirely inaccurate, historically, at least at the moment of the work's composition. *Le Roman de Mélusine* plays upon the pathological and British (a conjunction encouraged by the

Figure 5. Melusine in full winged-serpent form flies above the Poitevine tower of the castle of Lusignan. Rubric: "Comment la serpente se party de dessus la Tour Poittevine." Jean d'Arras, Le roman de Melusine. *Paris, MS Arsenal 3353, f. 155v. Photo: Service Photographique, Bibliothèque Nationale.*

text) origins of the dynasties that have ruled in the southwest of France. For the myth of Melusine, it draws not only on the generic *lamia* material found in English historians like Gervaise and Giraldus but also on a curious Anglo-Norman tale about the monstrous origins of Albion, the original name for Britain, founded in this account by a race of female giants who mated lasciviously with demons.

The Lusignan, in Jean d'Arras, descend from Elinas, variously the king of Scotland or, more interestingly, *roi d'Albanie* or d'*Alebine* (BN fr 1484), that is, king of Albion. *Elinas, roi d'Alebine* could not but signal to contemporary minds the pathological origins of Albion as recounted in the popular fourteenth-century Anglo-Norman poem, *Des grantz geanz (Of the Great Giants)*.[9]

Considering Jean's introjection of the duke of Berry as a real historical actor at the end of his *roman* and the taking of the castle of Lusignan as a real historical event, along with the unusually precise dating of the beginning and ending of the composition of the work by Jean, the nature of "history" in *Mélusine* and in *Des grantz Geanz* merits closer study, but not here.

Like Melusine's own hybrid form, the kind of "history" we find in these works more closely resembles a monstrous grafting of disparate discourse modes—chronicle, romance, crusade epic, epic, and so on—into one format rather than history as we understand it, or than as Froissart himself practiced it in books three and four of his *Chroniques* that deal *in extenso* with the duke of Berry's official doings (closely tied to English and French official policy) in the 1380s and early 1390s. Were not Jean so insistent on the historic foundation of his account, an historic grounding imparted to the tale of the English demon-bred giants, one might be content to let well enough alone and simply see it as typical of late romance.

But no other late romance so persistently interweaves real historical markers. Nor does another contemporary historical romance have so prominent a patron, so intimately involved in the English negotiations in the late 1380s and early 1390s that he personally escorted John of Gaunt, duke of Lancaster, Richard II's uncle and principal ambassador, into the Council of Amiens in early spring 1392. The duke of Lancaster was father to the not-so-future Henry IV who opposed and defeated his cousin Richard in 1399. The duke of Lancaster was also the father of a daughter for whose hand in marriage the duke of Berry, we are told by Froissart, spent a good deal of time in the first half of 1388 attempting to negotiate, losing out finally to a younger Spanish prince.

Such textual evidence for the importance of history for the work and its context suggests that we might think of Jean's *roman* as illustrating a new kind of literary work, borne out of the maelstrom of French/English politics of the late fourteenth century. That new genre, merging chronicle and romance, constitutes a powerful hybridization of classical themes with Celtic myth and indigenous folk beliefs, that empowers a form of allegory with the ability to probe the unconscious of contemporary political events.

The recourse to allegory motivates historiography as practiced during the period as a record of humans thinking history, studying it, making sense of it, in order to influence its course, at least the course of contemporary history. As Angus Fletcher put it, apropos of Shelley's *Prometheus Unbound*, great poets "give mankind the laws of thought, if not of expedient practicality. Allegory thus would reach its highest plane in a symbolism that conveys the action of the mind."[10]

Allegory is a figurative mode, perhaps the most figurative mode, and it makes use initially of deception for its effects. Without characterizing it as "pathological" in the sense we have defined the pathological image above, we might note that Fletcher does ascribe its agency to demonic forces. They are demonic in the sense Apuleius intends demons, as incorporeal abstractions, abstract ideas, as it were, capable of assuming the substantive form of historical events. "They may not actually create a personality before our eyes, but they do create a semblance of personality" (Fletcher, 27). The fairy realm whence issue Presine and her daughters has always, of course, been a natural, literary domain for the demonic agent of allegory. It is in Jean d'Arras, for perhaps the first time in vernacular European literature, that we find the fairy realm joined to the contemporary, political world for the purpose of making political allegory.

Notes

1. Quoted from *The Norton Anthology of English Literature*, ed. M. H. Abrams, 5th ed. (New York: Norton, 1987), 828–29.

2. For an informed discussion of Plato's demonology see Léon Robin, *La Théorie platonicienne de l'amour* (Paris: F. Alcan, 1907), ch. 3.

3. "Quippe, ut fine conprehendam, daemones sunt genere animalia, ingenio rationabilia, animo passiua, corpore aëria, tempore aeterna. Ex his quinque, quae commemoraui, tria a principio eadem quae nobis sunt, quartum proprium, postremum commune cum diis inmortalibus habent, sed differunt ab his passione. Quae propterea passiua non absurde, ut arbitror, nominaui, quod sunt iisdem, quibus nos, turbationibus mentis obnoxii." Lucius Apuleius (Apuleius Madaurensis), *De Deo Socratis.Apulée, Opuscules philosophiques et fragments,* ed. Jean Beaujeu (Paris: Les Belles Lettres, 1973), ch. 13: §148 (p. 33).

4. Saint Augustine, *De Civitate Dei,* 8:17. Quoted from translation of David S. Wiesen, *The City of God Against the Pagans,* vol. 3 (Cambridge, Mass.: Harvard University Press, 1968), 79.

5. "Eum nostra lingua, ut ego interpretor, haud sciam an bono, certe quidem meo periculo poteris Genium uocare, quod is deus, qui est animus sui cuique, quamquam sit inmortalis, tamen quodam modo cum homine gignitur, ut eae preces, quibus Genium et genua precantur, coniunctionem nostram nexumque uideantur mihi obtestari, corpus atque animum duobus nominibus comprehendentes, quorum communio et copulatio sumus." *De Deo Socratis,* ch. 15: §150–52 (p. 34).

6. "Est et secundo significatu species daemonum animus humanus emeritus stipendiis uitae corpore suo abiurans. Hunc uetere Latina lingua reperio Lemurem dictitatum. Ex hisce ergo Lemuribus qui posterorum suorum curam sortitus placato et quieto numine domum possidet, Lar dicitur familiaris; qui uero ob aduersa uitae merita nullis [bonis] sedibus incerta uagatione ceu quodam exilio punitur, inane terriculamentum bonis hominibus, ceterum malis noxium, id genus plerique Laruas perhibent. *De Deo Socratis,* ch. 15: §152–53 (p. 35).

7. The rubric for this miniature dramatically, albeit fortuitously, illustrates how the images conflate narrative sequence. While other rubrics for illuminations relate directly to the scene depicted, that of fol. 4v suggests a divergence between the rubricator and the artist who followed him. The rubricator wrote, "Comment le Roy Elinas fu esbahi quant il les vit ainsi partir" [How King Elinas was stupefied when he saw them depart]. Strictly speaking, this inner state of amazement would be difficult to render visually. The artist therefore chose to illustrate the sequel. And yet, the entombment of Elinas *does* somehow convey his confusion.

8. The whole quotation suggests the disarray of French affairs at the time and reads: "Des trois oncles de Charles VI, l'ainé, le duc d'Anjou, alla ainsi se perdre à la recherche d'une royauté d'Italie. Le second, le duc de Berri, s'en

était fait une en France, gouvernant d'une manière absolue le Languedoc et la Guienne, et ne se mêlant pas du reste. Le troisième, le duc de Bourgogne, débarrassé des deux autres, put faire ce qu'il voulait du roi et du royaume." Jules Michelet, *Histoire de France,* Livre 7, Chapitre 1er. *Oeuvres complètes de Michelet,* vol. 5, ed. Paul Viallaneix (Paris: Flammarion, 1975), 292.

9. *Des Grantz Geanz*—Anglo-Norman Text, 13th c., possibly beginning of 14th. *Des grantz geanz, An Anglo-Norman Poem,* ed. G. E. Brereton (Oxford, 1937).

10. Angus Fletcher, *Allegory: The Theory of a Symbolic Mode* (1964; rpt., Ithaca, N.Y.: Cornell University Press, 1990), 278.

Melusine's Progeny: Patterns and Perplexities

Jane H. M. Taylor

Most readers' acquaintance with the *Roman de Mélusine* is probably secondhand: there exists an agreed synthesis, privileging the relationship of Melusine and Raymondin, from which commentators like Markale and Lecouteux draw their conclusions. To read any particular medieval version of the romance, anchored in its specific time and place, can be a disconcerting, perhaps even disappointing experience. It is probably symptomatic, for instance, that most "popular" versions abridge: Michèle Perret's translation, for instance, omits some fifty pages of those parts of the text that most modern readers probably find rather rebarbative: the crusading adventures of the sons. For while the *Roman de Mélusine* as Jean d'Arras or Coudrette imagine it may indeed have at its core the synthesis I mentioned earlier, with Melusine the linchpin, it devotes a rather larger proportion of narrative space to the exploits of her sons than one would imagine were one to read only the secondary literature. What I propose to do is to redress the balance and look not at Melusine the progenitrix but at her progeny. Taking as a starting point the assertion of scholars that the romance's appearance at this particular point in time is an index of its political utility, I shall argue that the *Roman de Mélusine* is in essence a genealogy and that the textual strategies it employs in its treatment of Melusine's sons are characteristic of that *genre* in the late Middle Ages. On this basis, I shall then argue that the pragmatic function of the romance (its value as argument for Jean de Berry's pretensions in Poitou) and its schematic content are not, and indeed cannot be, resolved, and that this lack of resolution is detectable in a series of violations of narrative schemata: globally of the scheme adumbrated above, incidentally in constant violations of story schemata that are from time to time activated but never actualized. I use here, incidentally, a terminology and a model of story-grammars loosely derived from critics like R. N. Ross and Deborah Tannen.[1] What I mean by "schemata" are those "structures of expectation" that lead us, on the basis of our background knowledge of stories heard or read, to predict from a set of givens a likely story-structure and a likely outcome. Thus for instance—and to simplify somewhat—the given "There was an x who had three sons . . ." activates a scheme whereby I predict that the story will focus on the youngest son's search for fame and fortune. It is characteristic of the *Roman de Mélusine*, I shall suggest, that in the case of Melusine's progeny Jean d'Arras should, with some consistency, first activate but then block schemata of particular types, and I shall suggest that this recurrent pattern is most plausibly explained by the genealogical ambiguities that an ancestor like Melusine cannot but provoke.

First then, the genealogical "mission" of Jean's *Mélusine*. From knowledge of contemporary events, it seems plausible that this is indeed a work commissioned in circumstances calling for a convenient genealogy. Le Goff, Le Roy Ladurie, and Michèle Perret[2] for Jean d'Arras, Roach and Harf-Lancner for Coudrette,[3] set out clearly the relevance of Melusine for the Lusignan family and its castle, and in turn of the Lusignan family and its castle for Jean de Berry, the *commanditaire*, in 1393: useful ammunition, given his distant kinship with the family, in support of the Duke's uncertain hold on Berry in general and Lusignan in particular; one could talk, as it were, of a geographical genealogy feeding off a biological one. The centrality of biological genealogy to the *Roman de Mélusine* is also inscribed in the text by Jean d'Arras's insistance, lexically and thematically, on lineage. Its importance in the social structures imagined by Jean is surely betrayed by Count Bertrand's equation of identity and genealogy, and his incredulity and disquiet that Raymondin, with no idea of the lineage of his intended wife, has made no effort to remedy this ignorance: "Lors dist ly contes: Au moins, beau sire, nous dictes qui elle est ne de quelle *lignie.* Par ma foy, dist Remondin, tout en riant, vous me demandez ce dont je ne sauroye respondre, car onques je n'en enquis tant. Par foy, dist ly contes, veez cy merveilles. Remondin se marie et ne scet quelle femme il prent ne de quel *lignaige*" [Then the count said: "At the very least, fair sir, tell us who she is and what is her lineage." "Indeed," said Raymondin, with a laugh, "you are asking me a question to which I cannot respond, for I was never bold enough to ask her." "Indeed," said the count, "this is a quite extraordinary thing. Raymondin is to take a wife, and he has no idea of her identity nor of her lineage"] (*M* 36, italics added).

For Jean d'Arras, moreover, good government assumes a reliable, agnatic passage of power across generations: the people's reaction when Josselin is killed and Raymondin retrieves his inheritance is symptomatic: "Quant le peuple du païs scot que *cellui qui estoit filz de leur droit seigneur* estoit venus, si furent moult joyeux, et lui firent grans presens, a l'usaige du pays, comme de vin, de bestail, de poissons, de poulaille, de foings et d'avoines, et de moult d'autres choses. Et estoient moult liez, puis qu'il ne plaisoit a Remondin a demourer, ne a tenir la terre, quant ils estoient receuz *en la droicte ligne de leur seignourie*, et *hors de la lignie Josselin*" [When the people of the country knew that he who was the son of their rightful lord was come, they were exceedingly pleased, and gave him generous gifts after the fashion of the country: wine, cattle, fish, poultry, hay and oats, and many other things. And they were all the more pleased in that Raymondin was intending to stay and hold the country, and in that they were now to be back in their old allegiance, and freed from the lineage of Josselin] (*M* 69, italics added).

More revealing still, perhaps, are Jean's ramifying genealogies such that what is created is a pan-European, transhistorical, lateral and lineal network of interrelationships. The major role is of course the marriages and alliances of the sons, but this is not all. The frame story, for instance—that of Melusine and her two sisters—is already couched genealogically: Melusine will have a "lignie moult grant," Melior's *lignie* will be cursed to the ninth generation, Palestine can only be rescued from her imprisonment in the "montaigne de Coingo" by "uns chevaliers de vostre lignie" (*M* 13). The story of Raymondin's killing of his lord is accompanied by genealogical predictions: unexpectedly, Raymondin will be "ly plus riches, ly plus puissans, ly plus honnourez qui *feust oncques en son lignaige*" [the richest, the most powerful, the most honored that there has ever been in his lineage], and conversely, will give issue to "*une si tres noble lignie* qu'il en seroit mencion et remembrance jusques en la fin du monde" [a lineage so noble that it will be remembered and spoken of until the end of the world] (*M* 21, italics added). I do not need to point out, of course, the narrative subterfuges (all those heirless rulers with marriageable daughters!) with which Jean scatters Melusine's progeny across Europe and the East. But in addition, almost surreptitiously, he constructs an embryonic extratextual genealogical network. Distantly—and the family trees are, perhaps strategically, difficult to draw up—Raymondin is a kinsman of Saint Guillaume (a conflation of several saints of the name):[4]

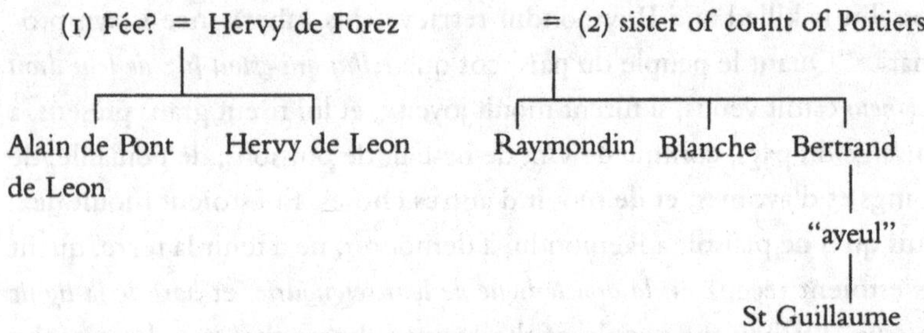

And similarly, according to one manuscript (Bibliothèque Nationale, fonds français, 1484) Melusine is distant kin to Alexander the Great (see *M*, introduction, 10, n. 2):

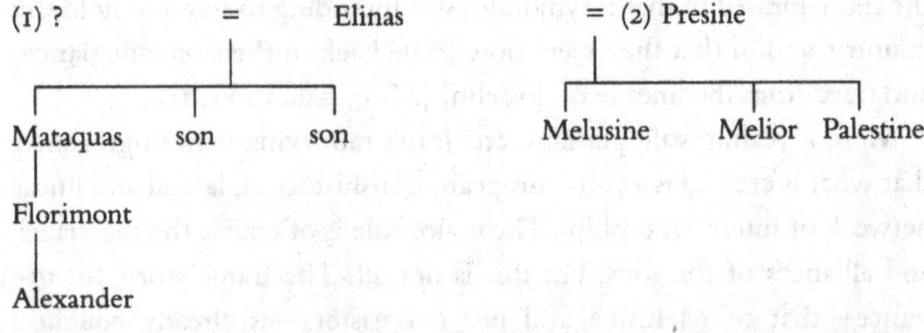

Indeed, on this last point, it is surely significant that the text appears with some consistency to have been understood genealogically by its readers. At the end of Jean's prefatory remarks—the self-justificatory explorations of Gervaise of Tilbury, and so forth—he foregrounds Melusine as *fondatrice* or *défricheuse:* "Je vous vouldray dire dont celle faee vint *qui fonda la noble place et forteresce de Lisignen* dessus dit" [I should like to tell you whence came the fairy that founded the noble castle and fortress of Lusignan that I spoke of above] (*M* 5, italics added). At this point, however, the scribe of B.N. f.f. 1484 and the editor/publisher of the 1478 edition, as well as the translator of the Middle English version of the romance, intercalate a full catalogue of the sons, prefaced, in the two French versions, by the words *Des generations*, and in the ME text by the formula: "Herafter folowen the names of the estates of the children whiche yssued of Melusyne" (see variants, *M* 5, n. 1). And that the constitution of a family tree, on the lines of the Tree of Jesse, with Melusine herself as the root, is a prime product of the text is interestingly recognized in the title page engraving of the Augsburg edition of 1480, which not only shows Melusine and her sons but hints at the lateral genealogies by showing Melusine's two sisters (fig. 1).

So far, I have been employing the words *genealogy* and *genealogical text* as though they were self-evident and unambiguous. It is to this question that I would now like to turn. Duby,[5] Guenée,[6] and others have noted the proliferation of genealogies as such in the twelfth and thirteenth centuries, meaning those essentially nonliterary texts that need do no more than record, often in the barest terms, the bloodline of a particular family. Duby notes the coincidence of this proliferation with new patterns of inheritance, and is inclined to attribute the new interest in genealogy precisely to a consciousness that unambiguous transmission is essential if a patrimony is to pass freely and without dispute from father to son. It is less this type of genealogy that interests me here, however, than the sort of genealogy that, from the thirteenth century, purveys genealogical *myth:* which establishes for a particular family a suitably momentous founding father, and demonstrates for the family concerned a "heroic consistency" traceable precisely to that founding father. Genealogies of this sort are more than the bare record, the family tree; on the contrary, it will be part of their strategy to invent or at least to embroider freely on originary myths, to demonstrate the valor, beneficence, justice, or authority of a founding father. They constitute a partisan record for a particular group, establishing and enhancing the group's collective image. Moreover, as Bloch and others have pointed out,[7] fictional genealogies, in epic or romance, have the advantage of

Figure 1. Augsburg: J. Bämler, 1480, now in the Library of Saint Gall, no. 999. Reproduced as plate 41 by Clier-Colombani, and as a frontispiece by Lecouteux, Mélusine.

building from the present; they are therefore also pseudopredictive. A family that can lay claim to a heroic founder confers on itself a retrospective inevitability and a prospective stability. What this means, of course, is that genealogically based histories, while appearing purely informative and antiquarian, are in fact tendentious in content and, in particular, strongly deictic in perspective.

No one, I imagine, would dispute this latter characteristic for the *Roman de Mélusine.* I would not wish to argue—as Roach does for Coudrette's *Mélusine*[8]—that the romance is a roman à clef, but it is surely only in Poitou that the list of Melusine's building exploits is comprehensible, and only in Poitou in the later fourteenth century that the burgeoning empire of the Lusignans—with the implied political message of indisputable claims to the crowns of Cyprus and Armenia, the network of aristocratic links with La Marche or Bohemia or Austria, along with intimations of the lineage's fragility—makes sense. More particularly, however, it is precisely on the pseudopredictive value of the myth of Melusine that Jean d'Arras can capitalize, by presenting as anticipated the fate of the family. That the House of Lusignan should have lost the castle that is its heartland, that the last Lusignan king of Armenia should be reduced to hawking his misfortunes around Europe, is presented as entirely predictable since predicted by no less an authority than Melusine herself. After their marriage, she thanks Raymondin for his discretion: "'Et sachiez de certain que, se vous le tenez desormais ainsi, que vous serez ly plus puissans et ly plus honnourez qui oncques feust en vostre lignaige. Et se vous faictes le contraire, vous et voz hoirs decherront petit a petit, et la terre que vous tendrez alors que vous ferez la faulte, se il est ainsi que vous le faciez, ce que Dieu ne veulle ja consentir, ne sera jamais tenue par nul de voz hoirs ensemble'" ["And let me tell you for certain that if you continue to behave in the same way, you will be the most powerful and the most honored lord that there has ever been in your lineage. But if you do not do so, then you and your heirs will decline little by little, and those lands of which you are lord at the time of your transgression, if indeed, and God forbid that it should be so, there is a transgression, those lands not one of your heirs shall ever hold as a single fief"] (*M* 42). Echoed, of course, by the dramatic and rather more specific prophecy that accompanies Melusine's final disappearance after Raymondin's transgression of the interdict: "Sachiez que après vous jamais homs ne tendra ensemble le pays que vous tenez, et auront moult voz hoirs aprez vous a faire. Et sachiez que aucuns par leur folie decherront moult d'onneur et de heritaige" ["Know that after you, no man will ever hold your lands as a single fief, and that your heirs will have much to do. And know that some of them, through their folly, will fall far below you in honor and inheritance."] (*M* 257–58).

What characteristics then may we attribute to the conventional genealogical myth? (And perhaps I may acknowledge here a particular debt to Gabrielle Spiegel for her article on genealogy in *History and Theory* and her book *Romancing the Past*.)[9] I would suggest that a genealogy is designed to *anchor* and to *explain*. By *anchor*, I mean that a conventional genealogy seeks to demonstrate what Spiegel (speaking of the *Grandes Chroniques de France*) calls "mythic homogeneity": that is, one or more self-perpetuating characteristics showing the family concerned as peculiarly suitable for the rank and function to which they are called. As a consequence, a genealogy will tend to privilege conformity:[10] as the generations fan out from the single originary and mythical ancestor, certain traits of character (and perhaps physique) will be perpetuated. By *explain*, I mean that the writer argues back from the current situation of the family concerned, rationalizing its present and setting back in some distant, but (pseudo-)historical, past its acquisition of fame and fortune. I am thinking here, for instance, of the sort of family myth constructed for the contes de Guines by Lambert d'Ardres, which traces the family's rise to a founding father, a *chevalier errant* of a romance sort, who wins the love of the daughter of the king of Flanders.[11]

If then we may imagine Jean d'Arras constructing a genealogy, we must also recognize that the strategy he has chosen is not without risks. True, whereas the majority of conventional genealogies are commissioned by the family concerned, this commission does not come direct from the Lusignan family, by now in steep decline, but rather from Jean de Berry, not himself directly a Lusignan. But as I suggested earlier, this is a distinction without a difference, since Jean de Berry's commission can best be explained, in the political circumstances of 1392/3, if we imagine that Jean d'Arras's romance was at least partly political propaganda in favor of a duke who, suggests Harf-Lancner, "récupère ainsi la légende, se posant en libérateur, en seigneur légitime de Lusignan et du comté de Poitou et en *descendant de la fée*."[12]

Legitimation of the sort offered by this romance is, however, a two-edged sword. After all, whereas the mythic homogeneity provided by some unambivalent Trojan hero[13] can only be to the honor of the family thus honored, Melusine's progeny is unavoidably ambiguous. They are perhaps necessarily so, merely because of the kernel story: their mother's possibly devilish, and at the very least uncanny, origin, their father's act of betrayal. I quoted above those prophecies that tend rather to project family instability precisely from these two factors as characteristic of the Lusignan family, but of course I am also thinking here of the physical or genetic inheritance represented by the presence among Melusine's sons of Geoffroy Big-Tooth and especially Horrible, and physically imprinted on the immediate progeny by the *tares*—the deformities consequent on Melusine's dual, human and fairy, nature. What Jean de Berry is appropriating is an ambiguous inheritance: his hold on the castle must be, like that of all the members of the Lusignan family, uncertain, and his "genetic" antecedents are physically repellent. It is in this context, I consider, that we must judge Jean d'Arras's treatment of Melusine herself and her progeny: his oddly consistent refusal to develop the schemata that his narrative syntax seems regularly set to activate.

Let me start with a simple example of what I mean. Melusine's ambiguity as a source of mythic homogeneity is of course her supernatural origin, her double nature as woman and serpent, her magical powers. These are demonstrated, of course, most strikingly in the building of the castle of Lusignan, the lavish provision of banquets and servants and armies. But a lineage stemming from a woman who dabbles in the supernatural surely loses its source of male heroic consistency. In this context, I am struck by two matching episodes where Jean instigates what seem to be particular narrative schemata. On two occasions, Melusine gives her sons magic rings that will make them victorious and impervious to any enchantments, provided that their motives remain pure: "Enfans, dist Melusigne, veez cy deux anneaulx que je vous donne, dont les pierres ont une mesme vertu. Sachiez que tant que vous userez de loyauté, sans penser ne faire tricherie, ne mauvaitié, et que vous les ayez sur vous, vous ne serez desconfiz par armes, mais que vous ayez bonne querelle; ne sort, ne enchantement d'art de magique, ne de poisons, de quelconque maniere, ne vous pourra nuire, que si tost que vous les regarderez, que ilz n'aient perdu toute leur force" ["Children," said Melusine, "here are two rings that I shall give you; each of the stones

with which they are set has the same potency. Know that as long as you behave with loyalty, and without a single treacherous or evil thought or act, and as long as you have the rings by you, you will never be defeated at arms, provided that your cause is good; no spell or magical enchantment, or poison, or any other thing, will be able to harm you, for as soon as you glance at such things they will lose all their power to harm"] (*M* 84; virtually identical episode, 155). The reader expects, surely, given acquaintance with the schemata of romance and folklore, that what is being instituted is indeed a scheme: will the sons lose the rings? have them stolen? use them to combat enchantments? will the rings lose their virtue because one of the sons becomes involved in a *querelle* that is not *bonne*? The plethora of magic rings in Guerreau-Jalabert's *Index des motifs narratifs*[14] is ample evidence of the potential fruitfulness of the schema. But in fact the narrative potential of the rings is never, in either case, exploited; a scheme, in other words, instituted, but blocked.

This pattern—institution and blocking of schemata—is curiously prevalent. The most striking instance, for the casual reader, is perhaps the sons' physical deformities. In a romance world, as we know, deformity of any sort is generally equated with moral turpitude, and any heroic figure who is initially portrayed as hideous will, if indeed he is noble, eventually turn out to be under an enchantment; I know of only one romance in which ugliness is no barrier to a noble soul: the *Roman de Perceforest*, where Le Bossu is portrayed with unusual sympathy.[15] And yet here the *romancier*, perhaps obliged to do so by the constraints of an existing legend, must needs make the founding fathers of the Lusignan family hideous. And yet, does he? True, the first eight of the sons are one-eyed or three-eyed, have ears like windmill sails, and so on. But is it symptomatic that the last two sons to be born have apparently no physical mark (*M* 196)?[16] We might put this down to exhausted invention, but I wonder if it does not rather indicate an authorial embarrassment, and relief—perhaps—at being able to forget about what are after all potentially disgraceful marks. This hypothesis is all the more tempting because throughout the text, Jean has in fact blocked the scheme that seems to be instituted by the deformities of the sons. By this I mean that he scarcely exploits, indeed even underplays, the interesting narrative potential offered by the sons' appearance, and in ways that are reminiscent of the treatment of the magic rings.

First of all, he ensures that deformity is never absolute: all the sons, apart from the unfortunate *tares*, are remarkably handsome at birth, and a characteristic syntax draws attention away from their deformities: Urian is "de toutes figures bien formez" but has "le visage court et large au travers, et avoit un oeil rouge et l'autre pers" [Urian had the most perfectly formed appearance, but his face was broad and flat, and he had one red eye and one blue] (*M* 47–48); Eudes has one ear much bigger than the other "*mais* de tous membres il estoit beaulx a grant devise et bien formez" [but all his limbs were most beautifully formed] (*M* 780); Guyon is a "moult bel enfant, *mais* il ot un oeil plus hault que l'autre" [a most good-looking boy, but with one eye higher than the other] (*M* 78); Antoine "grant fu et bien formez de tous membres. *Mais* il apporta en la senestre joue une pate de lyon" [was tall and with every limb most beautifully formed, but on his left cheek was a lion's paw] (*M* 790). More particularly, the sons' deformities—and again this is what I mean by blocking—have no effect whatever either on their careers or on others' perceptions of them. When Urian becomes King of Cyprus, none of his new subjects expresses a reservation about his appearance, none indeed is made explicitly to seem aware of it: "Et pour dire verité, chascun se donnoit merveille de sa grandeur, de sa fierté et de sa puissance de corps qu'il auoit, et bien disoient que c'estoit l'omme qu'ilz eussent oncques mais veu qui plus se faisoit a ressoingnier de le courroucier" [And to tell the truth, everyone was amazed by his height, his proud bearing and the vigor of his body, and everyone said that he was of all men that they had seen the one whose mere appearance made his anger most redoubtable] (*M* 123–24). When Florie first encounters Guyon, she appears to notice nothing odd about him (*M* 126–27); when a *gentilhomme du pays* reports on Renaud and Antoine to the Count of Luxemburg, he says no more than that they are "grans et fors et de moult fiere contenance" [tall and strong and of the fiercest appearance] (*M* 147); and even when an *escuier* does report on the deformities attached to Antoine and Renaud, he privileges their good looks: "cellui lui compte . . . de la beauté des corps et des membres des freres" [he told her of the beauty of the bodies and limbs of the brothers] (*M* 159). And indeed, I return momentarily to the Augsburg genealogical tree (fig. 1) to point out that the sons are pictured as perfectly ordinary, handsome young men, and that only Geoffroy's *grand dent* is in any way represented—and even here with the greatest of discretion: surely this too must reflect the fact that the artist has not had impressed on his consciousness the appearances (many of them, like three eyes or one, perfectly easy to represent pictorially) of the other sons? In addition, in the complete set of woodcuts from the edition of 1485 published by Clier-Colombani,[17] which show a number of the sons, not one shows a trace of any deformity.[18]

I am struck by this instance of blocking as confirmation that this is a romance that, as a whole, is reluctant to exploit its own narrative potential, especially as this potential relates to the supernatural. What, for instance, are we to make of the proliferating *dames de la fontaine* (*M* 6–10)—fées or mortal?—who become wives to first Elinas and then to the Count of Forez? Conventional narrative schemata would suggest that they would be doubles of Melusine herself, but Jean d'Arras, having introduced them with precisely those formulas that make it possible for us to recognize the scheme "mortal meets fée" (*une moult belle fontaine . . . une voix qui chantoit . . . la grande beauté;* the comparison with a *seraine*, etc.), then blocks the scheme and leaves it oddly inconsequential. And what, similarly, of the curious episode of the Château de l'Epervier (*M* 302–7), whose hero should, conventionally, by succeeding in his test, achieve fame and fortune, but who in this romance achieves success and is thereby doomed, along with his lineage, to failure?

The blocking of schemata is surely especially evident in the case of the two most ominous of the brothers, Horrible (or Eudes) and Geoffroy. The latter, as all scholars have pointed out, is of course a legacy of history; indeed, as Michèle Perret notes, some of the contradictions in the romance would suggest "l'hypothèse d'une composition d'ensemble, à partir d'une série de petites scènes disparates."[19] But what history imposed, it seems, was uncompromisingly negative: the Geoffrey of thirteenth-century history is a destroyer, a persecutor, an enemy of Saint Louis, perhaps even an atheist whose war cry was "Dieu n'existe pas." In consequence, perhaps, our initial introduction to Jean's Geoffroy institutes a scheme promising developments of the sort we might find, for instance, in the story of Robert le Diable[20] or Raoul de Cambrai;[21] certainly, the thumbnail sketch and prognostication made for him as it is for all the sons seems unambiguous: "Gieffroy au Grant Dent . . . fu grans, haulx, et fourniz et fort a merveilles, hardiz et crueulx. Chascun le doubtoit qui en ouoit parler. Et fist moult de merveilles" [Geoffroy

Big-Tooth was tall, well-endowed with force and strength, brave and cruel. Everyone who heard of him was afraid. And he was responsible for many remarkable deeds] (*M* 80).

It is this act—the burning of the monastery at Maillezais, for reasons that remain persistently obscure (why should Fromont's becoming a monk provoke such rage?)—that triggers Raymondin's transgression and the institution of "the Lusignan curse." Looked at schematically in this way, his role in the romance seems narratively consistent. And yet, once again, the scheme is blocked. The catastrophic outcome of the burning of the monastery is surely best motivated if it remains gratuitous, and yet Jean goes to considerable pains to short-circuit, as it were, the question of Geoffroy's guilt, by having Melusine justify it: "Se Gieffroy, vostre filz, a fait son oultraige par son courage merveilleux et fort, sachiez que de certain *c'est pour le pechié des moines, qui estoient de mauvaise vie et desordonnee; et en a Nostre Seigneur voulu avoir la punicion*, combien que ceste chose soit incongnoissable quant a humaine creatur" [If Geoffroy your son has done his appalling deed, in spite of his heart being so marvellous and strong, then be sure that *it was because of the sins of the monks, who were living a sinful and disorderly life, and because of this Our Lord wanted to punish them*—although such things are of course incomprehensible to mortal understanding] (*M* 255; italics added). In other words an act that had seemed blasphemous and that ought therefore to have instituted a scheme of "blasphemous progeny" has become meritorious and sanctioned. In all other respects, indeed, Geoffroy is portrayed as saviour: slayer of tyrannous giants, repentant sinner before the Pope, and finally guarantor of the rights of the Lusignan family over their own castle. Once again a narrative that seems set to conform to a particular scheme—one son as innately the evil heir to his mother's more demonic self—is curtailed: once the narrative usefulness of Geoffroy in this role has been exploited, Jean hurries to recuperate him rather for the glory of the Lusignan family.

The case of Horrible, or Eudes, is of course less clear-cut. He is introduced with hints of what *should* develop into a quite startling scheme: "Mais a la xj[e] annee, apporta un filz, le viij[e], grant a merveille. Cil apporta trois yeux sur terre, de quoy ly uns fu ou front; et fu si crueulx et si mauvais qu'il occist, ains qu'il eust quatre ans, deux de ces nourrices" [But in the eleventh year, a son was born, the eighth son, who was very large. He brought into this world a face with three eyes, of which one was in the middle of his forehead; and he was so cruel and so evil that before he was four years old, he had killed two of his nurses] (*M* 80). He reappears, briefly, cited by Raymondin as evidence of the evil progeny of Melusine: "Ne veez la Oruble qui n'a pas vij. ans acompliz, qui a ja occiz deux de mes escuiers, et avant qu'il eust trois ans, avoit il fait mourir deux de ses nourrices par force de mordre leurs mamelles?" [And consider Horrible who is not yet seven years old and yet has already killed two of my squires, and who, before he was three years old, had killed two of his nurses by biting their breasts?] (*M* 253). And finally, he is condemned to death by his own mother in her parting words before she flies out of the tower: "Gardez . . . que vous faciez tant que Eudes, nostre filz, qui a trois yeulx, dont l'un est ou front, soit mort priveement, car sachiez en verité, que il feroit tant de maulx que ce ne seroit pas si grant dommage de la mort de telz xx^{m} que de la perte que on auroit par lui, car certainement il destruiroit tout quanque j'ay ediffié, ne jamais guerre ne fauldroit ou pays de Poittou ne de Guyenne" ["Be careful to ensure that Eudes [Horrible], our son, who has three eyes, one in the middle of his forehead, is killed privily, for you should know for sure that he will be responsible for so many ills that we might lose through him the equivalent of twenty thousand men, for if he lives he will assuredly destroy everything that I have created, and never will war cease in Poitou or Guyenne"] (*M* 258). But of course his death, supervening very soon thereafter, means once again that we are never *shown* Horrible as other than potentially evil.

Now, in point of fact, the mystery that attaches to Horrible's curtailed career of evil—curtailed both in that he is smothered to death and in that his potential for evil is never exploited—is narratively and imaginatively successful. Indeed, lest anyone should imagine that in talking here and elsewhere of *schemata blocked* I am making a negative aesthetic judgment on Jean's romance, let me say that this is not my intention. What I wish to point out is what seems to be a consistent pattern, whereby those ominous incidentals of the story that derive from Melusine's dualities and that in other circumstances might provide a positive plethora of extraordinary narrative developments are systematically blocked. And I should like to finish by putting forward a modest hypothesis that sets the *Roman de Mélusine* (or rather, as Jean d'Arras consistently calls it, the *Histoire de Mélusine*) in its literary context.

Harf-Lancner, in the introduction to her translation of Coudrette's *Mélusine*, points to a proliferation in the twelfth and early thirteenth centuries of claims to genealogies stemming from the supernatural: the Bouillon family and the legend of the *Chevalier au Cygne*, the Plantagenet family and the legend of the Count of Anjou who married a *fée* (*M* 17). To these, we might add a miscellany of other legends that propose exotic or incongruous or ambivalent origins also likely to cast a bizarre or ambiguous or even ominous light on heroic founding fathers, and hence on historical families, such myths, characteristically, attaching especially to already existing dynastic or cyclic corpuses:

(1) The persistent legend that has the Capetian dynasty stem from a wealthy Parisian butcher, Hugues Capet's father or grandfather. Ribémont and Salvat, in a very recent article in *Le Moyen Age*, find the legend hinted at in the thirteenth century (reflected of course in Dante's *Purgatorio*), but fully developed in the *Chanson de Hugues Capet*, a late epic of the latter half of the fourteenth century.[22]

(2) The legend of Pepin's womanizing, and hence Charlemagne's two traitorous illegitimate brothers, Henri and Rainfroi. Horrent finds this legend fully developed in the fourteenth-century *Mainet*.[23]

(3) The equally persistent legend of the so-called *péché de Charlemagne*.[24]

What these may represent, perhaps, is something that Guenée[25] notes: a growing interest in the "dramatic" construction of genealogies, which, rather than an ancestry grounded in conformity, *une galerie de types exemplaires* as Duby calls it,[26] prefers one grounded in singularity. But to revert to a phrase I used earlier, this is a high-risk strategy for the historian or family genealogist in a world that believes in procreative determinism, where a linear consciousness of history supposes uniformity. Hence, perhaps, in the case of a number of these genealogies, a parallel tendency in later pseudohistorical versions of the stories to neutralize or at least attenuate any potential damage—Ribémont and Salvat use the interesting expression *décontaminer*.[27] Thus, it seems, the old shape-shifting motif of the swan-brothers is rationalized into the story of the knight *with* the swan ("le chevalier *au* cygne"): supernatural progeniture perhaps seeming to suggest a dubious lack of orthodoxy because of its dangerous proximity to an incubus story.[28] Hence too, perhaps, in the mid-fifteenth century David Aubert's neutralization of the story of Charlemagne's two bastard brothers, who become mere conventional traitors with no family connection to Charlemagne himself.[29] Hence finally, presumably, the authorial efforts that go into neutralizing the story of the butcher at the source of the Capetian dynasty, so that Jean d'Outremeuse, for instance, rather than have the ancestor of the Capetian dynasty a butcher, maintains simply that because of his (entirely noble) family's penury, Hugues was *apprenticed* to a butcher,[30] thus giving rise to the demeaning legend. And if I may be allowed an argument *ex negativo*, it is perhaps significant that I find no trace of the legend of the *péché de Charlemagne* in the histories of the fourteenth and fifteenth centuries.

What is characteristic in all these cases is the neutralization, indeed the denial, of genealogy as determinism. It is this sort of blocking of promising narrative schemata that, I suggest, also characterizes the *Roman de Mélusine.* A coherent causal narrative, based on the predictive model that family histories tend to suppose, would ensure a consonance across the whole range of Melusine's progeny: the *tares* acting in each case, and not only in the cases of Geoffroy and Horrible, as outward marks of an inner ambiguity. But the process of *mise en écrit* actualizes the deictic content of a myth or legend. The originary—folklore—myth of Melusine, as long as it does not impinge on the narrator's or patron's present, is a harmless, indeed a charming *fiction*. Once, however, the Lusignan family's continuity is stressed, for political or propagandist purposes, and in something that its author repeatedly calls the *Histoire de Mélusine* and for which he claims irrefutable chronicle evidence, the awkwardness of the originary story is inescapable. Hence, presumably, the welter of conquest and crusade. Jean d'Arras's loving exposition of the brothers' military might, strategic acumen, and crusading devotion is surely not just amplification or display of the Lusignans' historical antecedents but also, by sheer detail, a counterweight to schemata latent in myths of offspring tainted by a supernatural parent.

Is it not *also* significant that of all the children, only two (besides, of course, the monk Fromont) have themselves no offspring to carry on the line? As we have already seen, Geoffroy's career of evil is in any case curiously inconsequential: where a Raoul de Cambrai burns a nunnery as part and parcel of a history of violence, hotheadedness, and disloyalty, where a Robert le Diable consistently reduces monasteries and nunneries to ashes, Geoffroy is drawn just once, quite uncharacteristically, into an act of violence in which he serves, it seems, as God's avenging hand. But significantly, only he and Horrible leave no progeny, and the Lusignan line passes to Thierry, one of the two brothers who suffers from no *tare.* Ought we not to see these differing fates as a careful blocking of genealogy? I am even more persuaded of this in the case of Horrible, denounced by his mother in a move that makes her both the originator of, and the block to, genealogical logic.

The narrative scheme that the *Roman de Mélusine* adumbrates—the agreed synthesis, in other words, with its concomitant curse—sits uneasily with a pragmatic need to glorify Jean de Berry through a connection with the Lusignans. Just as it seems to have been perceived as an embarrassment by the historians of the later Middle Ages that Godefroy de Bouillon might have been descended from a swan-knight, Hugues Capet from a butcher, Roland—perhaps—from Charlemagne's sin, so Jean d'Arras minimizes the more uneasy consequences of Melusine's fairy image, and indeed her betrayal of her own father, for which her dual nature is a punishment. Schemata that could have had promising narrative consequences—the sons' appearance, Geoffroy's tendency to evil—are blocked, and in a dramatic, perhaps metonymic move, Horrible assumes the role of *bouc émissaire.* In this opportunistic romance—opportunistic both in its conception and in its seizing on every useful strand of contemporary historical and political life—Jean d'Arras blocks what can be blocked of peripeteia unlikely to advance his patron's cause.

Notes

The preparation of this chapter was supported by a grant from the British Academy. I am most grateful for its support. I am also grateful to Adrian Armstrong, who kindly read the paper on my behalf at the Colloquium "Mélusine at 600" at the University of Massachusetts, Amherst.

1. Tannen's model is designed for the analysis of oral narrative; see her "A Comparative Analysis of Oral Narrative Strategies: Athenian Greek and American English," in W. L. Chafe, ed., *The Pear Stories: Cognitive, Cultural, and Linguistic Aspects of Narrative Production* (Norwood, N.J.: Ablex, 1980), 51–87, and id., "Oral and Literate Strategies in Spoken and Written Narratives," *Language* 58 (1982): 1–21. Cf. also her "What's in a Frame? Surface Expectations for Underlying Expectations," in *New Directions in Discourse Processing,*

ed. Roy Freedle (Norwood, N.J.: Ablex, 1979), 137–81. The expression "structures of expectation" comes from R. N. Ross, "Ellipsis and the Structure of Expectation," *San Jose State Occasional Papers in Linguistics* 1 (1975): 183–91, which serves in some sense as the starting point for Tannen's work; some analogous research has been done by R. C. Anderson, "The Notion of Schemata and the Educational Enterprise," in R. C. Anderson et al., *Schooling and the Acquisition of Knowledge* (Hillsdale, N.J.: Lawrence Erlbaum, 1977), 415–31.

2. See Le Goff and Le Roy Ladurie; Michèle Perret, in the *postface* to her translation of Jean d'Arras's *Mélusine,* 315–18. See also Laurence Harf-Lancner, "Littérature et politique: Jean de Berry, Léon de Lusignan et le *Roman de Mélusine,*" in D. Buschinger, ed., *Histoire et littérature au moyen âge* (Göppingen: Kümmerle, 1991), 161–71.

3. See Roach's introduction to Coudrette, *Mélusine,* 50–52, and Harf-Lancner's introduction to her translation of Coudrette, 29–35.

4. See *M* 17, n. 1, and Stouff's note on St. Guillaume, M 330.

5. Georges Duby, "Remarques sur la littérature généalogique en France au moyen âge," in *Hommes et structures du moyen âge* (Paris and The Hague: Mouton, 1973), 287–98.

6. Bernard Guenée, "Les généalogies entre l'histoire et la politique: la fierté d'être capétien, en France, au moyen âge," in *Politique et histoire au moyen âge: recueil d'articles sur l'histoire politique et l'historiographie médiévales (1956–1981)* (Paris: Publications de la Sorbonne, 1981), 341–68.

7. See R. Howard Bloch's article, "Genealogy as a Medieval Mental Structure and Textual Form," in GRMLA XI/1: *La Littérature historiographique des origines à 1500* (Heidelberg, 1987), 3:135–56, and his *Etymologies and Genealogies: A Literary Anthropology of the French Middle Ages* (Chicago and London: University of Chicago Press, 1983).

8. See Roach's introduction to Coudrette, *Mélusine,* 16. Roach's identification of legendary with historical characters has had a mixed reception: positive in *Romania* 105 (1985): 545–50, and *Revue de Linguistique Romane* (1968): 254–57; relatively positive in *French Studies* 39 (1985): 451–52, and *Vox Romanica* 43 (1984): 320–22; and hostile in *Speculum* 59 (1984): 639–42.

9. "Genealogy: Form and Function in Medieval Historical Narrative," *History and Theory* 22 (1983): 43–53, and *Romancing the Past: The Rise of Vernacular Prose Historiography in Thirteenth-Century France* (Berkeley and Los Angeles: University of California Press, 1993).

10. André Vauchez adduces some interesting evidence to show that even sainthood is felt to be hereditary ("transmission d'un charisme"): "'Beata Stirps': sainteté et lignage en Occident aux XIIIe et XIVe siècles," in Georges Duby and Jacques Le Goff, eds, *Famille et parenté dans l'Occident médiévale* (Rome: Ecole Française, 1977), 397–406.

11. On Lambert d'Ardres, see Georges Duby, *Le Chevalier, la femme et le prêtre: le mariage dans la France féodale* (Paris: Hachette, 1981), 269–300, and cf. Jacques Le Goff, "Naissance du roman historique au XIIe siècle," *Nouvelle revue française* 238 (1972): 163–73.

12. See the introduction to her translation of Coudrette's *Mélusine,* 30; italics added.

13. For the prevalence of Trojan heroes as ancestors, see for instance Léopold Génicot, *Les Généalogies* (Brepols: Turnhout, 1975), 20–22.

14. For this as for most folklore motifs, I refer to Anita Guerreau-Jalabert, *Index des motifs narratifs dans les romans arthuriens français en vers (XIIe–XIIIe)* (Geneva: Droz, 1992). As she points out, magic rings serve in romance to confer invincibility, detect enchantments, render invulnerable, protect from harm and witchcraft, etc.

15. Ed. Jane H. M. Taylor (Geneva: Droz, 1979), 182–83, and cf. "La Chanson du Bossu," in *Les pièces lyriques du Roman de Perceforest,* ed. Jeanne Lods (Geneva: Droz/Lille: Giard, 1953), 28–29.

16. By what is either inadvertence or, as Michèle Perret suggests, failure entirely to coordinate two originally separate stories, Jean d'Arras calls these two sons *Fromont* and *Thierry;* in fact of course the birth of Fromont has already been described (M 80). Later (M 258), he uses the names *Remond* and *Thierry* (cf. Coudrette, who talks of *Raymons* and *Thierry,* ll. 2797–98).

17. Clier-Colombani reproduces the full suite of woodcuts from the edition of 1485 (Augsburg: Antoine Sorg); however, they are greatly reduced and therefore difficult to examine closely.

18. Laurence Harf-Lancner, "Le *Roman de Mélusine* et le *Roman de Geoffroy à la Grand Dent:* Les éditions imprimées de l'oeuvre de Jean d'Arras," *Bibliothèque d'Humanisme et Renaissance* 50 (1988): 349–66. There is also some interesting information in François Eygun, *Ce qu'on peut savoir de Mélusine et de son iconographie* (Puiseaux: Pardès, s.d.).

19. See the postface to her translation, 318.

20. Cf. *Robert le Diable,* ed. E. Löseth (Paris: Firmin Didot, 1903). Robert is the son of a *duc de Normandie* whose wife, despairing of conceiving a child, prays to the devil. Robert is therefore unequivocally the child of the devil. On the historical Geoffrey, see S. Roblin, "Le sanglier et le serpent: Geoffroi à la grand dent dans l'histoire des Lusignan," in *Métamorphose et bestiaire fantastique au moyen âge,* ed. L. Harf-Lancner (Paris: ENSJF, 1985), 247–85.

21. It is not clear whether Jean d'Arras could have known of Raoul de Cambrai other than by repute. The only known manuscript of the *chanson de geste* dates from the end of the thirteenth century; see A. Longnon's lengthy discussion in the edition done by him and P. Meyer (Paris: Firmin Didot, 1882), lxxvi–lxxix, and cf. Sarah Kay's remarks in her edition (Oxford: Clarendon

Press, 1992), xxvi–xxviii. There seems to be no trace of the work in the later Middle Ages: Georges Doutrepont finds no *mise en prose* (see his *Les Mises en prose des épopées et des romans chevaleresques du XIVe au XVIe siècles* [Brussels: Palais des Académies, 1939], 371), nor any mention in the inventories of the dukes of Burgundy.

22. Marquis de la Grange, ed., *Hugues Capet, chanson de geste . . .*, coll. Anciens poètes de la France 8 (Paris, 1864); cf. the translation by J. Subrenat and F. Suard, *Le Roman de Hugues Capet,* Trésors littéraires du nord de la France 5 (Troesne-la Ferté-Milon: Corps 9, 1987). The article to which I refer is by Bernard Ribémont and Michel Salvat, "De Francion à Hugues Capet, descendant d'un boucher: Légende des origines et encyclopédisme," *Le Moyen Age* 99 (1993): 249–62; one can also refer usefully to Ferdinand Lot, *Etudes sur le règne de Hugues Capet et la fin du Xe siècle,* Bibliothèque des hautes études, sciences historiques et philologiques 147 (Paris: Emile Bouillon, 1903), Appendix 7, "Légendes sur Hugues Capet," 324–50.

23. See Jacques Horrent, *Les versions des enfances de Charlemagne,* Académie Royale de Belgique, Mémoires de la classe des lettres 64 (Brussels: Palais des Académies, 1979).

24. See, among others, Rita Lejeune, "Le péché de Charlemagne et la *Chanson de Roland*: contes de gestes," in *Studia philologica a Damaso Alonso* (Madrid: Editorial Gredos, 1961), and more recently Suzanne Martinet, "Le péché de Charlemagne, Gisèle, Roland et Ganelon," in *Amour, mariage et transgression au moyen âge: Actes du Colloque des 24/25/26 et 27 mars 1963,* ed. Danielle Buschinger and André Crépin (Göppingen: Kümmerle, 1984), 9–16.

25. In "Les généalogies entre l'histoire et la politique," 341–68.

26. "Remarques," 259.

27. "De Francion à Hugues Capet," 261–62.

28. See H. Pigeonneau, *Le Cycle de la Croisade et de la famille de Bouillon* (Saint-Cloud: Veuve Eugène Belin, 1877), and more recently Herbert Kolb, "Die Schwanenrittersage als Ursprungsmythos mittelalterlicher Fürstengeschlechter," in *History and Heroic Tale: Proceedings of the 8th International Symposium organised by the Centre for the Study of Vernacular Literature in the Middle Ages, Odense University, 21/22 November, 1983,* ed. Tore Nyberg et al. (Odense: University Press, 1985), 23–50, and E. Emplaincourt and J. A. Nelson, "Le fond lotharingien de *La Chanson du Chevalier au Cygne,*" *Le Moyen Age* 99 (1993): 231–47.

29. *Les Versions,* 68–71.

30. *Ly Myror des histores,* ed. S. Bormans, Collection des chroniques belges (Brussels, 1977), 1:xciii, 4:165–67.

Fiction and History: The Cypriot Episode in Jean d'Arras's *Mélusine*

EMMANUÈLE BAUMGARTNER

Mélusine. To pronounce the name before a modern audience, to evoke the shrieking fay ("les cris de la fée") or her plight in the wake of her lament ("Mélusine après le cri"), is no doubt first of all to bring to mind Nerval's famous verse, or André Breton's meditation concerning the advent—how fervently desired?—of an age that would "valorize women's ideas at the expense of men's" and "give maximum prominence to everything pertaining to the feminine—as opposed to the masculine—world order."[1] Or perhaps the name simply conjures the image of a creature, half-woman and half-fairy, who would serve as metaphor for that shadowy, secret, unsettling side of sexuality that a woman must carefully conceal if she is to preserve her happiness. Whatever the case, if the Melusinian myth still seems very much alive at the end of the twentieth century, it is not apparent that the romances of Jean d'Arras and Coudrette, which played an important role in the myth's literary elaboration—Jean having provided the first French version in the form of an organized, well-developed narrative—were decisively influential in the legend's nineteenth-century "renaissance."[2] It was more plausibly in oral and popular traditions and in local legends that Romanticism rediscovered the ambiguous figure of the serpentine fairy, prior to its appropriation by historians of *mentalités.*

If we consider the story by Jean d'Arras in its entirety, taking into account its remarkably heterogeneous content, that view of the tradition's development would hardly seem surprising. However, even a cursory reading leads one to wonder whether the mythic dimension, so consistently valorized in contemporary criticism, is really what predominates, and whether, even for the medieval reader, that dimension was in fact of primary interest. Might one suggest, then, that the "Melusinian scenarios" have perhaps been excessively and too hastily detached from a more significant totality? That totality, dedicated as it is to the celebration of a lineage (in the manuscripts the text is entitled *La noble histoire de Lusignan* or *Le Roman* or *Le Livre de Mélusine*), does indeed recount the mythic origin and the founding role of Melusine; yet it also lingers at great length over the conquests and governance of the sons of Melusine, in Cyprus, Armenia, Luxembourg, and Bohemia, in pages more redolent of chronicle, chanson de geste, and crusade narrative than of tales and marvels of the fairy world. It is precisely this other aspect of the text, its embodiment of a fundamental tension between *History* and *Romance*—the polarity apparent in the various titles given the text—that I wish to examine here, beginning with the segments devoted to the exploits in the Near East of Urian and Guyon, then of Geoffroy. These episodes, we recall, are themselves interrupted by the "séquence 'similaire'" detailing the prowesses of Antoine and Renaud in Luxembourg and Bohemia, which are, in a way that seems to me symptomatic, even more frequently omitted from summaries of the work than are those of Urian and his other brothers.

As commentators have long noted, the Melusinian myth's literary reconfiguration at the end of the fourteenth century coincides on the one hand with the political turmoil of the Hundred Years' War and on the other with the attempted renewal of the Crusades, coordinated by Philip of Mézières and directly supported by the last of the Christian monarchs of Lesser Armenia, Léon of Lusignan, who had been deposed by the Turks in 1375 and who died in Paris in 1393.[3] The Lusignans' presence in the Near East dates from the twelfth century; the family distinguished itself in the defense of the Holy Land, where Hugh VII of Lusignan died in 1148 and where the historical Guy of Lusignan (1129–1194), the youngest son of Hugh VIII, had a remarkable career. Initially Count of Jaffa and of Ascalon (the county of Jaffa was to pass to his brother Geoffrey in 1191, thence to his other brother Aymeri), in 1180 Guy married Sibyl, the elder sister of Baldwin IV, the Leper King. Crowned king of Jerusalem in 1186, a title he retained until 1192 even though Jerusalem had been recaptured by Saladin in 1187, he became king of Cyprus in 1192, whereupon the title of king of Jerusalem was attributed to Conrad of Montferrat, the head of the rival faction (who in fact was executed in that same year by the leader of the Assassins). The Lusignans held Cyprus until 1489; they had acquired Lesser Armenia (Cilicia) in 1342. Jean d'Arras began his narrative in 1392 at the behest of his patron Jean, duke of Berry, who was related, by way of his mother, Bonne of Luxembourg, to the House of Lusignan. Jean de Berry had recaptured the fortress of Lusignan, the largest fortification in Poitou, from the English in 1374, but in 1392 he feared that he would again lose it to the English, and with it all of Poitou (see Harf-Lancner, Coudrette, 25–35). The important place that Jean d'Arras makes in his story for the seizure of Cyprus and Lesser Armenia by the Lusignan family can thus be seen as an exaltation of the lineage whose glory and pretentions to Poitou were both currently accruing to Jean de Berry, as well as an attempt to reawaken the spirit of the Crusades and, more precisely, to draw the attention of Christendom to the plight of Léon of Lusignan and his kingdom. It is thus not surprising that this story, whose folkloric elements were those that assumed primary interest over the ensuing centuries, devotes so many of its pages to the conquests by the fairy's sons, in the East of the Crusades as well as in Luxembourg, Bohemia, and elsewhere.

Jean d'Arras's account of that establishment in the Near East, however, becomes immediately problematic for the modern reader, and was so very probably for its initial public. Since the thirteenth century there had been numerous written accounts, in the form of chronicles, of the story that linked the Lusignans and Cyprus—a story that was set during the course of the Third Crusade. Although Jean d'Arras and his readers would have had access to these accounts, his own account of this "real" conquest, as well as of that of Armenia, is false on historical grounds.

This phenomenon is no doubt not an isolated one, but it is nonetheless surprising, as it concerns events that by no means hark back to time immemorial; it was composed, moreover, during a period that, from Jean le Bel to Froissart, saw a proliferation of chronicles that give a factual account of events without seeking at every moment to penetrate the private lives and the secrets of the protagonists.

If on the other hand we consider the work in terms of its narrative coherence as a romance, it is not difficult to understand why Jean d'Arras, instead of composing a story based on such accessible sources as the *Estoire de la Guerre sainte* by Ambroise, the *Continuation de Guillaume de Tyr*, or the *Chronique d'Ernoul et de Bernard le trésorier*, to cite only a few, chose instead to fabricate a story.[4] The answer is obvious: the vague and remote "Melusinian" age, the time of mythic origins and founding acts, antedates the historical period of the Crusades; Jean d'Arras could not submit a "biography," no matter how romanesque, of such historical personages as Guy and his brother Geoffrey I of Lusignan.[5] As we shall see, he takes care—not without bias, certainly—to locate the account of the conquest of Cyprus in an equally vague temporal context, though one prior in any case to the period of the Crusades. The matter at hand, then, is not to seek the immediate impetus for this historical "fraud," which stems from the narrative logic, but rather to attempt to identify the episode's raison d'être and the means used to cloud the issue, so as to give the invention the veneer and semblance of a page from history inscribed into the myth and to endow it with the exemplarity of a model.

After having recounted the origin and phenomenal ascent of the Lusignan lineage, and prior to announcing its decline, the story uses its new moorings in the Near East and the Crusades to break free from marvels and enchantments in order to offer an idealized narration of the foundation of an historical realm. The annexation to Christendom of Cyprus, an isle that, before the Third Crusade, was not under the dominion of the Arabs but of the Byzantine emperors, was in fact an achievement not of the Lusignans but of Richard the Lionhearted. The English king had seized the isle in 1190, expelling Isaac Comnenos, and made it a resupplying base for the siege of Acre. That the conquest was carried out with flair and vigor is attested by Ambroise's *Estoire de la Guerre sainte*, as well as by the *Continuation de Guillaume de Tyr* and the *Chronique d'Ernoul.* As for Guy of Lusignan, he acquired the isle through purchase in 1192, and with some sacrifice, having had to relinquish the throne of Jerusalem in order to become king of Cyprus. His access to power was thus hardly glorious, though the author of the *Continuation de Guillaume de Tyr* praises him for having followed the generous advice of Saladin concerning how best to populate his new kingdom, opening it to those whom the Saracens had despoiled of their fiefs, to wives, widows, and orphans, as well as to *corversiers* (cobblers), *massons* (masons), and "escrivains en sarazineis" (writers of the Saracen language), who, according to the Continuator, became "chevaliers" and "grans vavassors de l'isle de Cypre" (*Continuation* 139).

The story told by Jean d'Arras is entirely different. While historical writing is woven on the weft of chronology, the Cypriot episode as he tells it is a closed sequence that unfolds within a time long past, suggestive of the time of foundation myths or, more modestly, of that of the great Arthurian romances that Jean d'Arras could hardly not have known. Indeed, as in an Arthurian romance, an auspicious recurrent situation—"Et tousjours s'entretenoient compaignie Uriiens et Guyon. Et les amoient tant les nobles enfans du pays, et eulx aussi les nobles et les enfans, qu'ilz ne povoient plus, et fesoient armes bien souvent en joustes, en tournois et en bouhours" [Urian and Guyon always kept company with one another; the noble youths of the land esteemed them, and they in turn could not have been more admiring both of the noblemen and the youths, and they often jousted with them, in tournaments and other chivalric exercises] (*M* 81)—is disrupted when two Poitevin knights arrive at the court of Raymondin and Melusine and reveal that Cyprus and its Christian king are imperiled, besieged at Famagusta by the *soudan*, the Sultan of Damascus. The two inseparable brothers, Urian, the eldest, and Guyon, the third son, neither of whom stand to inherit the fief of Lusignan earmarked for Geoffroy, vow to remedy the situation. Their exploits on Cyprus, then in Armenia, their conquests, their happy and fertile marriages occupy a lengthy segment of the story, until the moment when another Poitevin knight returning from the Near East reports that Guy, the new king of Armenia, has been attacked by the Caliph of Baghdad and the Great Caraman, who are also threatening Urian. Geoffroy, coming to their rescue, providentially finds his brothers off Jaffa, seizes that city, then takes Beirut and marches on Damascus. At this point, in fact, as in many Crusade narratives and chansons de geste, the prowess of the Christians confronts the overwhelming superiority in numbers of the Saracens, though both armies, by now exhausted, negotiate a truce. Geoffroy, however, as heir of Lusignan and bound by his vow to return at the end of a year, returns to Poitou, leaving his brothers to settle definitively in Cyprus and Armenia. The story has in the meantime acquired a parallel thread, this time within the European sphere, in the segments devoted to Antoine and Renaud, who have gone to the rescue of Chrétienne of Luxembourg; Antoine will marry the lady, while Renaud will eventually win the hand and realm of Aiglentine of Bohemia.

The exploits of the three siblings in the Near East comprise segments of varying lengths: while Urian's liberation of Cyprus is described in considerable detail, the Armenian campaign, cast more or less in the same mold, is more quickly expedited; both culminate in the firm possession of the kingdoms. On the other hand, Geoffroy's intervention opens onto other perspectives. As heir of the patrimony, he cannot establish himself in the East, but the truce of one hundred years and a day that he negotiates with his adversaries reopens access to Jerusalem and to pilgrimage; his return voyage (*M* 237–38), from Jerusalem to La Rochelle via Jaffa, Armenia, Rhodes, and Cyprus, triumphally reverses the itinerary of the hero of the Third Crusade, Richard the Lionhearted, whose way was blocked at Acre.

Notably unlike the "historical" conquest of Cyprus by the English monarch—a conquest in the form of a raid, soon abandoned and turned over to the Templars, who were quickly overwhelmed and unable to hold the island[6]—the "conquests" of Urian and Guyon are ideally planned and executed territorial appropriations.

Again as in an Arthurian romance—the shadow of the Prose *Lancelot* seems to hover over the opening pages—we are first told of the awakening of the desire for remote realms and glory in the hearts of the heroes, a desire whose catalyst is the story told by the Poitevin knights. As for Melusine, she immediately assumes the Lady of the Lake's role in the *Lancelot*, in carefully planning the expedition, and especially in instructing her two sons in an artfully limned discourse on the art of governing and of maintaining one's eventual conquests. This discourse, moreover, is quite curious, in that it folds into her general counsel considerations of a newer and more realistic hue, for example on appropriate degrees of taxation and the dangers of borrowing. The blend bespeaks the evolution of a world in which power is no longer merely a matter of virtue—was it ever thus, in fact?—but of resources in gold and silver as well (*M* 84–87).[7]

As for the account of the conquest itself, we may find in it, without undue solicitation of the text, the avatar of a narrative format well attested in romance. Jean d'Arras has in sum transposed to the East of the Crusades the romanesque motif of the girl or young woman unable to defend her kingdom in the absence of her father. Hermine, the daughter of the king of Cyprus, and her cousin Florie, the king of Armenia's daughter, are perfect exemplars of the rich heiresses in need of protection and thus eminently marriageable, who offer the hero an opportunity to display the prowess required by such a situation. Smitten at the first exchange of glances, they are moreover given and taken legally, by the hand of the father, to the one whom he makes, by the same gesture, the heir and champion of his realm.

The stakes are clear. At the beginning of the story, Raymondin acquires a dubious/magical heritage whose obscure origins are beyond anyone's ken and that thus raises questions that will eventually lead to his downfall; here, in its place, are formal gifts duly proffered by fathers who have been able to gauge the merits of their successors. The first of these episodes, the most exemplary and detailed, is the conquest of Cyprus. Having overcome the Saracens, Urian emphatically refuses the status of "soudoyer" and the money associated therewith, accepting no other gift or recompense than to be knighted by the very king he has succored, who in turn "exacts," as recompense ("guerredon"), that he become his succesor and the husband of his daughter. This irreproachable father has, in addition, the good grace to expire from his poisoned wound only after the marriage has been consummated, thus obviating the potential for legal entanglements. Guyon's recompense is the same, though by way of a testamentary letter from the already deceased king of Armenia, bequeathing to the young knight both his realm and his only daughter.

Jean d'Arras's redeployment of a banal motif thus retains the idealistic, indeed utopian, dimension of the implicit narrative model: access to power, appropriation of the land and the lady, based on reciprocal love and prowess. Thus did Enéas espouse Lavinia, as did Yvain Laudine, to cite only two familiar examples of the pattern. In contrast to the *Chevalier au lion*, however, the rewriting is here framed within a universe of strict legality in which the heiress is given in marriage (rather than yielding her own hand, which might be retracted), where law and the licit desire of the father reign instead of the willfulness of fairies. In contrast to the *Enéas*, and to the *roman antique* generally, access to power no longer takes place in a mythic dimension but is renewed within a spatial and temporal framework familiar to the public, a known and believable world, yet one also tinged with a degree of glamour that might perhaps be called exotic. Above all, in the case of both sons, the story unfolds in contrast with the Melusinian schema. The heroes are not chosen by a fairy who, by ensuring their prosperity, would seek to neutralize the curse that weighs upon her. It is by dint of personal valor and heroism that the second generation—in fact the first in the "romance"—to bear the name of Lusignan and bring it renown, conquers kingdoms and wins heiresses fascinated by prowess and insensitive to physical monstrosity.[8] Their acquisitions are achieved with the utmost legality. The shady, perhaps diabolical, origin of the Lusignan fortune is thus reinvested by the story of conquests thoroughly permeated with the spirit and fervor of the Crusades, carried out heroically and in a most Christian manner under the auspices of the Master of Rhodes and his knights, who positively sanction every phase.[9]

The final episode, devoted to Geoffroy, appears to be the crowning achievement of this attempt to Christianize, legitimize, and justify the fortune of the Lusignans by relocating it within the context of the Crusades. Heir of the patrimony, Geoffroy has no need to pursue a wealthy heiress. He must on the other hand demonstrate his prowess in the service of God, as he does with panache over the course of his campaign. Of course, he never conquers Jerusalem. Just as the authors of the Arthurian corpus never dared lead Arthur to the conquest of Rome, Jean d'Arras never authorizes his hero to take possession of the Holy City. In fact, he provides him with better solutions: negotiation of a century's truce with the pagans (until the conquest of Jerusalem by the heroes of the First Crusade?); a tribute of thirty thousand gold besants that the Saracens promise to pay Urian; the friendship of a bedazzled Sultan of Damascus, who is "moult en amourez de Gieffroy, et lui tenoient tousjours compaignie, et lui offroit tousjours tout le plaisir qu'il lui porroit faire" [most enamored of Geoffrey, and always kept him company, and sought to please him in every possible way] and who takes the knight to Jerusalem where he spends three days "ou sepulcre en devocion" [worshiping at the Holy Sepulchre] soon joined by "le roy Uriien et le roy Guion son frere, et le maistre de Rodes, et moult grant foison de crestiens" [King Urian, his brother Guyon, the Master of Rhodes, and a very large contingent of Christians] (*M* 237). In sum, an inventory of "conquests" that lend the monstrous son of the serpent-woman an aura of the sacred, the prestige of a Godfrey of Bouillon, indeed of the legendary Charlemagne of the *Voyage à Jérusalem et à Constantinople.* Is it thus so surprising that a unique and very curious temporal notation occurs at this juncture? The Jerusalem that the Sultan of Damascus opens to his new friend and to the Christians escorting him is a city that "pour lors n'estoit pas reparee ne refremee de la destruction que Vespasien et Thitus son filz y orent faicte quant ilz vindrent vengier la mort Jhesucrist aprez son crucifiement" [was not yet repaired and restored after the destruction that Vespasian and his son Titus had inflicted when they came to avenge the Crucifixion of Jesus Christ] (*M* 237).

The narrator's intervention here is as interesting as it is problematic. While nothing provides any clue as to the temporal dating of this episode, nor even, seemingly, of the story as a whole, the reader is taken abruptly back to a time well before the First Crusade, before the conquest of a city not yet subjected to the profanations of Islam.[10] It is thus as if Geoffroy's expedition allowed the period in which the Holy City was physically marked by the Arabic presence and faith to be eradicated from historical time, as if there had been no solution of continuity between the historical moment when Vespasian avenged the death of Christ by destroying the Jewish city and that when Geoffroy of Lusignan, making it accessible to the Christian world, makes possible its restoration.

Here again, however, fiction seems to toy with history so as to remodel it to the advantage of the illustrious lineage. How could the friendship of Geoffroy and the Sultan not bring to mind the bonds created during the Third Crusade between Richard the Lionhearted and Saladin and the truce, historical but far more ephemeral, that enabled a few pilgrims, though trembling, harrassed, and ransomed by the Arabs, to make their way to sacred locales?[11] Might we not take this parallel still further by pointing out that in order to recover his kingdom, and with the help of his brother Geoffrey who had come by sea, the historical Guy de Lusignan had valiantly renewed the struggle against Saladin after the fall of Jerusalem in 1187? (Cf. supra note 8.) No doubt Jean d'Arras cannot exploit the full potential of his fictive history: just as the historical Guy never retook Jerusalem, Geoffroy never conquers it. Yet by conquering the cities leading to it—notably Jaffa, another fief once held by the Lusignans—and by concluding a lasting truce, the mythic Geoffroy, powerfully seconded by his brothers, provides a kind of reenactment of the exploits and victories of Richard the Lionhearted, the English king, during the Third Crusade, while at the same time chalking them up to the credit and exclusive glory of his own lineage.

Functioning as an etiological narrative, the episode thus gives an exaggerated account of the Lusignans' access to the kingdoms of Cyprus and Armenia and dispels any doubts that might have lingered concerning the descendants of this lineage. Its origin from the background of Melusine of course remains obscure, while nevertheless providing a necessary mythic aura. Yet the story of its expansion, into the Near East, Luxembourg, Bohemia, and so on, creates an image that is both idealized and devoid of enchantments. The magic rings Melusine gave her sons at their departure were never used (*M* 84). The human and material resources and moral and physical qualities of the three sons alone sufficed. Even beauty, of dubious value, was not a prerequisite. The conquest was carried out in the name of religion, the crusading spirit, and mutual support among Christians, through a sequence of gifts and recompenses emphasized at length in the dialogue between the old King of Cyprus and Urian.

Yet it would be simplistic and reductive to perceive in the Cypriot episode and its aftermath nothing more than a story designed to exalt the Lusignans and to celebrate, in this world in search of its roots that is France at the end of the fourteenth century, the old chivalric values and the fervor of the Crusades of yore. It seems to me that in this passage Jean d'Arras is also experimenting with a new form of writing, whose status is nevertheless difficult to characterize. The Cypriot episode is thus a suitable "locus" to be evaluated with regard to the ways in which romanesque prose fiction writes and renews itself at the end of the fourteenth century, on the margins of, and perhaps in rivalry with, those enormous Arthurian "machines" like the *Perceforest*, an undoubtedly earlier work, and Froissart's *Méliador*, its contemporary.

If not its savory aftertaste, at least the story's essential ingredients are easily identifiable. An initial noteworthy feature is the particular blend of precise geographical components and itineraries with the style and tonality of the chanson de geste. Jean d'Arras correctly locates Cyprus with respect to the African coast, Cilicia (Lesser Armenia), and the isle of Rhodes, an important locus in the story. He knows the key points on Cyprus: Famagusta, Limassol, Cape Saint Andrew at the northwest extremity, and so on (though Nicosia is never mentioned). His heroes' military strategy takes into account the authentic topography of the island. The relative precision of the geographical context evokes, among the chansons de geste, the subset of poems in the first crusade cycle, notably the *Chanson d'Antioche* and the *Chanson de Jérusalem*, which also take place, from Nicea to Antioch thence to Jerusalem, in a Near Eastern area located fairly precisely, and which involve the historical luminaries of the First Crusade. The text also borrows from the chansons de geste its characteristic tendency to report exaggerated information, in numerical statistics, descriptions of blows delivered, heated skirmishes, carnage, and the like. The reader may be more struck, however, by the precision of technical terms, notably those concerning maritime warfare, or by the acuity of the military strategies deployed, the takeovers of vessels and combats at sea, all so rare in medieval romance and epic, yet so evocative of nineteenth-century tales of the buccaneers.[12] Are these echoes of the great fourteenth-century naval battles, like the one involving the Ecluse in 1340? Realistic details appear elsewhere too, as in the clever combination of pitched battles and raids carefully laid out by a network of spies, or in a variety of methods that depart in realistic fashion from the technique of direct frontal assault characteristic of Arthurian romance—and used with disastrous consequences by French chivalry at Crécy (1346) and Poitiers (1356).

The use of epic style, on which contemporaneous historical chronicles also rely, is equally apparent in the frequency of stereotypical formulas, such as the "la veïssiez . . . "—that is, "had you been present, you would have seen . . . "—widely used in depictions of combat, or in the fairly frequent recourse to emotionally charged anaphoras that give the effect of *laisses similaires*, or again in the repeated use of certain motifs: collective jubilation at the moment of the fleet's departure; joyful, if not downright festive, warfare.[13] More fundamentally, Jean d'Arras here seems to recapture the spirit of the epic cycle of William of Orange, already evident in the way he portrays two pairs of brothers (not cousins) whose sometimes parallel, sometimes interlaced careers gain them control of a vast portion of the known world and thus serve to broaden the narrative's spatial and temporal parameters. It may well be that this entire central segment of the story including the diaspora of Melusine's sons and their worldwide conquests was inspired, consciously or not, by the generous impulse that in *Les Narbonnais* prompts the sons of Aymeri de Narbonne to relinquish the patrimony and take leave in different directions in order to parcel out the world among themselves in truly auspicious fashion.[14] Like the William Cycle, the *Histoire de Lusignan* is not the history of an individual or of a couple but that of a lineage whose various members disperse themselves spatially: to the frontiers of Christendom, whose limits they strive to push back; to the Near East, as to the East still under the European threat; and indeed to Northumberland, in the direction of a Scotland whose savagery had been a source of fascination over the course of the century for Jean le Bel and the Froissart of both the *Chroniques* and *Méliador*,[15] that Scotland over which Elinas, Melusine's father, long ago reigned, and where Geoffroy, after returning from the Holy Land, will venture in the guise of a civilizing hero, to slay the giant Grimaut. At the end of the fourteenth century, the Spanish *reconquista* was over, but the way had been opened for the defense of Christendom on a broader scale. Could we not allow, then, that in this segment of his story, which is both central and centrifugal, Jean d'Arras reawakens and unleashes the same spirit of conquest and colonization that already haunted the William Cycle?

Although skillfully woven into the fabric of events, the other, more discreet and less innovative recourse is to motifs that are more specifically romanesque. To lend a little substance to his two heiresses, Jean d'Arras equitably endowed both of them with the motif of a distant love (*amour de loin*) based on the hero's reputation and with love's torments, amorous interchange, hesitation between the grief of losing one's father and the joy of marrying his chosen successor. Taking advantage of the maritime decor, Jean expressly depicts Florie using the romanesque and epic motif of the lady at the window gazing ruefully toward the receding fleet that carries away her beloved, a motif that frames, from Guyon's departure to his triumphant return, the episode of the conquest of Armenia (*M* 127, 143).

We might well find many examples in earlier, especially Anglo-Norman, literature of stories whose heroes, or whose male characters in general, bear the names of historical personages or known families, stories that interlace love scenes and tales of prestigious conquest. *Waldef*, *Fouke Fitz Warin*, and *Guy de Warewic* show such tendencies. Jean d'Arras nonetheless uses them more subtly, and a first glance at the segment under analysis here might lead one to perceive it as a kind of first draft of what was eventually to become the "historical romance,"[16] for it conforms to the first prerequisite of that literary form, which is the depiction of a precise geographical framework. It also portrays characters whose familial identity (the house of Lusignan) and names coincide in part with the names of historical personages—Guy, Geoffrey—who lived and acted in the same framework. In addition, we find frequent recourse to reality effects; the writer describes military strategies, designates weapons, vessels, and other objects, with systematic anachronism. Reflections of a more theoretical bent on the art of government (Melusine's two discourses are good examples) blur temporalities while augmenting the verisimilitude of what might well serve as a fictionalized passage in a history of the Crusades. One also finds polyvalent usage of the technique of interlace and of the formula "Cy se taist l'hystoire . . . en ceste partie dit l'ystoire . . . " [Here the text falls silent . . . in this part the story says . . .] or its variant, "Cy vous leray de . . . et vous diray de . . ." [Here you will read that . . . and I will tell you about . . .], which are prominent in this part of the text.[17] In the romance, in fact, this technique is governed by the writer's own wishes as he determines the disposition of his material. In the chronicle, where it is in use since Villehardouin at least, it is an invaluable device of historical writing because it allows different spaces and different events to cohere, so as to capture the complexity of the real and to endow it with meaning. But if we wish to indulge in the game of naive reading, and in view of the fragments of discourse that refer to or mimic historical reality, how in Jean d'Arras's text do we determine, say, if the correspondence among various events, or the parallel then convergent spatial displacements of the heroes, or the opportune chance occurrences, are inventions in the author's fiction, or if instead they might be carefully managed retranscriptions of historical events?

One element, however, puts an end—though retroactively, at the end of the segment—to such indetermination: the narrator's aforementioned intervention concerning the state in which Geoffroy and his brothers found Jerusalem when they arrived there on their pilgrimage, which unquestionably prevents the reader from locating himself within the historical context of the conquest of Cyprus at the end of the twelfth century. Things thus become clear: Jean d'Arras was not offering his public a deliberately falsified account, nor would his public likely have been deceived thereby. Yet by leavening his account with imprecisions, has he not described, recomposed, as a superimposition upon historical truth, the past as it *might* or as it *should* have unfolded, as the ideal crusade of an illustrious lineage? And has he projected into a past and a space in which history and (Christian) myth mingle that which could, that which *should* recur in the near future in the name of Lusignan, the war cry still reverberating through the lands of the Crusades?

Notes

1. "Faire valoir les idées de la femme aux dépens de l'homme . . . de faire prédominer au maximum tout ce qui ressortit au système féminin du monde par opposition au système masculin" (*Arcane,* 17).

2. For a concise overview of the fortunes of Melusine after the Middle Ages, see Yves Vadé, "Mélusine dans la littérature, de la Renaissance à nos jours," in *Dictionnaire des mythes littéraires,* ed. Pierre Brunel (Paris: Editions du Rocher, 1988), 1005–9; ibid., Laurence Harf-Lancner, "Mélusine," 999–1004.

3. See in particular Harf-Lancner's introduction to her translation of Coudrette, and her article, "Littérature et politique: Jean de Berry, Léon de Lusignan et le *Roman de Mélusine,*" in *Histoire et littérature au Moyen Age,* ed. D. Buschinger (Göppingen: Kümmerle Verlag, 1991), 161–71.

4. *Estoire de la Guerre sainte d'Ambroise,* ed. and trans. G. Paris [Collection de documents inédits sur l'histoire de France] (Paris, 1897); *La Continuation de Guillaume de Tyr (1184–1197),* ed. Margaret Ruth Morgan [Documents relatifs

à l'histoire des croisades, 14] (Paris, 1982); *La Chronique d'Ernoul et de Bernard le Trésorier,* ed. M. L. De Mas Latrie (Paris: Société de l'Histoire de France, 1871).

5. Geoffrey I, who in 1188 joined his brothers Guy and Amaury in the Holy Land, was one of the heroes of the Third Crusade. Concerning his feats, see Ambroise, *Estoire.*

6. On these details, see *La Chronique d'Ernoul,* 284–88, or *Continuation,* 135–41.

7. An attentive mother, Melusine again provides counsel and gifts when Antoine and Renaud depart (M 152–54).

8. See Hermine's observation to herself that "se il avoit le visaige plus contrefait .C. foiz que il n'a, si est il tailliez, pour sa bonté et pour sa prouesse, d'avoir la fille du plus hault roy du monde a amie" ["Even if his face were one hundred times more deformed than it is, in terms of his goodness and prowess he is made to order to have as his sweetheart the daughter of the world's most powerful king"] (M 104).

9. The expression "Master of Rhodes" in this episode no doubt designates, very anachronistically, the Master of the Hospitalers of Saint John of Jerusalem, an order founded in 1099, ensconced in Saint John of Acre from 1197, on Cyprus from 1291, then at Rhodes from 1308 to 1522; when Charles V brought it to Malta in 1530, it came to designate the Knights of the Order of Malta. Might Jean d'Arras have wished, with deliberate anachronism, to lend a mythic past to this order whose founding was patronized by Godfrey of Bouillon?

10. However, the narrator of the *Livre d'Eracles,* for example, notes the presence in Jerusalem of religious edifices—mosques and minarets—constructed by the Arabs and subsequently demolished by the Christians. On this passage from the *Estoire d'Eracles,* ed. P. Paris, 2 vol. (Paris, 1879–80), bk. 8, pp. 267–68, see E. Baumgartner, "Jérusalem et l'écriture de l'histoire dans la Croisade: réalités et fictions," in *Actes du Colloque d'Amiens, 18–22 mars 1987,* ed. D. Buschinger (Göppingen: Kümmerle Verlag, 1989), 7–17.

11. See for example Ambroise, *Estoire,* vv. 12013–100.

12. For an especially colorful account of the takeover of a vessel, see *M* 218.

13. A fine example of anaphoric reprise occurs in the description of the last battle before Damascus (*M* 235–36). Or, for a different tonality, see the brilliant, lively, and colorful description (*M* 214) of the moment when the fleets of Guyon and the Master of Rhodes are reunited.

14. *Les Narbonnais,* ed. H. Suchier, 2 vols. (Paris: Société des Anciens Textes Français, 1898), vv. 1–301.

15. See E. Baumgartner, "*Ecosse* et *Ecossais:* L'entrelacs de la fiction et de l'histoire dans les *Chroniques* et le *Méliador* de Froissart," in *L'Image de l'Autre*

européen XVe–XVIIe siècles (Paris: Presses de la Sorbonne Nouvelle, 1992), 11–21.

16. On this question, see the fundamental article by Jacques Le Goff, "Naissance du roman historique au XIIe siècle?" *Nouvelle Revue Française* (October 1972): 163–73; more generally, consult the special issue of *Revue d'Histoire Littéraire de la France,* nos. 2 and 3 (March–June 1975), on "Le Roman historique."

17. On this type of formula see Michèle Perret, *Le Signe et la mention: Adverbes embrayeurs ci, ça, la, iluec en moyen français (XIVe–XVe siècles)* (Geneva: Droz, 1988), esp. ch. 8.

Writing History/Writing Fiction

Michèle Perret

The *Roman de Mélusine* by Jean d'Arras, a genealogical romance whose writing is accompanied by many protestations of the truth of its source-texts, presents itself as historical, written "au plus justement que j'ay peu, selon les croniques que je cuide estre vrayes" [as accurately as I could, according to the chronicles that I believe to be true] (*M* 2). The romance is incessantly set in relation to the true story, even though the reader is not taken in by this ruse on the part of an author who is perfectly aware that he is engaging in a creative work of fiction-writing, and even if, as we would willingly believe, there already existed sources containing the essential elements of the legend. In this volume, Emmanuèle Baumgartner undertakes to compare the romance's Armenian and Cypriot episodes with their historical sources. Here we propose to subject Jean d'Arras's text to intrinsic study, to show how in its very composition—in its writing—it falls within the category of fiction.

The question to be asked, then, is this: are there textual properties that permit us to identify a text as a work of fiction? If certain critics, like John Searle,[1] answer in the negative, others like Käte Hamburger, followed on this point by Gérard Genette,[2] consider that there exist *indices of fictionality* that permit discrimination between fictional and factual utterances, between narratives of reality and those of fiction, indices that are principally that "the most salient differences seem essentially to affect the modal perspectives most closely linked to the opposition between the limited knowledge of the historian and the supple omniscience enjoyed by the one who invents his account."[3] Thus, for Hamburger, the presence of detailed scenes, of extended descriptions, of dialogues reported in extenso are all indices of fictionality. The same holds for everything that gives access to the subjectivity of the characters: verbs of feeling and thinking attributed to third parties without need of justification, interior monologues, and free indirect style, the latter being "the most characteristic of all because it virtually permeates the totality of the discourse, which it insidiously attributes to the character's consciousness," adds Genette.[4]

We shall thus retain two elements as potentially characteristic of the writing of fiction: the massive presence of *direct discourse*, and the focus on internal process (*focalisation interne*) through the description of *psychological states* as well as, in some cases, through free indirect style. To these elements we shall add a third characteristic typical of the classic fictional narrative: the construction, with regard to the characters, of a *totally intradiscursive reference*, internal to the text.

In order to bring out the specificity of the writing of Jean d'Arras, we shall compare history and pseudohistory by contrasting the *Roman de Mélusine* with a contemporary historical text, Froissart's *Chroniques*,[5] and a text written almost a century earlier but typical of the utterance of reality, of factual utterance in a pure state: the *Vie de Saint Louis* by Joinville.[6]

The Construction of Reference

We know that there exist two types of reference: *situational reference*, which refers directly to objects in the world—to external reality—either by means of shifters (*I, here, now*) or, especially as concerns our inquiry, with proper nouns (=PN), and *contextual reference,* which, after establishing at the beginning of the text a referential pivot (generally an indefinite one) refers to it thereafter by anaphora. Very roughly (our textual analyses will provide a more nuanced distribution), the factual universe, describing the world of that which is, utilizes situational reference: names of cities, countries, known people, existing in external reality, while the fictional universe relies on contextual reference: in the "once upon a time there was a princess who was as beautiful as she was foolish" of the tale, the indefinite article creates the character in the fictive universe, so that one may thereafter refer to her by saying "the princess." The classical novel replaces the "once upon a time there was" of the tale by *a Noun (N) . . . the/this N . . . :* "a man entered . . . this man. . . ." The indefinite article extracts an element from an ensemble: the narrator produces *a man* who becomes the pivot of future reference. Finally, we find *mixed references*, in particular those constituted of *a Proper Name (PN) + a . . . .* My hypothesis is that, in modern French at least, the structure *a N + PN* ("a man of independent means, Jean Dupont") is fictional, while the structure *PN + a N* ("Jean Dupont, a man of independent means") is instead factual.[7]

It is through one or the other of these types of reference that a narrative constructs its temporal and spatial markers and introduces its characters, but we shall be concerned here primarily with the latter. In fact, in all three authors, spatial markers belong to situational reference by means of a proper name. As for temporal indicators, they are inexistent in the three works, except for those afforded by the progression of the story, punctuated by *lors* (then) and *quant* (when). *Mélusine* situates the events *jadis*, long ago (M. 5–6, 15), Froissart "apriés l'apaisement des guerres de Flandres" [after the Flemish wars abated] (Fr. 41); Joinville is satisfied with incomplete dates: "le jour Saint-Marc euvangeliste aprés Pasques" [the day of Saint Mark the Evangelist after Easter] for the birth of the king, "le premier dymanche des Advens" [the first Sunday of Advent] for his coronation.

As for the contextualization of characters, the author who comes closest to a situational reference in a pure state is Joinville. He proceeds first of all to establish a referential grounding in relation to the "I" of the narrator and the "you" of the audience (the inscribed addressee), that is, in pure situational reference, to define his principal character thus: "*nostre* saint roy Looys" (J. §1, emphasis added here and throughout essay). On occasion he adds other referential anchors in relation to "I/you": "mon seigneur Phelippe son filz, le pere au roy *qui ore est*" [my

lord Philip his son, the father of the present king] (J. §37); "le conte de Brienne *qui ore est*" [the present count of Brenne] (J. §88). In these last two cases, it is a question of distinguishing these characters who are currently in power from the multitude of others that appear and who hark back to the seneschal's own youth. But this type of referential anchorage with relation to the time of reading is not the most frequent. More uncommon is the type of contextual anchorage whose pivot is Saint Louis: "le conte Pierre d'Alançon *son filz*" (J. §4); "du conte de Bouloingne *qui estoit oncle le roy*" [the count of Bouloingne who was the king's uncle] (J. §72, 108).

In fact the mode of "construction"—if it may be so called!—of reference privileged by Joinville is the use of the proper name alone, with no qualification whatsoever: a pure situational reference, which requires the interlocutor's full complicity. That which, even in French, we call "name-dropping" in effect rests on the assumption that the proper name injected into the conversation will be immediately identified by the interlocutor because well-known to him. Hence, moreover, also the reverse: the "celebrifying" effect of an unknown proper name thrown into conversation.

In Joinville the proper name is either a true proper name (first name + place name)—"maistre Robert de Cerbone" (J. §31); "monseigneur Geffroy de la Chapelle" (J. §81); "Ertaut de Nogent" (J. §90); "monseigneur Jehan de Biaumont" (J. §150); and so on—or a title + first name + place name: "l'Evesque Guillaume de Paris" (J. §46); "le conte Perron de Bretaingne" (J. §79); "le conte Thibaut de Champaigne qui puis fu roy de Navarre" (J. §75). In addition, when the proper noun is accompanied by a relative or an appositive expansion, the latter does not referentiate: "Monseigneur Baudoin de Reins, un preudomme qui estoit descendu a terre" (J. §157); "au conte de Soisson, cui cousine germainne j'avoie espousee" [to the count of Soissons, whose first cousin I had married] (J. §238); "Madame Marie de Vertus, moult bone dame et moult sainte femme" [. . . a very good lady and saintly woman] (J. §605), hence the necessity of scholarly notes that explain the referent for the contemporary reader: the empress of Constantinople (= Marie, daughter of Jean de Brienne, wife of Baudoin II), the king of Armenia (= Jean de Brienne).

One soon sees that the *Vie de Saint Louis* not only speaks of Saint Louis but is also an exercise in name-dropping: "Après ce que il fu

croisié, se croisierent Robert le conte d'Artois, Auphons conte de Poitiers, Charles conte d'Anjou, qui puis fu roy de Sezile, touz troiz freres le roy. Et se croisa Hugue duc de Bourgoingne, Guillaume conte de Flandres, frere le conte Guion de Flandres nouvellement mort, le bon Hue conte de Saint-Pol, monseigneur Gauchier son neveu (. . .) Si i furent le conte de la Marche et monseigneur Hugue le Brun son filz, le conte de Salebruche, monseigneur Gobert d'Apremont son frere" [After he had taken the cross, so also did Robert count of Artois, Alphonse count of Poitiers, and Charles count of Anjou (who later was king of Sicily), all three of them brothers of the king. And also Hugh duke of Burgundy, William count of Flanders, the brother of the recently deceased count Guion of Flandres, good Hugh count of Saint-Pol, my lord Gauchier his nephew . . . There were also the count of the March and my lord Hugh le Brun his son, the count of Salebruche, my lord Gobert d'Apremont his brother] (J. §108–9); "Le nom de ceulz qui estoient chevaliers entour le roy sont tiex: monseigneur Geoffroy de Sargines, monseigneur Mahi de Marley, monseigneur Phelippe de Nanteul, monseigneur Ymbert de Biaujeu, connestable de France . . . " [The names of those who were knights of the king's entourage are these . . .] (J. §173). This is undoubtedly why it is so important for certain great French families to have been named in Joinville. The effect of nomination in his text will be taken up below.

However, there is a mixed form of reference, though quite rare, of the type *a N + PN:* "un preudomme prestre que en appeloit doyen de Malrut" [a venerable priest who was called doyen of Malrut] (J. §129); "un escuier que je fiz chevalier, qui ot a nom monseigneur Hue de Wanquellour, et deux moult vaillans bachelers dont l'un avoit a non monseigneur Villain de Versey et l'autre monseigneur Guillaume de Danmartin" [a squire that I knighted, whose name was my lord Hugh of Wanquellour, and two very valiant *bacheliers* one of whom was named my lord Villain de Versey and the other my lord William of Danmartin] (J. §154); "deux serjans le roy dont l'un avoit a nom Guillaume de Boon et l'autre Jehan de Gamaches" [two of the king's sergeants, of whom one was named Guillaume de Boon and the other Jehan de Gamaches] (J. §240). This mode of reference concerns humble personages or, say, Saracens: "il avoient fait chievetain d'un Sarrazin qui avoit a nom Secedine le filz au Seic" [he had appointed captain a Saracen named Secedine the son of Seic] (J. §196), sometimes both of these: "un autre Sarrazin qui avoit non Sebrecin" [another Saracen who was named Sebrecin] (J. §372). From which one may conclude that it is good to have one's ancestors named in Joinville but better yet to be so named by an abrupt mode of nomination with the proper name isolated: a nomination that is the privileged mode of constructing reference in Joinville, one that shows an awareness on his part of the notoriety of those whose names he thus thrusts into the narrative. The effect obtained, through the almost total absence of situational connivance between Joinville and the contemporary reader, is one of pronounced alterity.

In Froissart, reference is much more elaborated than in Joinville, and less bluntly rendered by proper names supposedly known to the reader. The only references abruptly introduced situationally, in relation to the "I/you" for whom the effect of connivance may be effective, are "the wars of France and England," the subject of the book presented as identifiable: "les grans mervelles et li biau fait d'armes, liquel sont avenu par *les guerres de France et d'Engleterre* et des roiaumes voisins" [the great marvels and splendid feats of arms, which came about because of the wars of France and England and the neighboring kingdoms] (F. 35), which become in the following pages "les guerres desus dittes" [the above-mentioned wars] (F. 36),[8] without having been particularly defined (there is no reference to the present time or indication of contemporaneity, for example, although the direct witness of the knights and squires who participated in the wars is evoked).

But at once there is created, in situational reference, a referential pivot to which all the other personages will be attached by contextual reference. From the prologue itself, Froissart in effect sets the theme of the transfer of prowess, which allows him to introduce King Edward I, supposedly known to the interlocutor (situational reference): "Apriés a resgné Proesce un temps en Engleterre par le fait *dou roi Edouwart et de la bonne roine Phelippe de Hainnau* sa femme" [Thereafter Prowess reigned for a time in England, due to King Edward and the good Queen Philippa of Hainault his wife] (Fr. 38), the use of the definite article indicating that the personages are immediately identifiable by the reader. In the first chapter, with regard to the partners in the battle of Courtray, we also find posited as known "li biaus rois Phelippes de France" [the fair King Philip of France] (Fr. 41). One can note, moreover, that the two personages are connected situationally to their place of origin: of England, of France.

The other personages are attached discursively to these referential pivots: "au roi Edouwart d'Engleterre, liquels rois desus dis ne fu pas de si grant sens ne de tel proesce comme avoit esté *li bons rois Edouwars ses peres*" [to King Edward of England, which aforementioned king was not of such great good sense or such prowess as had been good King Edward his father] (Fr. 41); "*ses fils* nonmés Edouwars" (Fr. 41); "ce roi Edouwart, dont je parloie maintenant, *liquels fu fils au bon roi Edouwart, qui tant fu de proece* plain que il desconfi par pluisseurs fois en bataille les Escoçois" [this King Edward, of whom I was just speaking, who was the son of the good King Edward, who was so full of prowess that he defeated the Scots in battle several times] (Fr. 43), with numerous repetitions of the referential anchoring: "Et qant chils bons rois Edouwars fu trespassés, *ses fils, nonmés aussi Edouwars,* fu rois" [and when this good King Edward had passed away, his son, also named Edward, was king] (Fr. 43); "chils rois Edouwars, fils au bon rois Edouwart" [this King Edward, son of the good King Edward] (Fr. 44).

Then, in chapter 2, occurs the contextualization of the characters in relation to Edward II and Philippe le Bel established in chapter 1 on the model: *kinship relation with referential pivot + PN*:[9] "Chils rois d'Engleterre dont je parole, qui rechut ce grant blame et damage devant Struvelin en Escoce eut deux freres de remariage, desquels li uns estoit appellés li contes Marescaus et fu homs de sauvages et diverse maniere. Li aultres avoit nom Ainmons et fu contes de Kent, vaillans homs et preudoms" [This king of England of whom I speak, who received this great reproach and harm before Struvelin in Scotland, had two brothers by remarriage, of whom one was named the count of Marescaus and was a man of wild and unusual manners. The other was named Ainmons and was count of Kent, a valiant and worthy man] (Fr. 45); "Chil rois Edouwars eut de sa fenme la roine Issabiel, fille au biau roi Phelippe deus fils et deus filles des quels li aisnné ot nom Edouwars . . . Li secons des fils ot nom Jehan de Eltem . . . Li ainnee des filles ot nom Issabiel . . . " [This King Edward had of his wife, Queen Isabel, the daughter of the fair King Philip, two sons and two daughters, of whom the eldest was named Edward . . . The second son was named Jehan de Eltem . . . The eldest daughter was named Isabel . . .] (Fr. 45); "Li biaus rois Phelippes de France ot trois fils avoecques celle dame Issabiel qui fu roine d'Engleterre . . . Si eut a nom li ainnés Loys . . . " [The fair King Philip of France had three sons with that lady Isabel who was queen of England . . . The eldest was named Louis . . .] (Fr. 45–46).

The other personages will be contextually fixed in relation to them: "Phelippe de Valois, fils jadis a mesire Carle, le conte de Valois et frere a ce biau roi Phelippe de desus dit" [Philip of Valois, in those days son of mesire Charles, the count of Valois and brother of that fair King Philip already mentioned] (Fr. 46); "avoit deus jones filles en France, desquelles li rois Carles estoit oncles. . . . Ces deus filles, li une fu depuis duçoise d'Orliiens et li aultre, Margerite, contesse de Flandres et d'Artois" [had two young daughters in France, of whom King Charles was the uncle. . . . Of these two daughters, one was later the duchess of Orleans and the other, Marguerite, the countess of Flanders and of Artois] (Fr. 51).

One does, of course, encounter numerous personages who cannot be attached to the two pivots that are Edward I and Philippe le Bel. The most frequently employed mode of introduction is then that of fiction: *a N + PN*, with the qualification that in the first part of the syntagm *a N* a place-name will often appear, one given abruptly like all the place-names in these narratives; the historical personages are defined also by their rule over a territory: "un conte d'Artois qui s'appeloit Robers" (fr. 41); "li rois d'Escoce, qui se nonma Robers de Brus" (Fr. 43), who later becomes "ce rois Robert de Brus" (Fr. 44). One also meets, with or without indication of origin, "uns chevaliers qui se nonma messire Rogier de Mortemer" (Fr. 50), and "un chevalier de Cambresis qui se nonmoit li sires d'Esne" (Fr. 57). Hugues Spencer, for example, is also introduced according to the traditional model of fiction *a N + PN:* "Et avoit dalès lui un chevalier, grant baron en Engleterre et rice honme et son cousin, lequel on nommoit messire Hue le Espensier" [and he had next to him a knight, a great noble in England and a rich man and his cousin, who was named messire Hugh le Espensier] (Fr. 47); he will later become "li dis messires Hues" (Fr. 48), "ce Hue le Espensier" (Fr. 49).

The abrupt use of a supposedly known proper name, frequent in Joinville, does not occur in Froissart. Here, when a proper name is introduced for the first time, it is immediately accompanied by a referential expansion such as "pape Jehan, qui, pour ce temps, resgnoit et demoroit en Avignon" [Pope John, who, in this period, reigned and resided in Avignon] (Fr. 52), where the relative carries simultaneously a discursive referential anchorage—"ce temps"—and a proper name of place; or in "le conte Thomas de Lancastre, qui estoit ses oncles" [count Thomas of Lancaster, who was his uncle] (Fr. 48), where the relative bears the anaphora of a referential pivot.

Finally, we find in Froissart, as in Joinville, nominative lists, but these are not made up of proper names abruptly introduced; rather, they proceed always by the indication of a title followed by the place-name: "et manda le signeur d'Antoing, le senescal de Hainnau, le signeur de Ligne, le signeur de Bailleul, le signeur de Barbançon, le signeur de Haverech, le signeur de Gonmegnies, le signeur de Vertain et moult d'autres" [and he sent the lord of Antoing . . . and many others] (Fr. 59). Instead of Joinville's effect of connivance (lost today), we find reestablished a sort of reference that is partially contextual: "the lord of X who lived in the times of the recounted events."

Thus, contrary to Joinville's usage, Froissart establishes a very explanatory, elaborate referenciation, in which one begins from what is known to introduce new personages, and where each is defined by the place that is his, the period in which he lives, his family relations. However, the introduction *a N + PN*, of a fictional nature, is not rare: it is no doubt indispensable, even in factual narratives.

Now this "fictional" construction of reference (the word will henceforth be set off in quotes, as we have shown that it is not excluded from historical texts) in *a N + PN*, which Joinville reserves for humble personages and Saracens and Froissant uses to introduce secondary characters, is the dominant construction of *Mélusine*, where it is utilized to establish—in fact, to create altogether—the primordial personages, the founding ancestors who will thereafter become referential pivots: "Il est verité qu'il ot jadis *un roy* en Albanie qui fut moult vaillans homs. Et dit l'ystoire qu'il ot de sa premiere femme pluseurs enfans, dont l'ystoire dit que Mataquas, qui fu pere Florimont, fu ses premiers filz. *Cellui roy ot a nom Elinas* et fu moult puissant et preux chevaliers de sa main" [It is the truth that there was formerly a king in Albania who was a very valiant man. And the story says that of his first wife he had several children, of which the story says that Mataquas, later Florimont's father, was his first son. That king was named Elinas, and he was a very powerful and courageous knight] (*M* 5);[10] "La vraye histoire nous raconte qu'il ot jadiz en la Brute Bretaigne *un noble homme*, lequel ot riote au nepveu du roy des Bretons. . . . et s'en vint sur haultes montaignes marchissans aux reffuges du Rosne. . . . Or advint que les nobles de son pays lui pourveirent une bien haulte gentilz femme, qui estoit sereur du conte de Poictiers qui pour le temps regna. Et en ot pluseurs enfans masles. Entre les autres, il y en ot *un*, le tiers, que on appella *Remondin*" [The true story tells us that there was formerly in Brittany a noble man, who had a quarrel with the nephew of the king of the Bretons. . . . and he came upon high mountains bordering on the Rhone basin. . . . Now it happened that the nobles of his land arranged for him to marry a very noble woman who was the sister of the then count of Poitiers. He had several male children. Among them, there was one, the third, that they named Raymondin] (*M* 15).

Not only is the construction of the type *a N + PN*, the proper name being here far removed from the indefinite syntagm—for "un noble homme" the proper name is given only several pages later, in Melusine's narrative—by which means the narrator effects the extraction of an element "roi d'Albanie" or "noble homme"; he also introduces them by means of the segment "ot jadis," equivalent to the initial segment of tales: "il était une fois" [once upon a time there was . . .] which Genette calls an invitation to enter into the fictional universe, an operator that strangely resembles the one used in mathematical language "Let there be a triangle ABC" (*Fiction et diction*, 49–52). In the second example, there occurs a redoubling of the operation: invitation to the fiction with "ot jadis," then a singling out from an ensemble: "Entre les autres, il y en ot un, le tiers, que on appela Remondin" [among the others, there was one, the third, that they named Raymondin].[11]

The proper name is not, moreover, always given at the time of the creation of the character but may appear surreptitiously, as in the case of the name of Presine, which appears for the first time in the direct discourse of her stepson: "Ma dame la royne Presine, vostre femme" [my lady the queen Presine, your wife] (*M* 9).[12] So too for the count of Poitiers, who is defined as "the count of Poitiers ruling when Raymondin was fourteen or fifteen years old" and who without warning becomes, a dozen lines later, "le conte Aymerys de Poictiers" (*M* 16). As for Melusine herself, upon her second appearance in the romance, she is simply "la plus seignourie" of the three ladies of the forest and—although we have recognized her, but hadn't we already recognized her in the lady of Forez?—she does not receive her proper name, here again in direct discourse, until the ceremonies of her marriage to Raymondin: "Sire, ma damoiselle Melusigne d'Albanie se recommande a vous tant qu'elle puet" [Sire, my lady Melusine of Albanie extends her warmest welcome] (*M* 38). Until that point, she had been named "la dame"—"the lady"—and Raymondin was said to have wished to marry without knowing who she was.

The opposite occasionally occurs, when the personage is introduced in the fictional universe by a discourse reported in direct style: "Nostre roy si a une moult belle fille" [Our king has a very beautiful daughter] (*M* 93), then the proper name is given in the narrative: "Hermine, la fille du roy de Chippre" [Hermine, the daughter of the king of Cyprus] (*M* 96). Here too, a very literary procedure.

The other principal personages appear by filiation (as in historical narrative), but contrary to case in historical narrative, these filiations appear not in retrospection but in the natural progression of the narrative: "Or il advint qu'elle fu enceinte de trois filles et les porta son terme et delivra au jour. La premiere nee ot a nom Melusigne, la seconde Melior, la tierce Palestine" [Now it happened that she was pregnant with three daughters, and carried them to term and delivered when the time came. The first-born was named Melusine, the second Melior, the third Palestine] (*M* 9). The children of Lusignan are all introduced in the same way: "Et estoit pour lors la dame enceinte, et porta son terme, et acoucha a son jour de son second enfant, et fu un filz, et fu baptisiez, et ot a nom Eudes" (*M* 78); "Et, au second an aprez, ot un filz qui fu nommez Guyon" (*M* 78); "ou cinquiesme an après, ot Melusigne un filz qui fu nommez Anthoine" [Then the lady was pregnant, and came to term, and gave birth to her second child; it was a son, and was baptised, and was named Eudes. . . . And the second year thereafter, she had a son who was named Guyon. . . . in the fifth year thereafter, Melusine had a son who was named Antoine] (*M* 79).

Only the secondary personages are presented as being defined by the form *title + PN of the region:* "le roy de Chippre, le soubdan de Damas" (*M* 81); "le maistre de Rodes" (*M* 90); "le gallaffre de Bandas" (*M* 127), which is to be understood as "qui pour lors estoient"—in contextual reference. It is only after their introduction in this way that they sometimes receive a forename: "le roy Gallaffrin de Damiette" (*M* 223).

In fact, in spite of its protestations of historicity, *Mélusine* creates a closed fictional universe in which the personages are posited by means of the fictional connector "il ot jadis," a closed universe within which reference is constructed. The only extra-discursive references found in Jean d'Arras are references to real personages: Jehan (. . .), duc de Berry et d'Ouvergne (*M* 1); Gervaise (*M* 3) (Gervaise of Tilbury), Cersuelle (*M* 308) (Creswell); Yvain de Galles (*M* 309): Jean d'Arras distinguishes perfectly well between the fictional universe and the real world.

Status of Reported Discourse

Perhaps even more than the construction of reference, the status of reported discourse will be pertinent to the definition of fictional writing: in effect, by virtue of the fact that it is creation and not reproduction, fiction can allow itself a great deal of direct discourse, which the historian would have been unable to record. In principle also—but we shall see that it is not the case in fact—only fiction, which can allow itself to focalize subjective states, should be able to include free indirect discourse.

The more a narrative pretends to render an objective account of events that really took place, the more it will reproduce the discourse that really occurred in *indirect style*, which does not pretend to literarity, or in narrativized discourse.[13] Now the importance of indirect discourse is in constant regression from Joinville (approximately 13 percent of the text) to Froissart (approximately 10 percent) and from Froissart to *Mélusine* (less than 1 percent),[14] at the same time that the space accorded to direct discourse increases and that one passes from factual writing to fictional writing.

In Joinville, indirect discourse occupies approximately 13 percent of the text. It is true that the testimonies that found the authenticity of the narrative are recorded in indirect style: "et disoit l'on que la royne Blanche le besoit ou front par devocion, pour ce que elle entendoit que sa mere l'i avoit maintes fois besié" [and people said that queen Blanche kissed him on the forehead by devotion, because she had heard that her mother had kissed him thus many times] (J. §96); "Mais j'oy dire que avec la terre [que] li roys emporta, [li quita li cuens de la Marche] dis mille livres de parisis que il avoit en ses cofres, et chascun an autant" [But I heard it said that with the land that the king claimed, he paid the count of la Marche ten thousand pounds in parisis from his coffers, and so much again every year] (J. §103). But numerous discourses by the protagonists of the seventh Crusade are also reported in this oblique fashion.

And if it is often said that indirect style—including complex sentences with many subordinate clauses—is difficult to handle for medieval authors, such is not at all the case for Joinville, who does not shrink from the use of complex propositions: "il respondi que il n'en vourroit mie avoit tiex mil, puis que il ne vousissent ouvrer de son commandement, aussi comme il avoit fait" [he replied that he would not at all wish to have such a thousand, since they would not want to carry out his order, as he had issued it] (J. §176) is one example among many. Joinville also handles without problems sequences in indirect discourse: "Et les barons li manderent et prierent que il son cors se vousist traire arieres, et il se iroient combatre au conte de Champaingne et au duc de Lorreinne (. . .) Et le roy leur manda que a sa gent ne se combattroient-il ja que son cors ne feust avec. Et il renvoyerent a li et li manderent que il feroient volentiers entendre la royne de Cypre a paiz, se il li plaisoit. Et le roy leur manda que a nulle paiz il n'entendroit ne souferoit que le conte de Champaingne y entendit, tant que il eussent vuidié la contée de Champaingne" [And the lords sent messengers to him and requested that he consent to withdraw, and they would go to fight against the count of Champagne and the duke of Lorraine. And the king decreed to them that they were not to fight against his people until he himself was present. And they sent him back word that they would gladly hear the queen of Cyprus in peace, if he pleased. And the king sent word to them that he would not hear of or allow any peace that the count of Champagne figured in, until they had emptied the county of Champagne] (J. §85).

Such sequences are much more rare in Froissart (approximately 3 percent less indirect discourse than in Joinville), but they can be found: "il li fu demandé ou l'abbé et li monne estoient. Il respondi que il ne savoit, et que il les quidoit ou moustier. Dont li fu dit que il les alast querre et asegurer, car il ne lor voloient que tout bien" [He was asked where the abbot and the monks were. He replied that he did not know, and that he thought they were in the monastery. Then he was told to go to seek and reassure them, for he wished them nothing but good] (Fr. 78). Froissart, however, prefers more varied sequences: indirect discourse + direct discourse, or the opposite.[15] And we have not found these sequences of indirect discourse in Jean d'Arras, for whom discourse reported in indirect style is most often limited to a single proposition.

In effect, in *Mélusine* indirect discourse occupies no more, in the first fifty pages (excepting the prologue), than twenty three lines of the 1867 lines of text, or 0.8 percent (to Joinville's 13 percent); this is a tiny proportion, especially if we think that in certain cases indirect discourse is obligatory, for example "nous dictes qui elle est" [Tell us who she is] (*M* 36). One notes that indirect discourse is used especially for reporting intransitive thought: "et dist a lui mesmes qu'il n'avoit oncques veu si riche" [he said to himself that he had never seen anything so rich] (*M* 7); "et disoit a soy mesmes que c'est quelque fantosme qu'il a trouvee a la Fontaine de Soif" [he said to himself that it was some phantom that he had found at the Fountain of Thirst] (*M* 37), and for discourse attributed to the public voice, to "what they say": "Et bien dient ly aucun que oncques mais n'avoient veu si estrange chace ne si merveilleuse, ne senglier courir si estrangement. Et disoient pluseurs que c'estoit un senglier estrange et forpassez de ses repaires . . . et tousjours venoient gens qui tousjours disoient comme les autres, et que ilz s'estoient esgarez toute la nuit contreval la forest." [And some said that they had never seen such a strange and marvellous hunt, nor a boar run so strangely. And many said that it was a boar from elsewhere, away from its usual territory. . . . and other people came who all said the same thing as the others, and that they had been lost all night down in the forest] (*M* 28). But even in these cases, Jean d'Arras so much favors direct discourse that it appears both in interior discourse—"Quant Uriien le voit, si fu moult doulens, et dist a soy mesmes: Par foy, c'est grant dommage que ce Turc ne croit en Dieu, car il est moult preux" [When Urian saw it, he was very sorrowful, and said to himself: By my faith, it is a great pity that this Turk does not believe in God, for he is very valiant] (*M* 112)—

and to report discourse attributed to the public voice: "Et quant les gens percoivent la fierté de son visaige, si dient: Cilz homs est dignes de soubzmettre tout le monde en son obeissance. Par foy, dient ly autre, il le monstre bien, car il est entré en ceste cité comme se il l'eust conquise. En nom Dieu, dient les autres, la rescousse du dangier dont il nous a ostez vault assez conqueste. Par foy, dit uns autres, combien que son frere n'ait pas si fiere phizonomie si semble il bien homme de haulte emprise" [And when the people noted the fierceness of his countenance, they said: This man is worthy of subjugating the whole world under his rule. In faith, said the others, he shows it well, for he entered this city as if he had conquered it. In God's name, said others, rescue from the danger from which he has removed us is worth as much as conquest. By faith, said another, although his brother does not have such a fierce physiognomy he certainly seems a man of high deeds] (*M* 117).

Direct discourse increases proportionally as indirect discourse decreases and as we come closer to fictional writing. It is, however, quite well represented in the historical texts and even in Joinville (slightly less than 9 percent), where its presence can almost always be justified. Thus, for example, it can represent a citation and its translation: "'Ad te levavi animam meam' . . . et [dit] ainsi 'Biau sire Diex, je leverai m'amme à toy, je me fie en toy' [and says thus: "Good lord God, I will raise up my soul to thee, I trust in thee"] (J. §70), "words" that demand to be cited textually, like these phrases that the Saracen mothers say to their children: "'Taiziez-vous, vez-ci le roy Richart . . . '" "'Cuides-tu que ce soit le roy Richart?'" ["Be quiet, see there King Richard . . . " "Do you think that it is King Richard?"] (J. §76), and interjections: "'Or a eulz, de par Dieu! car ce ne porroie-je plus soufrir'" ["Now have at them, for God's sake! for I could not bear it any longer"] (J. §186), but also in the dialogues, insignificant but animated, that seem to have been recorded as they were produced, for example the moment of embarcation: "Quant les chevaus furent ens, nostre mestre notonniers escria à ses notonniers qui estoient au bec de la nef et leur dist: 'Est aré[e] vostre besoigne?' [Et il respondirent 'Oil,] sire; vieingnent avant les clers et les proveres.' Maintenant que il furent venu, il leur escria 'Chantez, de par Dieu!' Et il s'escrierent touz a une voiz: 'Veni creator Spiritus.'" "Et il escria à ses notonniers: 'Faites voille, de par Dieu!' Et il si firent."

[After the horses were aboard, our master sailor cried out to his sailors who were in the fore of the ship and said to them: "Is your task completed?" [And they replied "Yes,] sire; let the clerics and priests come forward." As soon as they had come, he cried to them "Sing, for God's sake!" And they all cried out in unison, "Veni creator Spiritus." And he cried to his sailors: "Raise the sail, for God's sake!" And so they did] (J. §126). For this example one can raise the question of the reliability of memory: to what extent was this dialogue, to us trivial, of the utmost importance to Joinville on the verge of setting out on the unknown element, to the point that these very routine words uttered at that moment would have been emblazoned in his memory?

In principle, factual writing should stop there, with the exception of the reproduction of written texts. The reproduction of long discourses dear to archaic history, which is reconstitution, indeed invention, should be excluded from any narrative pretension to veracity.

It doesn't work out that way, even in the good Joinville who reconstitutes important pronouncements in direct discourse: his official speech to his men before leaving on crusade (§111); the failure of Saint Louis to respect the custom of dividing two-thirds of the booty among the pilgrims (§167–69); as well as discourses of less historicity: the cleric and the robbers (§116–18); a testimony concerning the abbot of Cheminon and the Virgin Mary (§120). One suspects, however, that it is we who attribute a lesser degree of historicity to these discourses that Joinville considered worthy of the status of official words. The majority of the anecdotes in the section devoted to "deeds and words of Saint Louis" (a section not included in my count) are in direct discourse, which would confirm the hypothesis that Joinville used this mode of reported discourse for remarks that he judged too important not to attempt to reproduce them textually.

In Froissart (in whose text direct and indirect discourse are practically equally represented, with a bit more than 10 percent for indirect, a bit more than 11.5 percent for direct), the use of direct discourse is no longer justifiable as in Joinville. Even if it is sometimes necessary to report a clever word literally—"On li demanda pourquoi elle ploroit: 'Por ce, dist elle, que mon biau cousin Edouwars d'Engleterre se depart de moi et je l'avoie ja apris'" [They asked her why she was weeping: "Because," she said, "my fair cousin Edward of England is leaving me and I have just learned it"] (Fr. 70)—it appears especially, in fact uniquely, to fulfill the literary objective of animating the narrative, as in the two following insignificant discourses: "Adont dist li contes a son frere 'Jehan, cevauciés jusques a Buignicourt, et nous amenés nostre cousine la roine d'Engleterre: nous le voulons festoiier en nostre pais.' Li sires de Biaumont respondi 'Volentiers.'" [Then the count said to his brother, "Jehan, ride to Buignicourt, and bring us back our cousin the queen of England; we want to entertain her in our country." The lord of Biaumont replied, "Gladly"] (Fr. 59).

But the inflation of direct discourse is especially notable in *Mélusine*, where it occupies slightly more than one line in three (approximately 34 percent). One finds insignificant dialogues rendered in direct style: "et dist le conte a Remondin: 'Beau nepveu, nous demourrons cy tant que la lune sera levee.' Remondin dist: 'Si comme il vous plaira, monseigneur'" [and the count said to Raymondin: "Good nephew, we shall remain here until the moon has risen." Raymondin said: "As it pleases you, my lord"] (*M* 19), instead of "they decided to remain until the moon had risen"; or else: "il encontra un homme qui portoit un sac sur son col, qui lui vint a l'encontre et lui dist: 'Sire, acheterez vous ce cuir de cerf que je tiens en mon sac? On en fera bonnes cottes chasseresses pour voz veneurs.' 'Par foy,' dist Remondin, 'oïl, se tu veulz; et que me coustera il, ainsi qu'il est?' 'Par Dieu, sire, vous en payerés cent solz, se vous voulez.' 'Amis,' dist Remondin, 'apporte le a mon hostel, et je te paieray.' Et cil dist: 'Voulentiers.'" [he met a man carrying a sack on his back, who came toward him and said: "Sire, will you buy this deer hide that I have in my sack? From it one will make good hunting boots for your hunters." "By my faith," said Raymondin, "yes, if you wish; and what will it cost me, just as it is?" "By God, sire, you shall pay one hundred sous, if it please you." "Friend," said Raymondin, "take it to my lodging and I shall pay you." And the man said: "Gladly"] (*M* 33)—instead of "he bought some leather from a man who was passing by." This is because direct discourse here has a function of animating the narrative, where Jean d'Arras's art of storytelling is evident. These utterances would be unthinkable in a factual narrative, where only highly significant utterances are retained.

One finds also in Jean d'Arras's romance long constructed discourses corresponding to classical rhetorical conceptions, such as Melusine's discourse to her children (edifying admonishments) that occupies almost four pages (*M* 84–88). We also encounter retrospections in direct discourse, such as the story of Hervy de Leon, the founding ancestor who is of a human nature, recounted in direct discourse by Melusine to Raymondin (*M* 48–50) and then by Raymondin to the king of Brittany (*M* 57–59), whence the inclusion of reported discourse, always in direct style, at the third level.[16] The direct discourse is sometimes also a monologue (a fact that will be considered in the following section concerning interior processes); thus, in the first pages, there occurs a long lament over the death of the count of Poitiers that reproduces the movements of Raymondin's state of mind rather than his words (*M* 22–23).

One can thus observe that in the historical romance of Jean d'Arras: 1) direct discourse no longer pretends to be the textual reproduction of utterances actually pronounced but rather involves an erasure of the I-origin of the narrator to the benefit of the personages; and 2) direct discourse is the object of such an inflation that it assumes functions that should be those of the narrating voice (what Käte Hamburger calls the narrative function): retrospection and the description of psychological processes. The fictional displacement of the I-origin of the characters results in an effacement, to their profit, of the narrative function.

Psychological Processes

This third point will merely be evoked in passing. It appears on first perusal that, considered as such, the presence or absence of verbs, nouns, or adjectives describing psychological processes is not pertinent in distinguishing history from fiction: Froissart makes considerable use of the exposition of inner motivation, and "psychological" verbs are not rare in his work. *La vie de Saint Louis*, on the other hand, contains virtually no incursion into the psychology of the characters, no indication of interiority, including that of the narrator. Michel Zink some time ago called attention to one of the rare psychological processes of the text—"je ne voz onques retourner mes yex vers Joinville pource que le cuer ne me attendrisist du biau chastel que je lessoie et de mes deus enfans" [I want never to turn my eyes back toward Joinville, so that my heart not be saddened on account of the fair castle that I left behind and my two children] (J. §122)—to show to what degree emotion is contained

and appears only by paralipsis.[17] Let us note in addition the joy experienced in discovering that the count of Poitiers is alive ("Lors fu la joie si grant comme elle pot estre plus entre nous" [Then the joy was a great as it could be among us]) (J. §389), but the misery of the prisoners, the fear of the Queen, who had remained in Damietta, and the sufferings of illness are always described in a purely objective manner. An action—the Queen who asks an elderly knight to sleep near her bed (J. §387–88) or Joinville who weeps each time he hears the "libera me domine" announcing a new death (J. §415)—alone betrays the intensity of an emotion never *said.*

Is this owing to the temperament of the good Joinville, to an extroverted and observant nature little inclined to introspection? Possibly; but in any case, one finds oneself in the presence of an objective writing, typical of what should be a purely factual account.

In Froissart, on the other hand, psychological notations are found to be quite correctly represented, and we notice also that the work of the historian (Joinville is not a historian but a camera!) requires the observation of psychological processes. How, in fact, does one justify the actions of men, those actions that make history, without talking of the tastes, the hopes, and the fears that motivated them?

Thus, the *Chroniques* begin by painting the character and the sentiments of the English, given in the present tense as general truth: "Englés sont de mervilleuse conditions, chaut et boullant, tos esmeu en ire, tart apaisié ne amodé en douçour; et se delittent et confortent en batailles et en ocisions. Convoiteus et enveius sont trop grandement sus le bien d'autrui" [The English are of a remarkable nature, hot and boiling, quickly moved to anger, slow to be calmed or moved to gentleness; and they delight and take comfort in battles and killing. They are exceedingly covetous and envious of the goods of others] (Fr. prologue, 42). One may again, in this case, speak of an outward glance, of generalizations about observations. But Froissart is very quickly led to reconstruct plausible psychological processes, which he renders by thoughts reported in oblique propositions: "La roine d'Engleterre veoit que li contes de Hainnau et la contesse li faisoient tant d'onnour que plus ne l'en pooient faire; si en looit Dieu et regratioit grandement *en soi meismes*, car elle esperoit bien que par euls et les Hainnuiers, elle seroit confortee et adrechie, ensi que elle fu si grandement, comme vous orés

recorder avant en l'istore" [The queen of England saw that the count of Hainault and the countess did her as much honor as they possibly could; she praised God for it and was greatly thankful *within herself*, for she had great hopes that through them and the people of Hainaut, she would be comforted and redressed, just as she was, in large measure, as you will hear further along in the story] (Fr. 67) and even in free indirect discourse: "Quand messires Hues li Espensiers en fu enfourmés, si se doubta grandement que la poissance dou roi de France ne le fesist tresbuchier jus de ses estas, car bien imaginoit au fort [que] ses sires li rois d'Engleterre n'oseroit courouchier le roi de France. *Et encores oultre, se cette aliance se faisoit, que le jones Edouwars d'Engleterre fust mariés en France et presist sa cousine germainne, il ne poroit longement estre ne demorer que, dou costé de France, il n'euist a faire,* avoecques tout ce encores que il sentoit bien que moult estoit hais en Engleterre" [When my lord Hugh li Espensier was informed of it, he feared greatly that the power of the king of France would cause him to be deposed, for he well imagined that his lord the king of England would not dare to anger the king of France. *And even more that if the alliance came about that the young Edward of England were to be married in France and take his first cousin, he could not long remain there for, on the French side, he would be powerless*, and with all that, moreover, he felt he was much hated in England] (Fr. 51).[18]

The appearance of free indirect discourse, very frequent in Froissart, is, let us recall, considered by Käte Hamburger as characteristic of the writing of fiction. This process of notation of inner discourse goes beyond the reconstruction of a plausible interiority. We should thus no doubt distinguish two types of description of psychological processes: the reconstruction of plausible motives of an action may appear in factual writing, while the depiction of successive emotions, internal deliberations, and contradictory reactions to an affect, especially minimal ones, would be reserved for fictional writing.

Psychological notations are not more rare in Jean d'Arras than in Froissart; they are even a bit more frequent in *Mélusine* than in the *Chroniques.* It may be a question of an isolated notation: "ly contes ot grant paour que ly porcs n'affoulast son nepveu" [The count was very fearful that the boar might attack his nephew] (*M* 19); "Remondin, ainsi pensif et plein d'ennuy et de meschief qui luy estoit advenu, qu'il ne savoit ou il aloit" [Raymondin, so thoughtful and full of grief and the misfortune that had befallen him that he did not know where he was going] (*M* 24) with occasionally an oblique construction, following a verb of reported thought: "une voix qui chantoit si melodieusement que il ne cuida pas pour l'eure que ce ne feust voix angelique, maiz toutes foiz il entendy assez . . . que c'estoit voiz femmenine" [a voice that was singing so melodiously that he thought for a moment it was none other than an angelic voice, but at the same time he heard well enough . . . that it was a feminine voice] (*M* 6). Or it may render complex interior processes: La contesse et ses enfans font grant dueil, le peuple et tous les barons font grant dueil, et en seurquetout Remondin fait greigneur dueil que tous les autres, *et se repentoit tant de son meffait que se ne feust l'esperance du confort qu'il prenoit de sa dame, il ne se peust estre tenus qu'il ne leur eust dit sa mesaventure, pour la grant contrition qu'il avoit de la mort son seigneur*" [The countess and her children mourned greatly, the people and all the nobles mourned greatly and especially Raymondin mourned more than all the others, *and repented so much of his misdeed that had it not been for the hope of comfort that he had from his lady, he could not have refrained from telling them of his misadventure, on account of his great contrition for the death of his lord*] (*M* 28–29); "Cy vous lerray d'eulx et diray de Gieffroy, *qui moult fut doulent de ce qu'il ot par son pechié ainsi perdu son pere et sa mere . . . Dont remort conscience a Gieffroy, et lui souvient comment il avoit ars les moynes de Maleres, et l'abbé, et son frere Fromont, sans raison, et que par ce pechié avoit esté sa mere perdue. Puis lui ramembre de son oncle le conte de Forests, lequel li fist saillir de la grosse tour de Marcelli le Chastel sur la roche, et le fist tuer. Lors commenca Gieffroy fort a penser a ses pechiez. Et dist bien que, se Diu n'a pitié de lui, l'ame de lui est en grant peril et en voye de dampnacion.* Lors entra Gieffroy en une chambre, et commence a mener grant doulour et a plourer ses pechiez. *Et la lui prist devocion d'aler a Romme confesser au Saint Pere*" [I will leave off speaking of them and tell of Geoffroy, *who was greatly sorrowful that through his sin he had thus lost his father and mother . . . For this his conscience troubled him, and he remembered how he had burned the monks of Maleres, and the abbot, and his brother Fromont, without reason, and that his mother was lost on account of this sin. Then he remembered his uncle the count of Forest, whom he had had hurled from the large tower of the Castle of Marcelli down to the rock and killed. Then Geoffroy began to think intently about his sins. And he said that, if God did not take pity on him, his soul was in great peril and risk of damnation.* Then Geoffroy entered a chamber and began to grieve greatly and to weep for his sins. *And he committed himself to go to Rome to confess to the Holy Father*] (*M* 274).

However, the grief of Elinas over the loss of his wife is described through external observation: "il ne faisoit que plaindre, gemir et souspirer, et faire griefz lamentacions" [he did nothing but moan, groan, sigh, and utter woeful laments] (*M* 10). Also in external observation is the description of the ambiguous sentiments that trouble princess Hermine: "Quant Hermine ouy celle nouvelle, elle ot si grant joye ou cuer qu'elle ne scot que faire. Mais elle n'en monstra nul semblant. Ains monstre qu'elle sente grant douleur ou cuer, et si faisoit elle. Lors prent congié de son pere, et le baise doulcement tout en plourant. Et s'en vint en sa chambre, et la commence a lui complaindre de la doulour que elle ot de son pere, et l'autre heure a grant desir qu'elle a de veoir Uriien, dont la demeure lui tarde. Et fu en ces pensers telement arguee que toute la nuit ne dormy oncques, et ainsi se passa la nuitiee jusques a l'endemain" [When Hermine heard this news, she felt such great joy in her heart that she did not know what to do. But she gave no sign of that. Rather, she showed that she felt great sorrow in her heart, and indeed she did. Then she took leave of her father, kissing him tenderly and weeping all the while. She went to her room, and there began to lament of the sorrow that she felt on account of her father, and then again of her great desire to see Urian, for whose arrival she was impatient. She was so torn by these thoughts that she did not sleep at all that night, and thus the night passed until the next day] (*M* 116). Her pain is exteriorized and we see that the expression of her contradictory sentiments is rendered by a brief monologue in indirect discourse.[19] Reported discourse is again the means most frequently employed to transcribe psychological processes, the sentiments that affect the characters of the fiction. Omnipresent in the unfolding of the narrative—used abundantly to name characters, for clarifications and retrospections, and to transmit the narrator's ethic and ideology—the direct style also contributes largely to the representation of emotions. The sentiments of the young Melusine who desires to take vengeance on her father are given in direct style; in direct style too are the emotions of the count of Poitiers, who reads his destiny in the stars, and the despair of Raymondin who has killed his uncle. We may also recall the heart-rending monologues and dialogues of Melusine and Raymondin at the moment of the curse and their separation (*M* 253, 255, 256, 257, 259).

At the end of this analysis, we can see clearly how Jean d'Arras situates himself deliberately on the side of fiction. This appears in the system of reference he adopts, drawing his characters from nowhere to establish them later as referential pivots internal to the text, as well as in his systematic use of reported discourse in direct style as an element of narrative progression. This use of direct style is contrary to historical objectivity and displaces the I-origin, from the narrator toward his personages, to whom, moreover, is delegated a part of the narrative function.

On the other hand, the paucity of elements expressing psychological processes does not seem convincing. Scarcely more frequent in the texts of fiction than in the historical texts, it attests instead to a system of representations in which interior analysis still has little place. One could almost propose as a hypothesis for further research that the description of sentiments and emotions might predominate in factual narratives: confronted with the stubbornness of facts, a need for clarification would arise, a need for justification a posteriori, useless in fiction, where the narrator remains the master of causes and effects. As with Chrétien de Troyes, novelistic writing at its origins is still unsuited for the description of sentiments and affects by focalization on internal processes, and prefers to utilize the procedure of the monologue in direct style. Only with the liberation of free indirect style and its proliferation will the complex play of fictional intrusions gain the upper hand.[20]

Notes

1. John Searle, "Le statut logique du discours de la fiction," in *Sens et expression* (Paris: Minuit, 1982).

2. Käte Hamburger, *Logique des genres littéraires* (Paris: Seuil, 1986); trans. of *Logik der Dichtung*, 1977; Gérard Genette, *Fiction et diction* (Paris: Seuil, 1991).

3. Genette, *Fiction*, 92: "les différences les plus nettes semblent affecter essentiellement les allures modales les plus étroitement liées à l'opposition entre le savoir relatif de l'historien et l'omniscience élastique dont jouit par définition celui qui invente ce qu'il raconte."

4. "le plus caractéristique de tous car il imprègne à la limite la totalité du discours, qu'il réfère insidieusement à la conscience du personnage" (76).

5. Jean Froissart, *Chroniques*, final draft of the first book; MS Rome Reg. lat. 869, ed. George T. Diller (Geneva-Paris: Droz-Minard, 1972), cited as Fr.

6. Joinville, *La vie de saint Louis*, ed. Noël L. Corbett (Québec: Naaman, 1977), cited as J.

7. See Michèle Perret, *L'Enonciation en grammaire du texte* (Paris: Nathan, 1994), 28.

8. Also appearing in situational references are the wars of Flanders which provide the story with an initial date: "apriés l'apaisement des guerres de Flandres" [after the Flemish wars abated] (Fr. 41).

9. This procedure exists, in embryonic fashion, in Joinville, where it remains very clumsy (J. 89, 92).

10. The minimum characterizers: "preux," "puissant," "vaillant" are introduced only to attenuate the suddenness of a pure and simple predication of existence.

11. The same holds for other personages: "En ceste partie dit l'ystoire que ens es parties de Allemaigne, entre l'Ostheriche et Ardeine, avoit en ce temps une moult noble terre nommée la terre de la conté de Lucembourc (. . .) Pour l'eure que je dy, avoit mort un moult vaillant prince qui fu nommé Assellin, lequel fu sire d'icellui pays. Et n'avoit demouré de lui nul hoir que une seule fille, laquelle estoit nommée Crestienne" [In this part the story tells that in Germany, between Austria and the Ardennes, there was at that time a very noble land called the land of the county of Luxembourg . . . At the time of which I tell, there had died a very valiant prince named Asselin, the lord of that land. He had no heir except a single daughter, who was named Crestienne] (*M* 146); "il ot, grant temps après le trespas du roy Guion, un roy en Armenie" [There was, a long time after the death of king Guion, a king in Armenie] (*M* 302).

12. Presine is first presented anonymously: "apperceut la tres plus belle dame qu'il eust oncques jour veu" [he perceived the most beautiful lady that he had ever seen] (*M* 6); then she is created by the discourse of Elinas.

13. *Discours narrativisé* (G. Genette, *Figure III*, 19) refers to verbs of speech implying that discourse took place but in no case giving the content, even in summary, of that discourse: for example, "s'excuser, prendre congié, mercier, conjoïr" [excuse oneself, take leave, thank, welcome].

14. These counts, as well as those pertaining to direct discourse, have been done manually, counting by lines and half-lines, on the first fifty pages of each text, not taking into account the prologues and, for Joinville, the first part about the king's words. Even approximate—one would need in fact a count by sign for the totality of the text—they indicate an order of magnitude, and the difference between *Mélusine* and the other texts is very significant.

15. "Et leur dist que elle et ses fils leur feroient droit et loi et bon jugement selonch lors fais et lors oevres. Adont respondi messires Hues et dist 'Ha! madame, Dieus nous voelle donner bon juge et bon jugement'" [And she told them that she and her son would render them justice and law and good judgment according to their deeds and their works. Then my lord Hugh replied and said "Ah! Madam, may God grant us a good judge and good judgment"]

(Fr. 85); "'Madame, monsigneur mon frere et madame ma soer la contesse de Hainnau vous prient et par moi que vous les venés veoir et lors enfans.' La roine respondi et dist que, de ce faire elle estoit toute preste." ["Madam, my lord brother and my lady sister the countess of Hainaut request of you through me that you come to see them and their children." The queen replied that she was quite ready] (Fr. 61).

16. Discourse of the third level: discourse reported within reported discourse. See for example *M* 49.

17. Michel Zink, "Joinville ne pleure pas, il rêve," *Poétique* 33 (1978): 28–45.

18. Another example: "Li dis chevaliers se consilla as aultres barons et chevaliers, et raporta par plainne sieute que il avoient bien mort deservi selonc la prise et la teneur de pluisseurs oribles fais que ils avoient la oy recorder, et les tenoient pour tous vrais et tous clers. *Et avoient deservi par la diverseté de lors fais a estre justichiet en trois manieres, c'est assavoir premiers trainnés, et puis decolés, apriés pendut en un ghibet.* Tout en la maniere qui il furent jugiet, furent il tantos justichiet." [The ten knights conferred with other lords and knights and formally reported that they had certainly deserved to die on account of the weight and gravity of several heinous acts that they had heard recounted there, and they considered them all true and unambiguous. *And according to the diversity of their acts they had deserved punishment in three ways, that is, first to be drawn, then beheaded, and finally hanged* (Fr. 86).

19. I found no free indirect discourse in my samplings.

20. The author has addressed this topic in "Histoire, nomination, référence," *Linx* 32 (1995): 173–88.

Interference in *Mélusine*

MARINA S. BROWNLEE

The interdependence between mythography and history during the Middle Ages is nowhere more visible than in Jean d'Arras's recasting of the Melusine legend to create an illustrious genealogy for the house of Lusignan. Such rewriting of popular myth as historical document is clearly audacious, though, of course, not unprecedented. It is, as we know, quite a familiar procedure, as Haydn White and others have demonstrated.[1] This being said, however, Melusine is not simply an audacious choice of ancestor made by Jean's patrons (the duke of Berry and his sister), she is a perilous one as well. The present essay discusses these perils and Jean's awareness of them. Rather than adopting the negative perspective of Guy-Edouard Pillard who sees Jean's text as illustrative of "les *ruines* d'un mythe beaucoup plus qu'une *survivance*,"[2] it is important to underscore Jean's distance from the subject—his awareness of both the benefits and dangers involved in the appropriation of this myth of origin by his patron.

Briefly stated, Jean creates a tension between these two aspects of the Melusine narrative. If Jacques Le Goff can claim that Melusine is "la fée de l'essor économique médiéval" [the fairy of medieval economic power] and that "elle apporte à la classe chevaleresque terres, châteaux, villes, lignages" [she endows the chivalric class with lands, castles, cities and lineages], that she is "l'incarnation symbolique et magique de leur [les milites] ambition sociale" [the symbolic and magic incarnation of their (the knights') social ambition] (Le Goff and Le Roy Ladurie, 603), we can, on the negative side, point out that she is also both a parricide and regicide whose aunt is the infamous Morgana.[3] How can these various attributes be reconciled? Why would then Jean and Marie de Berry choose to adopt Melusine as their ancestor?

Discrepancies such as these and others stem, in my opinion, from the crucial distinction between *myth* on the one hand and *allegory* on the other. Speaking of these two kinds of discourse, Harald Weinrich distinguishes the "aspect événementiel" of myth (its narrative essence) from the "caractère résultatif" (the a posteriori nature) of allegory. Allegory does not evolve, it is absolutely static; it constitutes a selective decontextualization of the myth from which it is taken. That is, it reduces the complexities of the myth to one of its aspects. Taking the example of Narcissus in Guillaume de Lorris's *Rose*, Weinrich explains his allegorical (rather than mythic) function. In this text: "le mythe est pour ainsi dire arrêté, réduite à une nature morte qui se révèle à mesure qu'un spectateur découvre et contemple le tableau qu'il a devant ses yeux. Les événements ne sont plus l'amour et la morte du héros mythique, mais les découvertes et réflexions que fait sur eux un personnage qui nous ressemble"[4] [the myth is, so to speak, reduced to the status of a still life that reveals itself as a spectator uncovers and contemplates the painting he has before his eyes. The events are no longer the love and death of a mythic hero, but rather the discoveries and reflections that a character who resembles us makes].

Jean d'Arras is called upon by his patron to write an allegory. Yet, aware of the axiological complexities inherent in the Melusine narrative, and of the fundamental discursive difference between the *histoire* of myth and the *discours* of allegory, Jean chooses instead to juxtapose allegory and myth—to build in a kind of *metacritical interference* between the two. While detailing Melusine's prowess as a builder of fortresses and cities, for example, he also includes her infanticide. She functions, therefore, simultaneously as the Mother Goddess and as the somewhat sinister mother figure.

In reviewing the scholarship devoted to this text, one finds (quite surprisingly and revealingly) that no consensus exists concerning the identity of the heroic figure at the center of it. According to Pillard, for example, the time during which the text was produced "fut l'époque courtoise . . . ce qui conduisit peut-être Jean d'Arras—ou ceux qui commandèrent son travail—à choisir Mélusine comme héroïne de son roman" [it was the courtly epoch . . . which perhaps led Jean d'Arras—or his patrons—to chose Melusine as the heroine of his romance] (308). At a different point in his study, however, he indicates that Geoffroy Big-Tooth is the hero: "[il] est un héros . . . le vrai fils de Mélusine; ses autres enfants étant des mortels ordinaires, simplement chanceux par la protection maternelle, et marqués de stigmates" [he is a hero . . . the real son of Melusine; her other children are ordinary mortals, simply lucky because of her maternal protection, and marked by birthmarks] (313). Perhaps it is because of the prodigious number of adventures undertaken by Geoffroy and also his putative association with the historically real figure of a certain Geoffrey who in 1232 burned the monastery of Maillers that this sixth son of Melusine is considered by some to be the principal hero of the text. Claude Lecouteux, on the other hand, offers a Proppian analysis that presents Melusine's husband—Raymondin—as the indisputable hero and true focus of the work (294–306). This lack of critical consensus is symptomatic, in my view, of the textual interference that characterizes Jean's enterprise.

Let us now consider the exemplary—allegorical—dimensions of Melusine's portrayal as well as the mythic, dark side that Jean includes. In this text, Melusine is known for her beauty as well as her remarkable talents as facilitator—the mother of ten sons who can construct not simply fortresses but entire cities in the twinkling of an eye. These attributes are highly desirable in terms of imperial concerns and also conform nicely with the Christian imperative to be fruitful and multiply. Her active role in annihilating the infidels through her sons is similarly laudable and appropriate to Jean de Berry's identity.

At the same time, however, Melusine poses a real threat on several counts. Key among these is her sexuality.[5] While she is unquestionably beautiful, a totally devoted wife, and an exemplary mother, she is at the same time monstrous for a variety of reasons. On the most obvious level she is monstrous because of her tail. This particular anatomical feature is somewhat mysterious in that we do not know whether or not it predates the imprisonment by Melusine and her sisters of their father, Elinas. In other words, is it a blemish, like the physical defects exhibited by at least eight of her ten sons, or a punishment meted out to her by her mother? While these questions are not explicitly answered by the text, the serpentine connotation is certainly troubling for a Christian axiology. Speaking of the polysemy of the serpent in myth, Mircea Eliade asserts that: "Il est immortel, parce qu'il se régénere . . . il distribue fécondité, science (prophétie) et même immortalité"[6] [It is immortal because it reproduces itself . . . it provides fecundity, science (prophecy) and even immortality]. Clearly, both her immortality and prophetic gifts interfere with Christian doctrine. One might in addition be tempted to speak of her in terms of the earth-mother who is eventually displaced by the sky-father who appears in more advanced societies. Of this pattern, Northrop Frye explains that "it is often assumed that the sexual and maternal myths are older [than those of the sky-father], being more appropriate for an agricultural society, as their rivals were for the patriarchal, tool-using urban society that came later."[7]

In any event, Christianity aside, Melusine is a phallic mother in that she entombs her father in a womblike cavern (rather than the accustomed imprisonment of a daughter by a king/father in a phallic tower). This phallic association is crystallized by Rabelais in chapter 38 of his fourth book where he makes the following remark about the provenance of *andouilles* (sausages): "Si ces discours ne satisfont à l'incredulité de vos seigneuries, praesententement (j'entends après boyre) visitez Lusignan, Partenay, Vovant, Mervant, et Ponzauges, en Poictou. Là trouverrez tesmoignes vieulx de renom et de la bonne forge, les quelz vous jureront sus le braz sainct Rigomé que Mellusine, leur premiere fondatrice, avoit corps foeminin jusques aux boursavitz, et que le reste en bas estoit andouille serpentine, ou bien serpent andouillicque."[8] [If these remarks do not assuage your incredulity, go (I assume after drinking) visit Lusignan, Partenay, Vovant, Mervant, and Ponzauges, in Poitou. There you will find elderly witnesses who are of good repute and lineage who will swear on the arm of St. Rigomé that Melusine, their first founder, had a female body as far as the navel, and from there downward that of a serpentine sausage, or rather of a sausagelike serpent.] (Translation mine.)

The father's imprisonment, moreover, is definitive—constituting parricide since Elinas is unable to escape his locus of bondage. Why, we may well ask, did his loving wife Presine allow him to die? As we know, Melusine imprisoned her father for his betrayal of Presine, which led to Melusine's banishment. Like Melusine's husband Raymondin, Elinas transgressed against his fairy wife by gazing at her during the time when she had forbidden him from doing so. At the moment of his betrayal, Presine takes her three infant daughters (Melusine, Melior, and Palestine) away to live in the company of her sister the Queen of Avalon—the sinister Morgana—and a third unnamed sister who inhabits the Ille Perdue. Thus there is a symmetry not simply between the two husbands who voyeuristically betray a mother and her daughter but also in the two generations of three females. Christian concerns are virtually absent from the narrative of Presine's betrayal, her flight, and the incarceration and causally related death of Melusine's father. I say virtually absent because Presine reflects an awareness of the Last Judgment when she explains, "en plourant: Filles, veez vous la le pays ou vous fustes neez et ou vous eussiez eu vostre partie, ne feust la fausseté de vostre pere, qui vous et moy a mis en grant misere sans fin jusques au jour du Hault Juge, qui punira les maulx et essaucera les biens" [weeping: Daughters, you see there the land where you were born and where you would have your part—were it not for the falseness of your father, who cast you and me into great misery until the Day of Judgment, which will punish evildoers and reward the good] (*M* 11).

Another unanswered question surrounding Elinas's betrayal of his wife and her putative recognition of the Christian ethos of divine retribution is that of why Presine chooses to punish the three daughters who were trying to avenge their mother of the terrible wrongdoing committed by their father. In response to Melusine's suggestion that the sisters imprison their father, the text reads: "les autres deux lui respondirent: Vous estes notre ainsnee, nous vous suivrons et avouerons ce que vous en vouldrez faire" [the other two answered her saying: You are our eldest, we will follow you and support that which you wish to do]

(*M* 11). Far from approving of this behavior, Presine punishes each of her offspring severely: by contrast with Melusine's prolific childbearing, her sisters must each remain celibate, Melior being confined to a castle in which she must care for a falcon until Judgment Day (*M* 10), while Palestine is entombed within a mountain along with her father's wealth, which, we are told, will be used to conquer the Holy Land (*M* 10). The most severe punishment is meted out to Melusine herself (either because the perfidy against their father was initially her idea or because she is the eldest, hence the most responsible) (*M* 9). Each Saturday she will be transformed into a serpent from the waist down and must never be seen by her husband in this state. If she is seen, she will be turned permanently into a serpentine form until the Day of Judgment. In addition, she is told that she will, three days before the fall of a Lusignan castle, circle around it howling in her bestial form. She will do likewise three days before the death of any family member (*M* 10).

Presine then disappears from the text, leaving us to contemplate the axiological disjuncture at issue between her discourse of the Last Judgment and God's omnipotent justice and her own pagan mythological retribution against her daughters and reluctance to save her husband. This clash of pagan (fairy) values and Christian ones reveals the interference that is visible between the complexity of the myth and the allegory of Melusine the builder and facilitator with whom Jean de Berry wishes to associate himself.

It is interesting to note that in the repeated event of the next generation (Raymondin's betrayal of Melusine) Christian concerns are conspicuously present and treated in a more coherent manner. In other words, a kind of generational progression is at issue, whereby Christian values become increasingly important.

If we consider Raymondin's surveillance of Melusine during the forbidden day, we see that Jean is careful to build in certain details that contrast boldly with the consequences of Elinas's transgression against Presine. First of all, Melusine feigns ignorance of the transgression, comforting Raymondin instead for his distraught condition: "Remond commence a souspirer comme cil qui grant douleur sentoit, et celle l'embrace et lui demande: Monseigneur, que vous fault il? Estes vous malade?" [Raymondin begins to sigh as if he felt a great pain, and she embraces him and asks: Sir, what is wrong? Are you ill?] (*M* 243–44).

She does so, we are told, because Raymondin has not revealed her serpentine identity to anyone else.

As we know, it is only when he learns that Geoffroy has burned down the monastery of Maillers, thereby immolating one hundred monks including his own brother Fromont, that Raymondin divulges the truth about Melusine, blaming her for her son's wayward behavior:

> Par la foy que je doy a Dieu, je croy que ce ne soit que fantosme de ceste femme, ne ne croy pas que ja fruit qu'elle ait porté viengne a perfection de bien; elle n'a porté enfant qui n'ait apporté quelque estrange signe sur terre. Ne veez la Oruble que n'a pas vii. ans accompliz, qui a ja occiz deux de mes escuiers, et avant qu'il eust trois ans, avoit il fait mourir deux de ses nourrices par force de mordre leurs mamelles? Et ne vy je leur mere, le samedy que mon frere de Forests m'accointa les males nouvelles, en forme de serpente du nombril en aval? Si fiz, par Dieu. C'est une esperite ou c'est toute fantosme ou illusion qui m'a ainsi abusé; premiere foiz que je la vy, ne me scot elle bien a dire toute ma mesaventure?
>
> [I swear by my faith in God that that woman is nothing but a phantom, I don't believe that she ever made anything good; she never bore a child who didn't have a strange birthmark. Don't you see Horrible, who isn't yet seven years old and has already killed two of my squires, and who before the age of three killed two of his wet-nurses by biting off their nipples? And didn't I see their mother, the Saturday my brother from Forez told me the bad news, in the form of a serpent from the waist down? I did, by God. She is a spirit or a phantom or illusion who has abused me; the first time I saw her, didn't she tell me my misfortune?] (*M* 253)

Melusine tries to console Raymondin for the grief he feels at Geoffroy's reprehensible behavior at Maillers, and in this her arguments are overwhelmingly Christian:

> Sachiez qu'il n'a si grant pecheur ou monde que Dieu ne soit plus grant pardonneur et plus debonnaire, quant le pecheur se repent et lui crie mercy de bon cuer et de bonne voulenté. Se Gieffroy, vostre filz, a fait son oultrage par son courage merveilleux et fort, sachiez que de certain c'est pour le pechié des moines, qui estoient de mauvaise vie et desordonnee; et en a Nostre Seigneur voulu

avoir la punicion, combien que ceste chose soit incognoissable quant a humaine creature, car les jugemens de Dieu sont si secrez que nul cuer mondain ne les puet comprendre en son entendement.

[Know that there is no sinner so great that God cannot pardon him, when the sinner repents and begs mercy with a sincere heart. If Geoffroy, your son, has committed his outrageous deed as a result of his extraordinary strength, know that the cause is really the sinfulness of the monks, who were living an evil life; and therefore Our Lord wished to punish them; God's will is inscrutable; the judgments of God are so secret that no human being can understand them.] (*M* 255)

Despite her words of Christian consolation, reminding him of God's inscrutability and capacity for forgiveness, Raymondin reviles her: "Hee, tres faulse serpente, par Dieu, ne toy ne tes fais ne sont que fantosme, ne ja hoir que tu ayes porté ne vendra a bon chief en la fin . . . [Fromont] est destruit par l'art demoniacle, car tous ceulx qui sont forcennez de yre sont ou commandement des princes d'enfer; et par ce fist Gieffroy le grant et horrible et hideux forfait d'ardoir son frere et les moines qui mort ne avoient point desservie" [Oh, false serpent. By God, neither you nor your deeds are anything but illusion; no heir that you have borne will come to any good . . . [Fromont] is destroyed by demonic power, since all those who are wrathful are so by order of the princes of Hell; that is why Geoffroy committed the horrible deed of burning his brother and the monks who did not deserve to die] (*M* 255).

Here, too, we find interference. Do the duke and duchess of Berry want to be associated with the serpent or her murderous progeny Geoffroy, whom his own father characterizes as similarly infernal and imperfect? The allegorical value of Melusine the builder, the symbol of social success Le Goff details, is considerably problematized by this episode. Both Melusine's discourse of *caritas* and Raymondin's rejection of it dramatize the distance that Jean d'Arras creates between the abstraction of Melusine the salutary builder (her static, allegorical function) and the narrative complexity of her myth—the narrative in all its organic complexity.

Upon hearing Raymondin's vituperation, Melusine collapses into a dead faint. Thereafter she is revived, but only long enough to offer her last will and testament. In an act of true devotion and Christian charity, Melusine forgives her husband for having cast her into eternal torment, rather than allowing her to live and die like a true Christian woman: "se tu ne m'eusses faussee, j'estoye gettee et exemptee de paine et de tourment, et eusse vescu le cours naturel comme femme naturelle, et feusse morte naturelement, et eu tous mes sacramens, et eusse esté ensevelie et enterree en l'eglise de Nostre Dame de Lusegnan, et eust on fait mon anniversaire bien et deuement. Or me r'as tu embatue en la penance obscure ou j'avoye long temps esté par ma mesaventure. Et ainsi la me fauldra porter et souffrir jusques au jour du jugement et par ta faulseté. Je pry a Dieu qu'il te veulle pardonner" [If you had not been false I would have been spared pain and torment, and I would have lived like a natural [human] woman, and I would have died a natural death, with all my sacraments, and I would have been buried in the church of Notre Dame de Lusignan, and my day would have been celebrated. But you have inflicted upon me an obscure penance that stems from my past misfortunes. And for this reason I must suffer until the Day of Judgment because of your falseness. I pray that God may forgive you] (*M* 256).

Melusine's stance as Christian apologist is surprising given both her monstrous physical nature and the lack of such discourse in the parallel episode of her mother's betrayal. Yet Jean prepares us for her spiritual perspective at the structurally important midpoint of his text—the moment at which Melusine articulates the values she deems to be the most important in life as she gives advice to her sons Antoine and Renaud before they depart. In a lengthy speech she instructs them, saying: "Ce que je vous diray et l'entendez et retenez bien, car il vous aura bien besoign. Premierement amez et doubtez et servez Dieu, vostre Createur, continuelment. Tenez les commandements de nostre mere Saincte Eglise et tous les degrez et commandemens de nostre foy catholique" [Listen to what I say and keep it always in mind, because it is important. First, love and serve God, your Creator, always. Obey all the commandments of our holy Church and all the teachings and commandments of our Catholic faith] (*M* 152–53). We see Melusine in this speech affirming the omnipotence of God and thus subordinating her powers as creator, builder, and seer, implicitly but clearly presenting her world as totally subservient to His. Midpoints are traditional *loci* of illumination for the reader and/or hero. In this text it is the reader who is meant to understand the greater importance of Melusine's Christian—rather than supernatural—identity. Nonetheless, the two identities are, in real terms, mutually exclusive. And, I submit, Jean intends for us to perceive this form of interference between the allegory of Melusine as creator and the complications stemming from her mythic narrative.

In romance, not only the midpoint sequence but also the themes of ascent and descent play a key role in interpretation. Descent episodes usually reveal the hero's true genealogical identity, as Northrop Frye reminds us: "In romance the descent theme often has a great deal to do with one's descent in a genealogical sense, where the crucial event is the discovery of the real relation of the chief characters and their parents" (122). Geoffroy's entry into his father's tomb conforms to this paradigm. Upon entering he sees not only a plethora of gold, precious jewels, and a statue of Elinas, but an inscription revealing Melusine's genealogy as well as the treason that she and her sisters had perpetrated upon their father. He also encounters a multitude of prisoners contained within the tomb, held captive by a hideous giant whom he slays (*M* 166–68).

While the lower world in this text functions both as a locus of cruelty and imprisonment and as an oracular cave, it also leads Geoffroy to the rather un-Christian vow to avenge his mother by killing his uncle (*M* 168), and he carries out this revenge shortly after its articulation. Here Melusine is clearly being presented as a victim of her perfidious brother-in-law, and not as a demonic creature. And yet, in terms of themes of ascent, all we find is her draconian flight, which seems menacing to say the least. Having instructed her husband to kill their demonic son Horrible, Melusine, we are told

> lors fist un moult doulereux plainte et un moult grief souspir, puis sault en l'air, et laisse la fenestre, et trepasse le vergier. Et lors se mue en une serpente grant et grosse et longue de la longeur de xv. piez. Et sachiez que la pierre sur quoy elle passa a la fenestre y est encores, et y est la fourme du pie toute escripte . . . Lors a fait la dame, en guise de serpente, comme j'ay dit dessuz, trois tours environ la fortresse. Et a chascune foiz qu'elle passoit devant la fenes-

> tre, elle gettoit un cry si merveilleux et si douloreux que chascun en plouroit de pitié, et appercevoit on bien qu'elle se partoit enviz du lieu, et qu'elle s'en partoit par contraincte. Et adont print son chemin ver Lusegnen, menant si grant escroiz et si grant enfreinte qu'il sembloit, par toute ou elle passoit, que la foldre et la tempeste y deust cheoir.
>
> [uttered a painful complaint and a great sigh; then she jumped into the air, leaving the window and crossing the garden. Thereupon she turned into a large serpent, fifteen feet long. And know that the stone she trod on the windowsill as she was taking flight is still there, and the shape of her foot remains there permanently embedded in the stone. Thus did the woman, in the form of a serpent, as I have explained above, circle the fortress three times. And every time she passed by the window, she let out a cry that was so doleful that everyone who heard it wept out of pity, and everyone realized that she was leaving in great sadness. She then took the road for Lusignan, making such a terrible noise that it seemed, wherever she passed, like a terrible hail storm.] (*M* 260)

If we consider the basic function of ascent themes, we find, as Frye notes, that "ascent themes introduce us to . . . a metamorphosis, the growing of identity through the casting off of whatever conceals or frustrates it. The simplest form of such ascending metamorphosis is the removal of enchantment, in which an animal disguise or something parallel is replaced by the original human form. The frog becomes the prince; Lucius the ass, in Apuleius, becomes Lucius the initiate of Isis, etc." (140). What we find in Jean's text, however, is precisely the opposite trajectory, the definitive bestialization of the valorous fairy—replete with the apocalyptic details of hail and lightning bolts falling from the heavens. Here Jean's transgression against the normative ascent pattern again serves to underscore his complication of the simple equivalence of Melusine and the house of Lusignan. He is once again standing back, as it were, from the subject matter imposed upon him by his patrons, in order to remind us of the considerable distance that often separates myth from allegory.

If this interference between mythic and allegorical discourse is operative in Jean's text, then it should very likely be reflected in the remarks made by the narrator as well. This is, in fact, the case in the devices upon which Jean relies to endow his enterprise with authority. Michèle Perret has analyzed with great insight the strategies by which he establishes the truth status of his narrative, identifying three principal ones: *garants de crédibilité*, *preuves métonymiques* and *témoignage médiatisé* (Perret, 27). The device of "mediated witnessing" refers to the attestation of an absent but respected enunciator whose stature is sufficient proof or authentification of the veracity of his statement (27). "Metonymic proof" involves the verification of one part of the narrative in order to underscore the truth-status of the whole. One of the most notable examples of this procedure is the detail that when Melusine took to the skies, pushing off into the air from a window, she left a footprint in the stone: "sachiez que la pierre sur quoy elle passa a la fenestre y est encors, et y est la fourme du pié toute escripte" [know that the stone she trod upon is still there, and the footprint is preserved] (*M* 260).

The third procedure, the "guarantees of credibility," concerns witnesses (often *auctores*) who swear to the validity of seemingly impossible occurrences. In order to render credible the genealogical succession between Melusine and his patron, the duke of Berry, Jean resorts to some very audacious arguments. As Perret puts it, "il accumule les garants dans une préface et une conclusion si spécieuses qu'elles en sont presque incompréhensibles" [he accumulates proofs in the preface and conclusion that are of such a suspicious nature that they are almost incomprehensible] (30). The prophet David, Aristotle, and Paul are invoked as examples of venerable figures who inspire us to marvel at God's inscrutability and his capacity for effecting extraordinary events. Gervaise of Tilbury, inhabitants of Poitou (including numerous eyewitnesses to Melusine's local and polymorphic identity—not to mention the duke and duchess of Berry, who would never have commissioned a mendacious work) offer further evidence of the work's truthfulness. Finally, the reader is told—rather coercively—that if he does not believe in the text's truthfulness it is because he is obviously ignorant, "grossiere." One should add that the disposition of these authority-endowing devices (found in the preface and at the very end of Jean's lengthy text) creates the effect of superficiality (or of an afterthought) since the body of the text makes little or no effort to present the fantastic events it treats as empirically possible. The text reflects the outrageous claims made by Jean in remarks such as the following, which clearly strain the reader's credibility: "selon ce que j'ay trouvé et peu sentir des anciens autteurs, tant de Gervaise comme d'autres anciens autteurs et philosophes, je repute ceste histoire et la chronique estre vraye, et les choses faees" [according to what I have found in the ancient sources, both in Gervaise and in other ancient authors and philosophers, I judge this story and chronicle to be true, and also the fairy matter] (*M* 310). I agree with Perret that Jean's arguments are so specious as to be "virtually incomprehensible"—but, by contrast with her reading, I see such remarks as part of a *programmatic function* whereby Jean calculatedly distances himself from his subject matter, doing here on the level of authority what we have seen him do with the interference he generates between mythic and allegorical discourse at so many junctures in his text.

Of Melusine's ten sons, all but the last two are described in terms of their notable deformities. The first, Urian, is distinguished by his physiognomy in that he has one brown and one green eye, as well as the largest ears ever seen on an infant; Eudes, the second son, has one ear much larger than the other; Guyon has one eye much higher in his head than the other; Antoine, for his part, has a birthmark in the shape of a lion's paw on his jaw; the fifth, Renaud, has only one eye; Geoffroy Big-Tooth is so called because of one inordinately long tooth that protrudes from his mouth like the fang of a wild boar, Fromont has on his nose a large hairy blemish; Horrible, the eighth, meanwhile, is born with three eyes, one of them in his forehead. Of the youngest two sons (Remonnet and Thierry) little is known regarding their physical appearance. What is striking in the case of the first eight, however, is that they are in each case described as being very handsome—a claim that seems hard to believe given their notable deformities. Moreover, as we know, in the world of romance, physical beauty or deformity mirrors the ethical fiber of the character in question. Thus it is shocking to find so many physical defects in Melusine's offspring, and also shocking to have these men function in a laudable—rather than sinister—manner. Equally shocking, of course, is the claim that they are all strikingly handsome given their readily discernible deformities. It does not matter here whether we adopt the romance equation of beauty with goodness and ugliness with evil; the physiognomic details we are given definitively preclude describing Melusine's sons as handsome.

Why then does Jean defy both the laws of romance ethics and of common sense so consistently in the presentation of Melusine's progeny? By his presentation, Jean treats the sons and their mother as creatures who pertain to the exotic marvelous, which Tzvetan Todorov describes as "supernatural events [or beings] reported without being presented as supernatural," as deviating from the norm.[9] In terms of audience, Todorov adds that "the implicit reader is supposed to be ignorant of the regions where the events take place, and consequently he has no reason for calling them into question" (55). Yet Jean's reader is familiar with the kingdom of Lusignan, thus here too we find another dimension of interference, another metacritical disjuncture intended to generate a degree of skepticism regarding the duke of Berry's genealogical association with Melusine. This surprising depiction is, in my opinion, yet another manifestation of the programmatic "interference" by means of which Jean both structures his text and defines his metacritical role as mediator between myth and allegory. That is to say, these defective children in some sense figure the willed "defectiveness," so to speak, of the text. Their physical appearance cannot be construed as allegory, just as Melusine's complexities cannot—in Jean's view—be reduced to the power-myth that his patrons envision.[10] Thus it would appear that Jean found the historically real defect of Geoffroy to be a particularly suggestive device for signaling the allegorical aporia that defines his text.

Pierre Mabille offers a succinct definition of the meaning of the marvelous: "Beyond entertainment, beyond curiosity, beyond all the emotions such narratives and legends afford, beyond the need to divert, to forget, or to achieve delightful or terrifying sensations, the real goal of the marvelous journey is the total exploration of universal reality."[11] The universal reality defined by Jean is the interrogation of allegorical paradigms—of their appropriateness—for the representation of human history. In the final analysis, Jean d'Arras wishes to highlight his patron's consummately human—rather than mythological—lineage, and, from this point of view, the duke of Berry is identified less with Melusine than with her husband, Raymondin—the *roy mondain*—the earthly king.

Notes

1. Hayden White, *Metahistory* (Baltimore: Johns Hopkins University Press, 1973).

2. Guy-Edouard Pillard, *La Déesse Mélusine. Mythologie d'une fée* (Paris: Herault, 1989), 328.

3. On this subject see Harf-Lancner, *Les Fées au Moyen Age.*

4. Harald Weinrich, "Structures narratives du mythe," *Poétique* 1 (1970): 30.

5. On the question of her complex sexuality see the study by Markale.

6. See Pillard, 282.

7. Northrup Frye, *The Secular Scripture* (Cambridge, Mass.: Harvard University Press, 1976), 112.

8. François Rabelais, *Le Quart livre*, ch. 38: "Comment Andouilles ne sont à mespriser entre les humains" in *Oeuvres complètes*, ed. Guy Demerson (Paris: Seuil, 1973).

9. Tzvetan Todorov, *The Fantastic: A Structural Approach to Literary Genre*, trans. Richard Howard (Ithaca, N.Y.: Cornell University Press, 1975). See also in this connection Ivy Corfis, "Beauty, Deformity, and the Fantastic in the *Historia de la linda Melosina*," *Hispanic Review* 55 (1987): 181–93.

10. It is significant that Jean develops the issue of Melusine's progeny so fully since, as Pillard notes, they have little direct bearing on the founding of the house of Lusignan (with the exception of Geoffroy). It is also significant that they appear to be developed by both Jean and Couldrette: "Si Couldrette et Jean d'Arras, dans leurs romans, content les aventures des fils de Mélusine—et même longuement—la tradition orale ne parle d'aucun d'eux, si ce n'est de Geoffroy; mais Geoffroy est un fils très particulier, et le peu qu'en colporte la tradition pourrait bien n'être qu'un apport historique récent. Ces fils semblent donc être une création littéraire et de ce fait n'intéresser que d'assez loin la fée de Lusignan. En réalité, tous, plus ou moins, révèlent des aspects de leur personnalité et de leur activité qui pourraient très bien les apparenter à des ancêtres mythologiques lointains. Il est vraisemblable que les romanciers du Moyen Age ne les ont pas intégralement créés" (72–73).

11. Pierre Mabille, *Le Miroir du merveilleux* (Paris: Minuit, 1962), 57.

Myths in Progress: A Literary-Typological Comparison of Melusine and Joan of Arc

Nadia Margolis

At the other end of the euhemeristic scale from Melusine and her analogues—that is, a real-life female figure, whose historical presence was transformed into legend, or legends, motivated by the artistic, political, and theological climate of the time—stands Joan of Arc, the Maid of Orléans. Yet both are national symbols, possessed of remarkably similar destinies: preexisting folk myths metamorphosing into literate ones within forty years of each other, under related patronage,[1] with at least a significant part of their careers unfolding around Poitiers. A literary-typological study of the two, at roughly comparable points in their formation, might provide greater insight into the interrelation between later medieval French mentalities and their respective texts in the creation of national myths, especially those of female heroism.[2]

Most of us are familiar with the substance of Joan's story, but its authorship is more elusive and fragmentary, requiring some redefinition for our purposes. The account of her life was rarely dialogical, but rather plurivocal and sequentially told. I submit that during her mission Joan was nevertheless her own author to a major extent, in a way far exceeding the platitude that we are all authors of our lives, and that this life was consciously self-fashioned[3] as a response to preexistent texts—some oral, some written, some popular, some more learned—especially prophecies, in which Melusine's legend may have participated.[4] Moreover, so powerful was her design, despite her appearance as a simple country girl, that even after being forced to relinquish control over her text to her enemies after her capture and execution, their ruthless tactics would only nourish her legend through her canonization.

Toward that end, just as Melusine's legend had undergone reworkings according to the various cultural contexts and registers through which she would pass before and after Jean d'Arras, Joan, within a much more compressed time frame, seems constantly to revise the book of her life with respect to these texts, thus making them premonitions of herself as divine agent already inscribed within contemporary consciousness. This she first attempted out of private, mystical inspiration, and then, as her mission became apparent to her, she invoked such authorizing texts under the duress of many confrontations with the outside world. She authored and authorized her own story by both word *and* deed in a manner distinct from traditional female mystics, who tended to lead passive lives, sometimes bedridden, devoid of historical agency. However, like them and to a greater degree—though never completely—she based much of the meaning of her mission on her death and its aftermath, as though this were part of her program as subcategory of God's grand design.[5]

Like Melusine, Joan derived her charisma from preexistent cults—satanic or benevolent, depending on the witness's loyalties—becoming a cult figure herself, even during her lifetime.[6] After Joan's capture, her trial testimony, though originally uttered by her, was authored by her enemies in a manner surpassing the normal practice of mere "scribal emendation." At her posthumous rehabilitation, her text would be revised by others, though sympathetically this time, at least on the surface, by Charles VII's notaries eager to improve his royal image by salvaging hers. Much later, the Church would do the same, for similar reasons. Each party claimed to present the truth about her. This plurivocal nature of the Book of Joan, while rendering our investigation more complex, is perhaps inevitable in any great real-life figure's transformation into legend, since myths must embody more truths than any one mortal person. Joan may well have impressed these powerful and sophisticated authors into the service of her myth more than they, or we, realized.

Jean d'Arras's *Mélusine*, though more synoptically, also derives much of its fascination from what Michèle Perret has called the "*fonction testimoniale*," as the author repeatedly assures us of having been a witness, and now chronicler, to the "truth" of what was presumed to be a folkloric tale.[7] By extending Perret's observations on the *espace* and *matérialité* in *Mélusine*, we can compare Jean d'Arras's use of these to similar phenomena, as controlled by Church and state over much time and many leaves of parchment, in Joan's story.

This investigation was inspired by some of the more obvious similarities and revealing contrasts in the formulation of the books of the two heroines. In their late medieval incarnations (Joan having been born only some twenty years after Jean d'Arras "gave birth" to the first cohesive story of Melusine), both were created from regional, folkloric oral culture to emerge as protective guardians: Joan of Lorraine, liberator of Orléans; "Mélusine, c'est l'une de nos grandes fées nationales" [Melusine is one of our great national spirits].[8] These popular figures of enchantment were appropriated and refashioned by the hired historians and poets of each realm, Lusignan and Armagnac France, for the common purpose of strengthening national pride and to help combat the English menace during the Hundred Years' War: whether under the aegis of Jean, duke of Berry, for whom Jean d'Arras's Saracens and perhaps even the Giants represented Anglo-Burgundians, or Charles VII, by whose time those same adversaries no longer required comparison with heathen foes to accentuate their ominous presence. Already we can discern a hierarchical layering of eventually fatal confrontations, each echoing the other from the outermost sphere of what we might simplify here as the Anglo-French conflict, to that of the Burgundians and Armagnacs—or between Berry and its neighboring adversaries—and down to the strife within Charles's court or Melusine's family.

Apart from their respective political and historical surroundings, both women are nurtured on earthly symbols of fecundity, renewal, and magic (trees, fountains), to become sweet and gentle maidens. At the same time, their often frightening, supernatural power also derives from these natural elements either by birthright (Melusine) or revelation (Joan). Each heroine's association with the supernatural is marked by a deformity or deformities mystifying to their real-world cohabitants: Melusine's Saturday-night serpentine seances and her variously blemished progeny, and Joan's male attire and lack of menses, all of which can be seen to connect with a common, primal system of male fears and fantasies.[9]

In this connection, though possessed of what we might term an Amazonian autonomy,[10] to achieve her ends as founder/savior, each woman also yields afterward a noble lineage to enrich and legitimize the blood royal of Lusignan and France as the chosen realm of God. This last constitutes a uniquely curious accomplishment, since each, by her very nature (or *super*-nature), threatened the Church's doctrines and credibility, and had first to be in a sense isolated and purified (in Joan's case, burned) and Christianized, with the aid of clerkly maneuvering. We note how frequently Jean d'Arras mentions Melusine's obedience to none but the Christian God, as the future mother of a line of crusaders, while on the other hand, Joan's ardent Catholicism was too personal, to say nothing of redoubtable; her idea of the Church differed from that of her persecutors. She who was burned as a heretic would wait more than 450 years to be canonized—the only figure in history to have endured such a discordant destiny.

Within the narratives of each heroine's life, at least three layers of binary exchange emerge: 1) the global one between learned and popular culture; 2) that between the discourses of author and his or her sources; and 3) the dual code of conduct and ritual exemplified by Melusine and Joan. This dual code operates in one way for the mortal, chivalric world and in another for the privileged, divine otherworld, known to each heroine at least in part, but unknown to the mortals she frequented. These levels of interpretation were not immune to a certain amount of manipulation by the various authors: Jean d'Arras, the trial notaries and memoirists, Christine de Pizan and the anonymous contemporary poets, and Joan herself.

One could continue to tease out a hodgepodge of such rapprochements, but to achieve a more systematic result, I should now like to align the two histories in parallel fashion according to a modified typological pattern combining the structural models established by Harf-

Lancner and Lecouteux for the Melusine stories.[11] Our schema includes the following stages:

(1) The *meeting* of mortal and enchanted worlds in the form of hero (Elinas/Raymondin's father/Raymondin) and heroine (Presine/Belle Dame/Melusine), each temporarily isolated from his and her origins, in a place specifically dominated by one or more *fountains* and *trees* (*M* 6–9, 15, 29, 33–34). Each meeting, as recounted in Jean d'Arras, foreshadows the next by repetition through succeeding generations in the families of both characters.

(2) The *pact* or *covenant* made between the two figures or worlds, often implying some sort of *interdiction* (*M* 9, 25–26). Melusine promises that she is sent by God to make Raymondin the most powerful mortal and to make all of his dreams for his domain and lineage come true. Raymondin must marry her and swear never to visit her on Saturday night. The pact is signified by a gift, as when Melusine gives Raymondin magic stones and empowering rings (*M* 27, 40, 259), after which the two figures begin life together, prospering in the mortal world. Such a pact seemingly redoubles the intensity and consequences of pledges the other mortals make among themselves (for example, Geoffroy and Remonnet, *M* 268), including Raymondin's and Melusine's wedding vows (*M* 37–38).

(3) The *transgression* or *betrayal* by the mortal (Elinas, Raymondin) in breaking his promise to Presine/Melusine, as instigated by an outside antagonist, such as the count of Forez (*M* 240–43). In committing the misdeed, the transgressing hero or heroine is never completely contemptible to us because he or she errs, at least partly, out of ignorance of the otherworldly secret germane to the pact. Although the mortal protagonist participates in the making of the pact itself, he or she, because of the secret history informing the otherworld side of things, remains unaware of the covenant's deeper causality and consequences. The mortal hero thus has less incentive to keep his word, and the mortal reader, made omniscient by the narrator, sympathizes with him.

(4) The *punishment* of the transgression, equal to *separation* of the two lovers/worlds, signified by a curse: Presine curses her daughter for her hubris in presuming to avenge her for Elinas's crime, which eventually will bring about the tragedy of Melusine's betrayal by Raymondin, who in turn can never see Melusine in "naturelle," "femmenine" form again

(*M* 256–59). Jean d'Arras's description of Raymondin's profuse tears at this moment of remorse, after which he and Melusine faint in unison, subtly recalls and subverts the fountain scene of their first, happy encounter (*M* 257).

The deformity of most of Melusine's and Raymondin's progeny is also perceived as a penalty, whose precise cause is left to various interpretations, as debated by Raymondin and Melusine (*M* 253–55).

(5) The *legacy to posterity,* the replication of the essence of these events through time and lineage (*M* 42–43, 260), and its evolving role in causality and etymology in the formation of regional mores and self-image: despite her imperfect children, some imperfect towers, and other misfortunes, Melusine is proudly adopted as the guardian, founding spirit of Poitou and especially the Lusignan people, reflected onomastically in "Mère-Lusigne."[12] Her literary posterity—the genealogy of her text in various European languages—to which Jean d'Arras is a major contributor, also pertains to this phase.[13]

To insert the comparable episodes from Joan's story within this structure:

(1) The most logical counterpart to the *meeting* phase in Raymondin's and Melusine's encounter at the Fontaine de Soif consists in the moments in Joan's life when she experiences her voices and visions of Saints Michael,[14] Catherine, and Margaret, also sometimes occurring near the "Fairy tree" (*arbre aux Fées*) and Oak Forest (*Bois chenu*), with a minimum of two fountains: that "of the Frogs" (*aux Rains*) and of the Fairies (Tisset-Lanhers, 1:65). By her third hearing of the voices, Joan knew them to be angelic (Tisset-Lanhers, 1:71), just as Elinas is struck by what Jean d'Arras describes as a *voix angélique* and "*femmenine*"—Presine's—as he approaches the fountain of their first encounter (*M* 6). Although angels are supposedly genderless, which governs Joan's discernment of the voice as merely "bel, bonne, et digne" [beautiful, good, and worthy] (Tisset-Lanhers, 1:62), their masculinity or femininity essentialized their inspirational attributes as visions. Her inability or unwillingness to describe their corporeality in further detail created grave credibility problems at her trial (Tisset-Lanhers, 1:87) while Melusine's amplified, hybrid body occurs as a result of Raymondin's failure to believe in her.

Masculine and feminine, worldly and otherworldly parameters also inform Joan's first meeting with the Dauphin, the Elinas/Raymondin

counterpart in her mission, at Chinon. Jean d'Arras and the Book of Joan bear detailed witness to the inception of each heroine's first encounter with the mortal she has been sent to save or help. Both deploy a similarly sibylline register, typical of the guide figure in heroic epic, since she, too, like the author, must convince her listener. Their slight interspersing of legalistic language, typical of later medieval French prose, intensifies this persuasiveness. Jean d'Arras thus records Melusine's first words to Raymondin at the Fountain: "Par Dieu, Remondin, je suiz, aprez Dieu, celle qui te peut plus aidier et avancier en ce mortel monde, en tes adversitez... Et saiches que je scay bien que tu cuides que ce soit fantosme ou euvre dyabolique de mon fait et de mes paroles, mais je te certiffie que je suiz de par Dieu... et vraye catholique... Et saiches de certain que sans moy ne mon conseil tu ne pues venir a chief de t'emprise... car je te feray le plus seignoury et le plus grant qui oncques feust en ton lignaige, et le plus puissant terrien" [In God's name, Raymondin, I am, after God, the one who can help and advance you the most in this mortal world, in whatever adversity befalls you... And may you know that I well know that you think me some phantom or diabolical creation in my deeds and words, but I assure you that I am sent by order of God . . . and a true Catholic . . . May you also know with certainty that without me or my advice you cannot accomplish your goals... for I will make you the most noble, most sovereign and greatest member ever of your lineage, and the most powerful mortal on earth] (*M* 25–26).

Unfortunately for the sake of parallelism, we have no record of what Joan said to the Dauphin at their first meeting, but her "Letter to the English" provides a good indication. All of Joan's letters, which she herself authored, reveal her self-awareness as an agent of divine intervention very early in her mission.[15] So powerfully was her sense of purpose expressed in these missives to the English and certain French cities that these no doubt helped her claims to attain reality, as exemplified in these words to the English on March 22, 1429: "rendez à la Pucelle qui est ici envoyée de par Dieu, le Roi du ciel, les clefs de toutes les bonnes villes que vous avez prises et violées en France. Elle est venue de par Dieu pour reclamer le sang royal. Elle est toute prête à faire la paix, si vous voulez lui faire raison . . . et si vous ne le faites ainsi, attendez les nouvelles de la Pucelle qui ira vous voir sous peu, à vos bien grands

dommages" [surrender to the Maid, who is sent here by God, the King of Heaven, the keys to all the good cities you have taken and plundered in France. She has come by order of God to reclaim the Blood Royal. She is most ready to make peace, if you are willing to do right by her . . . and if you fail to do so, expect tidings from the Maid who will shortly come to see you, and do very great damage to you] (Modern French trans. in Pernoud and Clin, 379).

Each message, full of untested prophecies from a mysterious woman to a nobleman, focuses upon certain remarkably similar ideas: that, despite the prince's doubts, the woman is sent by God, that she will restore the prince whom she has been appointed to defend to his rightful position as ruler, that she will sanctify his lineage, and that the prince must follow her words.

The outcome of Melusine's prognostication, as we know, is the essence of Jean d'Arras's romance-chronicle. Joan's message and others would reach the English before the famous liberation of Orléans on May 8, 1429, the first real test of her self-prophecy and the faith of her supporters. It also serves as the first test of Joan as an author of history, as a post-Melusinian restorer and builder of a key aspect of French national identity.

(2) The second, *covenant* phase actually happens on several occasions, but it essentially exists in Joan's initial promise to her voices never to renounce or betray them and God, and to fulfill the mission assigned to her, in a way reminiscent of Elinas/Raymondin toward Presine/Melusine. Joan in this regard acted primarily as warrior, while Melusine was a renowned builder—with each following a strenuous itinerary throughout major regions of France, far beyond their birthplaces and homes. During her trial, Joan went so far as to refuse to acknowledge this oath to her saints, particularly regarding the secret sign she gave the king at their private interview at Chinon[16]—another comparable meeting scene between both worlds in which a *covenant* is made, between Joan and Charles, only to be broken by the mortal king. The protective power of Joan's covenant with her voices is most cogently signified by *rings* bestowed upon or by both heroines. Melusine bestows rings upon her husband and later her sons to safeguard them in battle. Joan wears mysterious rings for the same purpose, following the cult of Saint Catherine of Fierbois.[17] She also receives other tangible symbols of

divine appointment, for example, the sword from the altar of Saint Catherine of Fierbois indicated to her by her voices, one of three swords discussed at her trials. The sword, her armor, and her harness were long sought after as relics, together with her battle standards, decorated with principal symbols of specific phases of her mission.

Charles's coronation at Reims, which Joan had promised him, bears special mention in that it betokens two more *covenants* between divine and temporal worlds. The first accords itself with standard practice as Charles's sacrament of ordination. But it is of another type, much more immersed in the idea of divine sanction, with Joan's active participation as Charles's sponsor, actually touching him at his anointing.[18] This rite as such probably meant more to Joan than to anyone else involved, perhaps in that the crown functions as a token from her to Charles symbolizing their covenant at Chinon. Of greater import to this analysis, Joan insisted on this ceremony as part of her own covenant with her voices as an essential phase of her mission, and because she had come to know of the Merlin and other prophecies, most likely during her pre-Orléans interviews at Vaucouleurs, Chinon, and Poitiers (Wood, 141), it became an integral part of her self-authored—or self-author*ing*—mythology.

(3) The third, *transgression* phase again arises at more than one time. Obviously, the prime betrayer is Joan's "gentle dauphin," Charles, for whom it ceased to be politically viable to save her from her captors, paradoxically because of the very qualities that enabled her to save him and his kingdom.[19] At this time what had been glorified as her divinely-inspired powers—her mystical authority—was then twisted by Anglo-Burgundian propagandists, and even some of Charles's jealous courtiers, as satanic and heretical, potentially threatening to his newly gained legitimacy and that of France.[20] Charles's abandonment of the ever-faithful Joan may be compared to Raymondin's angry posttransgression invective, in response to Melusine's gracious, reasonable letter, in which he retracts his belief in their pact at the fountain virtually point by point: "Hee, tres faulse serpente, par Dieu, ne toy ne tes fais ne sont que fantosme, ne ja hoir que tu ayes porté ne vendra a bon chief en la fin" [Alas, most false serpent-woman! In God's name, you and your deeds are nothing but phantoms, and none of the heirs you have borne will ever accomplish any good in the end] (*M* 255).

But interestingly enough, Charles's betrayal is not part of Joan's text as authored by her and her contemporaries, which records her own moral failings, such as her decision to attack Paris on a holy day (September 8, Feast of Our Lady's Nativity). This she must have known to be blasphemous, since she had been careful to avoid a similar misdeed earlier at Orléans, and also because she would later affirm that the Paris and other unsuccessful campaigns were ordered by her captains or "certain nobles," not by her voices (Wood, 144). She also may have violated military code by decapitating a prisoner, the unsavory Franquet d'Arras, rather than granting him due privileges, in a controversial episode whose circumstances remain unclear (Warner, 180–81), maliciously exaggerated by her interrogators (Tisset-Lanhers, 2:57, 130, 3:40) and by Monstrelet in his chronicle (Quicherat, 4:399–400). Such instances recall Melusine and her sisters presumptuously (in Presine's eyes) punishing their father out of righteous desire to avenge their mother, and Geoffroy's burning of the Abbey of Maillezais out of sheer fury at the monks for converting his brother, who also perishes in the fire. This happens simultaneously, according to Jean d'Arras's scene-juggling, with Raymondin's more central offense against Melusine that fateful Saturday night (*M* 240–43). What interests us in these moments is that, while Raymondin knows he has sinned, Joan reportedly avoids it by simply saying "passez oultre" [go on], only to deny it completely at her trial (Tisset-Lanhers, 2:57), probably because she felt this earthly blasphemy to have been necessitated by her higher mission.

There is also the vexed question of another of Joan's *transgressions:* the momentous Abjuration, in which, weakened by her prison ordeal and faced with a horrible death at the stake, she renounced her voices and male dress by signing a recantation at the St-Ouen cemetery, assuming female attire for four days, only to "relapse" into her previous state. The paradox of her situation encapsulates the tumultuous quandary of any otherworldly being striving to act virtuously in accordance with the codes of both worlds simultaneously. In preserving this dual loyalty, both Joan and Melusine inevitably force some sort of transgression, whether directly by themselves or indirectly by a mortal, Charles or Raymondin (or Geoffroy at Maillezais, *M* 251–53). If the late medieval (mortal) world tended to perceive of itself as postlapsarian, most of its mythical heroes, like Melusine and Joan, nevertheless attained their superior status by observing what we might term a *non*lapsarian code.

They often did this at the expense of traditional customs and laws, or at the risk of being considered satanic. More succinctly, one world's saintliness is another world's sin.

(4) The fourth, *punishment* stage again engages several levels of Joan's story. Because of the threatening nature of her voices and visions, two other types of biworldly confrontation occur. One arose between the Church Triumphant and the Church Militant, in which Joan refused to submit to the latter—presumptuous mortals—in favor of the former, since she believed herself closer to God.[21] The second resides in Joan's dual status as prisoner: though captured as a prisoner of war, she was actually tried as a religious criminal, a heretic. Melusine's penitential process is simpler, since Jean d'Arras has pre-Christianized her for his public. Her penance, achieved within the romance-chronicle arena, seems secondary to that of the male figures, in relation to whom she usually figures as the wronged party.

Premonition plays a major role in the punishment phase. We recall Joan's failure at Paris, because of having knowingly attacked on a holy day. Her later capture at Compiègne was due at least partly to betrayal by Guillaume Flavy, who many historians claim was paid off by the Burgundians to close the city's gates on her attempted rush to safety. This betrayal was predicted by her, just as Jean d'Arras portrays Melusine as omniscient on a par with himself as he articulates many ominous foreshadowings of transgressions against her and others. An example of the heroine's fate presaged by another author offers itself when Joan, having retracted her Abjuration and resumed male attire, returns before her judges to reaffirm her voices despite the penalty awaiting her—prompting the clerk to inscribe "Responsio mortifera" [the fatal response] in the margins of his notes (Tisset-Lanhers, 2:345–6; Warner, 141). If such suspenseful involvement reveals itself rarely in official record keeping, it is of course found quite frequently in Jean d'Arras's romance in portentous phrases like "Mais tantost le seront plus [doulentes], ainsi comme vous l'orrez en l'ystoire" [And now they will be all the more unhappy, as you will hear in the story] (*M* 28), and "Or commence une partie de la douleureuse tristece Raimond" [Now begins an episode in the painful sadness of Raymondin] (*M* 241).

On the most central level, both Charles and Raymondin are penalized by the loss of, or *separation* from, their heroines, both of whom spent much time in towers after the separation: Melusine, once the builder of many towers (*M* 294), ensconces her serpentine self within the Tour Poitevine (*M* 260–61); while Joan, who once captured many enemy strongholds, reaps the dubious reward of a variety of turreted lodgings during a protracted prison itinerary after her capture. Both women suffer painful repercussions after the separation, especially Joan, who, alternately losing Charles and her angels, endures martyrdom, while Melusine appears especially to miss her children and people, past and future (*M* 259–62). The exact moment of separation between heroine and mortal world is most dramatic in both accounts. Like Melusine who flies away shrieking dolorously, Joan's soul was seen to float skyward from her body in the form of a dove or lark, after she cried out wrenchingly "Jesus! Jesus!" (Duparc, 1:225; 3:212–13). Both heroines thus experience tragic departures toward eternity, leaving unmistakable, notably intact traces of their unique lives on earth: Melusine's famous "fourme du pied toute escripte" [form of her foot fully inscribed] (*M* 260) and Joan's unburned heart among the ashes—whole and full of blood, first attested by Jean Massieu, citing the executioner, at her rehabilitation (Duparc, 1:435; 4:116). Like relics to hagiography, such parting signs inevitably enriched each legend at least as much as the heroines' deeds on earth.

Meanwhile, in this more practical, though ethically shorter-sighted, mortal domain, it would seem at this point that Charles and Raymondin, despite their treachery, end up receiving more merciful treatment than do the heroines in the postpunishment phase according to the ideals of both Lusignan and Armagnac: Raymondin continues to benefit from Melusine's ring, and Charles's kingship continues to triumph. The men's remorse may linger, but so automatically do their rewards, because of their heroines' suffering.

(5) The *legacy to posterity:* Melusine and Joan enter into their histories as answers to men's prayers for salvation. Having made their own promises to the supernatural world, the future heroines have been endowed (or cursed) with omniscience, and in turn exact promises from men whose glory they prophesied. But these mortal men cannot keep their own promises; they betray the heroines, causing the loss of them as protective envoys from the supernatural world. For similar reasons Joan's life span is as abnormally brief as Melusine's is "unnaturally" eternal,[22] although Joan too would be the object of many sightings years after her death, as the False Pucelle(s).[23]

"We have burned a saint." Joan's executioner, Jean Fleury, reportedly echoed the crowd's sentiments, as he confessed to Ysambard de la Pierre to save his soul after the burning (Duparc 1:225; 3:212–13). This recalls Raymondin's lamentation of his betrayal of the virtuous Melusine: "Haa, Melusigne, . . . dame de qui tout le monde disoit bien, or vous ay je perdu sans fin" [Alas, Melusine, . . . lady of whom everyone said good things, now I have lost you forever] (*M* 243). The public sympathy for Joan, coupled with the persistent activism of her mother and other supporters, led to her rehabilitation in 1456 and eventual canonization in 1920. Her legacy, despite all the negative portrayals generated by the Anglo-Burgundian forces, endured as the "gift of fortitude," in the language of royal anointing (Wood, 141), to her king and compatriots as they continued the campaign to expel the English from France (1456). Armagnac propagandists represented such victories over the Anglo-Burgundians as proof that God favored them as the "true" French, just as Joan had foretold.

In a sense, Charles, by finally acting as an effective ruler, does try to fulfill Joan's expectations of him after her death in an atonement similar, we might say, to Raymondin's pilgrimage and related pious deeds after losing Melusine (*M* 260–62, 269–75), and Geoffroy's penance after his crimes (*M* 274–75). Charles's ordering commemorative celebrations of the liberation of Normandy in 1450, held in such extra-Norman places as Maillezais abbey (Beaune, 185), points to another Melusinian intersection with Johannic history. Like the rehabilitation proceedings he finally initiated two years later, these events took place as the English were withdrawing from France. Jean d'Arras's text was composed well after his patron's Lusignan campaign. Although Charles faced considerably more danger from the English than did the duke of Berry from the Lusignan, both rulers ordered these works to help establish an ideological equilibrium throughout their territories.

I should now like to explore our typology from another angle in conjunction with what I consider to be one of the most revealing indicators in comparing Melusine and Joan of Arc: the symbolism of place—the *locus amoenus* [pleasant place]—of the initiation and encounter scene(s), which in both lives pertains to a special forest near one or more fountains. Because the Book of Joan and Jean d'Arras both devote considerable attention to establishing the verisimilitude as well as the enchantment of each place, its function and relationship to other magical places past and present, especially via the invocation of prophecy, this invites a closer reading of the authors' different discursive techniques and the motives behind them.

In a meticulously documented study merging ethnography with Joan's trial testimony, Madeleine Jeay emphasizes the confrontation between folk custom and clerical glossing of the defendant's youthful experiences around the famous Fairy Tree near Joan's home, and how forest, fountain, and prophecy would suffer from politically hostile rereading by her Anglo-Burgundian judges and notaries.[24] As she examines the particular interaction of noble and peasant, clerkly and popular culture on several levels in this episode, Jeay observes how, through the changing politics of notarial mandate, the transcripts of the condemnation trial used Joan's testimony and that of witnesses to discredit her as a lone practitioner of heretical rituals around the tree and fountains. Jeay then explains how, in the nullification trial, previous testimony, together with new evidence from witnesses (whose memories were recorded as curiously fresher despite the twenty-five-year time lapse!), led to her rehabilitation, since it depicted this place's enchanted aura as part of ancient pre-Christian, common lore involving May and summer festivals, in which both lord and peasant—and not just Joan—participated (Tisset-Lanhers, 1:178; 2:145).

The geographical reality of place vs. the testimonial function in both women's histories elicits a telling paradox. Although Joan's locale was supposedly the real one, she and her witnesses barely corroborate each other's testimony as to precise physical geographic details and occurrences at each site (Jeay, 149–53). Indeed, Jean d'Arras's romance offers much more precise spatial information to make his fairy tale more credible, as he lavishly exploits the fountain-forest ambiance as a well-known, yet always appealing motif to his readers, one also steeped in regional folklore and related to the eternal feminine. He also uses this familiar repertory of motifs, laced with conventional assurances of the truthfulness of his *vrayes chroniques* and, more uniquely, references to *textual* time and space (for example, *cy avant* [before this], *cy après* [after this]) to engage and control the reader's belief in the reality of Melusine's marvelous capabilities, as Perret remarks ("L'espace romanesque," 179–80).

All of these discursive levels enable the author, as *romancier* [novelist, romancer] instead of *notaire* [legal notary], to function as a more pleasing disseminator of the *histoire* [history/story] supplied by his patron and the Duke's sister. And yet, if he professes to be neither "historian," "chronicler," nor "clerk"—all of whom would be theoretically confined to what "the history/story tells us" (*M* 8)—he equally avoids calling himself a "romancer," expressing his modest wish to leave the creating to God (*M* 2–3), while relegating his role to that of one who would *mettre en prose* [set to prose] or *traictier* [treat, handle] this story. Jean thus also renders his intentions more innocuous, to cover himself during a politically volatile era. In this lighter mode, as it suits him, Melusine serves as just another fairy princess, around whom fountains and forests become universalized as spatial harbingers of some exciting *adventure* to break the *merancolie* [melancholy, doldrums] (*M* 35) of the status quo.

By contrast, every stage of Joan's existence had become momentous by the time of her various trials. There was no place for amusement. The portentous trial-testimonial discrepancies in depicting her youthful revelatory landscapes may be due in part to the very dynamics of the Maid's self-authoring: her myth, still being processed, was so labile that even (or perhaps especially) her supporters were unsure of reality. Joan's own story, as created by the Poitiers preliminary and trial documents, the Fairy-tree/fountain episode and most notably the Oak Forest served to situate her within traditional prophecy to validate her mission: "Ex nemore canuto puella eliminabitur ut medelae curam adhibeat" [From out of the oak forest a maiden will be sent forth to devote herself to healing], which was cited somewhat differently at her trial.[25] We have already alluded to Joan's awareness of this and other prophecies related to her mission, whose symbolic authority she may have continually supplemented, not only in the period between Vaucouleurs and Chinon, as Wood suggests (143), but also after Orléans—at least allowing such details of preexisting lore to become assimilated into her own myth through rumors, reports, and commemorative poems at this time (for example, the "Anonymous Ballade on the Reims Coronation," July 17, 1429).[26] Melusine, however subliminally, may also have figured in that lore, as we shall attempt to show.

Two weeks after the coronation and commemorative ballad, Christine de Pizan, the author of the only nonanonymous French poem on Joan during her mission, the *Ditié de Jehanne d'Arc* [The Tale of Joan of Arc],[27] would combine these levels of myth and prophecy—"structures of authority," as Kevin Brownlee has rightly visualized them—and enfold them within her own self-image as another woman seeking recognition in a male profession or endeavor: writing, instead of bearing arms.[28] Much of what Christine says about Joan was actually taken from the reactions of Jacques Gelu, Jean Gerson, and others at Poitiers, combined with popular belief, as Fraioli and Lefèvre-Pontalis have noted.[29] Joan's highly mutable, varied usage of authority and prophecy perhaps most closely resembles Jean d'Arras's allusion to divine prophecy as a background to his tale: "David le prophete dit que les jugemens et punicions de Dieu sont comme abysme sans rive et sans fons, et n'est pas saige qui les cuide comprendre en son engin" [The prophet David says that the judgments and punishments of God are like an abyss without sides or bottom, and anyone who would presume to understand these by his or her own faculties is unwise] (*M* 2), together with his equivocal deployment of testimonial functions as elucidated by Perret.

Again on the subject of forest, fountain, and prophecy, both the anonymous *Ballade du sacre de Reims* and Christine's *Ditié* allude to another prevailing omen, seen by Charles while hunting: a flying stag [*cerf volant*], representing, in simplest terms, the power of the French king as descended from Caesar (Kennedy-Varty, 63–64), akin to the Second Charlemagne prophecy also mentioned in both poems on Joan. In Jean d'Arras we recall that Raymondin's domain promised him by the count, as foretold by Melusine, would be defined by a hart's skin at the fountain, whose perimeter would prove surprisingly large, but this time through *mortal* ingenuity (*M* 32–35). In both cases, the stag or hart functions as a deceptively majestic herald of the donation of royal dominion by previous generations.[30] Jean d'Arras's use of the hart's skin as the basis of his foundation story plays a bit more perversely or ominously with this *translatio imperii* [transference of imperial power] on a literary level, since, as a distinct Virgilian echo, Melusine's eventually tragic *engin* [ingenuity] can be viewed by the literate reader as descended from that of Dido, the ill-fated founder of Carthage: the anti-Rome.[31]

But such ingenious interpretations are fragile and usually vulnerable to the shifting motives behind them, even among the most passive witnesses. Jeay, toward the end of her study of Joan's folkloric background, makes a very brief allusion to Melusine: "Cet avatar des légendes mélusiniennes n'est-il pas la meilleure façon dont fonctionne le bricolage culturel?" [Might not this avatar of the Melusinian legends be the best example of how cultural tinkering functions?] (161). Independently of Jeay, Fraikin relates Paracelsus's later account of "les Mélusines" as princesses dispossessed because of their sins to testimony at Joan's rehabilitation explaining the fairies' desertion of the tree at Domremy (58–59). This would reinforce the Dido-Melusine connection while also incorporating the trial testimony concerning the evil or goodness of the Fairy Tree. Fraikin's association also causes us to wonder whether Joan might have known of Melusine in some form as early as ca. 1413.

However plausible that may be, we recall that Joan's mission was approved by a panel of distinguished clerics following a two-week examination of the Maid in the spring of 1429 at Poitiers, land of Melusine. Although no cleric wishing to keep his post would have cited Melusine over the canonical "Judith, Esther and Deborah," and even the pagan Tiburtine Sibyl—all mentioned by Gelu, Gerson and then Christine—as examples of women chosen by God for traditionally male heroic tasks, might we perhaps carry Jeay's "avatar" theory further, to suggest that the subjacent legendary patina of the supernatural serpent-woman facilitated acceptance of Joan's proposed mission at Poitiers, whether the Maid herself knew of her or not? This seems all the more likely since Jean d'Arras's "cultural tinkering," like Christine's, takes pains to infuse the preface to his romance with allusions to Old Testament prophecy—divine prophecy, unknown to mortals—and also that greatest of pagan philosophers, Aristotle (for example, *M* 2).

In his *Mélusine*, Jean d'Arras was attempting to gild the historical reputation of Jean de Berry's diplomacy (just as testimonial tinkering in Joan's rehabilitation was supposed to improve Charles's official aura) by reassuring the Lusignans that Melusine had not slithered over to the English during the long campaigns in the Poitou during the 1370s.[32] We can forgive—or perhaps not even notice—this political propaganda because of his artistry, a license to which his chosen persona and genre entitle him. His politics strikes us as harmless when compared to that with which the notaries infused their records of Joan's trials. The disparity arises out of the distinction in trust the reader makes between an author who purports to be "making" a story based on history, "de cuer diligent, de mon povre sens et povoir" [with diligent heart, with my feeble reason and intellect] (*M* 1), and supposedly dispassionate notaries such as Manchon and Courcelles, whose "patron" might be equated with the Anglo-Burgundian cause and more directly, Pierre Cauchon, the chief magistrate of the condemnation trial. Besides which, the rehabilitation notaries were no more honest and disinterested.

Jean d'Arras's episode of Geoffroy at the sepulcher (*M* 265) nicely illustrates the problematics of reading, trusting in, then heeding, clerkly wisdom. Having discovered a sepulcher by chance while fiercely pursuing one of the giants, Geoffroy enters it and reads the history of the family of "King Elinas of Albanie," which he fails to recognize as his mother's. The chronicle nevertheless captivates and moves him, though more in an aesthetic way, as does the beauty of the chamber, which, he learns, is guarded by the giant and open only to members of Elinas's lineage (*M* 266). Because he is unaware of his hereditary entitlement, Geoffroy commits a cruel misdeed while intending an act of prowess. Jean d'Arras calmly underscores the ironic discord between Geoffroy's observance of proper lance holding and making the sign of the cross before entering the crypt (*M* 265) and his unnecessary—but typical, for his generation—killing of the guardian giant (*M* 266–67). What should have been an archetypal scene of family *pietas* in the progress of an epic hero is transformed into an illustration of a family curse repeating itself, before which clerkly admonition stands helpless.

As authors, both Jean d'Arras and Joan's notaries must exhibit piety, learning, and some form of self-effacement. But only one, the notary, carries the power over life and death as a prerogative of *clergie* [learning]. Rather than diminish the qualities of their *sens* as Jean d'Arras does, however formulaically, such men qualify themselves in the records as quite the opposite: *in sacra theologia bachelarii* or some similar title, from which we expect truth, not fiction.

Thus, if for all their subtlety, both Jean d'Arras and Joan become tripped up by their own stories at times,[33] only Joan receives the death penalty for it. However, in assessing Joan's self-fashioning, we should not dismiss the difference too hastily. Unlike Jean d'Arras, she functions as both author and subject with respect to her story. As character, particularly after her capture, she seems of necessity to surrender control, yet as we observed in her Abjuration/Relapse and other decisive moments in her trial in which she knows the consequences of her actions, she manages to manipulate the discourse and deeds of her persecutors to her final advantage and thus retain some power of authorship. Even more than other mystics and zealots, she demonstrates awareness that her martyrdom would become her signal exploit, overshadowing even Orléans, as if her ordeal's dreadful pain would be recompensed by posthumous glory, for her and for France. Unlike the cases of religious and political suicides, history would prove her right, whatever her actual degree of control.

The books of Melusine and Joan have benefited and suffered from political revisionism. After Orléans, Joan resanctified not only the French "blood royal" but also that of her own family. If Melusine's dynastic fecundity is an integral part of her legend, Joan's achievements in these domains require more effort to prove. Yet they were accomplished through a series of *post hoc ergo propter hoc* maneuvers to legitimize Joan by lineage as rightful liberator of France. Charles VII issued letters patent in December 1429 ennobling her father, Jacques d'Arc. From this, and via her siblings, Joan founded her own noble line, through which Morant, in his hefty volume *Le Sang Glorieux de Jeanne d'Arc*, identifies among her descendants such illustrious figures as Fénelon and Marshal Lyautey.[34]

In a strikingly opposite cycle, the betrayed Melusine disconnects her progeny from any glory for the future lineage of Lusignan as part of her legacy (*M* 257–58) so thoroughly that, as we have seen, her son Geoffroy does not know himself to be a descendant of a sacred lineage at a significant point in the story (*M* 265). Despite her monstrous progeny's problematical exploits, and maybe because of her disavowal of them, Melusine has been "adopted" by the Lusignans as their guardian mother figure forever, not by letters patent, but on the folkloric level, awaiting validation for the nobility by Jean d'Arras's and Coudrette's work. Across the channel, as with Joan, the English associated Melusine with the devil: they may still have been smarting from the dynastic myth linking the Plantagenets with "Melusine, daughter of Satan."[35]

Morant's genealogy of Joan, published in 1912 and bearing the papal seal of approval, was composed for reasons similar to those of Charles's letters patent and also those of Charles du Lys in his genealogy of Joan (1610), in that Morant, himself a self-proclaimed member of Joan's "family," was one of a profusion of authors—some secular, some religious, learned or popular, right-wing, left-wing, Catholic, Republican, of varying levels of sanity—who sought to help finalize the long-awaited canonization (1920), in some form or other, of the recently beatified heroine. The process was temporarily halted by World War I, which only strengthened Joan's cause, as it turned out, since, like Melusine for the Poitevins/Lusignans, she again became a galvanizing symbol for the French during other dark, menacing periods in their history, as attested in numerous posters and pamphlets of both world wars.[36] By contrast, the many nineteenth-century writings on Melusine and similar figures diminished and were confined to literary circles by the years immediately preceding World War I, during which productivity ceased completely; they recommenced at around 1927, whereupon Hoffrichter and then especially Stouff began their scholarly textual "veneration" of her (Pillard, 43).

Further possibilities for comparison certainly exist, but the most haunting questions are already apparent: could Joan herself have known of Melusine, of her spectral presence around Domremy or Poitiers, while omitting mention of her at her trial for the same reasons she avoided other potential connections with witchcraft? Her examiners, though not Poitevins, might they nevertheless have heard about this strange female guardian? Or could both sides have had Melusine in mind, along with the named "respectable" heroines, prior to Joan's mission, thus making examiners and the examined latent, tacit accomplices in the search for another female protector from the enemies of France, a country whose rulers, whether weak or strong, had to be male by Salic law?[37] While this attempt to relate the two mythopoetic processes in France circa 1429–31 cannot be deemed conclusive, it shows that something was definitely in the air.

Notes

1. Politics and patronage weave a tangled web in this matter. Jean d'Arras composed his romance for Jean de France, duke of Berry, who was also a major patron of Christine de Pizan, author of, among other important works, the first nonanonymous French poem celebrating Joan of Arc during the heroine's lifetime. Because Christine wrote her poem to Joan during her "retirement" at Poissy abbey, it does not figure in the Duke's manuscript collec-

tion. However, Christine had previously addressed her *Lamentacion sur les maux de la France* [Lamentation on the Troubles of France] (1410) to the duke of Berry, urging him to act as peacemaker under the threat of civil war. Unfortunately, he did not heed her advice. The duke was also the brother and chief rival of Philip the Bold of Burgundy, grandfather of Philip the Good, originally an avowed enemy of Joan but, interestingly enough, also a major collector of Christine's pre-Johannic works.

2. While at least one other scholar has noted the resemblance between Joan and Melusine, such references have been made only in passing, with no attempt at a systematic, in-depth comparison. See Guy-Edouard Pillard, *La Déesse Mélusine: Mythologie d'une fée* (Maulévrier: Hérault, 1989), 328.

3. In using this term I am certainly indebted to the classic study by Stephen Greenblatt, *Renaissance Self-Fashioning: From More to Shakespeare* (Chicago: University of Chicago Press, 1980), which I find eminently pertinent despite its focus on a later period in English literature. I also do not mean to imply that Joan's self-determinism was of a Renaissance dimension.

4. Editions of texts comprising what may be termed the Book of Joan include: (trial testimony of Joan and contemporaries) Pierre Tisset and Yvonne Lanhers, eds., *Procès de Condamnation de Jeanne d'Arc,* 3 vols. (Paris: Klincksieck, 1960–71), henceforth "Tisset-Lanhers"; *La Minute française de l'Interrogatoire de Jeanne la Pucelle,* vol. 1 of Paul Doncoeur and Yvonne Lanhers, eds., *Documents et recherches relatifs à Jeanne la Pucelle,* 5 vols. (Melun: d'Argences, 1952–61); Pierre Duparc, ed., *Procès en nullité de la condamnation de Jeanne d'Arc,* 5 vols. (Paris: Klincksieck, 1977–89); (Joan's letters) Régine Pernoud and Marie-Véronique Clin, eds. in *Jeanne d'Arc* (Paris: Fayard, 1986), 377–90; (contemporary literature and chronicles) Jules Quicherat, ed., *Procès de condamnation et de réhabilitation de Jeanne d'Arc dite la Pucelle* (Paris: Jules Renouard, 1841–49; rpt., New York: Johnson, 1965), vols. 4–5; Pierre Champion, "Notes sur Jeanne d'Arc: III. 'Ballade du Sacre de Reims,'" *Le Moyen Age* 22 / 2nd ser. 13 (1909): 370–77; Paul Meyer, ed., "Ballade contre les Anglais 1429," *Romania* 21 (1892): 50–52.

5. Profound teleological self-awareness is not unusual in mystics, zealots, and similar charismatic personalities. Marguerite Porete (d. 1310) and Hildegard of Bingen (1098–1179) reflect this quality in different ways, while Joan was a contemporary of Margery Kempe: for a comparison of the two, see Clarissa W. Atkinson, *Mystic and Pilgrim: The "Book" and the World of Margery Kempe* (Ithaca, N.Y.: Cornell University Press, 1983), 181–89. The most famous example is Christ, as provocatively examined by Hugh J. Schonfield, *The Passover Plot: New Light on the History of Jesus* (London: Hutchinson, 1965). In several panegyrics and other encomia of Joan, she is equated with Christ. For an example

of nonmystical authors ordering their posterity, David Hult examines Guillaume de Lorris as such in *Self-fulfilling Prophecies: Readership and Authority in the First "Roman de la Rose"* (Cambridge: Cambridge University Press, 1986).

6. For the cult of Melusine through the ages, see esp. the pioneering studies by Le Goff and Le Roy Ladurie, Pillard and, most recently and concisely, Christine Ruby's updating of Bossuat's "Jean d'Arras," in Geneviève Hasenohr and Michel Zink, eds., *Dictionnaire des lettres françaises: Le Moyen Age* (Paris: Fayard, 1992), 744–45. For Joan as cult object in her own time, see Pierre Lanéry d'Arc, *Le Culte de Jeanne d'Arc au XVe siècle* (Orléans: Herluison, 1887), 13; for the negative implications of this cultism as used in her condemnation, see Marina Warner, *Joan of Arc: The Image of Female Heroism* (New York: Knopf, 1981), 14, who cites Tisset-Lanhers, 2:95. For her cult in recent times, see, e.g.: Michel Winock, Christian Amalvi, Guy Lobrichon, and Philippe Contamine in "Dossier: L'Affaire Jeanne d'Arc," *L'Evénement du jeudi* 392 (7–13 mai 1992), 68–81, 84–86. See also Winock's fuller treatment, "Jeanne d'Arc" in vol. 3 of *Les France*, vol. 3 of Pierre Nora, ed., *Les lieux de mémoire* (Paris: Gallimard, 1992), 674–733.

7. "De l'espace romanesque à la matérialité du livre," *Poétique* 50 (1982): esp. 179–80; see also Perret's "L'Invraisemblable vérité," esp. 26–29.

8. Pierre Gordon, "Mélusine," in *Essais* (Neuilly: Arma Artis, 1983), 15.

9. See (for Melusine) Robert Brechon, "Le Mythe de la fée Mélusine," *Obliques: "La Femme surréaliste"* 14–15 (1977): 37; and Klaus Theleweit, *Male Fantasies* (Minneapolis: University of Minnesota Press, 1987), 75; (for Joan) Warner, 19–22.

10. One thinks, for example, of Dido—post-Sichaeus and pre-Aeneas—when she rules and builds the city of Carthage, as an archetype of such autonomy.

11. Laurence Harf-Lancner, "Mélusine," in Pierre Brunel, ed., *Dictionnaire des mythes littéraires* (Monaco: Du Rocher, 1988), 999–1003; Claude Lecouteux, "La Structure." Harf-Lancner concentrates chiefly on Jean d'Arras's account, while alluding to other versions. Lecouteux, citing and applying Propp's morphological models, subordinates Jean d'Arras and Coudrette within the larger, more diachronic, international category of Melusin*ian* legends.

12. I have added the onomastic-etymological and literary-historical facet to my modification of Harf-Lancner's and Lecouteux's models. For a comprehensive treatment of Melusine's name, along with other facets of her legend and related ones, see Jean Markale, 145–70.

13. For the textual genealogy of Melusine before and after Jean d'Arras in France and Germany, see Leo Hoffrichter's still valuable dissertation, *Die*

ältesten französischen Bearbeitungen der Melusinensage (Halle: Karras, Kröber & Nietschmann, 1927), esp. diagram, 72. For Joan's shifting histories, see Gerd Krumeich, *Jeanne d'Arc in der Geschichte* (Sigmaringen: Jan Thorbecke, 1989), here consulted as *Jeanne d'Arc à travers l'Histoire,* trans. Josie Mély et al., pref. Régine Pernoud (Paris: Albin Michel, 1993).

14. Saint Michael became the patron saint not only of Joan's mission but of all those fiercely devoted to saving France at that time and throughout the reign of Louis XI. For the growing reverence for him during the foundation of France, see Colette Beaune, *Naissance de la nation France* (Paris: NRF/Gallimard, 1985), 195–96.

15. Some scholars accept that Joan was illiterate and could only sign her name at best (Duparc, 5:145–50); others assess her literacy more generously. She appears even to have used a secret code with her men, indicating whether or not her signed orders were to be followed (Pernoud-Clin, 377).

16. Tisset-Lanhers, 2:120. Joan's "sign" or "secret"—whether a red, lily-shaped birthmark, a prayer, or other possibility posing another unresolved point in her trial testimony—is discussed most recently in conjunction with surrounding prophecies and folklore by Jean Fraikin, "Regard sur l'au-delà de Jeanne d'Arc," *Tradition wallonne* 10 (1993): 5–116, esp. 101–2.

17. For a recent, fresh attempt along the well-trodden path of Joan's legend vs. reality, and specifically her attendant mystical accoutrements, see Michel Lamy, *Jeanne d'Arc: Histoire vraie et genèse d'un mythe* (Paris: Payot, 1987), 171–74, which treats her rings, sword, and the popularity of Saint Catherine de Fierbois as a pilgrimage site among soldiers.

18. For detailed discussion of Joan's shifting political usefulness to Charles, see Malcolm G. A. Vale, *Charles VII* (London: Eyre Methuen, 1974), ch. 3; for Joan's interpretation of Charles's coronation as compared to French and English customs, see Charles T. Wood, *Joan of Arc and Richard III: Sex, Saints and Government in the Middle Ages* (New York: Oxford University Press, 1988), esp. ch. 1, and 139–43.

19. I should like to thank Prof. Michelle Wright for her suggestion, given at the Colloquium "Mélusine at 600" at the University of Massachusetts, Amherst, that I clarify Charles's role in Joan's history.

20. For an analysis of the Anglo-French political significance of Joan's mystical authority, see Wood, esp. 145–47. Vale, ch. 3, explains why Charles could not help Joan and also why he was slow to effect her rehabilitation. Vale also shows to what extent Joan was a victim of France's civil war in addition to the English menace; see "Jeanne d'Arc et ses adversaires: Jeanne, victime d'une guerre civile?" in *Jeanne d'Arc: Une époque, un rayonnement,* Colloque d'histoire

médiévale, Orléans, 1979, ed. Régine Pernoud (Paris: Centre National de Recherche Scientifique, 1982), 203–16.

21. See Fr. François-Marie Lethel, "La Soumission à l'Eglise militante: un aspect théologique de la condamnation de Jeanne d'Arc," in *Jeanne d'Arc: Une époque, un rayonnement*, 181–90.

22. Melusine exclaims: "Las! Mon amy, se tu ne m'eusses faussee, je estoye gettee et exemptee de paine et de tourment, et eusse vescu le cours naturel comme femme naturelle, et feusse morte naturelement" [Alas, my friend! If you had not wronged me, I would have been set aside and exempted from all penalty and torment, and would have lived a natural, normal life span as a normal woman, and would have died normally] (*M* 256).

23. Based on a notion first attested by the Dean of the Collegiate Church of Saint Thiebault of Metz in his *Chroniques de la ville et noble cité de Metz*, in Auguste Calmet, ed., *Histoire ecclésiastique et civile de la Lorraine*, 2nd ed. (Nancy: A. Leseure, 1745–57), 2: cols. 121–22, 200; rpt. in Quicherat, 5:321–23, this theory holds that Joan was never burned at Rouen but managed to escape while some poor unknown perished in her place, and resurfaced in most popular form as the Dame des Armoises, who confessed to her hoax in 1440. This belief was nevertheless reborn in the work of Father Vignier (late 17C), and continues through the present day in numerous works. See, for a comprehensive treatment, Yann Grandeau, *Jeanne insultée: Procès en diffamation* (Paris: Albin Michel, 1973).

24. Madeleine Jeay, "Clercs et paysans au XVe siècle: Une relecture de l'épisode de l'arbre aux fées dans les procès de Jeanne d'Arc," in *Normes et pouvoir à la fin du moyen âge*, ed. M.-C. Déprez-Masson (Montréal: CERES, 1989), 145–63. My thanks to Thelma Fenster for bringing this article to my attention.

25. As Wood, 236, and others confirm, the primary source of this Merlinic prophecy is in Geoffrey of Monmouth, *Historia regum Britanniae*, ed. Acton Griscom (London: Longman, Green, 1929), 390–91. In Joan's trial records for Feb. 24, the prophecy reads: "quod circa illud nemus [Bois chenu] debebat venire quedam puella que faceret mirabilia" [that from around this forest should come a certain girl who would work miracles] (Tisset-Lanhers, 1:67). For Merlin and Melusine as prophetic male-female counterparts, see Bea Lundt, *Melusine und Merlin im Mittelalter: Entwürfe und Modelle weiblicher Existenz im Beziehungs-Diskurs der Geschlechter* (Munich: Wilhelm Fink, 1991). For fuller documentation of contemporary prophecies relating to Joan, see the notes to Angus J. Kennedy and Kenneth Varty, eds., *Ditié de Jehanne d'Arc, Christine de Pisan* (Oxford: Society for Medieval Languages and Literature, 1977), 68–69.

26. See Pierre Champion, n. 4.

27. Quicherat, 5:3–21; modern critical ed. by Kennedy-Varty. Several examples of Christine's imagery resemble that found in the "Anonymous Ballade on the Coronation." Kennedy-Varty, citing De Roche and Wissler in *Festschrift Louis Gauchat* (Aarau, 1926), 332, note that the *Ditié* is grouped with Joan's letters to the king of England, and the Poitiers *Consultation* in the Berne ms., the base ms. for their edition (3).

28. "Structures of Authority in Christine de Pizan's *Ditié de Jehanne d'Arc*," in Kevin Brownlee and Walter Stephens, eds., *Discourses of Authority in Medieval and Renaissance Literature* (Hanover/London: University Press of New England, 1989), 131–50.

29. Deborah Fraioli, "The Literary Image of Joan of Arc: Prior Influences," *Speculum* 56 (1981): 811–30; Germain Lefèvre-Pontalis, notes to Antonio Morosini, *Chronique: Extraits relatifs à l'histoire de France*, ed. and trans. Léon Dorez, 4 vols. (Paris: Renouard, 1898–1902), 3:38–46; 4: appendix. The texts of Gerson, Gelu, and other Poitiers examiners, including the summary of their findings, can be found in Quicherat, 3:298–410.

30. Michael Bath traces the evolution of "Caesar's deer" and the flying stag as royal-dynastic and ethnogenic myths most fully in his *The Image of the Stag: Iconographic Themes in Western Art* (Baden-Baden: Valentin Koerner, 1991), a prolegomenon to which may be found in "The Legend of Caesar's Deer," *Medievalia et Humanistica* 9 (1979): 53–66. These very thorough analyses nonetheless omit *Mélusine* and also Christine's allusion to the flying stag as a lover's barter—rather than an imperial one—in her lyric *Jeux a vendre* [Songs for Sale], no. 13 (ed. Maurice Roy, 1:190): "Je vous vens le cerf voulant / de bien aimer ne soiez lent" [I sell to you the flying stag / As a good lover, never lag].

31. Virgil's brief allusion to how Dido acquired the terrain for her empire by cleverly using an ox hide in *Aeneid,* 1:365–68 receives fuller treatment by Servius, who in his popular 4C–5C commentaries adds the details of how the ox hide was cut into bands, etc. The *Eneas* romancer combines both Virgil's and Servius's accounts in his retelling (ed. J. J. Salverda da Grave [Paris: Champion, 1925; rpt., 1985], vol. 1, 13) and is Jean d'Arras's most likely source. Perhaps mindful of the stag's richer symbolism (see n. 30 *supra*), Jean substitutes its hide for that of the ox.

32. Françoise Lehoux, *Jean de France, Duc de Berri: sa vie, son action politique (1340–1416)* (Paris: Picard, 1966), vol. 1, esp. 336; Michèle Perret, postface, *Le Roman de Mélusine*, 313–15. To the claim of Melusine's exclusively Lusignan origins, one might object that in Jean d'Arras's story, Elinas came from "Albanie" and others of Melusine's mortal ancestors came from Scotland—to

which we can answer in turn that the Scots also resented the English, for which reason they would later fight with Joan against them.

33. For inconsistencies in Jean d'Arras's narrative, see Louis Stouff, *Essai;* one of the most obvious is found in *M* 258. Since one of the primary objectives of Joan's condemnation trial was to entrap the heroine within inconsistencies in her own testimony, see the interrogation sections of the trial records, Tisset-Lanhers, vols. 1, 2, passim; and Doncoeur-Lanhers, 5:110–55.

34. Count Georges de Morant, *Le Nobiliaire du XX*[e] *siècle*, vol. 4 (Paris: Nobiliaire du XXe siècle, 1912). For letters patent ennobling Joan's family, see his introduction, 47.

35. Wood reminds us of this example of Melusine's nefarious presence in English royal genealogy, as he describes the efforts of twelfth-century English propagandists to sanctify Henry II's new Plantagenet lineage by canonization (of his Saxon ancestor, Edward the Confessor), the benefits of which were undermined years later by Henry's ruthless killing of the much-loved Becket. As a result, curmudgeonly chroniclers instead devised this most pejorative genealogy. Wood also commends the aptness of their negative revisionism by dubbing Henry's son, the murderous King John, "a true son of Melusine" (24).

36. For reproductions of medieval and modern popular images of Joan, see Warner and, most recently, articles by Michel Winock, et al.; see n. 5 *supra*. For Melusine's iconography, see Clier-Colombani.

37. When the Burgundians seized Paris, Charles and his administration fled to Bourges and Poitiers—without a copy of this quintessential law, which they finally were able to copy in 1430 (Beaune, 272). By saving Charles, Joan in a sense saved French male succession as well.

Configuring the Epilogue: Ending and the Ends of Fiction in the *Roman de Mélusine*

Donald Maddox

The epilogue of Jean d'Arras's *Roman de Mélusine* repeatedly attests to a remarkable preoccupation with ending the work in an appropriate manner. Happily for us, this effort left as part of its legacy the precise date of its completion: "le jeudi vij[e] jour d'aoust l'an de grace Nostre Seigneur mil ccc.iiij[xx] xiij" "ceste histoire. . . fu *parfaicte*" [on Thursday the seventh day of August in the year of Our Lord 1393 . . . this story was perfected] (*M* 307). Significantly, commemoration of "la *perfection* de ceste estoire" (*M* 307) at this prominent juncture in the epilogue echoes the very first sentence of the exordium, which draws a conventional contrast between the "*perfection* de bien"—the process of creation in conformity with the archetype of perfection in the mind of God—and the degrees of imperfection in evidence among created entities ("selon les vices des creatures"). Mindful of mankind's potential for imperfection, Jean d'Arras humbly beseeches God to grant him the capacity to complete ("achever") his own undertaking both to His greater glory and to that of his patron, Jean de Berry.[1] From the beginning of the work, it would appear that

Jean's conceptualization of the writer's role is based on an analogy between divine creation and poetic invention, whereby the "perfect" created entity is ideally elaborated in conformity with an archetypal model. This resonates with a well-established view of "perfection" in earlier medieval thought, one that refers, in Douglas Kelly's words, to "the attainment of an amalgam that is complete and whole" in terms of its replication of a model.[2] Unblemished by lacunae or corruptions, the "perfect" poetic text in this sense is one that has been realized to the fullest possible extent as an exemplar of the poet's mental conceptualization of the integral work. Accordingly, Jean's insistent reiteration of the term *perfection* in his epilogue, while obviously conveying authorial satisfaction with the outcome of an ambitious project, also resonates with the term's earlier usage by medieval narrative poets who thus designate, either literally or in metaphoric configurations, the positive outcome of textual production.[3] My question here concerns the precise nature of that maximal fulfillment: what in Jean's view constitutes an apposite sense of an ending?

Having identified the date of the work's completion, the narrator briefly encapsulates its contents, as if to confirm that the principal objectives behind its elaboration are now fully realized: "Or vous ay dit et devisé, selon les vrayes croniques et la vraye histoire, comment la noble forteresse de Lusegnen en Poictou fut fondee, et retrait la noble et puissant lignie qui en est descendue des nobles gens qui la fonderent, dont Dieu veuille avoir les ames recommandees en son saint paradis qui est es siecles des siecles. Amen" [I have thus given you an account, according to the authentic chronicles and the accurate history, of how the noble fortress of Lusignan in Poitou was founded, and I have detailed the noble and powerful lineage that descended from those who founded it. May God keep their souls in His saintly and eternal abode. Amen] (*M* 307). Here in a nutshell are the text's generic moorings as Jean sees them: not at all a "*roman* généalogique," as we modern classifiers might have it,[4] but rather an accurate, reliable *history* of a lineage, one that harks back to its very founding, a narrative that is both etiology and genealogy. We are again reminded, as so often previously, that this tissue of textuality intermingled with fictions is a reworking of chronicles and of a history that are all "vrayes" from the author's point of view. Moreover, we are frequently given to understand that it was recounted—"dit et devisé"—as part of an oral presentation; such evocations of a narrator's presence before an audience no doubt also connoted a considerable degree of credibility to a contemporaneous public.

Yet within the full context of the lengthy epilogue, which in the Arsenal manuscript occupies nearly 6 percent of the whole, this remarkable declaration of the work's "perfection" seems oddly out of place. On the one hand, it occurs relatively late in the epilogue (folio 164, recto, column one), long after the end of the work was first announced (folio 157, verso, second column). At that earlier point, the narrative proper culminates in a rapid, seemingly definitive manner, with the enumeration of the political fortunes of eight of the sons of Raymondin and Melusine, whereupon we read: "Et cy fine la vraye histoire de la noble lignie de Lusegnen en Poictou, et avez ouy ceulx qui en sont yssuz" [Here ends the true history of the noble lineage of Lusignan in Poitou, about whose descendants you have heard] (*M* 294). This announcement of the text's formal ending in fact marks closure on one important level, the substratum of a genealogical infratext whose primary ramifications through the offspring of Melusine and Raymondin have now been fully illustrated. Then, however, after listing five minor branches of the family, the narrator makes a completely new beginning: "Et combien que j'aye dit que l'ystoire soit finee, si vous veuil je encores parler de Gieffroy" [Although I said that the story has ended, I nonetheless wish to speak to you again of Geoffroy] (*M* 294). The "true history" has officially ended, but something compels the narrator to continue at great length, through three seemingly unrelated segments.

In the first of these (*M* 294–301), he tells the story of how, after Raymondin's demise, Geoffroy once did battle with the mysterious "Knight of the Tower." After ten prosperous years as Lord of Lusignan, Geoffroy had discovered to his astonishment that a yearly tribute of ten sous was being paid to an unknown individual to protect the ornamental orb ("pommel") atop one of the fortress's towers. Upon inquiring about this odd expenditure, he was informed that after Melusine's departure from Lusignan, on the last day of August of each year, an enormous hand would emerge from the heavens and seize the globe, causing costly damage to the tower. To prevent this, Raymondin had arranged to pay an annual tribute to a man who now identifies himself only as "De par Dieu" (*M* 298, 300), an emissary of God. In this episode, after Geoffroy had engaged in a long and finally indecisive battle with this mysterious being, the latter explained that the payment had been imposed upon Raymondin as penance for breaking his vow to Melusine. He further counseled that instead of making any more payments to protect his tower, Geoffroy should ensure the peace of Raymondin's soul by building a hospital and a chaplaincy. Once Geoffroy had done this, all traces of the mysterious figure vanished.

After completing that lengthy account, the narrator moves to yet another (*M* 301–7): "Et cy fenist nostre histoire de ceulx de Lusegnen, mais pour ce que les roys d'Armenie en sont extraiz, je vous veuil dire une adventure qui advint a un roy d'Armenie" [Here ends our story of the Lusignan family, but since the kings of Armenie descended from them, I do want to tell you about an adventure that befell a king of Armenie] (*M* 301). This second "adventure" relates in great detail the misfortunes of a latter-day king of Armenie at the Castle of the Sparrowhawk. Any knight who sojourned there and succeeded in keeping a sleepless watch over the sparrowhawk for three consecutive days and nights could ask of the lady of the castle any boon he wished, save the lady herself. He who prematurely fell asleep would remain her captive. The young king himself succeeded in keeping the vigil for the requisite period, yet thrice he foolishly refused any *don* other than the one proscribed from the outset, the lady's body. His obstinacy incurred disastrous consequences: the lady was Melior, Melusine's sister, and because she was the aunt of this monarch descended from Melusine through King Guyon, kinship ruled out their carnal union. To punish him for demanding the forbidden reward, she consigned his lineage to nine generations of progressive decline.

After this account comes the third announcement of the end. This is the aforementioned passage giving the date of the work's "perfection" and concluding with what in musical terms would perhaps qualify as a "deceptive cadence," a progression, not from a dominant to a tonic chord, as in a conventional closing line, but from a dominant to a sixth, so that the unanticipated suspension of the move toward closure can allow for further development. For indeed, there is still more to come: a long third segment (*M* 307–12) initially brings into prominence the patronage accorded the work by Jean, duke of Berry and his sister, the duchess of Bar, and then proceeds to document Melusine's latter-day manifestations in the material world, at moments when the lordship of Lusignan was about to change. Finally, a protracted commentary on the believability of the seemingly incredible yields to definitive completion of the long-deferred process of ending.

In sum, to echo Matthew Arnold, the epiloque "begins, and ends, and then again begins," repeatedly. Three episodic segments plus four utterances of conclusion surrounding them provide a veritable cascade of endings. Few would disagree, I suspect, that the three narrative segments, despite their apparent randomness, are among the richest and most arresting in the entire work. Apart from a few formulaic sutures, however, the narrator provides no explicit indications either of possible thematic relationships among them or of what they might mean as an amalgam. Yet these are not merely random fragments shored against a premature and imperfect ending. It can be demonstrated, I believe, that they in fact comprise a coherent and richly significant triptych that retrospectively configures and valorizes "la perfection de ceste estoire" (*M* 307).

In the first place, the epilogue attests to a familiarity with the conventions of medieval romance, notably with regard to the well-established narrative convention of the *coustume*. Though directly indebted to Mandeville's *Voyages,* the second episode featuring the Coustume de l'Epervier cannot fail to recall, if only by its name, one of the earliest *coustumes* in Old French romance, the Custom of the Sparrowhawk in *Erec et Enide* by Chrétien de Troyes.[6] Although the episode shows no other close affinities with the latter, it conforms in terms of its overall structure to a format used repeatedly by Chrétien and widespread thereafter, especially in thirteenth-century prose romance: the hero arrives at a castle or other remote locus featuring an obligatory test identified usually, though not always, as a *coustume,* which is often the result of some type of supernatural enchantment. Often, this perilous mechanism has led to the death, imprisonment, or shame of all previous contenders; the hero invariably demonstrates a surpassing degree of prowess or virtue in mastering or even in abolishing it. Not infrequently he accedes to lordship of the castle.[7] Jean d'Arras is clearly mindful of this format, which he has adapted to fit the context of the work he has just completed.

Although this is the only *coustume* designated as such in the epilogue, it is apparent that the first and third episodes also rely on fundamental conventions of the literary custom. In the first segment, the fortress of Lusignan is held under the constraints of an enchantment, the material and symbolic yoke of a "treuage" (*M* 297), or tribute, which the hero, in this case no outsider but the young lord and heir of the castle, abolishes by force of arms. Likewise in the third segment, Lusignan is again under an enchantment, this one maintained by Melusine herself, who becomes visible to mortals in order to signify the succession of a legitimate heir to Lusignan. This mechanism serves precisely the same function fulfilled by many a *coustume* in courtly romance, which is to test the eligibility for the lordship of the castle of all who vie for the privilege.

These episodes all bring to mind much earlier romances featuring conventional *coustumes* that, as Douglas Kelly has recently pointed out, are topically amplified episodes that recontextualize a *merveille,* a marvelous adventure of the sort found in Celtic *matière.* In so doing, the exotic qualities linking them to antecedent traditions give way to a new coherence tributary to the work's fundamental meanings.[8] The question thus arises as to what meanings, precisely, this threefold rehabilitation of the discourse of literary customs is tributary. As far as the "perfection" of the work's global coherence is concerned, what ends are served by recourse to the properties of customs?

On closer scrutiny, it appears that the three episodes provide a means of tying off the major "loose ends" of the main story, whereby the conventions of literary customs serve in each episode to dispel fundamental ambiguities lingering at the story's end. The greatest of these results from the curious blend of Christian and folk elements inherent in the figure of Melusine herself.[9] At the end of the story, residual curiosity persists as to whether or not this *faee,* for all her marvelous accomplishments, was in attitude and action perhaps a malefic being. This possibility does seem untenable if we recall how Melusine generally respected religious protocol and generously laced her two instructive *chastoiements* to her sons with traditional religious and moral precepts (*M* 84–87; 152–54). On the other hand, however, she consigned her father to permanent exile in the depths of a mountain, and the text repeatedly evokes the perdurable punishment she subsequently incurred.

Moreover, after Fromont, the only one of her sons to espouse a monastic life, had burned to death in the abbey of Maillezais, she readily excused Geoffroy's arson and inadvertent fratricide on grounds that the monks at Maillezais were in any case a sinful lot (*M* 255). Indignant, Raymondin cited Fromont's exceeding goodness, branded his spouse in public as a "tres faulse serpente," and lamented that Fromont perished through "l'art demoniacle, car tous ceulx qui sont forcennez de yre sont ou commandement des princes d'enfer" [demonic art, for all those who are overwhelmed with rage are at the beck and call of the infernal princes] (*M* 255). This public excoriation of Melusine's serpentine state is what destroys the conjugal bond; Raymondin's disclosure of her secret openly demonstrates that he had perjured his vow to avoid her on Saturdays. True to Presine's warning, this revelation of her dual nature deprives her of a normal human life span and access to the Christian sacraments; it also consigns her to perpetual suffering until the end of time (*M* 256). While her renewed penance is depicted as part of God's unfathomable doing, her husband recognizes the role of his broken vow in bringing this about and seeks to make amends.

Accordingly, the first segment of the epilogue reveals that he had begun to pay an annual tribute, identified by his own counselors as a "rente" (*M* 295), to prevent further damage to his tower by a supernaturally directed hand. Is the origin of this marvel divine or is it demonic? Are we to infer that Lusignan is under the aegis of malefic supernatural forces sympathetic to Melusine's plight? It has in fact been suggested that the Knight of the Tower with whom Geoffroy does battle is really a demon.[10] On the other hand, this mysterious figure repeatedly asserts that he has been sent on behalf of God (*M* 298, 300). He also tells Geoffroy that he had been collecting the annual "rente" because Raymondin had never completed the papal penitence for his perjured vow to Melusine (*M* 300). Moreover, if this emissary were really demonic he would hardly have prescribed that in place of the annual monetary payment Geoffroy should found a hospital and chaplaincy for the peace of Raymondin's soul. To assume that the knight is a demon would also run counter to Jean's own insistence, later in the epilogue, that all of the "choses faees" in the story, including Melusine's confinement to the state of a serpent-woman, stem directly from "les secrez jugemens de Dieu" (*M* 310–11; cf. 4).[11]

That over the course of the episode the mysterious figure is gradually assimilated to the sphere of Christian values is likewise apparent from the metamorphoses of this custom over time. Literary customs in medieval romance are seldom inspired by the minute details of contemporaneous feudal juridical procedures.[12] Instead, they recall their own ancestry in the *materia remota* of antecedent, often Celtic, literary traditions.[13] In this remote material, the primitive form of the literary custom often involved physical violence or material destruction. Reminiscences of this sometimes persist in the customs of medieval romance, in the form of homicide, ritual beheading, or pitched battle at some hallowed geographical locus, such as a passage or a ford. To forestall further carnage, some less violent form of compensation, such as the periodic taking of hostages, the exaction of a monetary tribute or *péage,* the solution of an enigma, or some test of heroic physical endurance, might be substituted. That the literary custom has frequently been made somewhat more "pacific" in medieval romances without losing all of its primordially violent traces is what makes it such a curious blend of archaic elements with feudal and Christian properties. The custom in this episode is particularly interesting in that regard, because we can actually see its successive substrata in quasi-"archeological" fashion. The primitive form featured the awesome and destructive retribution periodically inflicted upon the fortress, as the terrifying celestial hand seized the pommel at the summit of the tower. Then, during the crepuscular phase of Raymondin's lordship, this was obviated by substitution of a material payment—called a "treuage" and a "rente"—which Geoffroy in turn abolishes by substitution of works of Christian charity and piety. If there are "demonic" overtones in this episode, these derive from the custom's primitive substrata, but it is clear from context that they are progressively eradicated by the explicitly Christian meaning attributed to the debt which Geoffroy finally pays in full through charitable works.

Recourse to the format of custom in this episode thus provides an opportunity to clarify the axiological ambiguity that many readers find in the body of the work, so as to intensify a penultimate sense of disjunction between good and evil. Like the narrator's comments in both the prologue and the epilogue concerning Melusine's subordination to the ways of God (*M* 4, 310–11), Geoffroy's encounter with the Knight

of the Tower must be seen as an effort on the part of Jean d'Arras to liquidate any remaining uncertainty concerning Lusignan's relationships with the supernatural. It clearly demonstrates the divine origin of the marvel, as well as Lusignan's exclusive infeudation to a Christian universal order. It is especially significant that the locus of this clarification is a tower in the fortress, for the story proper had left the reader with a virtually indelible image, often commemorated by iconographers, of Melusine, airborne in the form of a serpent and in a tempestuous fury, assailing the Poitevin tower so violently that the entire fortress seemed on the verge of falling asunder (261).[14] As if to compensate for the potentially demonic overtones of this image, the epilogue makes the tower, and the custom associated with it, a locus of Lusignan's homage to Christianity.

While this first recourse to conventions of custom emphasizes the subordination of marvelous phenomena to a divine plan, the second addresses a potential ambiguity concerning kinship relations. Jean d'Arras, appropriating the episode at the Castle of the Sparrowhawk from the *Voyages* of Mandeville, introduces a fundamental thematic modification. In Mandeville's version the successful contender may request only an earthly boon; the king's descendants are punished unto the ninth generation because he failed to respect this constraint, the lady being not mortal but supernatural.[15] While no issue pertaining to kinship is involved here, in Jean d'Arras's romance the taboo of incest becomes the fulcrum of the entire episode, as Melior make clear: "Povre fol, n'es tu pas descendu de la lignie du roy Guion, qui fu filz Melusigne, ma seur, et je suis ta tante, et tu es si prez de mon lignaige, posé que je me voulzisse assentir a toy avoir, que l'eglise ne s'i vouldroit pas accorder" [You poor fool, are you not descended from the lineage of King Guyon, who was my sister Melusine's son? I am your aunt, and you are such close kin to me that even if I were to consent to have you, the church would not allow it] (*M* 305). Why does the epilogue make such a conspicuous point about the prohibition of incest? Might this be an effort to address and definitively dispel a potential ambiguity latent in the main story? Indeed, at one point early in the narrative incest does make a veiled appearance in the register of imaginary play concerning Melusine's own very murky past. After Raymondin's father Hervy de Leon had killed the king of Brittany's son in self-defense, he had fled to

the Forez where, according to Melusine's account, he had received "moult grant aide d'une dame de laquelle je ne vous veuil pas parler. Et après le departir d'elle, qui lui aida en son premier gouvernement a faire les forteresses et les villes et habiter le pays, il ot la serour d'un qui pour lors gouvernoit la conté de Poictiers, et en ot pluseurs enfans, de quoy vous estes ly uns" [a great deal of help from a lady about whom I don't wish to tell you. When he first began to govern she helped him build fortresses and cities and populate the land. After she left, he took the sister of the count of Poitiers and they had several children, of whom you're one] (*M* 50). Although Hervy had clearly married in noble and legitimately exogamous fashion, Melusine's fleeting, reluctant, and truncated discussion of the mysterious "défricheuse" who had helped him civilize the Forez bears an uncanny resemblance to the civilizing profile of Melusine herself, who is in fact remarkably well informed concerning the history of Raymondin's father, Hervy. There is thus a very suggestive hint of what did *not* come to pass in the story: that Raymondin, having killed his father-surrogate in the person of his maternal uncle the count of Poitiers, eventually married his father's spousal surrogate, the mysterious lady of the Forez, alias Melusine, his own mother. The story thus brings to mind, while at the same time denying it, a scenario with distinctly Oedipal overtones.[16] Perhaps we are in the realm of Freudian *Verneinung,* whereby a forbidden wish may find conscious expression only when it is uttered negatively.[17] While in the same breath Melusine pointedly forecloses on the potential for inferring that the central couple veils a mother-son union, incest remains as palimpsest in the text's "imaginaire." This enigmatic aspect of Hervy's past may well explain Jean's curious adaptation of Mandeville's anecdote to suit a desire for disambiguation in the epilogue. To counter suspicions that the dark lady of the Forez was really Melusine or that incest might lurk beneath the integument of the intrigue, Melior's custom provides a means of demonstrating that the ethic of Presine's fairy daughters excludes incest from the realm of the permissible.

Although the Custom of the Sparrowhawk closely adheres to the format of many nefarious customs at remote castles, the challenge provided to the hero in those episodes normally results in his *exaltation* following a definitive triumph. However, in an effort to bring the fiction of the custom into line with the real world, Jean d'Arras introduces a negative peripeteia so that Melior's prediction of the decline and demise of the Armenian branch of the lineage coincides with current events.[18] Melior predicts that the last king in the line will be known as "beste mue," wild beast (*M* 305).[19] The last monarch in the Armenian line was in fact Leon de Lusignan, who in 1393 was living in exile in France after being deposed, and he was to die in Paris on November 29 of that very year.[20] Melior's prophecy thus seems to have been deliberately designed to remind his contemporaries of the virtual exhaustion of the Lusignan line and to emphasize the unlikelihood of any pretentions to the lordship of Lusignan on the part of the last of the Armenian kings.

A preoccupation with the state of political affairs in 1393 becomes far more explicit in the third segment, which directly addresses ambiguous matters pertaining to the current lordship of Lusignan. Jean now exalts the figure of the Lord of Lusignan and the patron of his work, Jean, duke of Berry, and that of his sister, the duchess of Bar. Such an encomium of a *mécénat* is by no means out of place here, yet in the summer of 1393 its resonance with the contemporaneous political situation can hardly be mistaken: while the English claim to Poitou remains at issue and Leon de Lusignan is still alive and living in Paris, though unwell, there remains a critical need to dispel any ambiguity as to the legitimacy of the duke's lordship. Emphasizing that the fortress has "tant alee de main en main qu'elle est venue en la main" [gone from hand to hand until it has come into the hand] of his patron, we are to understand that nothing underhanded has enabled this succession, which took place "par raison et par conqueste d'espee" [legitimately and by force of conquest] (*M* 307). Historically, military conquest did effect Lusignan's passage from the hands of Creswell, who held it for the English, to those of the duke, following the siege that lasted from March 12, 1373, to October 1, 1374.[21] Yet, though the duke has held Lusignan for nineteen years after conquering it, the narrator notes that only descendants of the original line have held it for more than thirty years (*M* 308). To enhance the duke's prospects for governing Lusignan for another decade and beyond, it must be demonstrated that Jean de Berry is the rightful heir. Historically, his claim was at best marginal, based merely on an alliance, when only a few years earlier a relative on his mother's side had married a female descendant of Hugh of Lusignan.[22] Rather than evoke this tenuous link, Jean d'Arras once again recurs to a conventional feature of one type of literary custom prevalent in Old French romance, whereby the custom's sole function is to provide a *merveille* that serves to determine the accession to lordship of a castle. Jean thus evokes the current belief that Melusine makes her customary appearance three days prior to a change of legitimate lord (*M* 308): "Et sachiez que, toutesfoiz . . . quant la dicte forteresse doit changier seigneur, la serpente s'appert trois jours devant" [Know, nonetheless, that . . . when said fortress is to change lords, the serpent appears three days beforehand] (*M* 308). This topic is then illustrated with a series of anecdotes concerning such appearances within recent memory (*M* 308–10). When the duke had besieged Lusignan, the serpent had appeared to the English commander shortly before he was compelled to surrender the fortress. Other witnesses are cited, including one who twice saw the marvelous creature on the walls of Lusignan three days before the fortress was surrendered to Jean de Berry. Like the traditional custom, the marvel of Melusine's materializations at Lusignan provides a means of adjudicating and validating seigneurial candidates. This accumulated testimonial evidence—Jean calls them "preuves" (*M* 310)—signifying Melusine's approbation of the duke's succession implicity validates his status as a lineal heir and thus defuses any potential ambiguity as to the legitimacy of his claim.[23] Significantly, then, at the end of the fourteenth century we have in Jean d'Arras an author who recurs to the convention of a literary custom in an attempt to clarify a real-world juridical case of seigneurial succession.

In addition to customs, there is one further way in which the epilogue strives to end the narrative in an appropriate manner, and this has to do with time, as each segment in the epilogue makes its own particular contribution to an overall temporal synthesis. While in the first two episodes figures of temporality—*analepsis* and *prolepsis*—provide succint summaries of episodes within the story itself, in the third the figure of *metalepsis* makes possible a remarkable *conjointure* of the past time of the narrative and the present situation of the poet and his patron.

It should be noted that analepsis, which brings a moment from the past into the unfolding story, is twice used in highly significant ways in the main story.[24] In a remarkably long narration—a protodiegetic analepsis, introducing elements not previously recounted in the main story, or diegesis—Melusine provides Raymondin with a detailed account of the life of the father whom he had never known, Hervy de Leon

(*M* 48–51). As Raymondin grew up in ignorance of the patrilineal order, so will his sons long live in ignorance of the marvelous matrilineal order. In the case of Geoffroy, this void is filled much later in the story, when he discovers the truth about his mother's lineage in an analepsis recalling the first section of the main story. This moment is highly ironic, for when Raymondin had earlier recounted the deeds of his father to Geoffroy, the latter had expressed relative indifference concerning his ancestry: "Je ne scay ne ne vueil enquester des choses passees: puis que mes ancesseurs en ont eu l'onneur et en sont venus a leur dessus, il me souffist." [I know nothing about the past and don't care to inquire about it. Since it was my ancestors who had the honors and the upper hand, that's good enough for me] (*M* 239). Yet very shortly thereafter he makes his way into a mountain in Northumberland and discovers therein not only the tomb of his grandfather Elinas but also an iconic representation of the ancestral couple and a lengthy written account of their entire history (*M* 265–66). He soon recognizes that they were his maternal grandparents (*M* 268) and passes the word on to his brothers (*M* 282). Exclusively by means of these two analepses, which are instances of what I have elsewhere identified as the motif of "specular encounter," whereby self-discovery occurs in the discourse of the other, the principal figures in the dynasty learn the two stories of its bifurcated, patrilineal and matrilineal, origins.[25]

The first segment of the epilogue, examined earlier, also provides an analeptic glimpse into the world of Lusignan after Melusine's departure. An element not previously recounted in the main story, this window on the past puts us momentarily back into the era of Geoffroy Big-Tooth, though the ultimate emphasis is not so much on the temporal duration of Geoffroy's tenure as Lord of Lusignan as it is on how, during that period, the domain itself was brought into harmony with a timeless transcendence by virtue of a successful negotiation between Geoffroy and the ethereal emissary who does the bidding of the beyond. This episode is therefore akin to the type of biblically inspired event in which the divine intervenes punctually in human affairs. While such moments are widespread in medieval literature modeled on the eschatological format of salvation history as well as in texts that feature the so-called *merveilleux chrétien,* they are relatively rare in modern literature. This perhaps explains why narratology has no term by which to designate what I would call "heterolepsis," that is, the figural interaction of the temporal and the transcendent.

The effective use of analepsis and heterolepsis in this segment alone would have sufficed as a relatively simple yet fitting way to close off the diegetic temporality of Lusignan if it had been a matter of merely achieving the work's autonomy as a fictive romance. That such was not the case is clear from the way time is handled in segments two and three.

The second segment, like the first, delves back into the distant past. While the king of Armenie is exploring the Castle of the Sparrowhawk, he enters a room in which the murals depict the entire story of Elinas, Presine, and their three daughters (*M* 304). Here we find the epilogue rehearsing antecedent episodes of its own textuality. This *mise en abyme* of the first part of the story in the very midst of its epilogue provides a vivid means of recalling the mythic protohistory of the Lusignan dynasty, one in some respects reminiscent of the Tristanian "salle aux images" or of Lancelot's murals in the Prose *Lancelot* and the *Mort Artu.* Later, during the king's hapless encounter with Melior, the latter offers him in a succinct prolepsis a glimpse of the future of his own branch of the lineage, predicting that the line will decline unto the ninth generation. As we have seen, this proleptic account foreshadows the present, August 1393, five months, in fact, before Léon of Lusignan, the last in his line, was to expire.[26] Thus, by virtue of analepsis and prolepsis, the second segment of the epilogue surrounds the main dynastic story with evocations of the originary transgression from which it was spawned and the ultimate transgression that marked the beginning of its decline. Hence a remarkable symmetry between the two transgressions that mark the beginning and the end of the Melusinian myth as Jean d'Arras reconceptualized it: Melusine's malediction that incapacitated her father at the very beginning of the genealogy is analogous to Melior's malediction that incapacitates a king and initiates the genealogy's decadent phase. In both cases, the main emphasis is on kinship, in a manner reminiscent, as I have suggested elsewhere, of Lévi-Strauss's work on kinship in medieval romance.[27] In the former instance, Melusine's transgression by sending her father into permanent exile is an undervaluation of kinship relations that leads to interrupted communication between generations in the lineage. Consequently, her expiation in the main story will be taken up largely with successive childbirths, an appropriate valuation of kinship relations through their multiplication; she eventually gives birth to the hero, Geoffroy, who will restore communication between his generation and that of her parents, his matrilineal kin. In contrast, the brazen Armenian king's transgression involves an incestuous demand for Melior and is thus an excess, an overvaluation of kinship relations, the appropriate punishment for which is the progressive decay of the lineage.[28] The analepsis and prolepsis in this segment are thus complementary components of a full mythic cycle, marked at its inception by figures of lineal growth and at its close by figures of lineal decline.

While these reflexive components collectively provide an overview of the comprehensive temporality of the dynasty and of the fiction that depicts it, the final segment uses yet another rhetorical technique, this time in a stunning attempt to close the breach between the fiction and the reality of the author who created it. To obtain some idea of the nature of this device, we may recur to a different text that well illustrates it, the prologue to the New Testament book of Luke: "Forasmuch as many have taken in hand to set forth in order a narration of the things that have been accomplished among us, according as they have delivered them unto us, who from the beginning were eyewitnesses and ministers of the word; it seemed good to me also, having diligently attained to all things from the beginning, to write to thee in order, most excellent Theophilus, that thou mayest know the verity of those words in which thou has been instructed."[29] As in Jean's epilogue, the order of events alluded to in the prologue to Luke is identified as a construct of the past which is both true and continuous into the present experience of the enunciator. The principal objective is to establish a qualitative bond with a past that is not perceived as fiction but rather as a historical prelude that has culminated in the present moment of the speaker or writer.

In this enunciative stratagem whereby a narrated order of past events is assimilated into the present situation of the narrator we recognize the figure of metalepsis. In his late twelfth-century *Ars versificatoria,* Matthew of Vendôme had identified metalepsis in verse, either grammatically or metrically, as a "climactic arrangement of clauses."[30] While one could indeed view Jean's epilogue as a "climactic"—and thus also as a "metaleptic"—arrangement of episodes, it conforms more closely to the classic view of *narrative* metalepsis, as illustrated in passing by Pierre Fontanier and as more fully elaborated by Gérard Genette in his "Discours du récit."[31] Metalepsis in the narrative sense involves imbrication of the temporality of the story being told into the temporality of the narrator's enunciation, or vice versa, thus breaking down the barrier between the narrator's own world and the world he is narrating.[32] While Genette's examples from modern literature indicate ways in which the figure serves to achieve the ends of irony, humor, or the fantastic, Jean d'Arras's usage is clearly designed to heighten the reality-effect of the story as historical document. He demonstrates that this figure can indeed serve as a device for the recuperation of a legendary or a mythic past into contemporaneous historical reality. The fabulous genealogical narrative may thus come to serve familial or dynastic ends by creating what Gabrielle Spiegel has recently called "a usable past," a past that bestows power, privilege, and prestige upon the present generation.[33] By virtue of the metaleptic illusion, the narrative discourse representing the past not only seems to intersect with the present, it also appears to *interact* with the present, creating a mirage of temporal continuity between the pseudohistorical dimension of the narrative and the represented dimension of its enunciation.

Metalepsis has remained a relatively neglected figure in narratology insofar as it applies to earlier types of texts.[34] This remarkable example is indicative that it may deserve much more attention in terms of its usage as a vehicle of pseudohistoricizing configurations in medieval narrative. We can readily see how veridiction as a construct of the cognitive dimension of discourse also figures within a stratagem of manipulation: the Melusinian narrative is used as a persuasive device to substantiate the juridical foundations of Jean de Berry's lordship of Lusignan.[35] What we find in the "*outre*perfection du livre" is a clever investment of the figure of metalepsis whereby the narrative account of an illustrious, mythified, yet ultimately crepuscular, even decadent, line is made to culminate in the present reappropriation of Lusignan by a lord deemed worthy—even by Melusine herself—of restoring it to the level of prestige it once enjoyed. Jean's use of metalepsis thus becomes the discursive equivalent of a late medieval painter's conspicuous, anachronistic depiction of his patron in the corner of a tableau devoted to the subject matter of myth or religion.

The tripartite epilogue thus strives to create a literary "perfection" of a very special kind, by mediating the inconsistencies in the far from seamless story of the Lusignan dynasty and the politically precarious circumstantiality of Jean de Berry, so that the fictive vicissitudes, inconsistencies, and paradoxes of the former might in the end become accessory to the fortunes of the latter. In bringing his book to a close, the most important achievement that Jean d'Arras presents to his patron is not simply the "perfection du livre," which is the outcome of a process of literary production, but rather an array of narrative configurations of veridiction by which he attempts to provide a closing signification of the story's authenticity, both as an account of the past and as an index of the future. In its unfolding, Jean's remarkable story of the Lusignans had left a residue of ambiguity concerning the possible dark side of unexamined origins; the significance of physical *tares* and lineal decline ultimately remains unclear, as other contributions to this collection have frequently shown. To ensure the heuristic value of such unsettling fiction, the epilogue seems carefully contrived to lend the impression of a seamless whole, confirming the positive supernatural and divine sanction of Lusignan, and seeking to dispel any lingering reluctance to see in Melusine anything other than a reliable adjudicator for legitimizing the claim of Jean de Berry. Instead of ending his work with nothing more than a bald and unconvincing assertion of the legitimacy of his lord's lordship of Lusignan, Jean d'Arras carefully constructs his epilogue so as to recuperate legend to tendentious ends, and in so doing purports to confirm both the reality and the reliability of Melusine in a post-Melusinian world.

Notes

1. "En toutes choses commencier on doit appeler le Createur des creatures, qui est maistre de toutes les choses faictes et a faire, qui doivent *tendre a perfection de bien* et les autres pervenir selon les vices des creatures. Et pour ce, au commencement de ceste hystoire, je, cognoicent que je ne soye pas digne de lui requerir, supplie a sa haute dignité que ceste histoire je puise achever a sa gloire et louenges, et au plaisir de mon tres hault, puissant et redoubté seigneur, Jehan, Filz de roy de France, duc de Berry et d'Ouvergne" [Upon beginning anything one must call upon the Creator of beings, Master of all things made

or yet to be made, whether they are to achieve a perfect form or are to obtain according to the imperfections of beings. And thus, at the beginning of this history, cognizant of my unworthiness to ask His blessing, I beseech His High Majesty to grant that I may complete this history to His honor and glory, and to the satisfaction of my exalted, powerful, and feared lord, Jean, son of the king of France, duke of Berry and Auvergne] (*M* 1). On this passage, see also Pickens in this volume.

2. "*Parfaire* refers to the attainment of an amalgam that is complete and whole. Any mental projection (*status archetypus*) into *matiere* (*status sensilis*) could achieve virtual 'perfection' in the finished opus, just as the relative perfection of nature's creatures reflects their perfect archetypal *species* in God's mind. This model patterns all kinds of invention." Douglas Kelly, *The Art of Medieval French Romance* (Madison and London: University of Wisconsin Press, 1992), 134.

3. For examples of critical and literary usage of the term from the twelfth century on, see Kelly, 134–45.

4. The designation applied by Harf-Lancner, *Mélusine*, 22 (emphasis mine); Perret calls it a "roman généalogique à prétention historique" in "L'Invraisemblable vérité," 26.

5. During the colloquium on "Mélusine at 600," Michèle Perret suggested that Jean's organization of the epilogue into multiple phases may in fact reflect a more generalized tendency in late medieval narratives, as in the case of *Jehan de Saintré* by Antoine de la Sale.

6. Chrétien de Troyes, *Erec et Enide*, ed. M. Roques (Paris: Champion, 1966), vv. 557–80, 691–1079.

7. Variants of the pattern, to mention but a few, are found in the romances of Chrétien (the "Joie de la cort" in *Erec;* the "Pesme aventure" episode in *Yvain;* Gauvain's adventure at the "Roche de Canguin" in the *Conte du graal*, etc.), in the episode of the "Fier baisier" in the *Le Bel inconnu;* and, beginning with Lancelot's conquest of the Dolorous Garde, in numerous episodes of the Prose *Lancelot*. See D. Maddox: *The Arthurian Romances of Chrétien de Troyes: Once and Future Fictions* (Cambridge: Cambridge University Press, 1991); "La Représentation du droit coutumier dans les romans de Chrétien de Troyes," in *Le Droit et sa perception dans la littérature et les mentalités médiévales*, ed. D. Buschinger (Göppingen: Kümmerle Verlag, 1993) 133–44; and "Coutumes et conjointure dans le *Lancelot* en prose," in *Conjunctures: Medieval Studies in Honor of Douglas Kelly*, ed. K. Busby and N. J. Lacy (Amsterdam: Rodopi, 1994), 293–309.

8. Kelly, 240–46; see also his contribution in this collection.

9. This blend of traditions emerges as early as the prologue where, on the authority of the *Otia Imperialia* of Gervaise of Tilbury, we read of *lutins* who

indulge in nocturnal kidnapping, mutilation, and burning of children (*M* 309) and of *faees* similar to Melusine in that they marry mortals and in some cases periodically change into serpents. Gervaise is cited as believing that such beings result from divine punishment that surpasses human understanding (*M* 3–4). On the traditions reflected in the figure of the medieval Melusine, see Josef Köhler, *Der Ursprung der Melusinensage: Eine ethnologische Untersuchung* (Berlin: Pfeiffer, 1895); Stouff, *Essai;* Le Goff and Le Roy Ladurie; Lecouteux, *Mélusine;* idem, "Structure"; and Harf-Lancner, *Fées.*

10. See Perret, *Mélusine*, 331: "le diable . . . a pris possession du pommeau de la tour." She also cites Henri Dontenville, *Mythologie française*, who sees the Knight of the Tower as the demonic spirit of a former owner of the land (323).

11. This concern emerges clearly near the end of the epilogue: citing Gervaise of Tilbury's *Otia Imperialia*, along with other authors of seemingly incredible stories, the narrator states that "je repute ceste histoire et la cronique a estre vraye, et les choses faees. Et qui dit le contraire, je dy que les secrez jugemens de Dieu et les punicions sont invisibles a congnoistre a entendement humain" [I consider this story and the chronicle to be true, and the events the product of enchantment. To whomever says otherwise, I say that God's secret judgments and punishments are unknowable through human understanding] (*M* 310–11).

12. Though they are sometimes broadly evocative of them. Moreover, they suggest an implicit critique of oral protocols for determination of right, a critique that anticipates the progressive move to written customals. See D. Maddox, "Représentation du droit coutumier," pp. 142–44; and idem. *Arthurian Romances*, ch. 5.

13. See Kelly, 241.

14. For iconographic representations of this moment, see Clier-Colombani. See also Kevin Brownlee and Laurence de Looze, in this volume.

15. See Stouff, *Mélusine,* 301 n. 1, for citation of a Middle English translation of this passage from Mandeville (British Museum MS Cotton Titus c. xvi).

16. Michèle Perret has in fact called this a "situation subtilement oedipienne." Perret, *Mélusine,* 330.

17. See the discussion of "Verneinung" (Eng. "negation") in J. Laplanche and J.-B. Pontalis, *The Language of Psychoanalysis,* trans. D. Nicholson-Smith (New York: Norton, 1973), 261–63.

18. Cf. Jane Taylor's identification, infra, of this departure from convention as one of the "blocked schemata" that typify this work.

19. In his verse version of the poem a few years later, Coudrette will make him "king of beasts," a lion.

20. Harf-Lancner, *Mélusine,* 28–35.

21. Ibid., 29–30.

22. The duke was the son of Bonne of Luxembourg, whose kinsman, Jean of Luxembourg, lord of Beaurevoir, had married a descendant of Hugh the First of Lusignan, king of Cyprus from 1205–1218. See Stouff, *Essai*, 17.

23. The narrator insists that these and many other such incidents, incredible though they may seem, constitute as many proofs—*preuves* (*M* 310)—of the coexistence of the true *and* the marvelous, "les choses faees" (*M* 310) being always manifestations, ultimately, of "les secrez jugemens de Dieu" (*M* 311), which, while true, exceed our understanding. The fact that such manifestations occurred not just in one place but in other regions and lands and that they are also attested by "anciens livres"—Gervaise of Tilbury being mentioned in particular—merely increases the credibility of "le vif et le vray des choses semblans increables" (*M* 311). See also Perret, "L'Invraisemblable vérité," 27, who identifies Jean's inventory of Melusine's appearances in the epilogue as instances of "témoignages médiatisés," whereby testimony given the author by reliable witnesses is considered an adequate guarantee of credibility.

24. On this figure, see Gérard Genette, *Figures III* (Paris: Seuil, 1972), 82–105.

25. On the motif of "specular encounter" in earlier medieval texts, see D. Maddox "Specular Stories, Family Romance, and Old French Fictions," *Exemplaria* 3 (1991): 299–326.

26. On prolepsis, see Genette, 105–14.

27. D. Maddox, "Lévi-Strauss in Camelot: Interrupted Communication in Arthurian Feudal Fictions," in *Culture and the King*, ed. M. Schichtman and J. P. Carley (Albany: State University of New York Press, 1994), 35–53.

28. Lévi-Strauss's work on medieval grail narratives was featured in his Seminar on Structural Anthropology at the Collège de France in 1973–1974, abstracted in "Anthropologie sociale," *Annuaire du Collège de France*, 74e Année, 303–9 and republished in *Paroles données* (Paris, 1984), 129–37, with an addendum, 138–40, by André Zavriew, "The Waste Land and the Hot House," summarizing Lévi-Strauss's lecture on Chrétien de Troyes, Wolfram von Eschenbach, and Wagner at the French Institute in London, on October 3, 1975. He mentioned Perceval as early as 1960, in his inaugural address at the Collège de France; see also *Anthropologie structurale deux* (Paris, 1970), 31–35.

29. *The Holy Bible, Douay Version. Translated from the Latin Vulgate (Douay, A.D. 1609; Rheims, A.D. 1582)* (London: Catholic Truth Society, 1956), N.T. 73.

30. Matthew of Vendôme, *The Art of Versification*, trans. A. Galyon (Ames: Iowa State University Press, 1980), 96.

31. Pierre Fontanier, *Les Figures du discours* (Paris: Flammarion, 1968), 127–29. Genette, *Figures III*, 243–45.

32. Cf. Genette: "*Métalepse* fait ici système avec *prolepse, analepse, syllepse* et *paralepse,* avec le sens spécifique de: prendre (raconter) en changeant de niveau" (244, n. 4). "Le passage d'un niveau narratif à l'autre ne peut être assuré que par la narration, acte qui consiste précisément à introduire dans une situation, par le moyen d'un discours, la connaissance d'une autre situation" (243). Defining the "métalepse de l'auteur": "toute intrusion du narrateur ou du narrataire extradiégétique dans l'univers diégétique . . . ou inversement . . . produit un effet de bizarrerie soit bouffonne . . . soit fantastique. . . . Nous étendrons à toutes ces transgressions le terme de métalepse narrative" (244). Metalepsis involves play along the "frontière mouvante mais sacrée entre deux mondes: celui où l'on raconte, celui que l'on raconte" (245).

33. Gabrielle M. Spiegel, "Genealogy: Form and Function in Medieval Historical Narrative," *History and Theory* 22 (1983): 43–53; see also her *Romancing the Past: The Rise of Vernacular Prose Historiography in Thirteenth-Century France* (Berkeley and Los Angeles: University of California Press, 1993).

34. For an example of metalepsis in a twelfth-century work of fiction, however, see Michèle Perret, "Atemporalités et effet de fiction dans *Le Bel Inconnu,*" in *Le Nombre du temps, en hommage à Paul Zumthor* (Geneva: Slatkine, 1988), 225–35.

35. See Perret, "L'Invraisemblable vérité"; and D. Maddox, "Veridiction, Verifiction, Verifactions: Reflections on Methodology," *New Literary History* 20 (1989): 661–77.

Principal Works Cited

This list includes texts and studies frequently cited in the essays in this volume, indicated in the text by author or editor and page. It is supplemented by works cited in the individual essays.

Texts and Translations

Coudrette. *Le roman de Mélusine ou Histoire de Lusignan*. Ed. Eleanor Roach. Paris: Klincksieck, 1982.

———. *Le Roman de Mélusine*. Trans. into modern French by Laurence Harf-Lancner. Paris: Garnier-Flammarion, 1993.

Historia de la linda Melosina. Ed. Ivy A. Corfis. Madison: Hispanic Seminary of Medieval Studies, 1986.

Jean d'Arras. *Mélusine. Roman du XIVe siècle*. Ed. Louis Stouff. Dijon: Publications de l'Université, 1932; rpt. Geneva: Slatkine Reprints, 1974. Cited throughout as *M*.

———. *Le Roman de Mélusine ou l'histoire des Lusignan*. Trans. into modern French by Michèle Perret. Paris: Stock Plus, 1979.

Studies

Clier-Colombani, Françoise. *La Fée Mélusine au moyen âge: images, mythes, symboles*. Paris: Le Léopard d'Or, 1991.

Desaivre, Léo. *Le Mythe de la mère Lusine: Etude critique et bibliographique*. Saint-Maixent: Reversé, 1883.

Harf-Lancner, Laurence. *Les Fées au Moyen Age: Morgane et Mélusine. La Naissance des fées*. Paris: Champion, 1984.

Lecouteux, Claude. "La structure des légendes mélusiennes." *Annales: Economies, Sociétés, Civilisations* 33 (1978): 294–306.

———. *Mélusine et le Chevalier au Cygne*. Paris: Payot, 1982.

Le Goff, Jacques, and Emmanuel Le Roy Ladurie. "Mélusine maternelle et défricheuse." *Annales: Economies, Sociétés, Civilisations* 26 (1971): 587–622.

Markale, Jean. *Mélusine ou l'androgyne*. Paris: Retz, 1983.

Perret, Michèle. "L'Invraisemblable vérité. Témoignage fantastique dans deux romans des 14e et 15e siècles." *Europe: Revue Littéraire Mensuelle* 654 (1983): 25–35.

Stouff, Louis. *Essai sur Mélusine, roman du XIVe siècle par Jean d'Arras*. Dijon: Publications de l'Université, 1930.

Contributors

Emmanuèle Baumgartner is Professeur de Littérature française du Moyen Age at the Université de la Sorbonne nouvelle. She is particularly interested in twelfth- and thirteenth-century narrative in verse and prose and has published numerous books and articles, including studies of the Tristan romances, Chrétien de Troyes, and Arthurian prose romance, especially the *Quête du saint Graal* and the Prose *Tristan*. She has recently completed a study on *Le Récit médiéval (XIIe–XIIIe siècles)*.

Kevin Brownlee is Professor of Romance Languages at the University of Pennsylvania where he teaches medieval French and Italian literature. Major studies include *Poetic Identity in Guillaume de Machaut* (1984); he has recently completed a book on autobiography and literary models in Christine de Pizan.

Marina S. Brownlee is the Class of 1963 College of Women Professor of Romance Languages at the University of Pennsylvania. She is the author of *The Status of the Reading Subject in the 'Libro de buen amor'* (1985) and *The Severed Word. Ovid's 'Heroides' and the 'Novela Sentimental'* (1990).

Laurence de Looze is Associate Professor in the Modern Languages and Literature Department of the University of Western Ontario. He publishes on English, French, Icelandic, and Spanish medieval literature and has edited and translated Jean Froissart's *La Prison amoureuse*.

Douglas Kelly is Julian E. Harris Professor of French and Medieval Studies at the University of Wisconsin, Madison. His recent books include *The Arts of Poetry and Prose* (1991), *The Art of Medieval French Romance* (1992), *Medieval French Romance* (1993), and *Internal Difference and Meanings in the 'Roman de la rose'* (1995). He is at work on a book on rewriting in the transition from Latin to the vernacular.

Donald Maddox is Professor of French and Italian at the University of Massachusetts, Amherst. He has authored two books on Chrétien de Troyes, *Structure and Sacring* (1979) and *The Arthurian Romances of Chrétien de Troyes: Once and Future Fictions* (1991), *Semiotics of Deceit: The Pathelin Era* (1984), and many articles on medieval literature and critical theory. In preparation is a book on reflexive properties in romance and brief narrative from the twelfth through the fourteenth century.

NADIA MARGOLIS has authored articles on Christine de Pizan, whose poetry she has also translated, a sourcebook on *Joan of Arc in History, Literature & Film*, and other studies in Johannic reception history. She is currently at work on Christine de Pizan and the Franco-Italian tradition.

STEPHEN G. NICHOLS is James M. Beall Professor of French and Chair of the French Department at The Johns Hopkins University. He also directs the School of Criticism and Theory. Author of *Romanesque Signs: Early Medieval Narrative and Iconography* (1983, 1985), his recent projects include *Medievalism and the Modernist Temper* (1995), *The Whole Book: The Medieval Miscellany in Cultural Perspective* (1996), *Commentary as Cultural Artefact* (1992), *The New Medievalism* (1991), *The New Philology* (1990). He is presently completing *Le théâtralisation du rire au moyen âge* and *Marie de France's Common Places.*

MICHÈLE PERRET is Professeur at the Université Paris X–Nanterre (Sciences de langage). Her publications include *Le Signe et la mention, adverbes embrayeurs ci, ça, la, iluec (XIVe–XVe siècles)* (1988); *L'Enonciation en grammaire du texte* (1994); and modern French translations of Jean d'Arras's *Roman de Mélusine* (1979) and *Le Bel inconnu* of Renaud de Bâgé (1991, with Isabelle Weill). She is preparing a book on the construction of referential universes in Old and Middle French fiction.

RUPERT T. PICKENS is Professor of French at the University of Kentucky. His books include a study of Chrétien de Troyes's *Conte del Graal*, critical editions of the *Conte del Graal* and of Jaufré Rudel's songs, and a translation of the Lancelot-Grail *Merlin*; he has edited three volumes of scholarly essays and published articles on a wide range medieval and critical topics. He is currently at work on a comparative study of Marie de France's *Lais* and *Fables* and a scholarly translation of texts from the William of Orange Cycle.

GABRIELLE M. SPIEGEL is Professor of History at The Johns Hopkins University. She is the author of *The Chronicle Tradition of Saint-Denis: A Survey* (1978), *Romancing the Past: The Rise of Vernacular Historiography in Thirteenth-Century France* (1993), *The Past as Text: Studies in Medieval History and Historiography* (forthcoming in English and Italian), and numerous articles on medieval historiography and critical theory. She is working on a book on the writing of medieval history in America.

SARA STURM-MADDOX is Professor of French and Italian at the University of Massachusetts, Amherst, where she teaches medieval and Renaissance literature. Recent books include *Petrarch's Metamorphoses: Text and Subtext in the Rime sparse* (1985) and *Petrarch's Laurels* (1992); she is completing a study of Ronsard's response to Petrarch in three collections of the *Amours.*

Jane H. M. Taylor spent many years at the University of Manchester before moving back to St. Hilda's College, Oxford, where she holds a Fellowship in Medieval French Literature. She has published extensively on the literature of the late Middle Ages: romances (the *Roman de Perceforest* and *Le Petit Jehan de Saintré*), historians (Froissart and Joinville), and lyric poets (Charles d'Orléans, Machaut, and François Villon). She is currently preparing a major study of Villon's *Testament*.

Index

www.ingramcontent.com/pod-product-compliance
Lightning Source LLC
LaVergne TN
LVHW030909080826
845145LV00010B/2822

* 9 7 8 0 8 2 0 3 5 7 1 0 2 *